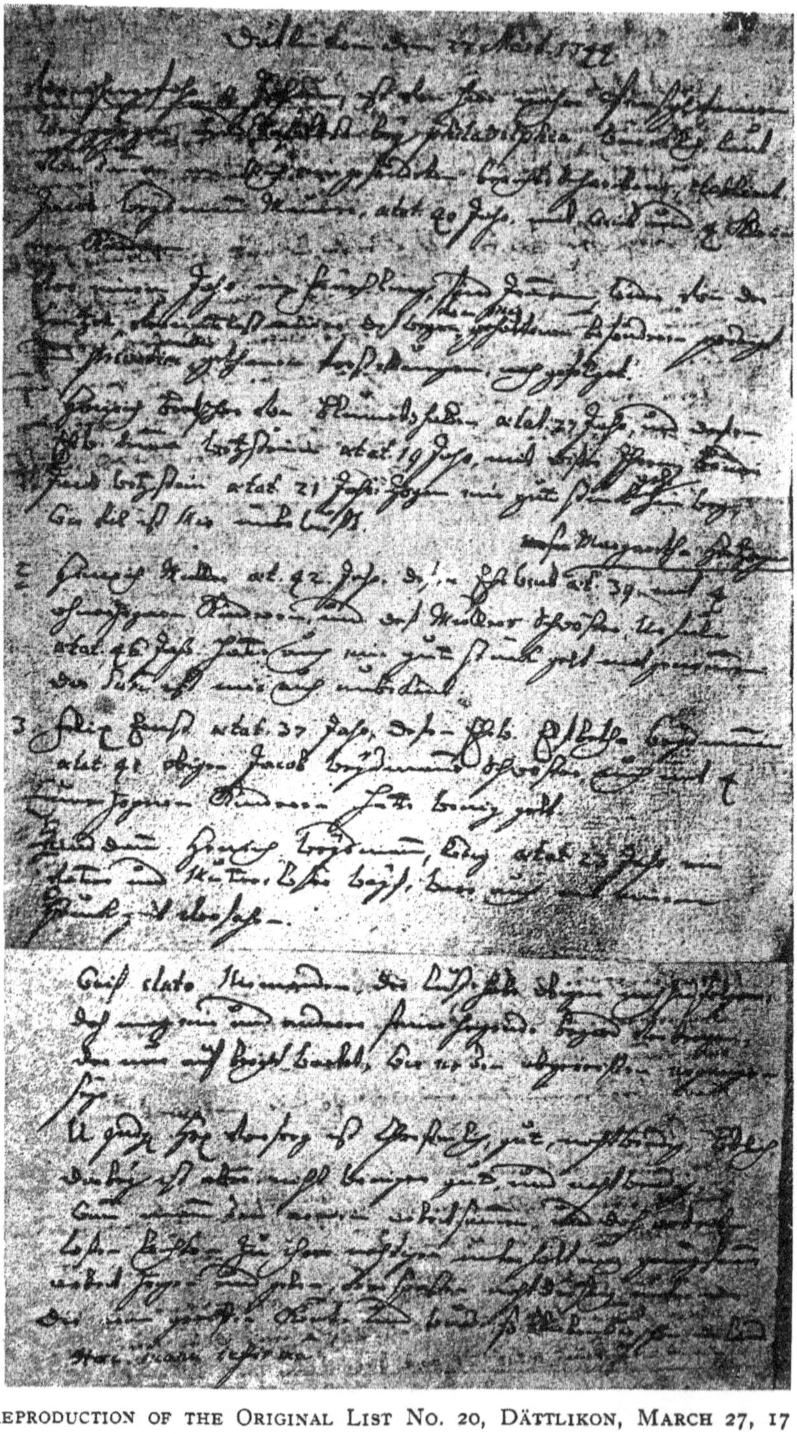

Plate 1

REPRODUCTION OF THE ORIGINAL LIST No. 20, DÄTTLIKON, MARCH 27, 17

Swiss Emigrants
in the
Eighteenth Century
to the
American Colonies

(2 Volumes *in* 1)

Compiled *and* Edited by:

Albert Bernhadt Faust, A.B., Ph.D.
and
Gaius Marcus Brumbaugh, M.S., M.D.

Southern Historical Press, Inc.
Greenville, South Carolina

Please direct all correspondence and book orders to:
SOUTHERN HISTORICAL PRESS, Inc.
PO Box 1267
Greenville, SC   29602-1267

Originally printed: Washington, DC 1920 & 1925
ISBN #978-1-63914-139-5
Printed in the United States of America

Lists of Swiss Emigrants in the Eighteenth Century to the American Colonies

VOLUME I

ZURICH, 1734–1744
FROM THE ARCHIVES OF SWITZERLAND

BY

ALBERT BERNHARDT FAUST, A.B., Ph.D.

PUBLISHED BY
THE NATIONAL GENEALOGICAL SOCIETY
GAIUS M. BRUMBAUGH, Managing Editor
WASHINGTON, D. C.

1920

Lists of Swiss Emigrants in the Eighteenth Century to the American Colonies

ZÜRICH TO CAROLINA AND PENNSYLVANIA, 1734–1744

PREFACE

THE manuscript here presented is contained in the State Archive of Zürich, and was discovered during a search it was my privilege to make after materials for American history in the archives of Switzerland.[1] The manuscript is in many respects the most valuable single document relating to America contained in the Swiss archives, being quite as important for its historical as for its genealogical and statistical materials. The whole history of Swiss emigration in the eighteenth century is epitomized in this valuable document.[2] The statistician finds in it the only reliable enumeration of Swiss emigrants of the early period, and is able to base far-reaching estimates thereupon. The genealogist is furnished with a large mass of family records, including about two thousand names with accurate data as to origin, distribution and destination.

This large body of names supplements the lists of I. D. Rupp, in his collection of *Thirty Thousand Names, of German, Swiss, Dutch, French, and other Immigrants in Pennsylvania*, from 1737–1776, compiled mainly from the ship lists in Philadelphia. Many of the names in the manuscript will be found also in Rupp's collection, and it is a pleasure to know that so many persons reached their destination. But a still larger number are not contained in Rupp's lists, partly because the Philadelphia ship-lists do not give a complete record of all arrivals even in that port, and partly because a great many of those named in the manuscript were shipped to Carolina. Many of those who landed in Carolina, however, sub-

---

[1] See *Guide to the Materials for American History in the Swiss and Austrian Archives*, by Albert B. Faust, Washington, D. C., 1916. The search was made under the auspices of the Carnegie Institution of Washington, Department of Historical Research, in the year 1913.

[2] A fuller understanding of this important epoch in American history may be secured through the reprinted *Swiss Emigration to the American Colonies in the Eighteenth Century*, herein reproduced (see below, pp. 1–25) through the courtesy of Dr. J. Franklin Jameson, Managing Editor of *The American Historical Review*.

sequently settled in Pennsylvania. An interesting example of this
is the case of the family Kölliker (Kelker), who very soon settled
four miles from Lebanon, Pennsylvania. Our manuscript tells us
that Heinrich Kölliker, with three sons and two daughters left
Herrliberg in 1743, destined for Carolina. This corresponds to
the family tradition which Rupp received from the great-grandson
Rudolph F. Kelker, whose ancestor's name is not in the Philadelphia
ship-lists.[3] Our manuscript moreover supplies not only the names
of the parents, but also of all the children and their ages.

In order to understand the manuscript before us, it is necessary
to bring before our minds the attitude of the European governments
toward emigration in the eighteenth century. The liberality of
view that developed in the nineteenth century, i.e., of toleration if
not encouragement, and a disposition to aid the emigrant to a
betterment of his condition, by means of transportation facilities
and an intelligent view of what was before him, this humanitarian
policy is modern. The old tradition was, that emigration was a
crime, and punishable as such, equivalent to desertion, a deliberate
shirking of one's obvious duty to the fatherland.

There were economic reasons for this policy. The loss of sturdy
people such as belonged to the emigrating class, meant so many
hands less for the farms and trades, so many soldiers less for the
protection of the country in a possible struggle for existence. The
danger of over-population was not present in the eighteenth century,
that became the problem of a later age. The enormous increase
in population in Europe during the nineteenth century is one of the
most remarkable facts in history, and brought to the foreground
entirely new economic questions. Certainly the point of view on
the question of emigration changed entirely. But in the manuscript before us we are dealing with an earlier age, when each
government, especially in Central Europe, with the instinct of self-

[3] See Manuscript (MS), No. 42, and I. D. Rupp, *Thirty Thousand Names*,
New edition, 1898, p. 167, note. Rupp reports a family tradition that Heinrich
Kölliker and his family were twenty-eight weeks crossing the ocean, that two
sons and one daughter died on the way, that they landed in Carolina, but that
Heinrich Kölliker was an elder of "Berg Kirch" near Lebanon as early as 1745.
The certificate of character given the departing Köllikers and preserved by the
descendants, is signed by the same pastor Conrad Ziegler who also sent in the
report to the Zürich government in 1744. The mother's name, according to our
MS was "Rägula" Brätscher, but "Barbara" Brätscheri, according to Rupp's
reading of the family certificate. It is probable that Rupp mistook the more
frequent name Barbara for the less common Regula (probably badly written),
and did not notice that the family name ended in "in" (not "i"), a (feminine)
termination frequently added to the names of women.

preservation, jealously guarded its population against leaving its borders. An egress though slight might bring up the horror of depopulation and resultant annihilation. Martin Luther read into the thirty-seventh psalm the duty to remain in the fatherland and make an honest living therein. The seventeenth and eighteenth centuries tried to prohibit emigration by law.

Thus we find in Switzerland that during the most critical emigration period, between 1734 and 1750, decrees or mandates were issued against emigration every few years, in 1720, 1735, 1736, 1738, and 1749, again in 1753, and 1754, repeated in 1771 and 1773. The populous Protestant cantons Bern, Zürich and Basel were most affected, and of these Zürich proceeded most energetically against the so-called "emigration fever." She published the first severe edict, November 3, 1734, forbidding emigration to Carolina, preventing property sales by those wishing to leave, and proclaiming punishments for agents and distributors of literature. This was followed shortly after by the mandate of January 29, 1735, which added sterner measures, deprivation of citizenship and landrights forever, penalties for purchasers of emigrant property and severe punishment of agitators. Bern and Basel did not act as promptly, the former retaining for a time the policy of favoring the emigration of the homeless and sectarian classes, the latter being obliged by her location to keep the gateway open. But as soon as they felt the dangerous force, they attempted by the same methods as Zürich to stem the rising tide.

Zürich had cause to be terrified. In some of her districts the "fever" of emigration produced something like a stampede, e.g., in the district of Eglisau, as the manuscript shows. It is hardly surprising therefore that, to get at the facts, the authorities of Zürich attempted to get a census of the emigrants. That is what the manuscript before us actually is. The central authorities, in the year 1744, sent a circular letter to all the districts of Zürich, which in turn sent the message to all the parishes, demanding to know the names, with dates of birth, departure etc., of every man, woman and child who had left the country between 1734 and 1744 with the purpose of going to Pennsylvania or Carolina. The persons who executed the order were the local preachers, whose signatures appear in the manuscript attesting the accuracy of their reports. Each report is numbered, and there are as many as ninety-eight numbers or reports in the manuscript.

The reports are not alike either in form or content. Each minister chose a scheme of notation as he pleased. In some cases the date of birth, in others of baptism is recorded. The name is usually given in full, often the father's name and profession is added, sometimes an additional, a familiar name appears, the habit of calling and even recording persons by their nicknames being still prevalent in some parts of Switzerland. In cases of bondsmen, the name of the estate, or of journeymen, helpmates (Gesellen), the master's name is given for identification. Very commonly the trade of the men is stated, carpenters, joiners, turners, wheelwrights, wagon-builders, blacksmiths, locksmiths, masons, glaziers, weavers, shoe-makers and tailors abound, also very special trades are mentioned, as tilers, menders, rope-makers, resin-scrapers, hedge-, and scabbard-makers. The reports vary in matter from a bare statistical catalogue of names, to a gossiping letter. Most of the reports contain some notes or data which add to the human interest or fill out the historical background of the manuscript.

Most of the reports betray great anxiety to serve the cause of obstructing emigration, and in some cases an objectionable display of fawning servility appears in the communications to superiors. Some emphasize the speed with which their reply to the circular has been returned, the record-time being less than twenty-four hours; very many feel the necessity of apologizing for the departure of emigrants, calling attention to their paternal admonitions and repeated warnings concerning the dangers of the voyage and the false reports circulated about a land of plenty ("Schlaraffenland"), where sluggards have but to open their mouths for roast pigeons to fly in. A tendency existed to damage the reputations of those that departed, at least to represent them as an undesirable class, who had better be got rid of. On close inspection of the manuscript, however, it will be seen that the disorderly persons enumerated generally fainted by the wayside and rarely succeeded in getting across. The great bulk of those listed went with permission (though reluctantly given), which implies a certificate of good character from the pastor, when the contrary is not expressly stated.

Some of the pastors do not wish to curry favor, and a few boldly speak out, as the venerable pastor of Dättlikon, who says, that while the spiritual care of the people is essential, it would also be wise and good, to provide some form of work for the industrious unemployed, and then they would not be forced to emigrate.[4] A sombre coloring appears in the report from Schlieren, where the emigrants left amid pitiable lamentations of several mothers. Touching in the report of the pastor of Wyl is the brief reference

---

[4] See report No. 20.

accompanying Heinrich Sigerist, who left with his wife and "a daughter ten years old, who can read and pray very well indeed."[5]

The manuscript reveals much of the circumstances under which individuals were moved to emigrate. A very large number of the young people have lost their fathers, thereby missing either the parental protection at home, or the authority to curb their youthful spirit of adventure or "Wanderlust." Divorced persons and widowers are frequent, and widows with numerous children, who are. allowed to go because of the fear that they might fall a burden to the community. Young couples leave their homes because of objections to their marriage, they are frequently united on the way or on ship-board. But economic distress exerts the strongest pressure. From Richtenschweil[6] we hear of a group of emigrants who frankly declare, that they had to work day and night at home and even then they could not earn their daily bread, hence they were forced to leave: The hope of escaping unbearable conditions is the greatest driving power. Some left secretly to avoid the emigration tax, imposed so as to rescue some of the money that was leaving the country through the large emigration. The tax became as high as ten percent,[7] and was exacted with rigor.

Favorable letters or verbal reports from returning travelers gave a great stimulus to emigration. This we see illustrated again in the manuscript before us. The voyage is dangerous, the death-rate high, but work and food are plentiful, and the hard-working succeed, that is the old story. Occasionally an offer of help is made, as when a successful settler[8] promises to pay the transportation from London to America, if it be paid back in work on his farm. Those had the best chance to succeed who had a little money of their own, paupers very often were stranded on the way, or lay hopelessly at the ports.

An interesting study is furnished by the names. We have here an abundance of familiar Swiss and Palatine names such as Frick, Huber, Näff, Kunz, Kägi, Bär, Albrächt, Brunner, Frey, Fritschi, May, Wirt, Meyer and Müller. The transformation of such names into American spellings, and the many variant forms that appear in Pennsylvania and elsewhere, have been admirably treated by Professor Oscar Kuhns in his article *Studies in Pennsylvania German Family Names*,[9] which will be reprinted in the new edition of his *German and Swiss Settlements of Colonial Pennsylvania*.

[5] Report No. 97.   [6] No. 68.

[7] See reprint from *American Historical Review*, below, p. 1-25.   [8] No. 80.

[9] The studies in P. G. family names were first published in *Americana Germanica*, Vol. 4, pp. 299–341. The new edition of the *German and Swiss Settlements* etc. will be published by the Methodist Book Co.

It is noticeable that Carolina is mentioned more frequently as the destination of emigrants than Pennsylvania. This is due to the fact that in Switzerland no part of the American colonies received more advertising than the Carolinas. The only two independent Swiss colonies in America were located, the one in North Carolina at New Bern (1710) by Graffenried,[10] the other in South Carolina at Purrysburg (1732) by J. P. Purry.[11] Naturally much of the emigrant literature had the Carolinas for its subject, and the old tradition held its own for a long time. The Orangeburg-Lexington district in South Carolina also received a quota of Swiss settlers,[12] but migrations from one locality to another were very frequent.[13] The great distributing center, however, for the whole colonial German population, was Pennsylvania.

It must be remembered, that the names in this manuscript do not give us a complete catalogue of all the Swiss who came to America in the eighteenth century, but merely those from the populous canton of Zürich at the time of the great exodus, 1734–1744.[14] The names are representative and will furnish many a family who have a tradition of Swiss descent with a clue to their Swiss ancestry. In many instances, as in the case of the Kelker (Köllicker) family, the manuscript will furnish a verification or correction of family tradition.

The German original of this manuscript was copied under the supervision of Professor Hans Nabholz, state archivist of Zürich, to whom grateful acknowledgments are due. The translation and editing of the manuscript in the form in which it here appears was done at Cornell University, under the direction and with the assistance of the undersigned.

ALBERT B. FAUST.

ITHACA, N. Y., July 30, 1919.

[10] Cf. V. H. Todd, "Christoph von Graffenried and the Settlement of New Bern, N. C." (*Jahrbuch d. D. A. Hist. Gesellschaft v. Illinois, 1912.*) Also: *German American Annals*, n. s., XI, 210–302; and XII, 63–190.

[11] Cf. H. A. M. Smith, "Purrysburgh," *South Carolina Hist. Mag.*, X, 187–219.

[12] Cf. A. S. Salley, *The History of Orangeburg County*, Orangeburg, S. C., 1898.

[13] Cf. A. B. Faust, *The German Element in the United States*, Boston, 1919, Volume I, Chapters VIII (Carolinas) and X (Frontier). For bibliography on emigrant literature, *Guide*, supra, pp. 29–31. For traits of early German and Swiss settlers, see O. Kuhns, *German and Swiss Settlers of Colonial Pennsylvania*.

[14] Certain other rare and important lists of *Emigrants to the American Colonies from Basel and Bern, Switzerland*, of about the same period, are to be published in a subsequent volume, similar in character to this volume. Advance subscriptions will materially assist in the consummation of this project.

G. M. B.

TABLE OF CONTENTS

ILLUSTRATIONS

Swiss Emigration to the American Colonies in the Eighteenth Century*

By ALBERT BERNHARDT FAUST, A.B., Ph.D.

THE many thousands of Swiss colonists who came to America in the eighteenth century directed their course mainly to Pennsylvania and Carolina, which they commonly believed to be parts of the West India Islands. Two colonies were founded under Swiss leadership, one in 1710 at New Bern, North Carolina, under Christoph von Graffenried, the other in 1732 at Purrysburgh, South Carolina, promoted by Jean Pierre Purry of Neuchâtel. These colonies encountered all the hardships of pioneer settlements, extremes of heat and cold, fevers incident to the breaking of new ground, hostility of the natives, deficiencies in material equipment. Emigrants of the eighteenth century, before their arrival in the land of hope, had to endure the perils of the sea for months with slight protection and provision, they faced at best a decimation of their numbers on the crowded ships that conveyed them across, they were too often the victims of fraudulent captains and agents, who robbed them and sold them into servitude. All these trials and difficulties were borne and overcome by the early Swiss in common with all other sturdy and heroic pioneers of the eighteenth century.

But there is something distinctive about the emigration from Switzerland and that greater area of eighteenth-century emigration, the Palatinate and the upper Rhine country, the story of which has not been told. This is a record of hardship and obstruction at home, of barriers placed in the way of the emigrant by governments, of social ostracism, and of deprivation of all his rights and privileges. The home governments feared the loss of their people by emigration as much as they might by war or pestilence, and employed all means in their power to prevent it. For a study of this subject the materials found in the Swiss archives seem to be richer than those that have survived in the archives of the Palatinate and southern Germany, where in the eighteenth century the same policy prevailed of restricting, and if possible prohibiting, emigration. Conditions

* [Reprinted from THE AMERICAN HISTORICAL REVIEW, Vol. XXII, No. 1, pp. 21–41, Oct., 1916, through the courtesy of Dr. J. Franklin Jameson, Managing Editor.]

in Switzerland, therefore, may be assumed to illustrate also the situation for the German emigrant of the eighteenth century.

The only occasion when a Swiss government of the eighteenth century encouraged emigration was at the very beginning, and by the Council of Bern. This happened in the following way: in the years 1701–1704 the Bernese traveller Franz Ludwig Michel made two trips to the American colonies, visiting Pennsylvania and Virginia mainly, with the object incidentally of selecting a site for a colony. His manuscript report[1] on his journeys concludes with a draft of a petition to Queen Anne, proposing a Swiss settlement of from four to five hundred persons in Pennsylvania or Virginia under certain liberal conditions. The principal promoters of this plan were Georg Ritter and Rudolff Ochs,[2] who succeeded as early as 1705 in interesting the Council of Bern and the English envoy Aglionby in the scheme.[3]

It is of importance to note the motives that impelled the government of Bern to take up the matter. Emigration of the virile and well-to-do elements of the population was not what they intended, but they saw an opportunity of ridding themselves of what seemed to them two very undesirable classes of people. One of these was a pauper element, the homeless *Landsassen*, squatters not citizens. The other was the sectarian class, Baptists, Anabaptists, or Mennonites (*Wiedertäufer, Täufer*). The latter particularly were considered a source of danger to both Church and State: their refusal to bear arms or hold office, their simplicity of worship and communistic tendencies, seemed to undermine the foundations of civil governments, of the Protestant and Catholic churches alike. The

[1] This interesting manuscript is preserved in the Stadtbibliothek of Bern. Much of the German text of the manuscript has been printed in an article by J. H. Graf, entitled "Franz Ludwig Michel von Bern und seine ersten Reisen nach Amerika 1701–1704: ein Beitrag zur Vorgeschichte der Gründung von New-Berne," in the *Neues Berner Taschenbuch*, 1898, pp. 59–144. A translation into English of the complete manuscript has appeared in the *Virginia Magazine of History*, beginning in January, 1916, done by Professor William J. Hinke. The unique illustrations of the manuscript, including maps, the first building of the College of William and Mary, etc., are there reproduced to accompany the text; explanatory notes are also given.

[2] Joh. Rudolff Ochs compiled a descriptive work on Carolina, entitled: *Amerikanischer Wegweiser oder Kurtze und Eigentliche Beschreibung der Englischen Provintzen in Nord-America, Sonderlich aber der Landschafft Carolina, mit Grossem Fleiss zusammen getragen und an den Tag gegeben durch Joh. Rudolff Ochs neben einer neuen u. correcten Land-Karten von Nord- und Süd-Carolina* (Bern, 1711). Fifty thalers were voted to the author by the Council of Bern for this printed work dedicated to them; see Ratsmanuale of Bern, March 21, 1711.

[3] Cf. Faust, *Guide to the Materials for American History in Swiss and Austrian Archives* (Washington, 1916), p. 37.

most terrible and relentless persecution by courts specially appointed (*Täufer-Kammer*) and spies tracking the suspected to their homes (*Täufer-Jäger*), executions by fire and water (drowning, with intended irony), compulsory service in foreign armies or on the galleys of the Mediterranean, could not stop the spread of the sectarian doctrines. Deportation to the American colonies seemed to offer a hope of relief. Accordingly, the Council of Bern welcomed the opportunity offered by Ritter and Company, though they presented a double face, recommending America to the Mennonites as a place where they could obtain an abundance of food, while at the same time warning others against Pennsylvania, a desert, in which food supplies were altogether lacking, and from which the government felt duty-bound to hold its people back until longer experience had been gained.[4]

The expedition of Ritter did not start until March, 1710. We find an entry in the Ratsmanuale of Bern, that forty-five thalers a head were to be paid to Ritter for every *Täufer* he succeeded in bringing to America, and five hundred thalers more for another group of about one hundred emigrants (pauper class), who desired to go to America.[5] The deportation of Ritter's group of Anabaptists proved a failure, though every possible precaution had been taken to prevent their escape. The Dutch Mennonites objected strenuously to the deportation of brothers of their faith, and refused to allow any to be carried through their country for the purpose of transportation to America, unless it were of their own free will. Of the forty-three men and eleven women composing the *Täufer* group, thirty-two were released at Mannheim owing to age and sickness, the remaining twenty-two gained their liberty at Nimwegen.[6]

Graffenried and Michel became members of the Ritter Company in 1710, the former's connections with influential men in England, and the latter's experience, being of value in rescuing the Bernese emigration scheme from complete failure. A total purchase of 17,500 acres was made and probably through the influence of the surveyor Lawson the land was located at the confluence of the Neuse and the Trent in North Carolina. At this time London was crowded with more than ten thousand Palatine emigrants desirous of being transported to the American colonies, and the problem of their sustenance and disposition was becoming very burdensome.

[4] Bern, Mandatenbuch, 1709, 1710; Bern, Ratsmanuale (RM.), XL. 238, 392.
[5] Bern, RM., XLI. 229, 281, etc.
[6] Cf. Ernst Müller, *Geschichte der Bernischen Täufer* (Frauenfeld, 1895), pp. 252, 278, etc.

Graffenried and Michel succeeded in getting about six hundred of them for their Carolina colony, and Graffenried had the privilege of choosing what seemed to him the most desirable persons. These and the remnant of Bernese emigrants made up several ship-loads of colonists for Graffenried's new settlement. The fortunes of New Bern in its beginnings have been told by the facile pen of the founder himself.[7] He built better than he knew, under a luckier star than Peter Purry, whose town, so promising before the Revolutionary War, has left but a name in colonial history.

From the point of view of aiding the government in the deportation of undesirables, the Ritter agency was a total failure. Such a scheme was again discussed by the Berner Rat in 1710,[8] with a proposition to buy land in one of the American colonies for this purpose. But the plan was dropped, and never taken up again. There was a return to the original position on the subject of emigration, that contained in the prohibitory decrees of the seventeenth century,[9] punishing returning emigrants with loss of property and citizenship.

The old tradition forbade emigration. Leaving the country of one's birth seemed equivalent to desertion, and as desertion from the ranks was paid for with loss of life, so emigration was punishable with loss of all that the state deemed worth having, citizenship, property, land- and home-rights. Banishment, social ostracism, refusal of permission to return, imprisonment for life if caught returning, these were the conditions on which the emigrant gave up his country. Characteristic is the categorical command in the Lutheran translation of Psalm xxxvii. 3: "Bleibe im Lande und nähre dich redlich," which in the English version is an indefinite

[7] The three manuscripts of Graffenried on the settlement of New Bern are described, and two of them printed, in *German American Annals*, n. s., XI. 205–302, and XII. 63–190. See also *Guide*, pp. 73–75. W. F. von Mülinen, librarian of the city of Bern, has written the authoritative account of the life and career of Graffenried, based throughout on the original manuscripts given him by the Graffenried family. Cf. *Christoph von Graffenried, Landgraf von Carolina, Gründer von Neu-Bern*, zumeist nach Familienpapieren und Copien seiner amtlichen Berichte, von Wolfgang Friedrich von Mülinen, *Neujahrsblatt hrg. v. Historischen Verein des Kantons Bern für 1897* (Bern, 1896). A trustworthy and very readable account in English of Graffenried's settlement of New Bern has appeared in the *Jahrbuch der Deutsch-Amerikanischen Historischen Gesellschaft von Illinois*, Jahrgang 1912, by Vincent H. Todd: "Christoph von Graffenried and the Founding of New Bern, N. C." The reprint is entitled: "Baron Christoph von Graffenried's New Bern Adventures."

[8] Bern, RM., XLI. 408.

[9] Bern, Mandatenbuch, 1641, 1643, 1660; see *Guide*, p. 33.

promise of reward for good deeds.[10]   Remain in the land of thy forefathers and earn an honest living therein, is the admonition which Luther reads out of the Psalmist's text, and which is spoken out of his own heart.   Emigration is sinful and its wages death, so judged the sixteenth, seventeenth, and most of the eighteenth century; the nineteenth introduced a more liberal view.

There were some good reasons for the policy of restricting, if not prohibiting, emigration in the eighteenth century.   An able-bodied emigrant meant the loss of a defender of the land, and of an agricultural or industrial worker.   Especially in the smaller countries of Central Europe a large loss of population might mean political or economic ruin.   An increase of population seemed the result of good government, a decrease an indication of unsuccessful or incapable rulers.   Many governments, particularly in Switzerland, assumed a paternal attitude toward their subjects, caring for their material and spiritual welfare, or at least pretending to do so.   They felt this duty very keenly when it was to their advantage.   Hearing that many emigrants were lost at sea, and that many others met insuperable difficulties after their arrival in the American colonies, they warned their subjects in fatherly fashion, and soon forbade their leaving, to save them against themselves.   Similarly the Protestant governments were very much concerned for the spiritual welfare of such as might in 1720 take service in a Catholic province,[11] or either church might object to its people going into a colony of sectarians.   In 1716 the Ratsherren of Bern passed a resolution to allow only those to emigrate who could prove that they were well taught in religion (and were poor).[12]   Thus they endeavored to save the souls of their people, and at the same time to prevent the spread of heretical doctrines.

After the colonization scheme of 1710 had quickly come to an end at Bern, no further attempts were made for a decade.   The initiative then twice came from the neighboring principality of Neuchâtel (Neuenburg).   In 1720 a captain in the regiment Karrer by the name of Merveilleux (alias Wunderlich) attempted to secure recruits for service in (the island of) Mississippi.   He seems to have succeeded in getting "several whole families of poor people,"[13] but

---

[10] Psalm xxxvii. 3 in the Lutheran Bible reads: "Hoffe auf den Herrn und thue Gutes; bleibe im Lande und nähre dich redlich."   The English Bible interprets: "Trust in the Lord, and do good; so shalt thou dwell in the land, and verily thou shalt be fed."

[11] Expedition of Merveilleux, service in Mississippi region; see *Guide*, p. 41, etc.

[12] Bern, RM., LXVIII. 36.

[13] *Ibid.*, LXXXIV. 378; Erlach-Buch D., p. 661.

2

his scheme was vigorously opposed by Bern and other governments, partly owing to a distrust of overseas service, and partly on religious grounds, as described above. The other attempt was far more successful in course of time. It was the plan of Jean Pierre Purry of the firm Purry et Compagnie in Neuchâtel to found a colony in Carolina. He began to advertise as early as 1725 for three or four hundred workingmen of different professions, all Swiss Protestants of good reputation and manners, between the ages of twenty and forty. In spite of his advertisements,[14] spread broadcast and posted wherever possible, in which South Carolina was praised as one of the "finest countries in the universe," Purry did not make much headway until about five years later. He also published a book descriptive of Carolina, which was feared with good reason by paternal Swiss governments. In 1732 Purry established his colony of Purrysburgh with ninety-three colonists, to which there were soon added several hundred more.[15] The settlement had a prosperous beginning in comparison with many others, and is noted in colonial history for its experiment in silk growing and manufacture.

Social and economic conditions favored an increase in emigration during the thirties and forties of the eighteenth century. In Bern, Zürich, Basel, Luzern, Appenzell, Fribourg, Vaud, and elsewhere, the ruling classes, often composed of a few patrician families, bore down heavily upon the city and country folk, depriving them of all possibility of rising above their wretched economic condition, and enacting offensive laws, such as those forbidding artisans to carry wares under the arcades (*Lauben*) of Bern, so that the patricians might walk through them in comfort, or closing the vegetable market to all but the noble class until 11 a. m. Rebellion was the consequence, but unfortunately victory always remained with the aristocrats until the French Revolution awakened the Swiss people to a united stand for their liberties.

During this period Switzerland remained the recruiting ground for the powerful nations of Europe. Young Swiss noblemen found it a profitable business to equip and lead regiments in foreign armies, while their recruits, good soldiers who did not spare themselves,

[14] See Documents, F. DOCUMENTS A–F, referred to on this and following pages, are contained in *American Historical Review*, Vol. XXII, No. 1 (October, 1916), pp. 88–132. Found in the state archives of Basel and Bern, they were published to accompany this article, and to illustrate problems relating to the Swiss emigration of the eighteenth century.

[15] Lists of their names are given in the authoritative account of the colony by Judge Henry A. M. Smith, entitled "Purrysburgh," in the *South Carolina Historical Magazine*, X. 187–219 (1909). See also *Guide*, p. 169, etc.

received none of the bounteous rewards. A large percentage of officers and men, however, never returned to their homes. Swiss fought against Swiss on the battlefields of Europe, in the War of the Austrian Succession, as often before. It was estimated that in 1740 about 69,000 Swiss mercenary soldiers served in foreign armies, about 22,000 in French, 2400 in Austrian, 13,600 in Spanish, 10,600 in Sardinian, 20,400 in Dutch service.[16]

Add to these conditions periodic failures of crops, due to hailstorms and floods, as in the Bernese Oberland, and no sentimental ties nor governmental restrictions could restrain the desire for emigration. It is not surprising that at times this desire rose to a passion, that threatened to depopulate large sections and gave the governments good cause for alarm. Such an emigration epoch existed in Switzerland between 1730 and 1750, the high tide coming between 1734 and 1744.

What started the movement it is difficult to say. Perhaps the continuous advertisements of J. P. Purry had the effect of touching the match to the powder-barrel. Perhaps favorable letters from colonists happy in the new country had been coming in for a long time, with the natural suggestion to follow after. At all events the emigration fever gave visible signs of becoming epidemic.

Zürich acted quickly, issuing a decree, November 3, 1734,[17] forbidding her people to travel to Carolina, preventing the sale of property by those wishing to emigrate, proclaiming punishment of agents enticing people to emigrate or distributing seductive literature. This was followed after a few months by the decree of January 29, 1735, which repeated the previous commands, and added sterner measures, deprivation of citizenship and land-rights forever, punishment also of the purchasers of property sold by emigrants, close watch over and severe punishment of persons enticing others to leave. The decrees were read from all the pulpits in town and country, they were posted in public places, yet Zürich, as the records show, found it necessary to let large numbers depart.

Bern did not act as promptly, nor with the same decision. She hesitated before sending an order, July 6, 1734, to all the districts, warning against emigration to Carolina, restricting emigration to the homeless class and to sectarians, who were even to be assisted with

[16] Cf. *Eröffnungsrede*, gehalten in der Helvetischen Gesellschaft zu Langenthal, den 31. Mai 1843, von Regierungsrat Fetscherin in Bern, pp. 84–85. Cf. also: Johannes Dierauer, *Geschichte der Schweizerischen Eidgenossenschaft* (Gotha, 1912), IV. 234.

[17] This decree and the one of 1735 are printed in full in the *Guide*, pp. 15–17.

funds to get away.   The policy of 1710 seems still to have held sway in the minds of many of the Ratsherren, that of using America as a colony for deportation of undesirables.   A letter is written to Unter-see, urging the *Amtmann* to explain to those desirous of leaving, that the "printed book on Carolina" contains falsehoods; those who can not be persuaded to remain, shall be taxed five per cent. of the value of their property (a tax raised to 10 per cent. shortly after). In the meantime the gun-maker Striker (Stryger) of Steffisburg is suspected of being an emigrant agent, he is commanded to surrender his list of names, and in December he is banished from the country. Anxiously Bern inquires of Zürich, what she is doing to cure the "emigration fever."   Zürich sends copies of her decrees forbidding emigration, whereupon Bern is roused to publish her first decree, January 12, 1735,[18] warning her people of the Oberland against the trip to Carolina.   It is a document altogether different from the Zürich decrees, in that it attempts to use persuasion rather than force.   The *Amtleute* are to explain to those desirous of seeking their fortunes in Carolina, that the printed accounts on the subject are misleading, that the sea-journey is a long one, the change of air, the strange food, the lack of fresh water, occasion sickness and death among Swiss people, pirates on the sea sell them into slavery, and arriving in Carolina as paupers, they are obliged to sell them-selves into servitude.   Those who in spite of these warnings were determined to go, should not be prohibited from doing so, nor would they sacrifice the government's good-will, except those who pos-sessed means valued at over five hundred pounds, who should be compelled to give up their citizenship and land-right.   Emigration was not to be prohibited, but made distasteful, and the country was to be guarded against loss, as when persons of the homeless class were put into the places of those citizens who had left the district.

The records of the year 1735 at Bern show continuous emigra-tion.   Investigations concerning Carolina are ordered and reports are received.   On February 3 a vote is recorded that no more pass-ports shall be given to emigrants, but on March 2, on their petition, 322 persons are allowed to leave for the American colonies, and on the next day another group of emigrants from Oberhasli are given permission, provided they have means to the extent of five hundred pounds, defraying their expenses, and provided children left behind be cared for.   On March 13 three ships are designated to transport the greater part (*Hauptschwarm*) of the emigrants.[19]   On March

---

[18] The decree is printed in full in the *Guide*, pp. 34-35.

[19] Bern, RM., CXLVI. 215, 266, 270, 337.

17 a group are given back the ten per cent. tax which they had already paid.   If any of them desire to return, they can still buy back their property.   If children do not desire to go with their parents, they are to receive a part of the family property.   March 23 a complaint is received from the financial agent May in London concerning the distressing condition of Swiss (especially from Bern, Zürich, Graubünden) emigrants arriving there.   Money is voted to bring them back, with one exception, for whom a guinea is sent to continue her journey to America.   April 25 some success is reported in keeping back a group of highlanders of Oberhasli and Interlaken, and advice is asked concerning methods of providing for them. But, a few months after, the *commissaire* in London reports that a number of Bernese, desiring to go to Georgia, had arrived in England.   On September 26 measures are taken against a certain person named Quinche of Neuchâtel, who is trying to entice people to go to Carolina (probably in the interests of Purrysburgh).   This completes the record of the excitement at Bern for the year 1735. The pressure of emigration proved irresistible.[20]

A vacillating policy in regard to emigration continued at Bern for a number of years more.   An optimistic view was recorded on May 5, 1738:   The emigration tax (*Abzug*) should not be increased, first, because of the attention thereby directed to it and consequent dissatisfaction, secondly, because emigration was on the decline, "the RABIES CAROLINAE" had happily disappeared, and the people had allowed themselves to be persuaded by the sad fate of the best of the emigrants rather than by the paternal advice of the Ratsherren.[21]   But emigration had by no means stopped, it was destined to flow again, triumphantly, especially after 1740.   In 1741 Hans Riemensperger of Toggenburg is planning to induce people to go with him to Carolina and Georgia, and his arrest is ordered.   Neuchâtel is warned against him.   Peter Huber is under suspicion the following year, when the "emigration fever" seems to start anew. "Auswanderung wieder lebhaft im Gang," is an entry in the record book on March 1, 1742.   The Bernese highlanders are emigrating again in large numbers.   Some are diverted from their purpose by offers of work in the French parts of the canton.   In view of the danger the policy of Bern changes.   A decree is issued April 26, 1742, forbidding all emigration to Carolina or elsewhere in America, under heavy penalties.   A period of three months is allowed in

[20] See *Guide*, pp. 43–45.
[21] Säckelschreiber Protokolle, Y., Bern, May 5, 1738.

which emigrants may return, after which loss of citizenship, land-right, and property will be enforced. Property shall not be sent out of the country, but shall be forfeited to the community which the emigrant has left. Children under age (at the time of emigration) may return to their rights at any time, others shall be treated as agents attempting to entice people to emigrate. The decree yielded nothing in severity to those of Zürich published in 1734–1735 and re-enforced in 1739, 1741, and 1744.

In spite of all exertions on the part of the government, so it is recorded February 17, 1744, people from the Oberland go to Carolina in hordes (*haufenweise*). They are allowed to go, but such as return are to be put into prison. Peter Inäbnit, returning from Carolina, is under suspicion and is thrown into prison. On the same day, March 17, 1744, eighty emigrants, who have already paid their tax (*Abzug*), pass by the city of Bern in a boat. Other agents (*Amerika-Werber*) appear, Jakob Walder of the canton of Zürich, Jacob Joner of Basel, and others. Reports having appeared in newspapers that many thousands of emigrants had arrived in Basel ready to go to America and Nova Scotia, Bern requests Basel, Zürich, and other cantons, on June 26, to suppress such newspaper reports (whether true or false). Similarly a French paper of Bern is rebuked in 1750 (February 26), for publishing an article on Carolina and Pennsylvania, "where people make their fortunes." In the same year, after a group from the Oberland has succeeded in egtting a ship at Yverdun to take them over the lake, emigrants are thenceforth forbidden to take ship at this point. Letters are constantly searched for and confiscated; in 1753 the bearers of letters, Hans Zurflüh and Hans Wyss, are imprisoned for twenty-four hours, and then compelled to leave the country within a week.

Preachers who came to Switzerland soliciting funds for churches or Bibles, or seeking ministers for churches in America, were thought to be especially dangerous, since they could not be punished by the laws, yet their presence had the effect of enticing people to emigration. Therefore they were given the *consilium abeundi* and to facilitate their speedy departure, their hotel and travelling expenses (to the border) were given them. This happened to Michael Schlatter (prominent organizer of Reformed churches in America) in 1751, and to Pastor Gasser (minister of the Reformed church at Santee Forks, South Carolina) in 1755, who shortly after was ordered to be arrested on the charge of influencing people at Interlaken. Thus the Ratsherren of Bern had troubles unceasing in the attempt to keep their people at home, and even in 1766 and later complained of losing their population.[22]

Basel felt the pressure of emigration immediately because of her location at the gateway of travel.   She had cause to complain of emigrants arriving in a pauperized condition, waiting to be transported.[23]   A large number of emigrants were examined as to the causes of their leaving,[24] the most common reasons given being poverty, lack of employment, and failure of crops, while the hope of bettering their condition, or making their fortunes appears very seldom.   The government of Basel commonly allowed emigrants to pass on, though vigorous efforts were made to discourage wholesale emigration.   As early as 1735 difficulties were created for emigrants who wished to sell their property (*Vergantung*, or *Ganten*); the ten per cent. tax[25] also, and an additional sum for manumission in the case of those in bondage, were exacted, except that those whose possessions amounted to less than one hundred pounds[26] were released from all payments.   Many there were who had not a penny, which circumstance is also faithfully recorded in the official lists,[27] sometimes with a spark of unconscious humor, as: Hans Jacob Märcklin from Dürnen has 1 wife, 4 children, and otherwise nothing (*sonst nichts*).   Martin Gass from Rothenflue has 1 wife, 8 children, and nothing more (*weiter nichts*).   The same list reports that: Hans Rudi Erb from Rotenflue is unmarried, has a bad face, and 130 pounds worth of property.   To avoid the tax or for other reasons many emigrants left their homes in secret, leaving behind letters to their friends, or sending them regretful notice of their departure after having crossed the border.   These are referred to as *Heimliche Emigranten* in the records of Basel.[28]

The decrees of Basel, finally forbidding emigration to America, resemble those of Zürich and Bern.   The one of 1749, printed in full among the Documents[29] accompanying this article, prohibits the securing of an inheritance by anyone who has left the country; the emigrant is to be considered as "dead," and bereft of rights.   This

[22] The subject may be followed in detail by consulting the Ratsmanuale, in *Guide*, pp. 40–53.

[23] Cf. *Guide*, p. 101, etc.

[24] See Documents, D, 1 and 2.

[25] Cf. Kaspar Hauser, "Ueber den Abzug in der Schweiz," in *Jahrbuch für Schweizerische Geschichte*, hrg. auf Veranstaltung der Allgemeinen Geschichtsforschenden Gesellschaft der Schweiz, Bd. XXXIV. (Zürich, 1909).

[26] The value of the pound, Basel currency, was about two francs.

[27] See Documents, D, 1.

[28] For a specimen of such a letter, see Documents under B, no. 4.

[29] See under Documents, E, 1.

mandate was renewed in 1771, and an additional decree was published in 1773, aimed particularly at crafty emigrant agents, attempting to collect inheritances for friends in America. The word *Neuländer* is here[30] used for *Werber*, agent. The petitions and records at Basel show that the high tide of emigration at that city occurred between 1734 and 1752; another wave started about 1767 and lasted until 1773, when it was interrupted by the Revolutionary War. Emigration started again, though feebly, in 1786.[31]

The archives of Schaffhausen give evidence of emigration from that quarter in large numbers between 1734 and 1748. The Chronicle of the city (*Harder Chronik*) refers to this emigration several times, *e.g.*, September 8, 1738:

> In June many poor people from neighboring districts, notably Merishausen and Reiat, emigrated to North America. When then also some [of our] subjects at Rüdlingen and Buchberg made the unseasonable resolve to leave their fatherland and travel to far distant lands, and thus in thoughtless manner expose themselves to great discomfort and extreme wretchedness with repentance coming too late, the government "stepped in" and forbade emigration on penalty of the loss of land-right.

The cantons of Aargau, Solothurn, and especially Graubünden also furnished a quota of emigrants in the eighteenth century, though the records have been lost. There was emigration also from Luzern and the forest cantons, though the emigration from Catholic was smaller than from Protestant cantons. Interesting plans were proposed from time to time, to employ those desiring to emigrate in some remunerative industry, or to use the undivided land (*Allmend*) or the forests (*Hochwald*) for the benefit of the hopelessly poor. Almost without exception, however, these plans were never put into execution, and in the very few cases when they were carried out, they lived only a very short time.[32]

The archives of Switzerland throw new light on the character and methods of the emigrant agent. Owing to the severe penalties placed upon the trade, he appears as a far more subtle individual than the traditional *Neuländer*. The latter (so he is generally depicted), having failed as a colonist and finding "emigrant-hunting" a far more profitable means of livelihood, affected the appearance of wealth, with his conspicuous attire and heavy gold watch and

---

[30] See under Documents, E, 2.

[31] See *Guide*, pp. 101–107.

[32] Cf. Dr. E. Lerch, *Die Bernische Auswanderung nach Amerika im 18. Jahrhundert*, separate print from the *Blätter für Bernische Geschichte, Kunst, und Altertumskunde*, Jahrgang V., Heft 4, December, 1909, pp. 19–31. Cf. also Bern, Responsa Prudentum, *Guide*, p. 55.

chain, and loudly proclaimed tales of easily acquired wealth, bearing forged letters in witness of his claims. Such a figure may have existed and flourished at the seaports of Europe and America, but he could not have survived longer than a day in the upper Rhine country or in Switzerland. Watchful eyes would have been upon him, and the reward would have been collected for his capture twice before he could have earned a single fee for bringing an emigrant to port. The successful emigrant agent was a person of an entirely different description, shrewd, tactful, inconspicuous, denying any purpose of his visit, except to collect a debt or inheritance for a friend in America. He was careful not to arouse suspicion, and gave information only when asked for it. A good view of his methods can be derived from the records at Bern and Basel of trials (*Verhöre*) of persons suspected of enticing emigrants. Two of these are of particular interest, the examination of Peter Huber at Basel and Bern in 1742, and of Peter Inäbnit at Bern, in 1744. The verbatim reports of these trials, found in the archives of Bern and Basel, are published here for the first time, accompanying this article.[33]

Peter Huber was taken captive at Basel on the request of Bern. The examination at Basel reveals that he was a native of Oberhasli in the Bernese Oberland, about thirty years of age, and by trade a shoemaker. He was on his way back to Carolina, accompanied by his wife and two children, whom he had come to fetch the foregoing summer. One daughter had gone with him to Carolina on his first trip, about eight years before (1734), and she had remained in Carolina. To the question, whether he had any other travelling companions, he answered that his sister was bringing his baggage for him, and another woman, Barbara Horger, expected to go with him to Carolina. He denied knowing aught of the group of emigrants who had arrived at Basel, and affirmed positively that he had not urged anyone to make the journey with him. A number of emigrants at Basel were examined,[34] one of whom declared that he had been enticed by Huber, but that now, yielding to the advice of the authorities, he would prefer to remain. All ten others denied that Huber had put the idea into their heads, and all but two insisted on being allowed to go. So far no damaging evidence was brought against Huber. He was then taken to Bern in custody, and subjected to a more searching trial. The questions show that a body of facts had been collected against him that might indeed

---

[33] See Documents, A, 1, 3, 4.
[34] See under Documents, A, 2.

arouse suspicion, but such was Huber's skill in answering them, that he could not be convicted on the first examination. Some of the questions and answers were as follows:

Q.: Could he [Huber] deny, that he had desired to take some people away with him?

A.: He had desired to take no one away, except his sister, and the foreigner Jacob Lanu, who had worked in the mines for seven years. The latter had frequently approached him asking to be taken along, but he [Huber] had refused, saying that such a thing was prohibited. The inspector of the mines had, however, told Lanu that, being a free man, he could go wherever he wished. [Lanu was not a Bernese subject.]

When Lanu was confronted with Huber, contrary to his previous statement, he declared that Huber had not enticed him, but that he wanted to go on his own free will.

Q.: Did not Peter Scherz of Aeschi come to him [Huber] at Unterseen, and ask, whether a weaver could with wife and children make a living in Carolina?

A.: Scherz had come to him at Zollbrück, crossed the lake and spent the night with him, but that he [Huber] had told him there were enough weavers in Carolina, moreover that Scherz had not enough money for so long a journey. Subsequently he had received two letters from Scherz, which he had not answered.

Q.: Whether he did not urge Hans Aebiger to go to Carolina?

A.: Aebiger had come to him and asked how the hunting was in Carolina? Upon this he had described the country. Aebiger also asked him about a gun, which Aebiger offered him.

Aebiger affirmed, when examined, that Huber had awakened in him the desire to emigrate, and especially in his wife, who left him no peace about it, but that he was willing to remain, rather than incur the ill-will of the government. Several others also were examined.[35] Those who decided to remain, perhaps in order to better their chances with the authorities, threw the blame on Huber, while those who were firm in their resolution to go, exonerated Huber from any attempt to entice them.

After a number of other questions on individual cases, the court declared that it was very plain that Huber had enticed the poor people by praising Carolina; he should therefore confess in order to secure more gracious treatment. Thereupon Huber boldly affirmed, that he had spoken nothing but the truth; he had given up his citizenship and land-right, and had enticed no one; no person would

[35] See under Documents, A, 3 (at the close).

dare to confront him with such a charge.   Huber was remanded to prison.

A few days later a slip of paper was discovered, which Huber had thrown out of the prison window, and on which he told those who were still minded to travel with him to Carolina, to go and tarry for a while in the neighboring Neuchâtel; as soon as he was set free he would come to them and take them along with him to Carolina.   Upon this new evidence Huber was tried again.   The examiners skillfully concealed their discovery at first, in the hope of extracting more information, and cautioned him to adhere strictly to the truth.

Q.: What route had he [Huber] taken on his previous journey to Carolina?

A.: By way of Burgundy [i.e., Neuchâtel-Besançon], and France to Calais.

Q.: Why then did he take a different route this time, and go by way of the Brünig Pass, Unterwalden, Basel?

The question was a critical one, for there was suspicion, that he was taking people from the Oberland by the mountain route to Lucerne, and thence to Basel, keeping them out of the jurisdiction of Bern.   Otherwise they would have to come by way of Thun and pass Bern, on the way to Neuchâtel.

A.: He had intended to take his former route, but in order to avoid suspicion, and being followed by emigrants, he preferred the other route.

Q.: Whether he did not know that people had gone ahead to Basel to await him there?

A.: No, he had heard that one or another had gone down from the Oberland, but where they intended to go he did not know, except in the case of Barbara Horger, who accompanied him.

Q.: He should tell truthfully, whether this was not a plan, to meet at Basel, and then go together to Carolina?

A.: No!   He had nothing to do with those people, for he expected to take his usual route from Basel by land to Calais, while those people were going to take the Rhine route, and a ship had already been engaged for them.

New evidence was now brought against him; his baggage had been examined and a most interesting device for concealing letters was found therein.

Q.: Was he [Huber] not in possession of a wooden vessel [hölzernes Geschirr], the top of which would hold drink, and the bottom of which could be used for concealing letters?

A.: Yes, such a one was made for him by Hans Roth in Carolina, and could be found in his baggage

Q.: Had he not given Landsvenner Sterchi[36] at Zollbrück a ring and seal, by which he could recognize letters coming from him?

A.: No! He had, however, brought with him a letter of Peter Zaugg in Carolina to Sterchi; he knew not if anything of the sort were contained therein.

Q.: Since he [Huber] had thus far been very obstinate in denying answers to questions, at the same time had assured the court, that he would gladly confess all that was true, they wished now to see how earnestly he loved the truth: Did he not, the day before yesterday, throw [from his prison window] toward a woman of his part of the country [Oberland], a piece of paper, on which was written, that those that still had a desire to travel with him, should go to Neuchâtel and tarry there a while, that he hoped his case was not so bad that he might not soon be free, and when at liberty he would come and in passing take them with him, they would then directly be in Burgundy, and could pass on unhindered?

A.: At this question he seemed altogether terrified, looked about him to one side and another, and for some time did not know what to say, and the tears came to his eyes. Finally he answered: Yes! He could not deny this; he had thought, that when once free and finding these people outside of the jurisdiction of Bern, he could take them along without doing any wrong, but he confessed being grievously at fault in this, and humbly besought God's and Their Graces' pardon. [Act. March 21, 1742.]

Huber was taken back to prison, but was evidently set free soon after, and banished forever, perhaps under threat of the death penalty if he were caught attempting to return. We learn from the testimony of Peter Inäbnit, two years later, that Huber arrived in Carolina with a small number of emigrants, perhaps with more than the examinee was willing to state.

Peter Inäbnit (Imäbnit, In Äbnit, or Im Äbnit), brought to trial in 1744, was not so fortunate. He lost his life in the venture, though equally clever and perhaps better instructed, for Jnäbnit left Carolina after Huber had returned, and probably received directions from him. Peter Inäbnit had left Switzerland in 1734 with his parents and their children, when he was still under age. He was therefore privileged to return to his home in Grindelwald, and could lawfully remain there if he wished, for the law debarring an emigrant from all rights did not apply to his children leaving under age. It

---

[36] Landsvenner (Bannerträger) Sterchi was a friend of emigrants; see his name mentioned in a letter, Documents, C, 2.

was very clever on the part of Inäbnit to declare that he wished to live in Switzerland, and not return to Carolina. He was about twenty-five years of age in 1743, when he reappeared in the Oberland, to collect some money from a relative in his native town of Grindelwald. He was observed moving from place to place, notably in the districts of Hasli and Interlaken, whence most of the emigrants had always come. He also visited Reichenbach (located near Bern on the peninsula of the river Aare), then the seat of the English envoy. He had been seen surrounded by large crowds of people, especially on Sundays, and he was asked all sorts of questions by them, but was moderate in his speech. He was also reported to have brought letters from Carolina. For all of these circumstances he was under suspicion, and was soon brought before a court for examination.[37]

Many a prisoner fell a victim to his inquisitors on the initial question, why have you been taken captive? Not so, Peter Inäbnit. He expressed ignorance and surprise.

Q.: Why was he still remaining in the country, though his business must have been settled long ago?

A.: He expected to remain in Switzerland. In Carolina he had lived nine years, and suffered from illness all but the first two, for that reason he did not like the country, and did not expect to return.

Q.: There were reasons to doubt this, for it was known, that he had come with a very different purpose; he should tell squarely, whether he had not come to entice some of his countrymen, and engage them to go with him to Carolina?

A.: God forbid! He had not come to take anybody with him.

Q.: How could he explain, that wherever he appeared in the Oberland, crowds of people gathered about him, and since then it was found that a great many desired to emigrate?

A.: Of that he knew nothing, but he could tell no other reason, than that they wanted to hear something about how their relatives in Carolina were getting along.

Q.: Had he not praised the country, or talked about it to anyone?

A.: To many who asked out of curiosity, he had spoken about the nature of the country, but no one could prove, that he had advised anyone to go there.

Q.: Whether he did not write a letter to the English envoy with this intention?

A.: At this he was somewhat taken aback. Finally he confessed having written the letter,[38] saying he never intended delivering it to the

---

[37] See Documents, A, 4.

[38] The letter in question has survived; it is printed in full under Documents, A, 4. It reported to the English resident at Reichenbach, that there were about

envoy, but merely wished to satisfy those who urged him to do so. No sensible person, said he, would ever think, that anything could be accomplished in this way.

Q.: Would he deny having been at Reichenbach, in order to speak with the envoy?

A.: To be sure, he had been there, but had had no audience with the envoy.[39]

Q.: Whether he did not, at Grindelwald, station himself in the churchyard on Sundays, and commend Carolina to the people?

A.: He never staid long in the churchyard, but many people came to him in the inn, but he told them nothing more than what they asked about Carolina.

Q.: Whether he had not brought letters from Carolina, that undoubtedly gave a favorable enough account of the country?

A.: Yes. Eight letters, one to Grindelwald, and seven to Oberhasli.

Questioned about the letters in another examination, he said he knew not the contents, except that Christen Brauen wrote to his father, that he had arrived safely, but not having had sufficient means, he had been obliged to serve for four years. People in Carolina, Inäbnit declared, had tried to overload him with letters, but he had refused except in behalf of his nearest friends, because only trouble came of it.

Q.: Who had told him to write to the English envoy?

A.: He could not tell, but he had been urged from many quarters.

Q.: Why did he wish to speak to the English envoy personally?

A.: He wanted to offer his services, since he had heard that the English resident desired a servant who could speak English. But he did not succeed in seeing him.

Q.: What had he told the people about Carolina, making so many of them anxious to go there?

A.: He had not said anything specially about it, except in answer to questions; moreover, he had neither praised nor blamed the country, but of course told them what the conditions were, and that over there as here, whoever brought nothing was in a bad way, and although as a carpenter he had earned 15 batzen a day, he did not wish to go back, because he could not pull through very well.

200 persons ready to go to Carolina, if the Hon. Ambassador would open his generous hand, but that most of the people were poor, and some that were not did not know how to get their property away. Some had small children and did not know how to go about the matter of the journey. They wanted also to know something about the period of service.

[39] It would have been very unwise for the envoy to receive a person offering to violate the laws of the country to which he was accredited.

Q.: Had not in the preceding year Peter Huber taken people to Carolina? [An attempt to connect him with the convicted agent.]

A.: There were nine or ten persons who arrived with him, but he
[Huber] could not have derived any benefit therefrom, especially since
some, for their travelling expenses, had to serve those who had released
them from the ship.

Q.: He should once for all tell the truth, and say, whether he had
not been sent expressly to bring people into the country?

A.: No, he had merely wished to see his fatherland again, and remain
here, or in Germany.

The document goes on to say, that after the prisoner, in spite of
expostulations, threats of torture, and confrontation with the exe-
cutioner, had refused further statement or confession, he was taken
up to the torture-chamber and once more vehemently urged, and
threatened with the application of torture—nevertheless he adhered
firmly to his previous statements, *viz.*, that he had not come to entice
anyone to go to Carolina, that he did not know what was contained
in the letters he brought with him, that he himself did not intend to
return to Carolina, and no one could charge that he had lured anyone to go, on the contrary he had rather advised against than in
favor of emigrating.   For the rest he realized that he was in the
power of the high authorities, they could do with him whatever they
wished, however he begged that they graciously give him his liberty.
Upon that he was condemned to stand in the stocks, and then banished forever.   This was in February, 1744.

In spite of his cleverness, courage, and firmness, Peter Inäbnit
failed, for he lacked the quality of caution.   He made the mistake
of writing too many letters, dangerous instruments, for they could
easily get into the wrong hands.   Instead of leaving Switzerland at
once, he was discovered at Basel during the following month, and
brought once more to Bern.   There he was forced to confess that
he had written letters to Hans Nägeli, Christen Brunner, and Hans
Müller, instructing them how to go about preparing for the journey
to Carolina.   He claimed that he was greatly urged to do so, was
under the influence of drink, and believed he was doing no wrong,
since he was banished anyway (not a convincing argument).   He
confessed having written also to Grindelwald for the money which
was coming to him, and to his cousin Christen Feller, near Thun,
inviting him to go with him to England to visit a relative.   Concerning the letter from Philip Wild of Rotterdam,[40] he explained

[40] This letter to Peter Inäbnit was captured, according to a record in the Ratsmanuale of Bern, February 20, 1744.   It seemed to prove that Inäbnit had insti-
gated about 70 families to emigrate.   On this evidence he was ordered to be
arrested again.   See *Guide*, p. 47.

that the blacksmith Jacob Ritschard[41] had for several years back planned to go to Carolina, and had requested him to write for information to Rotterdam, which he did, asking Wild to reply to Ritschard.   For himself he had done nothing, and was not minded to go back to Carolina, and no one could bear witness against him, saying that he had enticed anyone.   Therefore he prayed for his release.   This was on March 27, 1744.

The court sent Peter Inäbnit back into confinement.   His prison was one of those picturesque old towers still standing in the city of Bern, the one still known as the *Käfigturm* (the cage-tower, *i.e.*, prison-tower).   The prisoner had many friends, and they were willing to aid him.   They brought him food and wine; a tool for boring was smuggled in to him and a rope, by which he planned to let himself down and make his escape.   Unfortunately an accident prevented the successful issue of his daring venture.   The rope seems to have been securely fastened, but either the rope broke or the prisoner lost his hold.   He was discovered lying bleeding and unconscious at the base of the tower.   The abettor of emigration was carried to a neighboring inn, but never recovered speech or consciousness from after nine in the evening, when he was found, until seven in the morning, when he died.   No sympathy was wasted on him by the rulers of Bern.   "Owing to clearly proven and partly confessed crimes of the deceased, the body was ordered to be buried under the place of public execution," thus abruptly ends the chronicle of the career of Peter Inäbnit.[42]

Both men, Peter Huber and Peter Inäbnit, will be pardoned for their crimes by the American historian.   Though dangerous to the interests of their home governments, they were indispensable helpers in the building up of the new colonies, of a new people.   They were unselfish in the main, aiding the poor to a condition of self-support, and their friends to social and economic betterment.   There were many agents who were not of as high character, *e.g.*, Jacob Joner, whose selfishness and greed led him to attempt to acquire the inheritance of a fellow-countryman, as his trial at Basel in 1750 proved.[43]   There were agents good and bad, and their activities

[41] Ritschard was examined with others of the Huber group.   As stated by Peter Inäbnit, Ritschard had for several years been anxious to go to Carolina. He denied that Huber had influenced him, but that a book on Carolina had started his interest.   Ritschard claimed to have relatives in Holland (Leiden), whom he wished to see and from whom he expected assistance.   See Documents, A, 3 (end).

[42] In Documents, A, 4, at the end, will be found statements of fellow-prisoners concerning Inäbnit, who is given a good character by them.   Their accounts add a touch of intense realism to the tragic close.

[43] See *Guide*, p. 112 ff., etc.

were far more hidden, their methods far more subtle than has generally been supposed.

Next to emigrant agents, letters from colonists with favorable comments on the new country were considered the greatest danger. Letters of this kind as early as 1711 have survived,[44] and these were probably not the first.[45] These letters are typical for most that follow, telling of the agricultural wealth, the opportunities for cattle-raising, the liberty of body and soul, the high wages, also the hard work but sure returns. They do not conceal the perils of the sea, the loss of life, the scarcity of spiritual guidance, comforts, and pleasures, but all these drawbacks fade away in the presence of the heroic pioneer spirit, the colonial optimism, that pervade the letters. The example of one successful pioneer has greater force than the discouragement of half-a-dozen that fall by the wayside. The effect of such letters was not fully realized until the great waves of emigration set in during the early thirties of the eighteenth century. Then all possible causes of the "emigration-fever" were searched into, and letters were discovered to be a disease-breeding germ, if not the responsible bacillus. Measures were at once taken for their capture and extermination, letters were hunted and kidnapped, the bearers and recipients were punished if they refused to give them up. A few illustrations of governmental action will suffice. In 1737 Hans Georg Striker wrote a report on Carolina for Lieutenant Rubi in Thun; this letter was ordered to be seized and laid before the government of Bern.[46] In 1742 Peter Stoker's letters from Carolina were demanded of him. In the same year a letter from Carolina addressed to Daniel Kissling of Wattenwyl was ordered to be surrendered by the Ratsherren of Bern. On March 4, 1744, the police of Bern were instructed to prevent the luring of emigrants by means of letters; it was the same day on which Bern asked Basel to take Peter Inäbnit prisoner. A fine of thirty pounds was to be inflicted on anyone who would not surrender such a letter without delay. On April 29, 1752, letters from Pennsylvania were ordered to be opened and copied. Anything unfavorable to the

---

[44] Cf. "Copia Underschiedlicher Brieffen auss Nord Carolina" (1711), included in the article: "The Graffenried Manuscripts," *German American Annals*, n. s., vol. XI., nos. 5, 6, September–December, 1913. The letters are here printed in full.

[45] The earliest Swiss settlers in America were probably some who had left their homes in the seventeenth century for the Palatinate, and subsequently joined groups of Palatines emigrating to America. From such, letters may have been received in Switzerland before 1711.

[46] Bern, RM., CLIII. 40–443.

3

colonies should be published in the next issue of the annual calendar
(*Der Hinkende Bote*).[47]   The policy was widespread of suppressing
the favorable passages of letters and publishing whatéver was
damaging.   Thus one of the most critical, in parts vituperative,
epistles,[48] one written by a disappointed woman, Esther Werndtlin,
the widow of Pastor Göttschi (who died shortly after arriving in
Philadelphia), was printed and widely circulated by Zürich and
Basel.[49]   Basel ordered (April 2, 1738) that copies be sent to all
the country districts, to the preachers in every parish, and be made
known to every subject desirous of emigrating to Pennsylvania.
The number of letters with tidings of fortunate experiences in
America was undoubtedly very much greater, judging by the mass
of letters contained in the state-archive of Basel.   Most of these
unquestionably were confiscated letters,[50] held in the archives to
prevent their circulation.   It is not surprising, therefore, that Peter
Huber (the country-folk of the Bernese Oberland were noted for
their cleverness) carried letters in the false bottom of a drinking-
vessel, specially constructed for the purpose of concealing written
messages.

The policy of suppressing favorable news was also forced upon
the newspapers.   On October 8, 1736, the Council of Bern gave
the following order: "Since the *Avis-Blättlin* [*Intelligencer*] has
recently brought an article on Carolina, the editor is directed in
the future not to publish any more reports on Carolina and the
condition of the emigrants there.   In any case nothing favorable
about them shall be printed." [51]   On February 6, 1738, the *Avis-
blätter* of Bern and Lausanne are commanded not to publish any of
the reports coming from the neighboring Neuchâtel, in view of the
propaganda coming from there.[52]

A further danger existed in the numerous books and pamphlets
descriptive of the American colonies.   The earliest actually received
encouragement from Swiss governments, because information was
desired.   Thus Kocherthal's report, and Ochs's *Amerikanischer
Wegweiser* (1711) were welcomed, and the latter rewarded.   But

[47] See *Guide*, pp. 46–49, etc.
[48] This letter dated Philadelphia, November 24, 1736, is reprinted among the
documents accompanying this article, see Documents, C, 1.   Some of the letters
published in the *Hinkende Bote* of Bern, have also been included, see Documents,
C, 2.
[49] Cf. *Guide*, pp. 30, 103, etc.
[50] A number of these appear in print for the first time among the accompanying
Documents, see B, 1–6.
[51] Bern, RM., CLII. 224.
[52] *Ibid.*, CLVII. 122.

though at that time emigration was not feared, even these did not
fail to arouse a protest, as in the booklet: *Das verlangte und nicht
erlangte Canaan bei den Lust-Gräbern . . . absonderlich dem . . .
Kocherthalerischen Bericht wohlbedächtig entgegen gesetzt* (1711).
Later it became the general practice to reply to every book that gave
a favorable account and gained a circulation. Thus the eulogistic
account of Carolina published in 1734: *Der nunmehro in der Neuen
Welt vergnügt und ohne Heim-Wehe lebende Schweitzer*, provoked
the equally curious book: *Neue Nachricht alter und neuer Merk-
würdigkeiten, enthaltend ein vertrautes Gespräch und sichere Briefe
von der Landschafft Carolina und übrigen Englischen Pflanz-Städten
in Amerika* (1734). The latter was in effect a denial of the one that
went before, and was widely circulated by the governments to
counteract the influence of its predecessor. Another booklet
adopting the catching dialogue form of the *Neue Nachricht* and
equally impressive in its warnings against the American colonies,
was *Der Hinckende Bott von Carolina, oder Ludwig Webers von
Wallissellen Beschreibung seiner Reise von Zürich gen Rotterdam*
(1735), suggested by the unfortunate experiences of Pastor
Göttschi's group of emigrants from Zürich. The *Neu-Gefundenes
Eden* (1737) was followed in the same year by *Christholds Gedanken,
bey Anlasz der Bewegung, welche die bekannte Beschreibung von
Carolina, in Amerika, in unserm Land verursacht*. In this a Kingdom is named superior to the New Eden, toward which there is a
beautiful voyage without sea-sickness, where there is eternal peace
instead of wars, and where there is a great and just king, better
than any ruler on this earth—and the reader is cautioned not to
lose this Kingdom, which he might do by yielding to the seductions
of the New Eden.[53]

The large amount of attention given to emigration, and the severe
restrictive measures adopted by the Swiss governments of the
eighteenth century, indicate that they were not contending for a
mere abstract principle, but were dominated by the fear of an ever-
present danger. It was not to them a question of losing a few
hundred people annually, but of depopulation of whole country districts, as was threatening in the case of Eglisau in the canton of
Zürich, or Oberhasli in the highlands of Bern. Had this panic fear
sufficient foundation in fact? This question is difficult to answer,
owing to the lack of accurate statistics. In the decade from 1753
to 1763, which was a period of only moderate emigration, about

[53] For a list of books and pamphlets belonging to this eighteenth-century
emigration period, with full titles, see *Guide*, pp. 29–31, etc.

10,000 persons left the canton of Bern, 4000 of whom were men entering foreign military service, and 6000 men and women emigrating to other countries.[54] The loss of 1000 persons annually was at least appreciable. The fact also, that recruiting in foreign regiments was constantly draining the country of men, undoubtedly made the governments more eager to stop the leakage caused by emigration.

The only accurate statistics which the writer was able to find in the Swiss archives, bearing on the question of the number of Swiss who came to the American colonies in the eighteenth century, was a carefully compiled list of emigrants from the canton of Zürich during the years 1734–1744.[55] The list furnishes names, with dates, home districts and destinations, and claims to be complete. The total number it records is 2300. This one reliable source furnishes a reasonable basis for an estimate of the total emigration to America in the eighteenth century. If there were 2300 names of recorded emigrants from the canton of Zürich, we must add about two hundred more for secret migration (those leaving without permission); this would give Zürich 2500. Since the canton of Bern was more populous, and emigration very prevalent, we may assign to Bern the number 3000. Basel in proportion to her population might be given 1500. Other cantons whose archives contain most evidences of emigration in the eighteenth century are: Aargau, Schaffhausen, Graubünden, and Solothurn. Together they probably equalled Zürich in population, therefore the number 2500 would fairly represent their emigration. The remaining cantons, mostly Catholic, did not have as large an emigration in the eighteenth century, if we can trust the fact that very few records of emigration from those quarters appear. The number 2500 would perhaps more than do them justice, though the population represented is more than three times that of Zürich. This would give a total of 12,000 emigrants for all of the Swiss cantons during the period 1734–1744. Now, these eleven years represent the high tide of Swiss emigration to the American colonies. It is not likely that the total emigration for the eighteenth century was more than twice this figure, judging by the records in the archives. It is the writer's opinion, therefore, that the emigration from Switzerland to the American colonies in the eighteenth century amounted to something like 25,000 persons,

[54] Cf. Dr. E. Lerch, *Die Bernische Auswanderung nach Amerika im 18. Jahrhundert*, p. 31.

[55] Staatsarchiv, Zürich, A. 174. "Verzeichnisse der Ausgewanderten nach Carolina und Pennsylvanien 1734–1744." See *Guide*, p. 14. This is the list printed below, and here published for the first time.

though the discovery of additional data might change this estimate to a figure above or below the one assumed.

Numerical estimates of eighteenth-century emigration appear strangely diminutive when compared with the statistics of the nineteenth century. The United States reports, running back to 1820, show a total Swiss immigration up to 1910 of over 250,000. A strong current set in about 1816, during a period of economic depression (*das Hungerjahr*). The emigration from Switzerland fluctuated in the nineteenth century. From hundreds annually it rose to over 1500 in 1828, dropped, and rose again to about 1400 in 1834; starting again strongly in 1852 with nearly 3000, it rose to 8000 in 1854, dropped to 4500 in 1855, and much lower in succeeding years, until the high-water mark came in the eighties, beginning with over 6000 in 1880, and reaching the crest in 1883 with 12,751. From 1880 to 1886, over 61,000 Swiss arrived in the United States. Recently the average has been about 3000 annually. The embargo upon emigration was removed by the Swiss cantons in the nineteenth century. Periodic conditions of overpopulation, failure of crops, and hard times, recurring in certain districts, showed plainly that, far from being a cause of fear, emigration might prove an advantage to a vigorous people increasing rapidly, yet confined within narrow borders. Complaints from seaport towns in France, Holland, and Germany, calling attention to the congregating of masses of poor people waiting to embark, and subsequently the objections of the United States to the deportation of undesirable classes, brought about a regulation of emigration from Switzerland. The policy was adopted, neither to encourage nor to discourage emigration, but to let it take its course, and to protect the emigrant against the selfishness of speculators, and the consequences of his own ignorance. The business of transporting the emigrant was left in the hands of agencies, who were required to secure a license and to obey the laws. In 1880 the Federal Emigration Bureau (*Eidgenössisches Auswanderungsamt*) was established at Bern to control the licensed agencies, to enforce justice and provide helpful information. This represents the modern solution of a problem so exasperating to the cantonal governments of the eighteenth century.

LIST OF EMIGRANTS TO CAROLINA AND PENNSYLVANIA, 1734–1744

No. 1. List of those Persons, who between 1734 and 1744 left the Territory of Zürich, in Order to Travel to America

Lake-District

Stäfan	0
Humbrächtikon	1
Mänedorf	0
Uetikon	0
Meilan	12
Herrliberg	24
Ehrlibach	0
Küssnacht	16
Zumikon	0
Richtenschweil	23
Wädenschweil	7
Schönenberg	0
Horgen	3
Hirtzel	0
Dallweil	0
Langnau	0
Kilchberg	0
Rüschlikon	0
Wollishofen	0
Altstätten	2
Schlieren	41
Sax	0
Sennwald	0
Salez	0

Frey

Kappel	15
Hausen	16
Knonau	24
Maschwanden	6
Augst	0
Rifferschweil	24
Metmenstetten	16
Affholteren	52
Hedingen	7
Ottenbach	7
Bonstätten	19
Stallikon	0
Birmenstorf	15
Urdorf	2
Ütikon	0

STEIN

Stein	0
Stammheim	0
Andelfingen	49
Ossingen	0
Dägerlen	61
Drüllikon	7
Lauffen	0
Benken	0
Martelen	36
Feuerthalen	0
Dörfflingen	0

WINTERTHUR

Winterthur	0
Oberwinterthur	17
Töss	15
Seüzach	9
Neftenbach	31
Hettlingen	7
Dorf	1
Henkhard	39
Berg	15
Flach	10
Embrach	73
Lufingen	4
Rorbas	34
Dättlikon	24
Pfungen	1
Brütten	14
Feltheim	2
Wülflingen	31
Buch	7

ELGG

Elgg	47
Elsau	22
Wisendangen	32
Seen	32
Rikenbach	0
Dynhard	15
Altikon	43
Zell	44
Turbenthal	2
Schlatt	0
Wyla	9
Wildberg	23
Sternenberg	15

WETZIKOM

Gossau	9
Grüningen	0
Hinweil	5
Wetzikon	9

Wald.. 0
Bärentschweil................................... 1
Dürnten... 0
Rüthi... 0
Fischenthal..................................... 0
Egg... 0
Bubikon... 0
Bauma.. 0
Oetweil... 4

KYBURG

Greiffensee..................................... 3
Pfäffikon....................................... 10
Hittnau... 2
Kyburg... 0
Fehr-Altorff.................................... 1
Jlnau... 44
Russikon.. 4
Weisslingen..................................... 12
Lindau.. 23
Wangen... 4
Schwertzenbach................................. 8
Dübendorff...................................... 6
Fällanden....................................... 24
Mur... 35
Uster... 7
Münch-Altorff................................... 0
Volketschweil................................... 18

REGENSBERG

Höngg.. 0
Weiningen....................................... 0
Regensperg...................................... 0
Dällikon.. 9
Otelfingen...................................... 14
Buchs... 5
Regensperg...................................... 10
Niderhaslen..................................... 15
Oberglatt....................................... 10
Rümlang.. 24
Kloten.. 11
Basserstorf..................................... 69
Affholteren..................................... 4
Dietlikon....................................... 18

EGLISAU

Weningen.. 32
Schöfflistorf.................................... 22
Steinmaur....................................... 116
Bachs... 56
Stadel.. 138
Bülach.. 111
Eglisau... 24
Glattfelden..................................... 53

Wyl.. 26
Rafz... 66
Weyach.. 36

DEPENDENCY

Wallisellen.. 61

Total...2,310[1]

No. 2. LIST OF THOSE FAMILIES AND PERSONS WHO, FROM 1734–1744, LEFT THE PARISH AFFHOLTEREN AT MT. ALBIS FOR (A) CAROLINA, (B) PENNSYLVANIA

(A) LEFT FOR CAROLINA

1734 (a) Family. Hans Grob with his wife Cathrj Ruestin, a son and two daughters.
1739 (b) Elsbeth Muller, grown-up daughter of Jacob Müller, deceased.

(B) LEFT FOR PENNSYLVANIA

1736 Two grown-up help-mates. Hans Jacob Dups, Heiri's (man), and Rudolff Haug, Uli's (man). N.B. Their first trip.
1743 (a) Families.
    1. Caspar Schnebelj Ottlis with his wife Verena Dups and four little children.
    2. Conrad Wyss, cooper, with his wife Barbara Dups and four young children.
    3. Felix Wyss, carpenter, with his wife Anna Huber and five little children.
    4. Johannes Epprecht with his wife Verena Walder and one little child.
    5. Conrad Näff with his three sons.
    6. Hans Heinrich Hurter with his wife Verena Huber and one young child.
  (b) Grown-up Help-mates.
    1. Hans Jacob Dups, Heiri's.
    2. Rudolff Haug, Uli's. N.B. Their second trip.
    3. Hans Dups, the above Hans Jacob's brother.
    4. Leonhard Schnebelj, Heiri Schnebelj's, the inn-keeper's (man).
    5. Heirj Epprecht, Joose's (man).
    6. Hans Heinrich Epprecht, Jacob's (man).
    7. Heinrich Suter, the deceased Hans' (man).
    8. His brother Hans Suter.
    9. Hans Jacob Suter, the deceased Rudi's (man).
    10. Hans Schnebelj, Rüetschj Heiri's (man).
    11. Heinrich Rudolff, the deceased Jacob's (man).
    12. Hans Jacob Schärer, Krämer's (man).
  (c) Boys under age.
    1. Leonhard Haug, Färber's.
    2. Conrad Epprecht, Joose's.
    3. Rudolff Kleiner.

[1] The total of the figures given is 2,262, not 2,310. The discrepancy may be accounted for by the omission or loss of the names of one or more parishes in the tabulation.

(*d*) Grown-up daughters.
  1. Barbara Haug, Uli's.
  2. Ana Schnebelj, Rüetschj Heiri's.
       Total 52 souls.
Affholteren at Mt. Albis,   Attested by
     April 22, 1744.   HANS ULRICH WYSS, *p.l.*
                                 (*i.e.*, pastor loci. *i.e.*, pastor in the parish.)

No. 3. THE FOLLOWING PERSONS FROM THE PARISH AFFHOLTEREN
    AT HÖNGG HAVE, AS FAR AS IS KNOWN, WITHDRAWN WITHIN A
    FEW YEARS, AND GONE TO PENNSYLVANIA OR CAROLINA

1. Jacob Matthysen's (in Unter-Affholteren) daughter, aged 28, withdrew six
   years ago.
2. Caspar Merkj (in Ober-Affholteren), smith and drummer, aged 29, with
3. His wife: Anna Dietschj, of the same age, left on account of debts. 1743.
4. Johannes Clingler, aged 29, left the same place, without the knowledge even
   of his parents, leaving behind wife and child, in the aforesaid year 1743.

No. 4. FROM THE PARISH ALTIKON THERE JOURNEYED TO
          CAROLINA, BETWEEN 1734–1744

FROM ALTIKON
1734. 1
Rudolff Meyer,   aged 30 years and ⎱ Married couple.
Anna Hasenfraz,   "   28   "   ⎰
     Children:
Magdalena, aged 4 years.
Maria,   "   1 year.

1735. 2
Rudolph Baumer, Felix Baumer's son, aged 26 years.
3
Jacob Ammann, Jacob Ammann's son, aged 24 years.
4
Christoph Müller, aged 30 years and ⎱ Married couple.
Barbel Baumer,   "   28   "   ⎰

1743. 5
Jacob Kreysz,   aged 46 years and
Anna Bachmann,   "   42   "
     Children:
Hans Ulrich, aged 18 years.
Hans Jacob,   "   16   "
Hans Felix,   "   8   "
Anna,   "   6   "
     Total from Altikon: 14 Persons.

FROM DORLIKON
1738. 1
Hansz Nüssli, Oeler, aged 42 years and ⎱ Married couple.
Angelica Meyer,   "   37   "   ⎰
     Children:
Elisabeth, aged 14 years.

Barbara, aged 12 yeaes.
Angelica,　　"　10　"
Verena,　　　"　7　"
Anna,　　　　"　5　"
Heinrich,　　"　3　"

2

Conrad Basler, aged 33 years and } Married couple.
Anna Baumer,　　"　35　"
　　　　Child:
Conrad, aged 7 years.

3

Christoph Weydmann, aged 37 years and } Married couple.
Elsbeth Schmid,　　　　"　34　"
　　　　Children:
Heinrich,　　aged 11 years.
Ulrich,　　　　"　6　"
Hans Caspar,　"　½ year.

1743. 4

Hans Ulrich Müller, aged 41 years and } Married couple.
Verena Bolsterlj,　　　"　42　"
　　　　Children:
Dorothea,　aged 11 years.
Anna,　　　　"　4　"
Hans Ulrich,　"　1 year.

5

Rudolph Epprecht, aged 44 years and } Married couple.
Anna Grügis,　　　　"　46　"
　　　　Children:
Jacob,　aged 21 years.
Rudolph,　"　18　"
Anna,　　　"　14　"
Margreth,　"　12　"
Elisabeth,　"　8　"
Verena,　　"　5　"
　　　　Total from Dorlikon: 29 Persons.
Altikon, April 15, 1744.　　　　CASPAR ULRICH, *Minister.*

No. 5.　FROM ALLTSTÄTTEN THERE WENT AWAY ON THE 23. JULY, 1743, WITH THE PURPOSE OF GOING TO PENNSYLVANIA

Margrethe Hindermann's two sisters, of the same name, the one 39, the other 36 years old.

Otherwise no one.

Which report herewith, because of no better opportunity known, is sent to accompany the Circular,—while commending himself most respectfully to His Grace, the Dean, by

　　　　　　　JOH. CASPAR HESS, *p.l.*

From WOLLISHOFFEN none, God be praised, have gone away.　God grant, that also in the future no one's mouth will water for this country.

From KILCHBERG no one has gone away, "principiis obstandum fuisset."

From RÜSCHLIKON also no one has left.　As far as I know, the thought never entered anyone's mind to go away from here.

No. 6. WITH THE INTENTION OF GOING TO CAROLINA THERE WENT
AWAY FROM THE PARISH ANDELFINGEN

1734, the 1. November. Anna Bretscher, from Atlikon, unmarried, aged 26.
But the report came later that this disorderly person got to Piedmont
and died there.

1738, the beginning of September. Adam Angst, tailor, from Niderwyl, aged 36.
His wife Barbara Räss, aged 35. Child: Elisabetha, aged 2½.

" Hans Jacob Schaub, from Niderwyl, unmarried, aged 26.
His sister Anna, unmarried, aged 21.

" Anna Moser, from Öhrlingen, unmarried, aged 26½.

" Jacob Bucher, from Alten, who left his wife, aged 58.
His son with him, Hans Conrad, aged 26.

" Hans Jacob Ullman, from Altlicken, aged 32.
His betrothed Anna Landolt from Kl. Andelfingen, aged 29.
These, however, did not get farther than Basel, and from there to the
district of Durlach, where they were married. He is said to be in service
there still, but the woman returned to her parents pregnant, in December
1741, where she gave birth to a child that died, subsequently she went
into service again.

1743 Went away Tuesday after Witsuntide.
Heinrich Schaub from Niderwyl, aged 51.
His wife Anna Barbara Bertschinger, aged 33½.

Children by the first marriage:	Anna,	aged 22
	Hans Ulrich,	" 20
	Adam,	" 18½
	Jacob,	" 16
	Johannes,	" 10
	Hans Conrad,	" 8
Child by the second marriage:	Susanna,	" 2¼

There also left at that time:
Heinrich Angst from Niderwyl, unmarried, ⎫ Both without a pass
aged 27½. ⎬ and certificate from
His sister Elsbeth, unmarried, aged 26. ⎭ pastor.

1743 Anna Hagenbuch, from the same place,
unmarried, aged 27. ⎫ Both of these left with-
Her brother, Hans Jacob, aged 18, who ⎬ out pass or certificate.
has not yet received the communion. ⎭

" the 13. June. Hans Ullmann, from Atlikon, aged 41½.
His wife Magdalena Hirt, aged 30½.
His child by first marriage Johannes, aged 3½.
He died in London, and according to a report received a week ago, which
sounds lamentable, she is still there with the step-child in a despicable
condition of poverty. The letter has come through Rieslimann of
Winterthur.

" the 6. July. Hans Conrad Schaub of Niderwyl, aged 29½.
His wife Anna Frey, aged 32½.
Children: Hans Conrad, aged 3½, Hans Jacob, aged 2½.
Also with him his sister Ursula, aged 23, and brother Heinrich, aged 21
(unmarried).

" the 1. April. Jacob Meisterhans, mason, from Andelfingen, aged 51.
His wife Verena Bernhardt, aged 41.

Children: Hans Conrad,	aged 12½.
Anna Elsabetha,	" 9½.
Hans Jacob,	" 4½.

1743   With him there left also, without desiring from me a certificate:
    Hans Jacob Islicker, from Klein-Andelfingen, aged 50.
    His wife Anna Himmel, aged 58.
    Their illegitimate daughter Anna Hegin from Cappel, unmarried, aged 25½.
"   Jacob Sigg, also from Kl. Andelf., aged 46.
    His wife Regula Eigenheer, aged 34.
    Children: Margaretha, aged 8½; Hans Jacob, aged 6.
"   Heinrich Süsstrunk, shoemaker from Humlicken, aged 29½.
    His wife Ursula Üly, aged 25.
    Child: Hans Ulrich, 8 months.
    He also took with him his sister Barbara, aged 17½, who has not yet
       received the communion.
    Testified from Andelfingen, April 10, 1744.   JOH. SCHOOP, *Minister.*

No. 7.   LIST OF THOSE PERSONS WHO SINCE THE YEAR 1734 JOURNEYED FROM THE PARISH BACHS TO THE NEW WORLD

Junghans Maag, born July 15, 1703, secretly left his wife and child.
Junghans Meyer, son of Jacob Meyer, deceased, unmarried, born March 28, 1706.
Heinrich Keller, born January 2, 1684.
Margeth Scheur Mejer, his wife, born February 6, 1687.
Margeth, his child, born June 12, 1729.
Hans Jacob Schüz, the deceased Hans Jacob Schüz's son, unmarried, born April 17, 1718.
Rudolff Schüz, Rudolff Schüz's legitimate son, unmarried, born July 17, 1715.
Felix Kunz, born October 13, 1695.
Anna Dutweiler, his wife, born November 6, 1681.
Vrena Pfister, wife of the deceased Schüz, born September 24, 1682.
Felix, son, born May 21, 1716, unmarried.
Rudolff, son, born April 23, 1719, unmarried.
Hans, a brother, born October 22, 1713.
Vrena Bleüler, his wife, born September 3, 1713.
Hans Caspar, her son, born February 8, 1739.
Klihans Kunz, Heinrich Kunz's (the rope-maker's) legitimate son, unmarried, born August 26, 1716.
Jacob Pfister, Klihansen's legitimate son, unmarried, born September 27, 1716.
Klihans Vrener, born May 21, 1714.
Regula Bräm, his wife, born December 19, 1699.
Caspar Vrener, his brother, unmarried, born October 6, 1720.
Barbara Kunz, Hans Kunz's legitimate daughter, born March 9, 1721, unmarried.
Hans Kunz, her brother, unmarried, born September 14, 1730.
Jacob Bucher, born April 10, 1696.
Barbara Albrecht, his wife, born October 12, 1695.
    Children:
Jacob, born September 1, 1725.
Heinrich, born May 17, 1728.
Jacob Schüz, born April 1, 1697.
Margeth Huber, his wife, born August 10, 1706.
    Children:
Anna, born May 28, 1730.
Elsbeth, born August 31, 1732.
Heinrich, born February 13, 1725.
Hans Heinrich, born May 26, 1735.
Barbara, born October 9, 1740.

Magdalena, Felix Majer's legitimate daughter, unmarried, born July 8, 1714.

{ Jacob Mejer, born August 18, 1703.
Susanna Hug, his wife, born March 7, 1697.
    Her child:
Vrena, born March 22, 1728.

Hans Jacob Weidmann, Felix's legitimate son, unmarried, born October 22, 1720.

{ Hans Weidmann, born October 8, 1702.
Anna Surber, his wife, born December 15, 1700.
    Children:
Anna, born May 21, 1732.
Anna, born August 29, 1734.
Rudolff, born September 12, 1737.

{ Hans Bernhardt, born May 14, 1699.
Vrena Schüz, his wife, born October 26, 1704.
    Children:
Cleophea, born December 14, 1728.
Heinrich, born September 14, 1730.
Hans Heinrich, born February 20, 1735.
Hans, born January 1, 1738.
Anna, born August 16, 1740.

{ Anna, born July 3, 1707.
Heinrich, born February 2, 1718.   } all unmarried, the deceased Hans Weid-
Johannes, born May 4, 1724.   mann's children.

{ Felix Mejer, born January 1, 1705.
Barbara Hollenweiger, his wife, born September 25, 1698.
    Child:
Regula, born May 19, 1737.

Total: 56 Persons.

Attested from the record-book of baptisms, March 25, 1744.
      BY JOHANN CASPAR SCHWEYZER, *Minister at Bachs.*

No. 8.   FROM THE PARISH BÄRETSCHWEIL IN 1742

Hans Heinrich Meyer from the Hinderberg went to Carolina, leaving his wife behind somewhere about Lake Zürich, got possession of about 50 florins and absconded.   He was baptized in February 1697.

                                   Attested,
Bäretschweil, April 18, 1744.   PASTOR SCHMID.

No. 9.   LIST OF THOSE PITIABLE PERSONS, WHO CONTRARY TO FAITHFUL WARNINGS AND ADMONITIONS OBSTINATELY WENT AWAY FROM THE PARISH BASSERSTORFF, with the intention of seeking their fortunes in Carolina or Pennsylvania.

1734

1. Heinrich Brunner, son of Jacob, deceased, called the trumpeter of Basserstorff, born May 3, 1716.
2. Susanna Keller, illegitimate daughter of Caspar Keller, deceased, born May 25, 1715.
3. Heinrich Dübendorffer, called Christen Hugen, born October 3, 1695.
    Barbara Meyer, his wife, born in Wallisellen.
        Children:

Rudolff, born April 22, 1726.

Anna, born February 18, 1731.

Barbara, born April 25, 1734.

4. Hans Jacob Dübendorffer, called Krebser, born April 12, 1696.
His wife Magdalena Krebser from Wallisellen.

5. Hans Heinrich Enderli, called Schörulis, born July 28, 1700.
His wife: Anna Keller from Oberembrach.
   Children:
Heinrich, born August 12, 1725.

Regula, born July 18, 1728.

6. Heinrich Dübendorffer, the mason's son, born May 8, 1698.
His wife: Verena Widmer from Ottikon.
   Child:
Felix, born November 17, 1733.

7. Hans Dübendorffer, called Küeffer, the tailor's son, born February 2, 1701.
His wife, Lisabeth Keller from the parish Embrach.
   Children:
Rudolff, born January 19, 1727.

Hans Geörg, born January 23, 1729.

Elsbeth, born December 25, 1731.

Katharina, born June 27, 1733.

8. Kilian Dübendorffer, called Krebser, born February 19, 1704.
His wife, Verena Krebser from Wallisellen.
   Children:
Abraham, born December 5, 1728.

Anna, born March 22, 1733.

9. Heinrich Hug, wainwright, a widower, born September 27, 1668.   Died on
the ship to Pennsylvania.

10. Christophel Leimbacher from Oberwil, Heinrich's son, born June 25, 1713.

11. Felix Leimbacher from Oberwil, born September 14, 1684.
His wife: Anna Meyer, born October 12, 1689.
   Children:
Felix, born March 15, 1711, is in the Dutch Service.

Hans Heinrich, born July 6, 1717, with his parents.

Anna, born October 30, 1725.

Lisabeth, born April 11, 1728.

Barbel, born February 18, 1731.

12. Hans Heinrich[2] Brunner, son of the deceased Heinrich, tailor, unmarried,
born December 19, 1728.
   [2] Heinrich is written above the name Ulrich, crossed out.

1743. Left Sunday, May 5

1. Heinrich Dübendorffer, called Krebser, born March 5, 1702.
His wife: Anna Wegmann from Tagelschwang, born 1703.
Married December 19, 1728.

2. Hans Jacob Reutlinger, Kaspar's son, unmarried, born July 30, 1719.

3. Salome Brunner, Hans Brunner's deceased wife (née Hursel), called Link's
daughter, born June 11, 1724.

4. Heinrich Leimbacher, deceased Jacob's son from Oberwil, unmarried, born
November 26, 1719.

5. Elsbeth Vetter, daughter of Jacob, left with Hans Jacob Brunner from
Kloten, since the parish Kloten objected to their marriage. Born August
8, 1717.

6. Jacob Altorffer, deceased Kaspar's son, from Birchwil, unmarried, born
October 5, 1727.

7. Leonard Altorffer, smith from Basserstorf, born August 10, 1700.
His wife, Anna Frener from Wangen, born May 17, 1706, married February
5, 1731.
Children:
Kaspar, baptized, January 18, 1739.
Hans Jacob, July 15, 1742.

8. Susanna Bachmann, the deceased Jacob Ringger's widow, from Nürrenstorff.
Born August 20, 1707, left with her own son, Heinrich,
Baptized March 13, 1735, and three sons by her first marriage.
Born by Barbara Morff from Effretikon.
Hans Jacob, baptized September 24, 1724.
Hans Caspar, baptized December 25, 1727.
Jacob, December 4, 1729.

9. Left the 11th of May.
Hans Jacob Leimbacher, Hans Heinrich's son, from Oberwil, unmarried,
born April 30, 1724.

10. Hans Jacob Brunner, called Trumpeter of Basserstorff, born September 22,
1709.
Anna Meyer, from Embrach, his wife, born June 12, 1707.
Left the 15th of May.

11. Heinrich Brunner, son of Rudolff, deceased, from the Hub, unmarried, born
January 9, 1718.

12. Jacob Hess, Caspar Hess' (from Ettenhausen) illegitimate son, lived at Basserstorff with his mother Anna Hugg, baptized here January 26, 1719.

13. Ulrich Brunner, tailor, surviving son of Kilian Brunner and Verena Altorffer,
from Basserstorff, unmarried, born February 22, 1722.

14. Hans Brunner, cooper from Basserstorff, born May 18, 1690.
His wife: Barbara Redinger from Höngg. Married August 26, 1727.
Children:

Hans Jacob,	baptized,	December	27, 1727.
Hans Ulrich,	"	June	14, 1730.
David,	"	August	17, 1732.
Abraham,	"	October	24, 1734.
Felix,	"	December	13, 1739.
Anna Margreth,	"	October	22, 174-.

15. Left July 4th.
Felix Bachmann from Oberwil, born December 18, 1701.
His wife: Regula Morff from Hakab, born May 10, 1711.
Children by the first marriage are:
Anna Hinen from Dietlikon.
Rudolff, born December 21, 1732.
Anna, born April 7, 1735.

Attested,

HANS ULRICH GESZNER, *Pastor at Basserstorff.*

No. 10. IN ACCORDANCE WITH THE MAGISTERIAL ORDER RECEIVED,
THE MINISTER OF BÄNKEN INFORMS HIS HONOR, DEAN
BRUNNER, THAT NO ONE HAS LEFT THE PARISH OF BÄNKEN
FROM 1734 UNTIL NOW: that at present, however, three families
have the wish to leave, to wit:

1. Johannes Studer with three children and his wife.
2. Jacob Meister, locksmith, with his wife.
3. Johannes Meister, the glazier, with his wife and three children.

These, however, have been held up by His Honor, the Chief Magistrate (Kreis-Obervogt) in Lauffen, until after Easter, and as a result will probably have to remain.

April 3, 1744.   Pastor WUNDERLIJ at Bänken.

No. 11. FROM THE PARISH BIRMENSTORFF THE FOLLOWING HAVE GONE TO CAROLINA AND PENNSYLVANIA

Lisabeth Haffner, the deceased Hans Haffner's daughter, born April 1, 1706, left two years ago.

Eva Hedinger, the deceased Hans Hedinger's daughter, born August 30, 1705, left in 1738.

Felix Wintsch from Landicon, born October 7, 1724, left in 1743.

Katharina Wintsch, his sister, born April 14, 1726.

Hans Stierlin from Aesch and his wife Anna Rasi, together with the 4 children: Jacob Stierlin, born October 21, 1715; Hans Stierlin, born January 26, 1718. Gregorious Stierlin, born November 22, 1722; and Ursula Stierlin, born February 25, 1725.

Hans Gut from Aesch and his wife Elsbeth Beerlj, with their daughter Margaretha Gut, born December 24, 1714.

Caspar Hoffstätter, born October 1, 1713.

Hans Jacob Meyer, also from Aesch, born September 19, 1707.

Total 15 Persons.

No. 12. LIST OF PERSONS WHO LEFT THE PARISH BONNSTETEN TO GO TO CAROLINA AND PENNSYLVANIA

Withdrew in September 1738.

Born:

October   28, 1701. Caspar Toggweiler, called Schwab.
December 10, 1709. Anna Huber, his wife.
   Their children:
February   12, 1730. Barbara.
June   24, 1731. Margreth.
July   21, 1737. Hans Heinrich.
June   24, 1703. Felix Glätlj, Chlyrüdis.
October   4, 1691. Catharj Huber, his wife.
January   9, 1689. Felix Frey.
September 23, 1688. Barbara Blikenstorffer, his wife.
   Their children:
September 13, 1718. Jacob.
March   6, 1725. Hans Heinrich.
   Also the following unmarried people.
April   17, 1717. Heinrich Aeberlj, son of Hans.
July   26, 1696. Heinrich Glätlj, son of the purser, deceased.
April   22, 1714. Hans Jacob Huber, son of the bailiff.
August   16, 1711. Heinrich Glätlj, son of Caspar deceased.
February   14, 1723. Anna Huber, daughter of Marti deceased.
   Withdrew in May 1743.
August   19, 1716. Cilian Gilg.   ⎤ They were in service in the
December 17, 1720. Hans Aeberlj, son of Hans ⎬ district of Knonau.
                            deceased.   ⎦
   Withdrew April 1, 1744.
December 18, 1714. Regul Gilg, daughter of Chlyjoggen deceased, left Knonau
                            where she served.

4

No. 13. There have gone to Carolina from the Parish Brütten

1. 1740. Heinrich Käller, born 1718, April 20, unmarried.
2. 1743. Felix Gross, born March 24, 1715, unmarried.
   Verena Stäffen, born April 4, 1718, unmarried.
   Hans Conrad Gross, born April 6, 1721, unmarried.
   Barbara Stäffen, born April 9, 1717, unmarried.
   Lisabeth Baltensberger, born August 20, 1720, unmarried.
   Hans Heinrich Baltensberger, born August 18, 1715.
   His wife, Barbara Sommer from Rümikon, born in the parish of Elsauw
   February 17, 1711.   She was in an advanced state of pregnancy at
   her departure.
   Finally there left Rudolf Gross, born September 26, 1716.
   His wife was Barbara Städeli from Basserstorff, born August 9, 1703.
   The children are:
   Heinrich, born 1732.
   Rudolf, born April 6, 1734.
   Lisabeth, born 1738.
   Hans Ulrich, born April 9, 1740.

No. 14. From the Parish Bubikon there withdrew for Carolina

1738. Conrad Zollinger and Lisabeth Zollinger with eight children, got as far as
   the Markgrafenland (S.W. section of the Black Forest, in Baden),
   where they remained for two years on fief-land.   The father died and
   the mother returned with eight children.
   Regula is married in the city of Basel.
   Hans Rudolf is in service in Basel.
   Hans Heinrich is also serving in Basel.
   Hans Rudolf is working also in the Basel-district.
   Hans Caspar died.
   Hans Ereth ⎫
   A. Barbara ⎬ These three are being brought up in our parish.
   Hans Jacob ⎭
1743. Hans Hürliman and Maria Keller with three young children got to Basel
   and after he had spent all his money, returned.   He wishes to burden
   the church with the bringing up of his three children:
   Maria,   born September 30, 1736.
   Heinrich,   "   April   3, 1738.
   Elsbeth,   "   March   17, 1740.

No. 15. List of Persons who from the Parish Bülach between 1734 and 1744 Journeyed to Carolina and Pennsylvania

From Bülach

1734. Hansz Jacob Kern, the deceased sexton's son, unmarried.

From Bachenbülach

1734. Abraham Bäninger, carpenter.
   His wife, two sons.
1738. Hansz Maag.
   His wife, three children.

1738. Salomon Mejer.
His wife.
Hansz Jacob Maag, Alexander's son.
His wife, three children.
Salomon Mejer, tailor.
His wife, four children.
Heinrich Zander.
His wife, three children.
1743. Jacob Maag.
His wife, two children.
Andreas Maag.
His wife, two children.

Total from Bachenbülach 35 souls.

There went from Eschenmosen

1738. Johanes Steiner, Caspar Steiner, both unmarried.
1743. Johannes Hildbrand, the deceased Jacob's son, together with his wife.
Johannes Hildbrand, the deceased Hans Jacob's son, unmarried.
Jacob Maag, resin-scraper.
His wife, three sons, two daughters.

Total: 12 persons.

There went from Winkel

1738. Hans Dutweiler.
His wife, two children.
Jacob Mejer, the deceased Conrad's son.
His wife, three children.
Hans Conrad Mejer, wainwright.
His wife, one child.
Barbara Dutweiler, unmarried.
Anna Mejer, also unmarried.

Total from Winkel: 14 persons.

There went from Hochfelden

1738. Joseph Volkert.
His wife Frena Friesz, two sons, one daughter.
Junghans Maag.
His wife Anna Herzog, one daughter.
Catharina Mejerhofer, Hans Heinrich Mejer's widow.
One son, one daughter.
Junghans Frälj.
His wife Barbara Engel, one son, one daughter.
1743. Junghans Mejer.
His wife Verena Huber, two daughters.
Hans Jacob Mejer, the above-named's broth r, unmarried.
Daniel Horner.
His wife Anna Kern.

Total from Hochfelden: 22 persons.

There went from Hörenen
Endhörj

1734.
Hans Heinrich Gaszmann, died on the way.
His wife Magdalena Frölj.
One child, Barbara Gaszmann.

1734.   Heinrich Gaszmann, died on the way.
    His wife Verena Engel.
    Two sons, Hans Jacob and Heinrich.
1739.   Hans Gaszmann.
    His wife Anna Bertschj.
    One son, Hans Martin, one daughter Anna Catharina.
    Junghans Pfister, tailor.
    His wife Babelj Gaszmann.
    One son, Heinrich, two daughters Dorothe and Barbara.
    Junghans Pfister, the deceased Jacob's son, unmarried.
    Hans Heinrich Oertlj.
    His wife Regula Oertlj.
    Two sons, Felix and Heinrich, two daughters, Kljverena and Anna.

NIDERHÖRJ

Hans Jacob Frölj.
His wife Elsbeth Brunner.
Two children { Elsbeth died in Rotterdamm.
             { Barbara died on the sea.

                            Total from Hörj: 27 persons.

    The grand total of all souls, that emigrated from the parish Bülach is III
souls. Attested by Pastor SIMLER. Bülach, April 11, 1744.

No. 16. LIST OF THE PERSONS WHO WENT FROM THE PARISH BUCHSZ TO PENNSYLVANIA

1734.   September 27.
    1. Hans Conrad Meyer, born 1682.
    2. Magdalena Weidman, born 1682.
        Son.
    3. Melchior Meyer, born 1720.
    4. Jacob Murer, born 1687.
    5. Elsbeth Murer, born 1690.
        Children:
    6. Margeth, born 1720.
    7. Anna Margeth, born 1727.
    8. Hans Heinrich Murer (cousin of the above). Deceased Jacob Murer's
       son, born 1720.
    9. Heinrich Huber, born 1698.
   10. Ursula Grendelmejer, born 1707.
        Boys:
   11. Hans Rudolff, born 1732.
   12. Hans Jacob, born 1733. Died in Rotterdamm.
   13. Jacob Schmid, born 1692.
   14. Cathrina Koch, born 1697. Died in Rotterdamm.
        Children:
   15. Anna, born 1719.
   16. Jacob, born 1720.
   17. Felix, born 1722.
   18. Kly Anna, born 1729.
   19. Johannes, born 1731. Died in Rotterdamm.
   20. Felix, born 1733. Died in Rotterdamm.
1738.   August 22.
   21. Heinrich Grendelmeier, born 1701.
   22. Margeth Grendelmeier, born 1705.

Children:
23. Heinrich, born 1727.
24. Margeth, born 1728.
25. Elsbeth, born 1730.
26. Felix, born 1733.
27. Barbara, born 1735.
28. Anna, born 1737.
29. Heinrich Meyer, born 1701.
30. Anna Vogler, born 1707.
    Children:
31. Vrena, born 1726.
32. Cathrina, born 1730.
33. Barbara, born 1732.
34. Felix, born 1734.
35. Anna Barbara, born 1738.
36. Hans Heinrich Meyer, born 1698.
37. Vrena Grendelmeyer, born 1706.
    Children:
38. Conrad, born 1729.
39. Elsbeth, born 1735.
40. Regula, born 1737.
41. Felix Meyer, born 1704.
42. Vrena Meyer, born 1705.
    Boys:
43. Jacob, born 1734.
44. Felix, born 1737.
Buchs, March 31, 1744.　　　　Attested, HEINRICH ULLRICH, *Pastor.*

No. 17. Cappel. From this Parish there Journeyed to Carolina in August 1734

Jacob Müller, baptized March 19, 1713. ⎫ Brother and sister.
Vrena Müller, baptized January 13, 1715. ⎬
Rudolf Lier, baptized May 18, 1718, was unmarried.

In May 1739 another group left for Carolina:
Rägul Hägj, baptized December 22, 1715. ⎫
Barbel Hägj, baptized March 30, 1718. ⎬ Unmarried brothers
Hans Jacob Hägj, baptized May 12, 1720. ⎪ and sisters.
Jacob Hägj, baptized September 24, 1721. ⎭
Johannes Hägj, baptized April 30, 1719, unmarried. ⎫ Brother and sister.
Vrenelj Hägj, baptized December 7, 1721, unmarried. ⎬
Jacob Grob, baptized November 9, 1708. ⎫ Married couple.
Susann Furrer, baptized August 19, 1708. ⎬

In April 1743 there went to Pennsylvania:
Heinrich Müller, baptized February 14, 1720, unmarried.
Thommen Lier, baptized September 26, 1725, unmarried.
Jacob Bär, baptized April 28, 1720, unmarried.
Ulrich Vollenweider, baptized December 5, 1723, unmarried.
　　April 25, 1744.　　　Attested, MATTHEW ESZLINGER, *Local Pastor.*

No. 18. List of those Persons who left for Carolina from the Parish Dägerlen

Dagerlen, 1743

Parents: *Ages.*
Heinrich Müller.................53
Susanna Geügisz.................51
Children:
Adam..........................22
Hans Jacob....................21
Anna..........................19
Barbara.......................15
Heinrich......................14
Johannes......................12
Hans Ulrich.................... 8
Hans Conrad................... 6

Rutschwill, 1743

Parents:
Johannes Hagenbuch............43
Margretha Schmid..............47
Children:
Jacob..........................17
Johannes......................16
Hans Heinrich.................15
Junghansz.....................10
Margretha..................... 8
Ulrich........................ 6

Parents:
Verena Schnider, Ulrich Müller's
   widow.......................36
Children:
Hans Heinrich.................14
Ulrich........................12
Jacob.........................11
Barbara....................... 9
Ursula........................ 6
Ulrich Waser, unmarried son of
   Joseph Waser................30

Parents:
Ursula Gischberger, whose hus-
   band had run away...........29
Children:
Ulrich Müller, stepson..........20
Rudolph....................... 2
Anna.....................3 weeks

Berg, 1734
Jacob Hagenbuch...............36
Barbara Bachmann..............37

Berg, 1738
                                    Ages.
Verena Wolfer, unmarried........24

Parents:
Anna Dändliker, Jacob Wolffens-
   berger's widow...............51
Children:
Anna..........................38
Hansz.........................14
Jacob.........................12
Regula........................10

Bänk, 1743
Hans Ulrich Schwarz, Jacob
   Schwarz's son................18

Oberwill, 1738
Parents:
Jacob Stuki...................46
Barbara Hugenbergerin..........47
Children:
Daniel........................20
Jacob.........................18
Johannes......................16
Peter.........................13
Ulrich........................ 7
{ Laurenz   Blatter,   unmarried;
   Andreas Blatter's son........21

Oberwill, 1743
Parents:
Andreas Blatter...............56
Maria Dietrich................54
Children:
Johannes......................17
Verena........................15

Parents:
Bernhardin Erzinger...........39
Barbara Blatter...............47
Children:
Barbara.......................17
Kathrina...................... 3

Parents:
Adam Blatter..................45
Margretha Wuhrmann............44
Children:
Verena........................12
Johannes...................... 9
Barbara....................... 5
Magdalena..................... 3

1743
Barbara Weber, Daniel Morff's
   wife.........................54
                    Total: 61 persons.

No. 19.   Dellickon.   List of those Persons, who left for the Country Carolina

September 27, 1734, Regula Weisz left for that place, legitimate daughter of Rudj Weisz and Barbara Schwällj, both of Dellickon.   She was baptized September 18, 1712.   (Documentary proof.)

After this daughter had given promise of marriage to the carpenter's mate, Johannes Matthysz of Watt, these two persons were united in marriage on my recommendation in the city of Basel, by Mr. M. Andreas Merian, candidate for the ministry.

August 27, 1738, there journeyed to the aforesaid land the following persons:
1. Heinrich Spillmann, wainwright, from Dellickon.   Baptized December 25, 1692.   (Documentary proof.)
2. Elsbeth Rümeli, from Seebach, wife of the preceding.   Baptized July 24, 1687. (Documentary proof.)
    Children:
3. Heinrich, baptized October 20, 1722.
4. Verena, baptized February 18, 1725.
5. Caspar Spillmann, brother to the above, baptized August 7, 1701.   (Documentary proof.)
6. Anna Müller, from Schlieren, baptized December 8, 1700.   (Documentary proof.)
7. Hanseli Spillmann, the son of the last-named brother, baptized July 9, 1730.

From the above-mentioned Heinrich Spillmann, wagon-maker, a letter has come, dated May 19, 1743, from Carolina, concerning the truthfulness of which there is doubt, owing to various causes.

Dellickon, April 2, 1744.   Hans Jacob Oerj, *Pastor.*

No. 20.   Dättlikon, March 27, 1744.   (See Plate 1)

About nine years ago, there journeyed from here to Pennsylvania, and established himself near Philadelphia, as a report to me from there shows:

Jacob Weydmann, a mason, aged 40, with his wife and four small children. In spring, a year ago, there followed after him, contrary to my admonition, preached from the pulpit in a sermon specially devoted thereto, and in spite of remonstrances in private:
1. Heinrich Bretscher from Blumetshalden, aged 27, and his wife Anna Wetzstein, aged 19, with her brother Jacob Wetzstein, aged 21.   They carried a good sum of money along with them, how much I do not know.
2. Heinrich Müller, aged 42, and his wife Margaretha Herzog, aged 39, with four small children, and the sister of Müller, Ursula, aged 46.   He also took along a good amount of money, the sum is not known to me.
3. Felix Ernst, aged 37, and his wife Elsbetha Weydmann, aged 41.
4. The above Jacob Weydmann's sister, also with four small children; she had little money.

Then Heinrich Weydmann, unmarried, aged 23, was also provided with a sum of money.

I do not know of anyone who has a desire to follow the above, but one or another may be concealing his wish, cherished within, and be waiting only for a report as to how those fared who left.

The paternal care of our gracious rulers is Christian, good, necessary, praiseworthy.   But along with this, it is no less good and necessary, if one gives to the poor industrious but unemployed people enough work for their necessary sustenance, or otherwise gives them some needy assistance, then they would be glad to remain in their native land.

This is written with my feeble hand.   (Haec manu infirma.)

No. 21.   From the Parish Dielstorff the Following Family has gone away to Carolina

Heinrich Kuhn } Parents.
Regula Zöbelj }

Felix Kuhn }
Heinrich Kuhn } Children.
Peter Kuhn }

    Total five persons.   Attested,
    Dielstorf, March 31, 1744.   HANS HEINRICH WIRTZ, *Pastor.*

No. 22.   From the Parishes Dietlikon and Rieden the Following Families and Persons have left for Carolina and Pennsylvania

1734.   1. Jacob Hunen, called Bieler's, born 1700.
      2. His wife Elsbeth Mejer, born January 10, 1699.
      3. Regula, their daughter, born November 2, 1727.
      4. Ulrich Schwarzenbach, from Rieden, born September 1, 1705.
      5. His wife Barbel Hänslj, from Brütten, born May 29, 1798.
      6. Felix, their son, born April 12, 1733.
      7. Heinrich, their son, born September 19, 1734.
1739.   8. Caspar Kuhn, from Rieden, born October 10, 1713.
      9. His wife, Anna Magdalen Mejer, from Rümlang, born January 21, 1714.
   10. Anna, their daughter, born April 29, 1739.
1743. 11. Kilion Hinnen, mason, a widower, born December 16, 1694.
   12. Jacob Rathgeb Schneider, from Dietlikon, born April 15, 1703.
   13. His wife, Anna Wintsch, born January 19, 1712.
   14. Hans Rudolff, their son, born September 9, 1734.
   15. Regula, their daughter, born March 23, 1737.
   16. Heinrich, their son, born July 6, 1738.
   17. Hans Conrad, their son, born October 2, 1740.
   18. Hans, their son, born April 22, 1742.

                  Thus attests,

             JOHN JACOB UTZINGER, *Pastor.*

No. 23.   From Dübendorff there left for Carolina in the Year 1734

		Born:
Jacob Dänzler, tailor } Married couple	{ July	15, 1703
Magdalena Pfister }	{ December	26, 1698

Children:
Jacob	July	28, 1726
Hans Rudolff	May	9, 1728
Margaretha	January	5, 1730
Jacob	May	24, 1733

                  Pastor MANZ.

No. 24.   Dürnten

No one has yet gone from this parish either to Carolina or Pennsylvania. There are some indeed who wander about wretchedly as homeless people, thus a dismissed judge from Dürnthen, viz.: Hans Caspar Hotz. Also a certain Dändliker from Grüningen, who for several years had settled in the village and also had spent everything, he is with a wife and child.

From Ober-Dürnten a certain Keller from the parish Mur is also wandering about in misery as a wretched head of a family with a wife and six children. Then, a certain Letsch, with wife and child, but who still has means to maintain himself; he is a saddler by trade.

ZELLER, Minister.

No. 25.   List of Those Who Left the Parish Dynhart for the New World

Heinrich Bosshart, from Dynhart, born December 22, 1695.
Anna Schaub, his wife, born November 12, 1694.
Children:
    Kaspar, born October 2, 1718.
    Heinrich, born December 26, 1725.
    This Bosshart with his wife and two boys left in 1734.
Ulrich Brunner, from Aeschlikon, born February 8, 1686.
Anna Ernin, his wife, aged 65 years.
Children:
    Heinrich, born October 8, 1719.
    Rudolff Brunner, also Ulrich's son, born August 27, 1713.
    Elsabetha Geyer, his wife, born January 12, 1715.
Child:
    Hans Ulrich, born December 17, 1741.
    These two households left together in 1743.
Ulrich Huggenberger, from Wetzikon, born January 23, 1698.
Magdalena Duttweiler, his wife, born July 7, 1700.
    This couple had no children and left in 1743.
Ursula Sommer, Jacob Sommer's (deceased) daughter, from Aeschlikon, born March 24, 1712, was in service at Stein and left with the above, in 1743.
Anna Ammann, Ulrich Ammann's daughter, from Wetzikon, born October 29, 1713, served at Berg, the parish Dägerlen and left with several from this parish in 1743.
    These are the persons, who against all warnings left the parish of Dynhart, with the purpose of going to Carolina.
    Dynhart, April 10, 1744.   Attested by John Rudolff Büeler.
    On further inquiry it appears that also Anna Stapfer, the daughter of the deceased Hans Jacob Stapfer, from Sulz, born October 5, 1704, left with several from Ellikon, where she served, without giving notification in the parsonage of Dynhart, in the year 1743.

No. 26.   The Following Persons Left the Parish Eglisau in June, 1743

Born   Family
                              1.

1692 Ulrich Hartmann, turner, at the Steig, July 24.
1695 Anna Fehr, December 25.
Children:
    1728 Anna Barbara, May 22.
    1730 Heinrich.
    1732 Hans Jacob, August 10.
    1737 Anna Catharina, February 10.

2.

1699   Hans Marthj, inn-keeper, boatman at the Burg, February 28.
       Verena Keiser.

3.

1717   Hans Ullrich Sprenger, September 12.
1716   Verena Schnetzer, December 26.

4.

1679   Regula Utzinger, April 20. Deceased Rodolf Schneider's wife from
       Oberriedt.
       Her son.
1712   Jacob Schneider, boatsman, February 26.
1717   Regula Hartmann:
Children:
       1740   Anna, August 2.
       1742   Hans Jacob, February 13.

5.

1705   Jacob Keiser, January 28.   Weaver at Oberriedt.
1711   Regula Braitter, April 15.

6.

1694   Fronnyk Keiser, October 27, Ulrich Bechtold's wife from Oberriedt.
With two children.
       1724   Magdalena, November 19.
       1729   Barbara, March 13.

7.

1717   Johannes Jauschlj, at the Staig, March 2.
       Ursula Meyer.,
       Rodolff Keiser, Marthj Keiser's (deceased) son at Oberriedt.
1721   Elisabeth Meyer, Jacob Meyer's (forester) daughter at Seglingen, April 13.
                                             Total: 24 persons.

No. 27.   List of Emigrants from the Parish Elgg for Penn-
                     sylvania and Carolina

1737

Hansz Ulrich Hofmann, from Schottiken, baptized September 18, 1718.

1742

Hansz Conrad Brunner, from Schottiken, baptized October 18, 1711.
Anna Barbara Speker, baptized June 2, 1715.
                          Same year
Hans Ulrich Vogler, from Elgg, glazier, baptized February 11, 1703.
Anna Maria Trachsler, baptized May 31, 1702.
Children:
       Anna Magdalena, baptized August 8, 1728.
       Hansz Heinrich, baptized April 11, 1731.
       Caspar, baptized July 28, 1737.
       Hans Ulrich, baptized April 15, 1739.
       Hans Jacob, baptized April 19, 1741.

1743

       Journeyed to Pennsylvania together with two persons from Veldheim, to
claim an inheritance of 7500 fl. from their cousin Hans Ulrich Hagmann at the
time in Germantown.
Rudolf Büchi, from Schottiken, Zürich, messenger's son, baptized December 1,
       1720.

Anna Barbara Peter, Hans Ulrich Peter's daughter in Schneit, baptized December
29, 1720.
Atque/eodem anno/alio Patriam quaerunt hub Sole jacentem.
(And in the same year there sought a fatherland cast under another sun):
Caspar Büchi, hatmaker, from Elgg, baptized December 3, 1693.
Anna Barbara Hegnauer, baptized April 24, 1697.
Children:
    Margaretha, baptized December 16, 1725.
    Heinrich, baptized November 17, 1726.
    Anna Barbara, baptized August 13, 1730.
    Hans Jacob, baptized January 6, 1732.
    Caspar, baptized August 1, 1734.
    Hans Ulrich, baptized April 11, 1743.

The same year

Ulrich Büchi, from Elgg, a widower, baptized February 6, 1698.
Daughter:
    Susanna, baptized February 1, 1728.
Sister:
    Maria, baptized December 2, 1708.

The same year

Bernhard Keller, from Elgg, baptized December 6, 1711.
Lisabeth Büchi, baptized February 15, 1711.
Children:
    Joachim, baptized November 10, 1737.
    Lisabeth, baptized March 11, 1739.
    Susanna, baptized April 1, 1742.

The same year

Joachim Peter, from Gündliken, baptized September 11, 1704.
Lisabeth Lieber, baptized September 26, 1711.
Children:
    Elsbeth, baptized September 10, 1730.
    Rudolf, baptized December 9, 1732.
    Joachim, baptized December 13, 1733.
    Melchior, baptized July 15, 1736.
    Hugo, baptized October 20, 1737.
    Anna Barbara, baptized November 15, 1738.
    Anna Magdalena, baptized February 24, 1743.

The same year 1743

Jacob Buchmann, from Schottiken, baptized March 22, 1696.
Margaretha Schwizler, baptized December 25, 1698.
Children:
    Jacob, baptized September 28, 1721.
    Hansz Ulrich, baptized July 26, 1723.
    Heinrich, baptized January 13, 1726.
    Salomon, baptized August 25, 1729.
    Anna, baptized August 24, 1732.
    Margaretha, baptized April 11, 1734.
    Joachim, baptized June 30, 1737.
    Hansz Conrad, baptized July 10, 1740.
      Total: 47 Persons.
Delivered in May, 1744.   By J. CONRAD WIRZ, *Minister at Elgg.*

No. 28. List of those Persons who went from the Parish Elsau to Carolina and Pennsylvania, Anno 1734-1744

| Date of Birth | | **1** | Left for Carolina |

Deceased Hans Ulrich Huber's sons
from Rümiken:

October   6, 1716.   Hans Conrad......................November 4, 1734
October   1, 1719.   Samuel...........................November 3, 1734.

2

July   9, 1699.   Andreas Brüncker from Rümiken.....November 4, 1734.
September 8, 1695.   Regula Herter, his wife.
   Children:
July   10, 1722.   Hans Heinrich.
March   5, 1724.   Hans Conrad.
April   14, 1726.   Hans Ulrich.
November 9, 1727.   Jacob.
August   6, 1730.   Maria Lisabeth; N.B. Died.
July   20, 1734.   Abraham.

3

March   23, 1697.   Salomon Ruckstul from Rümicken....November 4, 1734.
March   23, 1682.   Barbara Büchj.
   Children:
November 30, 1704.   Joachim.
October   9, 1707.   Salomon.
July   14, 1709.   Hans Conrad.
September 17, 1713.   Cleophea.
March   13, 1718.   Barbara.
January   9, 1724.   Hans Heinrich.
June   21, 1727.   Hans Ulrich.

N.B.   We have heard that the first three sons, Joachim, Salomon and Hans Conrad changed their intention and stayed behind in Alsace.

4   Left for Pennsylvania

August   18, 1700.   Melchior Ruckstul from Rümicken.
February 20, 1698.   Margreth Egg, his wife..................July 4, 1743.
   Children:
1737, baptized.   Verena Marithi, *spuria,* child of Verena in Winterthur, and Schupisser in Oberwinterthur.
   Elsau, April 16, 1744.   Attested: John Caspar Freüdweiler, *Pastor.*

No. 29. The Following People have left Embrach for Pennsylvania and Carolina

1. Hans Zollicker with wife and seven children.
2. Elsbeth Fäsi, Heinrich Zollicker's widow, with 2 children.
3. Kilian Zollicker with his wife and six children.
4. Heinrich Cappeler of Oberembrach, with one son and son's wife.
5. Rudi Cappeler's widow, Elsbeth Büchi, from Oberembrach.
6. Jacob Bachmann from Untermetterstetten and his wife.
7. Ulrich Huber, from Loch, with his wife and two children.
8. Jacob Bosserth, of Mülliberg, with his wife and four children.
9. Caspar Huber's (deceased), of Oberwageburg, son and daughter.
10. Felix Bentz's two sons (Bentz, who was killed by accident).
11. Peter Bänningers son, Ulrich, of this place.
12. Hansz Conradt Heuszer, with his wife and three children.

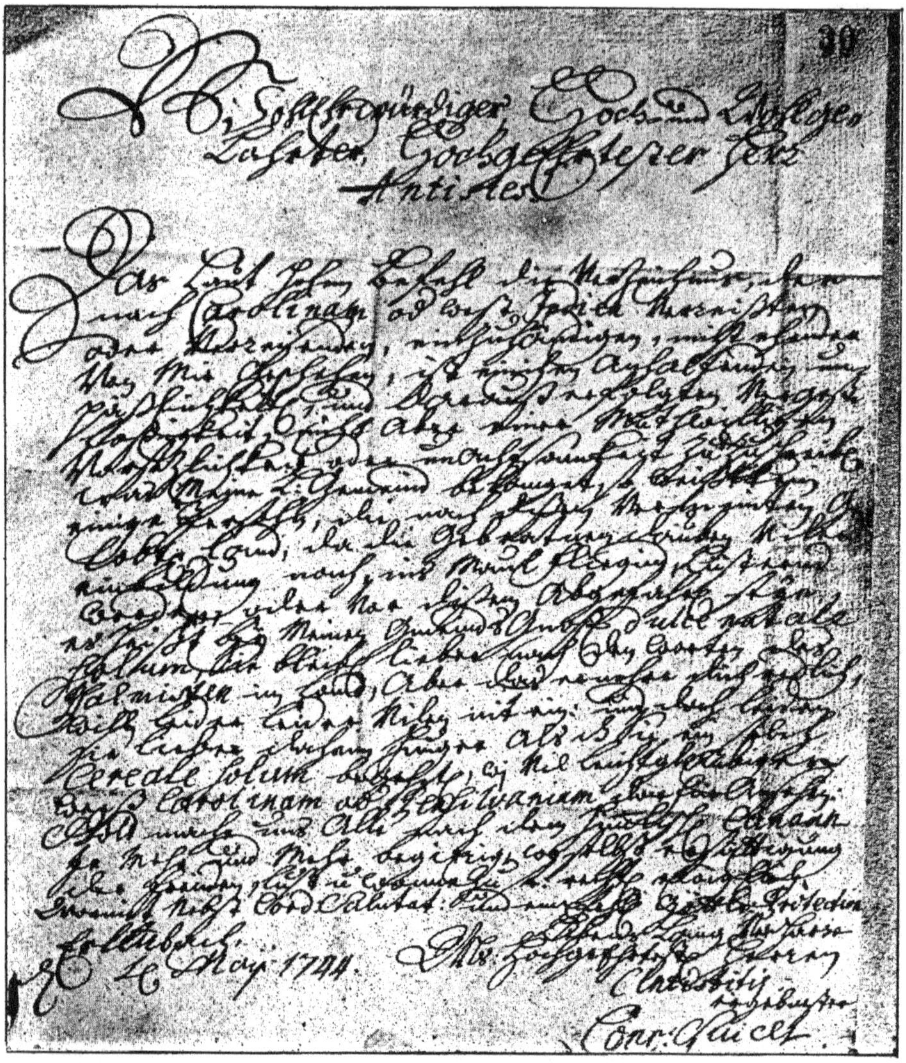

Plate 2

REPRODUCTION OF THE ORIGINAL LIST No. 30, ERLENBACH, MAY 1, 1744

13. The wife of Bernet Wipfen who was killed by accident, with one child.
14. David Leimbacher, with his wife and three children.
15. Ulrich Huber, of Underwagenburg, with wife and 4 children.
16. Rudolff Bosserth, of Mülliberg, with wife and 3 children.
17. Ruedi Cappeler's daughter.
18. Hansz Heinrich Bosserth's, of Mülliberg, one son and daughters.
19. Catarina Meier, daughter of Hans Meier of Embrach, deceased.
20. Ursel Bosserth, daughter of Heinrich Bosserth of Mülliberg, who has disappeared.
21. The son of Jacob Bosserth ab der Stiegen, deceased.
22. Heinrich Krebser's, of Rottenfluh, son Rudolf.
23. Johannes, son of Jacob Krebser, deceased.
24. Jacob Bänninger, son of Ulrich Bänninger of Embrach.
> Total: 73 people.
> Received March 28.   Sent the 30th.

No. 30.   From Luffingen.   (See Plate 2)

In 1738 Hans Ulrich Meyer with his wife and two young children journeyed to Carolina.   Because of my remonstrances no one has dared to do it since.

Most Honorable, Most Learned, and Most Revered Superior:

That I have not sooner, according to your command handed in the list of the people who have left or are leaving for Carolina or the West Indies, is due to certain restraining inconveniences and consequent forgetfulness, but not to stubborn insubordination or carelessness.   As far as my parish is concerned, I do not know of a single person who has cherished a desire for this so-called promised land, where, according to some people's fancy, roast pigeons fly into one's mouth, nor one who has departed thither.   My parishoners believe in the proverb "dulce natale solum" (Sweet is one's native land).   They prefer to remain in the land, according to the words of the psalmist, but the making of an honest living, alas! alas! has not always proved true, and still they prefer to suffer hunger at home than to desire such a "fruitful land," as many frivolous persons believe Carolina or Pennsylvania to be.   May God make us all long more and more for the Heavenly Canaan, where there is completeness of joy, happiness and bliss forever at His right hand.   With heartfelt greetings, and committing you to divine protection, I remain, for the duration of my life, my Most Honorable Superior's humble servant   CONRAD SUICER, *Pastor.*

Erlenbach, May 1, 1744.

No. 31.   List of those Persons who went from the Parish of Fällanden to Carolina

1. Jacob Aepplj, born July 10, 1701, his wife Anna Fenner, born March 31, 1705. Children:
   Margreth, born December 5, 1728.
   Johannes, born August 16, 1735.
2. Hansz Jacob Aepplj, born January 6, 1704, his wife Verena Wetstein, born September 26, 1706.
   Child:
   Rudolff, born September 25, 1735.
3. Christoph Hauser, widower, born May 10, 1691, the daughters:
   Barbara, born November 30, 1717.
   Anna Barbara, born May 2, 1719.
4. Hans Rodolf Bodmer, born May 1, 1692.
   His wife, Regula Gachnang, born July 9, 1703.

Children:
  Hans, born June 16, 1726.
  Heinrich, born November 14, 1728.
  Cleophea, born June 14, 1733.
  Regula, born April 8, 1736.
5. Hans Ulrich Bosshart, born March 25, 1717. ⎰ Brothers, legitimate sons of
   Heinrich Bosshart, born March 23, 1721. ⎱   Jacob Bosshart.
6. Johannes Bachmann, George's legitimate son, October 4, 1712.
7. Barbara Bosshart, deceased Jacob's legitimate sister, born February 17, 1711.
     The above persons all left Anno 1738.
   Anno 1743 there departed:
8. Heinrich Gachnang, born March 21, 1717.
   His wife, Susanna Fischer, born July 24, 1707.
   Their children:
     Christoph, born September 27, 1739.
     Salomon, born November 5, 1741.
                              Written by JOHN FÄSI, vicar.
     Fällanden, March 30, 1744.

NO. 32.   FISCHENTHAL

Names of those families and persons from this parish who from 1734 till the
present have been living in foreign lands.
  1. Regula Brunner, widow of Heinrich Egli, ab dem Rohr, with six children,
     named: Hans Jacob, Caspar, Barbara, Anna, and Regula, as well as
     Maria, who was married to Marx Kägi. This couple is wandering about
     the country and no one really knows where they are. The mother, how-
     ever, with the other children intended to go to Carolina, but came home
     poor; and will not be received by the parish until she can obtain the official
     permission to stay here.
  2. Salomon Egli, a son of the above-mentioned woman, has been in Holland
     for three years.
  3. Abraham Zuppinger from Müllibach has also been in Holland for about
     three years.
  4. Hansz Jacob Kägi from Lenzen hired out in Holland about two years ago.
  5. Rodolff Bischoff from Wald has been in Holland for three years.
  6. Hans Jacob Ryser from Leimaker has been in Holland for two years.
  7. Hans Ulrich Schönenberger from Heussli has been in Holland for a year.
  8. Jacob Kägi from Oberhoff has been in Holland for a year.
  9. Hans Jacob Bischoff auf der Bodmen has a wife and four children, deserts
     them, and the children are put upon the care of the parish and are supported
     by alms or from the church property. Where this man is, no one knows.
     It has already been four years since he disappeared.
 10. Hans Jacob Zuppinger, from Müllibach, has also been out of the country,
     no telling where, for four years.
   This is the specification made, according to the official command, of those
families and persons from the parish of Fischenthal who are residing abroad.
   Fischenthal, April 7, 1744.   Attested: S. WEISS, Pastor.

NO. 33

DORFF. On May 15, 1743, an unmarried man, named Martin Roth, aged
27 years, started from here toward Pennsylvania with 150 florins. He sent word
from London that he hoped to arrive there safely, but, to my knowledge, there
has since then been no further word from him. This circular I received at half

past two in the afternoon and I am sending it with respectful greetings to Rev. D., Pastor in Flaach.

FLAACH.   The past year three families left my parish: Jacob Fissler with his wife and two young men, Conrad Fehr with his wife and two children, and Conrad Gugler of Volken with his wife without children.   But four families have decided to leave next week unless an official prohibition prevents them, which will be immediately reported to the District Governor (Kreis-Landvogt) at Andelfingen.   We are sending the circular on the same day on which we received it.   With greetings, Rev. D's vicar, Berg.

BERG.   Anno 1738, the following persons left for Carolina: Jacob Bucher with his wife and three children,—took about 15 florins with him.   Also Jacob Meyer with his wife and four children,—also took about 15 florins with him. Also Ulrich Schmid who took about 30 florins with him.   Also Jacob Fehr, the weaver, and his wife who took about 15 florins with them.   Also Catharina Egg, unmarried, born in Seen.   These parties left in September of the given year 1738, but no report of them has ever reached us.   This circular is being sent as quickly as possible with respectful regards to the Pastor in Buch.

BUCH a/ Irchel.   Eight or ten years ago there left my pa ish for Carolina, Heinrich Meierhofer, an unmarried man of 30 years, with about 30 florins.   He is at present in Carolina in the service of Mr. Samuel Augspurger, a citizen of Bern.   Thereafter Caspar Schurter with his wife, both 30 years old and with young children,—took with them 40 to 50 florins.   Where they went we do not know yet.   At present no more from here have any desire to start out.   A year ago my son, Elias, vicar of Hengart, in a sermon to that purpose, tried to make the dangerous journey to Carolina distasteful by every conceivable and striking argument, and to prevent it, but he found a poor hearing with many.   I received the circular March 26, at one o'clock in the afternoon and am sending it the following morning with greetings to the honorable pastor in Neftenbach.

No. 34.   SPECIFICATION OF THOSE PERSONS WHO EMIGRATED FROM THE PARISH OF GLATFELDEN TO CAROLINA

1738

Parish Glatfelden.

Parents:	Ages.
1. Heinrich Meyer	40
Zusanna Meyer	35
Children:	
Susanna	6
Lisabeth	4

1740

2. Steffen Keller, deceased Hans'	49
Elsbeth Frey	40
Children:	
Salomea	20
Heinrich	12
Hans Jacob	6
Parents:	
3. Brother of the above-mentioned Steffen Keller,	
Felix Keller	45
Vrena am Berg	40

Children:

Hans...15

Vrena..12

Susanna.. 6

N.B. This Felix Keller has with him his mother, Margaretha Meyer (aged 75), wife of Hans (Meyer) deceased: also his unmarried brother, Caspar Keller (aged 38).

1740

Parish Zweidlen.

Parents: Ages.

4. Abraham Keller...................................41

Margaretha Koffel..................................39

Children:

Bernhard... 9

Vrena... 7

Barbara... 5

Glatfelden.   1743

Husband and Wife.

5. Hans Peter Lee....................................60

Vrena Meyer.......................................60

6. Parents:

Felix Lee..40

Vrena Martelerj...................................39

Children:

Hans..12

Anna..10

7. Husband and Wife.

Hans Jacob Huszer.................................20

Madalena Azenweiler..............................28

8. Parents:

Caspar Glatfelder..................................36

Lisabeth Lauffer...................................34

Children:

Anna Margareth...................................13

Anna..11

Salomon... 9

Johannes.. 7

N.B. Has with him his father-in-law,

Hans Jacob Lauffer.................................70

Parents: 1743

9. Heinrich Walder...................................30

Dorothea Lauffer..................................20

10. Husband and Wife.

Hans Peter Glatfelder..............................45

Salomea am Berg...................................40

N.B. Has with him his brother Felix Walder, unmarried..............25

Children:

Elsbetha..16

Barbara...14

Felix..12

Lisabeth..10

Hans Rudolf....................................... 9

Johannes.. 4

Zweidlen.
11. Parents:
    Hans Schmid..40
    Margaretha Schüz..38
    Children:
        Caspar..10
        Johannes... 8
        Hans Ulrich....................................... 4
Reinszfelden.
12. Heinrich Guth..28
    N.B. His wife, Anna Scherrer, with whom he lived until that time in the parish of Neftenbach is at present trying to obtain a separation from him from the Matrimonial Court.
    Total Number of persons—53.

No. 35. FROM THE PARISH GOSSAU THERE HAVE LEFT FOR CAROLINA

Anno 1734. From Bertschiken:
Rudolf Walder, baptized April 10, 1698, with his wife, Anna Stuzin and little son, Jacob, aged 4 years, took money with him, 50 pounds.

Anno 1739. From Ober-Ottiken:
Jacob Zollinger, baptized April 27, 1697, with his wife, Lisabeth Frey:
Children:
    Anneli, aged 10 years.
    Casperli, aged 6 years.
    Andres, aged 4 years.
    Babeli, aged 2 years.
He raised money on his farm and took with him 500 pounds.
             Attested: JOHN HEINRICH DÄNIKER, *Pastor.*

No. 36. LIST OF THOSE PERSONS FROM THE PARISH OF GREIFFEN-SEE who, from the year 1734 until this present year 1744, either have emigrated to Pennsylvania or have intended to go there, but are staying at present in other places or have returned home.

    Anno 1734, in October, Margaretha Vogel, daughter of the late Heinrich Vogel, the mason, left this parish for Pennsylvania, being then 30 years of age. She is said to be there at present.
    Anno 1738. Hans Jacob Wolffensperger, at that time 34 years old, and his wife, Susanna Danni, 30 years old, with three children: Elsbeth, then 7 years old, Maria, then 4 years old, and Margaretha, then ¾ year old. This family left our parish in August of that year. Went as far as Basel, from there back to Aarau, where they stayed almost two years. Since then they have been living again in our parish.
    Anno 1738. Heinrich Drachssler, the hedge-maker, then 23 years old, and his wife, Catharina Danni, then 24 years old, also left here in August of the specified year, went as far as Basel, from there back to Aarau where they stayed not quite a year, but since then they have been living again in our parish.
    Anno 1743. Johannes Bleuwler, son of Hans Heinrich Bleuwler, the butcher, 28 years old, left here in May. Went as far as Basel, where he is now working in a mill, as journey-man miller.

Felix Bleuwler, brother of the above, 20 years old, left here in May, went as far as Basel and has been since then in the French army.

Hans Jacob Brauch, son of Hans Conrad Brauch, 22 years old, left here in May, went as far as Basel and came back from there in a few weeks to our parish.

Hans Conrad Burckhard, son of Hans Conrad Burckhard, the scabbard-maker, 14 years old, a very poor boy; the three people above-mentioned allowed him to go with them to Basel (because he could not find a master hereabouts), where he has been living ever since. According to a written report which we have received, he is behaving himself very well and, through the kindness of some compassionate people there who have interested themselves in him, has been apprenticed for five years without apprentice-fee, to a ropemaker, to learn the trade.

Anno 1743.   Hans Jacob Wüest, the son of the district judge, Hans Conrad Wüest, 22 years old, learned the locksmith's trade and gave out that he was going travelling as a journeyman, but left Basel in May with some fellow countrymen to go to Pennsylvania, and is said to have married a woman from the Oberen Strass, who once stood in the pillory in Zurich.

Anna Wolfensperger, daughter of Jacob Wolfensperger, the joiner, 28 years of age, went from here to Basel in May and started from there with some fellow countrymen to go to Pennsylvania and is said to have married a fellow from Affoltern in the Albis.

Greiffensee, April 1, 1744.   JOHANN JACOB ORELL, *Pastor at Greiffensee.*

There was omitted above: Anno 1738.   Magdalena Drachszler, daughter of Heinrich Drachszler, the hedge-maker, deceased, then 17 years of age, travelled from here to Basel in August with the intention of going to Pennsylvania, but is said not to have gone on from there, but to be wandering around elsewhere—now here, now there—like a good-for-nothing woman without reporting definitely where she is at present.

No. 37. SPECIFICATION OF THOSE PEOPLE WHO WENT FROM THE PARISH HUSEN AM ALBIS, TO CAROLINA AND PENNSYLVANIA

Jacob Ringker, born August 16, 1707, son of Captain Werner Ringker, deceased, of Husen;—to Carolina September 1, 1741.

Heinrich Grob, born May 23, 1723, son of Julius, of Hirtzwangen;—to Carolina July 24, 1742.

Sergeant Heinrich Hitz, from the Bäuder-Albis, born July 11, 1697, with his wife, Elsbetha Frick, of Knonau, born April 18, 1711, and four children: Verena, born March 16, 1727, Adelheid, born February 10, 1732, Heinrich, born September 13, 1733, and Anna, born May 11, 1738;—to Pennsylvania.

Heinrich Lier, of Ebertschwyl, born August 7, 1707, with his wife, Verena Suter, also of Ebertschwyl, born October 6, 1705, and little son, Beat, born September 27, 1733.   Both parties to Pennsylvania April 29, 1743.

Sergeant Johann Conrad Schmid, son of the mason, of Heist, born June 24, 1717, with his wife, Susanna Hügi, also of Heist, born December 6, 1716, and three children: Hans Jacob, born September 17, 1741, Hans Rudolf, January 6, 1743 and Regula, March 1, 1744;—to Pennsylvania April 1, 1744.

April 27, 1744.

Attested: JOHANN JACOB HIRTZEL, *Pastor.*

No. 38. Anno 1743, from the Parish Henkartt, with the Knowledge and Consent of the Two Honorable Governors of Kyburg and Andelfingen, the following families and persons journeyed to the new-found land—I do not know whether to Carolina or to Pennsylvania.

1. Jacob Frauenfelder, shoemaker, called Gabriel, baptized October 30, 1707, with his wife, Elsbetha Meyer von Buech, far advanced in pregnancy.
   N.B. He was the instigator and the seducer of the others from the County.
2. Deyes Frauenfelder, brother of the above, baptized March 17, 1705.
   Verena Schaub, his wife, baptized February 18, 1703.
   Children:
   1. Mathias, baptized March 11, 1732.
   2. Jacob, baptized June 23, 1733.
   3. Ursala, baptized July 18, 1734.
   4. Johannes, baptized January 29, 1736.
   5. Barbara, baptized September 8, 1737.
   6. Heinrich, baptized November 15, 1739.
   7. Conrad, baptized October 8, 1741.
   They took all these seven children with them. This family resided in the Estate.
3. Jacob Frauenfelder, called Gräzli, baptized December 20, 1705.
   Anna Weyer, his wife, of Seen, baptized November 9, 1701.

From the County

Children:
   1. Anna, baptized January 22, 1732.
   2. Barbara, baptized May 20, 1734.
   3. David, baptized October 16, 1735.
   4. Elsbetha, baptized June 16, 1737.
   5. Hans Conrad, baptized September 10, 1741.
      Took them all with them.
4. Mathias Frauenfelder, son of Jonas, baptized December 10, 1712.
   Barbara Müller, of Hettlingen, baptized August 24, 1710. Far advanced in pregnancy.
   N.B. He sent back from London, where his wife recovered from the birth of a daughter, a lamentable letter, in which he could not write enough concerning how miserably they had been deceived, warning everyone against this journey. Threatens to come home again, as soon as it is possible.
   He resided in the Estate.
   These four families emigrated in June, but the two following ones in August. Nothing seemed so sad to me as this obstinate, unscrupulous emigration of these heartless parents with so many innocent little children. I was seriously ill at the time or I should have taken desperate measures to prevent the same, and would have sent the Elders immediately to the Honorable Governors on their account, but all was in vain, and my sickness was made all the more bitter for me,—and these people were as if bewitched and desperately resolute, for most of them were poor and could hardly get together sufficient money for the journey; and, what was worst of all, in their answer to our warnings they laid the blame—indirectly, indeed—upon our gracious masters. Note the following: If this were true and our gracious masters had allowed so many of their subjects to emigrate from their country, and if the aforesaid lamentable letter and other sad reports had not reached the country, and become known, a good many might have decided to emigrate.

Each of these six families has an official certificate of baptism from the pastor of the parish with them. The first four were written in my own hand the last two in the schoolmaster's hand, but signed by me and with these two words added: sponte et audacter (voluntarily and rashly).

5. Hans Jacob Frauenfelder, called Pfeiffer, baptized November 15, 1711.
Anna Frauenfelder, his wife, baptized July 29, 1712.
Children:
 1. Ursala, May 27, 1736.
 2. Pantaleon, March 4, 1738.
 3. Barbara, July 17, 1742.

6. Jacob Frauenfelder, son of Gabriel, the tailor, baptized December 3, 1713.
Elisabeth Brätschger of Aesch, born 1709.
Children:
 1. Barbara, baptized March 18, 1736.
 2. Hans Heinrich, baptized November 24, 1736.
 3. Elsbetha, baptized April 10, 1740.
 4. Anna, baptized September 23, 1742.

Anna Frauenfelder, a respectable young woman, unmarried, sister of Jacob Frauenfelder, above-mentioned, baptized March 29, 1716. These two families—Nos. 5 and 6—resided in the County.

In all six families, four from the County, two from the Estate. Persons—32.

Moreover, under my predecessor, deceased Anno 1739, there left here for Carolina; Felix Frauenfelder, son of Felix from the monastery, baptized November 13, 1701, and his wife, Elsbetha Mäder, from Schleittheim in the District of Schaaffhausen, baptized April 14, 1701, with five children, including four boys, the oldest about ten years old.

Henkertt, March 31, 1744.   LEONHARD HOLZHALB, *Pastor.*

No. 39. THE FAMILIES AND PERSONS FROM THE PARISH OF HEN-KERTT, residing abroad or wandering about here and there, March 31, 1744.

1. Adam Müller, baptized December 27, 1672, widower since July 19, 1733; resides in Schaaffhausen on a vine-raising estate.
Children:
 1. Ursula, baptized December 29, 1713.
 2. Hans Ulrich, baptized July 25, 1715. They are all said to have been
 3. Barbara, baptized December 22, 1717. baptized at Schaaffhausen.
 4. Rodolff, baptized May 23, 1720.

2. Adam Müller, son of the above, baptized January 1, 1705.
Verena Süesstrunk of Wisendangen, March 10, 1716. Married April 26, 1735. They also resided in the District of Schaaffhausen, but they are said to have settled permanently in the District of Basel.

3. Heinrich Weni and Ursala Chym of Schlatt. The former's wife died last year at Schaaffhausen on the vine-raising estate which he had leased; and he returned this year again to this parish with honorable testimonials and considerable means, aged 78 years.

4. Deyes Steinmann, a shoemaker, baptized October 4, 1687, was married in the margravate of Weil, an hour's distance from Basel, to Sara Seiffert, February 2, 1717. According to a letter which we have received, he died September 3, of last year, and his death has been published here. He leaves behind his wife and four children, two sons and two daughters, of whom the one son and the one daughter are already married. The children are called:
 Anna Maria,
 Lorenz Simeon,
 Johann Conrad.

5. Hans Jacob Frauenfelder, smith, baptized February 14, 1698.   He, it appears, disappeared suddenly and since then no one has heard the slightest word from him.   His wife, Anna Blickenstorffer, baptized August 20, 1699, wanders about the country with her daughter, Margaretha, baptized January 16, 1734, an illegitimate child, conceived in adultery, and spends much of her time in the districts of Baden and Bern.   The son, Hans Ulrich Frauenfelder, baptized March 29, 1722, also wanders around begging.

Hans Jacob Frauenfelder, son of the younger Graz, baptized January 8, 1690.

Joseph Frauenfelder, brother of Gräzli, baptized December 6, 1711.

Hans Conrad Frauenfelder, son of Baschi, baptized January 30, 1701.

Hans Conrad Steiner, brother of Seepe, baptized June 14, 1705.

Unknown

Also some people 60–70 years old or more, some of them discharged soldiers, some of them vagrants, of whom nothing is known, Baschi, David, Hans Conrad, Jacob, Isaac Frauenfelder.

Hans Ulrich Frauenfelder, son of Joseph, deceased, is living in Strassburg.   He was here in this country two years ago, living with a woman whom he is since said to have married.   Baptized May 4, 1719.

Hans Jacob Frauenfelder, called Weber, baptized August 16, 1696.

Barbara Frauenfelder, baptized November 14, 1797.

Children:
1. Hans Ulrich, baptized October 7, 1725.
2. Anna, baptized April 4, 1728.
3. Barbara, baptized January 1, 1730.
4. Hans Jacob, baptized March 21, 1734.
5. Hans Peter, baptized July 13, 1738.

Sold his property here and established himself with his family in Buesingen.

There are also three or four women missing who are said to have gone to the lowlands, or to be wandering about elsewhere, or to be in the realms of the dead. At any rate, we do not know anything about them.

The soldiers, who are at present serving in Holland or elsewhere, have been listed in another place.

LEONHARD HOLZHALB, *Pastor.*

No. 40.   LIST OF THOSE PERSONS WHO HAVE GONE TO CAROLINA FROM THE PARISH OF HEDINGEN, ANNO 1743

1. Barbel Hunn, wife of Heiri Schmid, deceased, from the District of Bern.
   Children:
   Maria, born February 14, 1723.
   Heiri, born September 14, 1727.
   Tomas, born June 23, 1733.
   With them went Uli Stähli, born January 9, 1706.   He is a poor stupid fellow, good for nothing.
   Also
   Catri Hubschmid, daughter of the miller at Hedingen, born 1700.
   Also
   Elseli Hedinger, daughter of Heiri Hedinger, born December 15, 1720.
2. Heiri Meili, son of Heiri, went with his wife and children either there or to Pennsylvania.   Many years ago he sold all that he had in Hedingen and since then h as not been living in Hedingen, but in Maschwanden with his wife and children, so that he should be reported from Maschwanden.

Attested: JOHANN FÄSI, *Pastor.*

No. 41.   In Answer to the Official Command which I received from the Honorable Dean Fäsi at Hedingen, to give an Account of the Persons from this Parish of Rifferschwül who have gone to Carolina and Pennsylvania, I Report the Following to the Honorable Dean:

Oberschweil

The first left April 28, 1739, namely:
Johannes Schleipffer, baptized January 8, 1719.
Johannes Bär, born January 31, 1723.
Elsbeth Bär, born August 27, 1719.
Bat. Rudolff Bär, born May 14, 1719.
Hans Heinrich Bär, born December 11, 1720.
Rudolff Bär, born May 17, 1722.
Hans Jacob Huser, born February 9, 1716.

Under-Rifferschweil

Hans Jacob Widmer, born December 6, 1722.
Anna Bär, born October 13, 1715.
Johannes Wäber, born April 14, 1720.
Ulrich Wäber, born May 12, 1720.

In August

Heinrich Weber, born October 6, 1715.
Anna Urner, born November 6, 1718.
Jacob Weber, born December 30, 1725.
    There also left in 1743 in May:
Jacob Frick, born August 22, 1697.
Verena Bär, born July 10, 1718.

Also from Ober-Rifferschweil

Henrich Schleipffer, born May 17, 1705.
Also his wife, Anna Grob, born August 1, 1706.
Also their children:
    Jacobli, baptized in Meria, in Flanders, Anno 1735.
    Cathri, born January 20, 1743.

Also from Under-Rifferschweil, April 1, 1744:

Henrich Urner, born June 10, 1702.
His wife, Anna Näff, born January 14, 1694.
Their children:
    Verena, born December 17, 1730.
    Johannes, born August 7, 1735.

No. 42.   Herrliberg

The following left for Carolina in 1743.   Before this there were none.
Born.

1704.   { Rudi Wy-man.
        { Dorothea Sennhauser.
    Children:
1721.   Elsbeth.
1723.   Barbara.

1725. Jacob.
1729. Verena.
1732. Heinrich.
1735. Hans Heinrich.
Parents:
1705. Heinrich Kölliker.
1704. Rägula Brätscher.
Children:
1732. Antoni.
1734. Heinrich.
1736. Anna.
1739. Susanna.
1742. Hans Caspar.

From Berg

Father:
1702. Heinrich Haab   (Name not entirely legible.)
Children:
1727. Rodolf.
1732. Hans Rodolff.
Parents:
1702. Heinrich Hermetschwyler.
1701. Barbara Erzinger.
Children:
1726. Anna.
1728. Barbara.
1731. Elsbeth.
1734. Jacob.

CONRAD ZIEGLER, *Pastor.*
(Signature added in modern hand-writing.)

No. 43. Hinweil

From this parish there emigrated Anno 1743, with the intention of going to Carolina:
Caspar Honegger, from Unterbach, baptized February 26, 1708.
Anna Schneider, his wife, baptized July 4, 1706.

With three children { Marx, baptized February 18, 1733.
Caspar, baptized April 18, 1734.
Hans Jacob, baptized January 1, 1736.

He took about 160 florins in money with him since his brothers bought him out about five years ago for 180 florins.
Hinweil, April 7, 1744.   JOHANN LUDWIG MEYER, *Pastor.*

No. 44. Hittnau

Honorable, Learned, Highly-Revered and Gracious Dean:
    In accordance with an official order, I am to send to the Honorable Dean a report of those persons from this parish who have gone to Carolina, in order that it may be sent to the official board.   I am glad to be able to do this in "three words," as they say, since there is only one married couple:
Heinrich Zwik, tradesman, from Oberhittnau, born November 3, 1709, and Anna Rüegg, born in Wollnau, in the parish Bauma.
    I have to report that they were married Anno 1737, and are still without children.   These people became so rich from the shop-keeping that they set up,

that they made a great pile of debts, which yield their creditors only the trouble of looking after them. And they knew how to craftily conceal their design and to secretly carry it out, so that they could sell their remaining possessions and their household belongings with the plausible excuse that they must have money for the Whitsuntide Fair at Zurzach (about a year ago); with which excuse they exacted payment of their outstanding debts, as far as possible,—from some they got but a little. So they escaped with considerable money without letting any-one know, and their departure was not noised abroad until some time after they had gone, when they were probably already safe in Holland.

That is all that I can say concerning the emigration from our beloved parish. I commend this notification to the Board and the Honorable Dean and my humble self to their continued favor. Committing you to the protection of Heaven and of Our Saviour, in dutiful submission,

The Honorable, Highly-Learned, and Gracious Dean's humble servant,

HEINRICH FÄSI, *Pastor.*

Hittnau, April 1, 1744.

NO. 45. FROM THE PARISH HOMBRECHTIKON

Caspar Muschgg from Brauslen, who formerly worked at Wollishofen, un-married, left for Carolina Anno 1734 in October. He appeared before the Magis-trates of the Estate Stäffen and acted against their advice. No one else so far as I know. No one from Stäffen has gone to America.

NO. 46. HORGEN

From this cherished parish there left last year for Carolina or Pennsylvania:
1. Hans Jacob Grundel, son of Jacob auf dem Bergli, baptized November 14, 1719, the son of a poor man who had worked as a hired hand.
2. Jacob Sträuli, son of Caspar deceased, from Käpfnach, baptized December 24, 1724.
3. Heinrich Stünzi, son of Marx, the tile-maker, from Käpfnach, baptized August 22, 1719.

Horgen, April 2, 1744.   JOHANN KELLER, *Pastor.*

NO. 47. FROM THE PARISH ILLNAUW the persons below described left for the so-called new-found land during the last few years:

7. Hanss Wezstein, wheelwright, from Kemleten, aged 38 years. Anna Frauenfelder, his wife, aged 36 years. } They left Anno 1737 with five children, of whom the old-est was 6, the youngest ¾ year.

7. Conradt Denzler, from first, aged 37 years. Anna Wezstein, his wife, aged 35 years. } They left with the above, also with five children, of whom the oldest was 6, the young-est 1 year.

5. Jacob Graaff, of Rykon, left with wife and three children, of whom the oldest was 7, the youngest 3 years, Anno 1738.

5. Margaretha Keller, widow of the schoolmaster, of Ottikon, aged 34, left Anno 1738, with four children; the oldest 15, the youngest 4 years.

4. Felix Widmer, of Ottikon, aged 36 years. Barbara Berüther, his wife, aged 40 years. } They left Anno 1743 with two children, the oldest 8½, the youngest 4 years.

5. Jacob Wägmann, of Rykon, aged 36 years. Dorothea Haffner, his wife, aged 34 years. } They left Anno 1743 with three children, the oldest 6, the youngest 2 years.

5. Mathias Frauenfelder, of Rykon, aged 45 years.
Anna Trindler, his wife, aged 50 years.

} They left Anno 1743 with three children, the oldest 14, the youngest 7 years.

2. Hanss Würgler, of Rykon, aged 21 years.
Verena Morff, his betrothed, aged 20 years.

} They left together Anno 1743.

3. Vrena Brändtlin, aged 22 years.
Regula Wägmann, aged 30 years.
Anna Hindermeister, of Effretikon, aged 40 years.

} Of Rykon { These three unmarried women left Anno 1743.

1. Barbara Schlumpf, of Horgen, aged 23, whose husband, Caspar Windsch, with her knowledge and consent entered the army for service in Holland 1742. She went back to her relatives at Münch-Altorff, where she became unfaithful to her husband and was made pregnant by another man, with whom she departed, Anno 1743, with her father's help. From the ship in Zürich she sent her legitimate little son back to his poor grandmother in Horgen. Total 44 persons, including 25 children.

Illnauw, April 2, 1744.   Attested: BALTHASSAR PEYER, *Pastor.*

No. 48. List of those Persons who have left the Parish Kloten for Carolina

KLOTEN

Anna Kern, wife of Jacob Brunner, with two children, after having faithlessly forsaken her husband, went with Heinrich Götschi to Carolina.

Jacob Brunner departed with the daughter of his cousin, Stüdli, of Basserstorff, whom he had made pregnant and with whom he had begotten an illegitimate child. Because the marriage-court refused to sanction their union they emigrated. He was 44 years old. He left behind in the parish five children, two sons and three daughters, who have fallen as a great burden upon the church and the parish for support.

Hanss Kleinpeter's son, by trade a carpenter, 24 years old, went to Carolina two years ago with people from Wallissell.

OPFIKEN

Felix Wismann, born June 19, 1707, and Verena Foster, born November 26, 1707, left with their child, Anna, born 1740, with the people from Wallissell two years ago.

Barbara Eberhardt, daughter of Felix Eberhardt, the cooper, of Opfiken, born May 22, 1707, emigrated nine years ago.

No. 49. List of those Persons who have gone from time to time from the Parish Knonau to Carolina and Pennsylvania

To Carolina, 1739

Heinrich Walder, son of the assistant magistrate, deceased, aged 32 years. Is said to have died on the journey.

Heinrich Sytz, son of the village watchman, aged 34 years.

Anna Walder, his wife, aged 30 years.

Heinrich Sytz, Jr., brother of the above, aged 24 years.

Caspar Frik, son of Ulrich, aged 31 years, is said to have died.

Veronica Hitz, his wife, aged 32 years.

Anneli Frik, their little daughter, aged 1 year, is also said to have died.

Johanes Frik, brother of the above, aged 20 years.
Ursala Frik, daughter of Caspar, aged 21 years.
Rudolf Frik, son of Felix, deceased, from Utenberg, an estate in the parish of Knonau, aged 29 years.
Anna Barbara Frik, daughter of Heinrich, from Utenberg, aged 24 years.

LEFT FOR PENNSYLVANIA, MAY 1, 1743

Leonhard Walder, of Knonau, aged 37 years.
Anna Weiss, his wife, aged 39 years.
Their children:
> Hanss Jacob, aged 16 years.
> Anna, aged 13 years.
> Hans Jacobli, aged 9 years.
> Vreneli, aged 7 years.
> Dorotheli, ten weeks old.

Elssbeth Frik, daughter of Ulrich, aged 39 years.
Anna Frik, her sister, aged 32 years.
Anna Sytz, daughter of Heinrich, aged 21 years.
Regula Sytz, daughter of Heinrich, deceased, aged 30 years.

Anno 1744, April 1, at 9 o'clock at night there left secretly without the knowledge of the Honorable Governor or of the pastor.

N.B. Barbara Niehvergelt, wife of Heinrich Sytz, whose husband is still alive and 56 years old. She, his disloyal wife, is 43 years old.

Hanss Jacobli Sytz, her 9 year old son.

> April 6, 1744.

This is attested by CHRISTOPHEL ZIEGLER, *Pastor at Knonau.*

No. 50. SPECIFICATION OF THOSE PERSONS WHO EMIGRATED FROM KÜSSNACHT FOR CAROLINA, ANNO 1743

From the Küssnachterberg, from the Hoch-Rüti	Born.
Elsbeth Tobler, wife of Hans Erzinger, deceased	1679

Children:
Regula, November 3	1715
Hans Jacob, April 3	1718
Maria, March 3	1720
Hans Rudolff, October 13	1722

From Küssnacht

Caspar Elliker, November 15	1700
Anna Wirz, June 16	1705

Children:
Anna, May 26	1729
Violand, April 27	1732
Caspar, January 10	1734
Hans Heinrich, May 21	1737
Lisabeth, October 13	1739

With him is his brother-in-law, Jacob Wirz, April 10	1671
Johannes Gimpert, September 28	1699
Barbara Bertschinger, May 4	1710

Children:
Anna, February 14	1730
Barbara, August 22	1734
Heinrich, September 8	1735
Johannes, January 18	1739
Lisabeth, November 6	1740

These went as far as Basel where the father entered the French service. The mother came back with the children and since the community would not receive her, she left the children in the parish and went away again.

Anna Wirz, who was divorced from Conradt Meyer, born January 15, 1714. She is said to be in Basel.

Salomo Werder, son of Bernhardt Werder, deceased, born January 2, 1724. He went to Holland and came back again.

This is attested in accordance with the official command by

H. ARMINGER.

Note on the back: From the parish of Stäffen no one has gone to the West Indies.

From the parish of Männedorf no one.

Probably no one has left from these parishes since I have received no report in answer to my repeated requests.

No. 51.   LIST OF THOSE PEOPLE WHO WENT FROM THE PARISH OF LINDAU TO THE SO-CALLED NEW-FOUND LAND

1738

Joachim Häussli, of Winterberg.
His wife, Elsbeth Ochssner.
Children:
    Jacob, aged about ten.
    Heinrich, born October 27, 1736.
        In the same year:
Sarah Bläuler, widow of Jacob Keller, deceased, of Winterberg, with her son, Heinrich Keller.

1743

Hans Felix Widmer, shoemaker, of Lindau, born September 6, 1696.
His wife, Elsbeth Bänninger, in October, 1708.
Children:
    Jacob, born February 27, 1725.
    Elssbeth, October 24, 1728.
    Margaretha, June 18, 1730.
    Kley-Jacob, October 12, 1732.
    Elisabeth, December 19, 1741.
        In the same year:
Hanss Kuhn, of Graffstahl, aged 52.
His wife, Barbara Dentzler, aged 53.
        In the same year:
Hans Ulrich Wägmann, of Dagelschwangen, January 2, 1699.
Anna Huber, his wife. In October, 1702.
Children:
    Barbara, December 9, 1726.
    Heinrich, April 3, 1728.
    Hans Jacob, April 14, 1730.
    Anna, January 1, 1732.
    Hans Caspar, November 18, 1733.
    Margaretha, September 20, 1737.
        These last were living on a feudal estate in Mur, from whence they emigrated.
The first two families went to Carolina, I am told, the last three to Pennsylvania.
    Lindau, April 1, 1744.   Attested: JOHANN HEINRICH ULRICH, *Pastor*.

No. 52. LIST OF THOSE PERSONS WHO HAVE LEFT THE PARISH OF
MARTHALEN FOR CAROLINA SINCE 1735 OR WHO HAVE DE-
CLARED THEIR INTENTION TO GO THERE

September 24, 1738

Hans Ulrich Binder, guide, baptized October 23, 1698
Magdalena Mökli, his wife, October 20, 1700.
Children:
    Hans Ulrich, July 11, 1728.
    Barbara, November 19, 1731.
Theopel Binder, carpenter, October 9, 1698.
Barbara Leüw, his wife.
Children:
    Elsbeth, stepdaughter, January 9, 1727.
    Hans Heinrich, January 1, 1731.
    Hans Ulrich, March 14, 1734.
Hans Ulrich Mantz, Sprungen, January 20, 1697.
Anna Bachmann, his wife.
Children:
    Anna, November 9, 1732.
    Hans Jacob, October 31, 1734.
    Hans Ulrich, October 6, 1737.
Jacob Binder, carpenter, June 28, 1696.
Ursula Spallinger, July 17, 1695.
Children:
    Magdalena, April 25, 1728.
    Rudolff, May 13, 1731.
    Susann, July 30, 1734.
Conrad Mantz, Sprungen, September 3, 1699.
Magdalena Ritter, his wife, July 14, 1700.
Children:
    Barbara, July 1, 1724.
    Magdalena, February 13, 1729.
    Margreht, October 9, 1731.
    Hans Jacob, March 27, 1734.
    Anna, July 31, 1735.
    Verena, March 9, 1738.

Single Persons

Johannes Wipf, saddler, June 17, 1694. Leaves behind a wife and one son.
Heinrich Spallinger, unmarried, April 4, 1717.
Johannes Mökli, unmarried, October 8, 1714.
Barbara Wipf, daughter of Georg, deceased, unmarried, September 25, 1716.
    From all those who left Anno 1738 not the slightest reliable report has reached
Marthalen as to where they are or whether they are still living.

Anno 1743

Heinrich Wipf, wheelwright, September 25, 1692.
Anna Dietrich, his wife.
Children:
    Elsbeth, March 10, 1726.
    Hans Jacob, September 25, 1735.

Anno 1744

Georg Spullinger, carpenter, January 21, 1696.
Margreht Sägenmann, his wife.
Children:
    Anna, December 29, 1728.
    Barbara, May 27, 1730.
    Hans Jacob, October 11, 1739.

This woman came back last week with the children and says that the man was taken by the soldiers down in Basel.

The two families who left Anno 43 & 44, gave out first that they intended to go to Carolina, then to the Palatinate, then to Alsace, so it is uncertain where they did settle.

Reported by KORRODI, *Pastor at Marthalen.*

No. 53. LIST OF THOSE PERSONS WHO WENT FROM THE PARISH OF MUR TO CAROLINA

Anno 1738 there emigrated from Mur

Parents:
Hans Jacob Zürcher, baptized June 16, 1692.
Anna Schmid, of Grüningen.
Children:
    Hans Ulrich, baptized August 10, 1717.
    Elsbetha, baptized October 3, 1718.
    Leonhardt, baptized June 5, 1723.
Conrad Aeppli, son of Jacob Aeppli, deceased, baptized February 7, 1700.
Hans Aeppli, son of Jacob Aeppli, baptized March 4, 1708, unmarried.

From Esch

Caspar Kunz, son of Conrad Kunz, deceased, baptized October 16, 1703.
Rudolff Egg, son of Hans Rudolff Egg, deceased, baptized June 7, 1705.

From Ebmattingen

Felix Meyer, with his wife.

Anno 1743, in May there emigrated

From Mur

Parents:
Heinrich Aeppli, baptized October 23, 1692.
Elsbeth Hotz, baptized 1690.
Son:
    Heinrich, baptized July 31, 1729.
Parents:
Heinrich Steiner, baptized June 14 , 1705.
Angelica Jud, baptized May 2, 1706.
Daughter:
    Barbara, baptized February 27, 1742.

From Esch

Mother:
Anna Hämmig, wife of Felix Fenner, deceased.
Children:
    Hans Caspar, baptized May 14, 1719.
    Hans Heinrich, baptized July 12, 1722.
    Felix, baptized November 3, 1725.
Hans Jacob Brunner, son of Heinrich Brunner, baptized March 9, 1712, unmarried.

From Uessikon

Parents:

Felix Zollinger, baptized July 10, 1698.

Elsbeth Reiff, of Uster, 1697.

Children:

    Anna, baptized July 20, 1723.

    Hans Jacob, baptized November 7, 1728.

    Felix, baptized September 13, 1733.

From Binz

Jacob Bantli, son of Rudolff Bantli, baptized March 13, 1718, unmarried.

Parents:

Bernhardt Wunderli, baptized August 21, 1693.

Elisabeth Brunner, August 27, 1693.

Children:

    Bernhardt, baptized November 29, 1730.

    Magdalena, baptized January 28, 1733.

    Elsbeth, baptized February 13, 1735.

    Heinrich, baptized December 15, 1737.

From Höll

Father:

Heinrich Trüb, baptized January 22, 1702.

Child:

    Anna, baptized June 5, 1741.

JOHANNES CASPAR AMMANN, Pastor.

No. 54.   From the Parish of Meylen the Following Persons Have Gone to Carolina

June 25, 1743

Born.

1710, August 19, Andreas Haab.

1712, March 28, Dorothea Dolder. } Husband and wife.

With their children:

    1732, January 22, Regula.

    1734, January 10, Barbara.

    1735, July 17, Heinrich.

    1740, December 20, Hans Jacob.

    This family paid the emigration tax.

June 23, 1743

There left without permission from the honorable magistrate, or the knowledge of the pastor,

1678, March 10, Hans Jacob Widmer, widower.

With two daughters,

    1703, April 22, Anna. She took with her an illegitimate child by Conrad Wunderli, named Maria, born 1736, November, 17.

    1719, March 12, Elsbeth.

In July or August 1743 there left:

1716, September 20, Heinrich Widmer, shoemaker and his wife.

1712, September 4, Verena Kölliker, of Herrliberg.

    They have no children.

    Total from this parish, 12 persons.

    April 6, 1744. PASTOR TOBLER, of Meylen.

From the parish of UTIKON no one has emigrated.   (Written by another hand.)
Attested: DEAN USTERI.

No. 55. FROM THE PARISH OF METTMENSTETTEN THERE EMIGRATED EITHER TO CAROLINA OR TO PENNSYLVANIA

September 4, 1738, from Rossau

Hans Buchmann, May 9, 1702.
Regula Windisch, March 20, 1707. } To Carolina.
Hans Heinrich, July 28, 1737.

May 30, 1739, from Untermettmenstetten

Heinrich Huber, April 14, 1715. } To Carolina.
Anna Ruetsch, December 1, 1720.

Verena Rüetsch, her unmarried sister, November 3, 1715.
Anna Gallmann, daughter of Heini, deceased, of Heffertschweil, born June 5, 1695.

To Pennsylvania:

May 1, 1743, from Obermettmenstetten

Heinrich Ruetsch, March 8, 1708.
Verena Meier,
    Barbara, January 26, 1738.
Johannes Haug, from Untermettmenstetten, February 14, 1723.
Heiri Sutter, from Grosholtz, October 16, 1712.
Hans Jacob Rosell, of Hefertschweil, March 16, 1727.
Jacob Buchmann, of Dachlesen, September 14, 1721.
Unmarried Women:
Elsbeth Buchmann, daughter of Jogli, of Dachlesen, December 24, 1724.
Anna Ringer, daughter of Jacob, deceased, from Rossau, 1713.

No. 56. NEFFTENBACH

Has lost the following families on account of Carolina.

I. Martin Gutknecht, of Hüniken, aged 39, who, with his wife, Margareth
Bertschinger, aged 40, and six children, Barbara, aged 13, Elsbeth, aged 11,
Heinrich, aged 9, Johannes and Andreas, twins aged 7, and Susann, aged 2,
left, Anno 1736, with the intention of going to Carolina, but is said to be
staying around Basel with them.

II. Barbara Müller, of Hüniken, an unmarried woman, aged 23, who went from
here to Carolina in 1738.

III. Jacob Keller, from the Oeden-Hoff, aged 43, who, with his wife, Susann
Stephan, aged 36, and seven children, Andreas, aged 13, Rudolff, aged 12,
Jacob, aged 10, Felix, aged 8, Heinrich, aged 7, Hans Jacob, aged 4, Hanss
Rudolff, aged 3, also left in 1738, and no one has been able to find out any-
thing about them since then, although they promised to write.

IV. Jacob Scherer, from der hintern Hub, aged 52, who, with his wife, Susann
Bertschinger, aged 54, and three children, Barbara, aged 25, Hans, aged 23,
and Adelheit, aged 20, also left in 1738.

V. Also Gottfried Scherer, also from der hintern Hub, aged 27, and his wife,
Elisabeth Huber, aged 30, who however, had no children, left in the same
year.

VI. Finally Hans Ulrich Hagenbucher, of Hüniken, aged 41, who, with his wife,
Barbara Frauenfelder, of the same age, and three children, Elsbeth, aged 13,
Margareth, aged 10, and Magdalena, aged 2, left here for Carolina June 14,
1743, because he had been severely punished, at Kyburg, in the previous

6

spring for blasphemous speeches and in addition to that had been obliged to hear from the pulpit a sermon expressly directed against him, and consequently was ashamed to live longer among the people here.

I received the circular on Good Friday morning and am sending it on before noon with many greetings to Pfungen.

Pfungen has not lost anyone to the new-found land except Rägula Eberhart, an unmarried wench, who died in Philadelphia in 1741. Moreover, the mandate of 1741 cannot be read in public here because the heirs of pastor Schellenberg, deceased, have not left it in our hands.

With many greetings to the Honorable Board...........

No. 57. Some Years ago there left the Parish of Nieder-hasslen for Carolina, not without official consent and permission, the following families from Nider-Hasslen:

Heinrich Volkhart who was baptized March 8, 1691.
Elsbeth Schütz, of Bachs, baptized October 6, 1695.
Their children were:

Hanss, September 18, 1717.
Felix, November 14, 1723.
Margreth, September 16, 1725.
Heinrich, June 27, 1728.
Hans Heinrich, October 30, 1729.
Anna, April 5, 1739.

Some years later the following family also left Niderhasslen, also not without the knowledge and official consent of our revered superiors. They had previously moved here from Ober-Embrach.

Hanss Conrad Müller, tailor. ⎱
Rägula Bosshart.   ⎰

N.B. They took with them four daughters, the youngest still in the cradle, but their names have been forgotten since their departure.

Also Hanss Fröli, son of Ulrich Fröli, baptized November 6, 1718, left as a hired hand, Anno 1738.

Niderhasslen, April 3, 1744.   Written in conformance with
                                      official orders by
                                      Hanss Caspar Usteri, *Pastor.*

No. 58. From Oberglatt, according to the report of the pastor, the following persons have emigrated to Carolina or Pennsylvania:

Anno 1739

Two daughters of Hans Gassmann, deceased.
1. Catharina, born February 9, 1717.
2. Anna, born October 5, 1721.

Anno 1743

1. Hans Därer, carpenter, born October 2, 1692.
2. His wife, Dorothea Bertschi, born 1694.
3. Hans Ulrich Brunner, son of the smith, born October 7, 1713.
4. His wife, Barbel Kern, of Bulach, born March 12, 1712.
5. Chilion Maag, son of Chili Maag, deceased, born January 11, 1722.
6. Hans Bertschi, son of Felix, deceased, born November 24, 1720.
7. Maria Marqualder, daughter of Melchior, born July 2, 1719.
8. Elssbeth Bertschi, daughter of Hans Bertschi, of Hofstetten, born January 24, 1723.   Attested: Johann Caspar Hegi, *Pastor in Oberglatt.*

No. 59. Oberwinterthur

Greetings from the Source of Salvation. Most Revered, Most Learned Brethren, Beloved in the Lord:

Yesterday evening the inclosed communication concerning the emigration of our beloved parishioners reached me. You will read for yourselves what our honored and solicitous Superiors desire from us all,—and that without delay. I ask you therefore, to send this circular on as soon as possible, and to set to work upon it immediately, and to send me the document on a clean half sheet of paper so that each can send it to his neighbor and all can be sent to the parsonage at Winterthur, from whence I shall have them collected. I am sorry that this request has to be made in this busy Holy Week. I beg you again not to delay with it. With God's blessing and hearty salutations to the brethren,

Committing myself under God's grace to your love, I remain,

My honored and revered brethren's humble servant,

March 23, 1744.   SALOMON ZIEGLER, *Pastor in Oberwinterthur.*

WINTERTHUR, WÜLFLINGEN, FELDHEIM, SEUZACH, HETLINGEN, HENGART, DORF, FLACH, BERG, BUCH, NEFTENBACH, PFUNGEN, DÄTLIKON, RORBAS, EMBRACH, LUFINGEN, BRÜTTEN, TÖSS, WINTERTHUR, CALLED OBERWINTERTHUR

WINTERTHUR does not need the circular, for no one is thinking of emigrating from the country, and in such case the magistrate would have to speak with the citizens. We send this with many greetings to the good pastor at Wylflingen.

WÜLFLINGEN. From the beginning I know of about 3 persons who have emigrated to Carolina, one single unmarried workman, Christof Bosshart from the Thal, born the 31. June, 1717, a shoe-maker's boy, who was persuaded by some people from Blumetshalden from the parish of Pfungen, who paid all his traveling expenses. He followed his mother and brother who had gone before him. I know of none who desire to travel at present. I received the circular at night of the 23., and am sending it with my enclosure the morning of the 24th, with respectful greetings.

FELDEN. A year ago two persons left here with an official pass. Hans Ulrich Freyhofer, a weaver, thirty years of age; and Verena Freyhofer, his niece, twenty-four years of age, together with two relatives of theirs from the parish of Elg, at the request of a cousin who lived in Germantown in Pennsylvania, who has gained considerable means and has no children. I received letters from them two weeks ago saying that they had arrived safely after a difficult and dangerous trip. They advised no one to undertake this journey unless it was necessary, for on their ship and one other, over 200 Swiss people died because they could not endure the sea-sickness. They reported further, that if anyone is sick upon his arrival he is not permitted to leave the ship, so that many die in the harbor because of poor care. They also report that the present war has made the trip dangerous. Because of this report many have been kept back who otherwise were intending to follow them.

Received this circular, March 24, 9 in the morning, and sent it at 10 to the neighboring Seuzach.

SEUZACH. A year ago Jacob Müller, called Saxer, aged 40, with his wife Barbara Fritschi of Hettlingen, and three children, Heinrich, aged 13, Martha, aged 11, Jacob, aged 7, left for Carolina against all my expostulations. Only a short time ago a young unmarried man of 35 years of age, who is working at Hüntwangen, Jacob Ackert, by name, has presented himself to me with a similar intention, and contrary to my advice, because of the good reports which have come back from there again recently, which induce many other people from his neighborhood and the country around it to leave for another land, has resolved to start thither in company with them, without heeding the fact that his own father, who is still alive, advises him against it and refuses his consent.   The former and this latter (especially the former) are, to be sure, poor people who have persuaded themselves, among other things, that they cannot lose much either way etc., etc.   I do not know whether I should add to these another man who was driven out of the country a year ago because of his debts, and who also has reported that he is going there, but who is still said to be staying near Basel, Sc. Christen Waaser, aged 40, with his wife Barbara Kleiner, and a boy, Jacob Waser, aged 5.

Received this circular at 11 o'clock and sent it at 12, to the neighboring Reverend Dean, Pastor Hetling.

HETLINGEN.   On the 30th of June the following persons left here for the West Indies, whether to the South or North they did not know themselves.
Franz Müller, aged 33.
Anna Herter, his wife, aged 37.
Children:
> Kungold, aged 10 years.
> Anna, aged 6 years.
> Franz, aged 1 year.

Margretha Kündig, Franz Müller's mother, born in Volken, aged 63.
Jacob Müller Egliss, aged 38, unmarried.   As far as I know these are the first persons, who have left here as colonists.

HENKERT.   As far as concerns the emigrants to Carolina: Before the sacred festival days are over, shall send a separate list of these.   At this time I report merely, that last autumn a letter was received from such an emigrant out of my parish, dated London in England, in which he makes clear the misery of such emigrants, indicating that everything was true which the pastor had previously told him, moreover that they had been wretchedly misled by the false statements of other people, etc., and he threatened also, if at all possible, to return home with his wife and child.

People are talking now of another Carolina to which some wish to go, saying more of Schlesien,[3] or Schlessingen as the peasants pronounce it, and allow themselves to dream very favorable things about such a land.

No. 60.   FROM OBERWINTERTHUR THERE WENT TO CAROLINA WITH THE PERMISSION OF THE HIGH AUTHORITIES

Anna Tobler, widow, with two sons, Heinrich, born in 1726, and Caspar, born in 1729.
Anno 1743, with permission, for Pennsylvania,
Jacob Sporer, a boy, born 1719.
Hans Heinrich Rugstul and his wife with one son, Samuel, 19 years old.
Jacob Schupisser, bleacher, with a five year old son.
From Stadel, Heinrich Bryner, a youth, 26 years old.
From Rüttlingen, Ulrich Ehrensperger with his wife and five children: Clephe, born 1721, Anna, 1723, Johannes, 1724, Lisabeth, 1726, Ulrich, 1728.
> Total 16 souls.   God preserve them!

March 25, 1744.   Pastor ZIEGLER in Oberwinterthur.

[3] Colonists were being solicited by Prussia for her province of Silesia, newly acquired from Austria.   A.B.F.

No. 61. List of those Persons who have left the Christian Parish of Detwyl for Pennsylvania

Anno 1743

1. Jacob von Tobel, from Willikon, baptized June 9, 1679. He was before this a churchwarden. Finally he gave over to his three sons his estate, and took from them besides a quantity of vines and grazing for a cow, for eight years annually 80 florins rental. He had a second wife, Elsbeth Frey from Uster. This man, without the knowledge of his people or of anyone else, left Sunday morning May 12, 1743. His people estimated that he took with him about 65 florins.
2. Adjutant Hans Rudolf Egolff, baptized at Egg, in 1678. He had with the knowledge of the authorities of Stäfa sold his fine little estate and after paying many debts and the emigration tax of 21 florins, 8 shillings, in opposition to the governor's and my kindly admonitions left here, with his second wife Elsbetha Pfister from Üetikon, baptized January 11, 1692, and his legitimate son by his first wife, deceased, Hans Rudolff, baptized July 31, 1729. Left on Monday, June 24, 1743.

Total of all persons who went to Pennsylvania 4.

Attested by most obediently, Pastor Salomon Hirzel.

Otweil, April 6, 1744.

No. 62. Osslingen

Highly Revered, Learned and Honorable Mr. Dean:

In reply to the command and mandate which has come from my gracious master and superior, in respect to those who have gone into the so-called new-found-land, I notify you most dutifully and properly that at the present date there is no one in my parish who wishes to commit such folly. A year ago Alexander Haussrad with his wife and their children wanted to leave, but he returned poor as a beggar, gave over his wife and three children as a burden to the parish, while he treacherously and secretly went into military service in Savoy, which is all that has been reported in regard to this questionable affair. I have the honor to subscribe myself, with the highest conceivable respect, the Dean's life-long most humble servant,

A. Burkhard.

Osslingen, April 3, 1744.

No. 63. List of those Persons who left the Parish Ottenbach to go to Pennsylvania

From Ottenbach

Hans Ulrich Hegetschweiler, Heinrich's son.
Hans Jacob Sydler, Marx's son.
Anna Hegetschweiler, deceased Heinrich's daughter.

From Wolsen

Caspar Frey, Felix's son.

From Ober-Lunneren

Heinrich, and Hans Bär, brothers, Heinrich's sons.

From Under-Lunneren

Johannes Gut, deceased Heinrich's son.

No. 64. Description of the Three Families that left the Parish Ottelfingen to go to Carolina

Anno 1738 in August there left the following families:

Parents:

Born: 1697, Heinrich Weltj, from Poplizen.
" 1693, Barbara, from Reütj.

Children:

" 1726, Rudolff.
" 1727, Hans.
" 1729, Anna.
" 1732, Clein-Anna.

Anno 1743, May 3d, there left the following families:

Parents:

Born: 1711, Hans Meyer.
" 1715, Elsbeth Bopp.

Children:

" 1735, Elsbeth.
" 1736, Barbara.

Anno 1743 in May there left the following families:

Parents:

Born: 1713, Caspar Meyer.
" 1716, Anna from Reütj.

Children:

" 1740, Caspar.
" 1742, Anna.

No. 65. From the Parish Pfäffikon in the Summer of 1733 the Following left for the New World

Heinrich Ernj, from Pfäffikon, baptized April 10, 1707, and Susanna Brunner, his wife, together with a child: Babelj, aged 2 years.

Anno 1734 there also went there:

A. Magdalena Mäntzin, the deceased Hans Hermetschweiler's wife, with the following children:

Annelj, baptized, January   7, 1714.
A. Magdalena,   September 29, 1715.
Babelj,   November 21, 1723.
Margreth,   October   2, 1725.
Regelj,   October 28, 1727.
Heinrich,   June   3, 1731.

April 25, 1744.   Attested, John Feer, *Pastor.*

No. 66. List of all Persons, who since 1734 went out of the Parish Raffz, thus Leaving their Home and Fatherland:

1738, September. According to the report received, the following persons left, with the purpose of going to Carolina:

Hans Ulrich Angst, son of Andersen, and
Barbara Sigerist, his wife. These have taken with them
Johannes Sigerist, a ten-year old boy, the brother of the wife.
Hans Jacob Graaf, shoe-maker, and
Anna Schweizer, his wife. These left with 5 children.

Barbara Meyer, Jacob Meyer's legitimate daughter, born August 21, 1707.

Total 11 persons.

N.B.   These left my parish of Rafz, and I know no more to say about them, except that up to the present I have not been able to find out what destination they reached.

1741, April 19.   Franz Neuchum, the joiner, born 1694, left the country with his oldest daughter.

Verena, his daughter, born January 7, 1725.

N.B.   He has left behind his wife with three small children, because he was angry that the meagre means of his oldest daughter, whom he was taking along, were not permitted to pass through.   I do not know of what those means consisted.   This man, so a report was received concerning him, died a few days after his arrival in the capital city of Philadelphia.   The remaining wife and children are being supported by alms.

Total 2 persons.

1743.   May 16.   The following left Rafz with the intention of going to Pennsylvania:

Hans Ulrich Baggenstosz, mason, born 1700.

Susanna Baur, his wife, born 1699.

Children:

Verena, 1725.

Hans Ulrich, 1726.

Johannes, 1734.

Susanna, 1737.

Heinrich, 1738.

Hans Jacob, 1741.

In addition to this there left with this mason:

Franz Graaf, the deceased mason's son, born 1733.   This boy was the above-named Baggenstoss's deceased sister's son.

Catharina Neüchum, 1718. } Franz Neüchum the shoe-maker's daughters from
Verena Neüchum, 1720.   } Sulgen.

Johannes Reutschman, deceased Conrad's son from Rafz, 1716.

Total leaving in 1743: 12 persons.

N.B.   Of these nothing has been heard up to date.

1744, March 31.   There left from Rafz, wishing to go to Pennsylvania the following:

Franz Neüchum, born 1710.   ⎫ N.B.   These families could have
Anna Siggin, from Glatfelden, his wife, born   ⎬   subsisted very well at home.
1705.   ⎭

Children:

Verena, 1734.

Heinrich, 1735.

Verena Neüchum, Hans Graaf's, the bailiff's widow, born 1704.

N.B.   This poor widow with her children has very little money with her, relies upon, besides God, her brother Franz Neüchum and her brother-in-law, John Neüchum, who have promised her all needed assistance.   Did not give heed to any warnings.

Children:

Barbara, 1729.

Franz, 1734.

Johannes, 1737.

Hans Jacob, 1740.

Hans Ulrich, 1742.

Johannes Neüchum, wagon-maker, 1697.

Susanna Neüchum, his wife, 1698.

N.B.   This family might have found an honest living at home.

Children:
Verena, 1732.
Heinrich, 1735
Johannes, 1737.
Susanna Schweizer, deceased Hans Baggenstoss's widow, 1700.
N.B.   Also this widow might have had a modest subsistence.
Children:
Hans Jacob, 1731.
Johannes, 1736.
Hans Ulrich Sigerist, called Melchers, 1698.
Elisabeth Baur, his wife, 1706.
Barbara, 1734.
N.B.   The needed subsistence was not lacking also in the case of this family.
Furthermore:
Hans Graaf Lehmens, 1697, weaver.
N.B.   This poor man, who has been able to take very little money along, goes away with his large family, forced by necessity.
Elsbeth Frey, his wife, 1698.
Children:
Elsbeth, 1726.
Barbara, 1728.
Heinrich, 1730.
Hans Ulrich, 1733.
Hans Jacob, 1737.
Dorothea, 1741.
Hans Sigerist, son of Hans Jö_lis, born 1705.
Anna Wildberger, from Neükirch, his wife, 1709.
N.B.   This man has had respectable means, but has been a poor manager, and as a result could not for long have kept up.   Therefore he was also ill-provided at his departure.
Children:
Hans Jacob, 1731.
Franz, 1738.
Anna, 1740.
Susanna, 1742.

Grown up-unmarried children

Heinrich Meyer, tailor, Heinrich Mejer's son, 1724.
Heinrich Baur, carpenter, the shoe-maker Jacob Baur's son, 1724.
Hans Conrad Hänseler, deceased Kestl's son, 1722.

Unmarried daughters

Verena Graaf, deceased Hans Jacob's daughter, 1716.
Catharina Neüchum, deceased Salomon Neüchum's daughter, 1723.
Total of all of those who from 1738 up to the present date have left Rafz—66 persons.
The truth of the above attested April 1, 1744, by JOHN HEINRICH HOLZHALB, *Pastor at Rafz.*
N.B.   These last named grown-up boys and daughters, have, to be sure, left with the above, but not exactly with the intention to settle in Pennsylvania, but to travel, in part supporting themselves by their trades, in order to gain experience, or in part being people of little means, to seek their fortunes elsewhere, if possible, and they entertain the hope, that if they return as free men and with good testimonials of their behavior, they may return without prejudice to their landrights.

No. 67. REGENSPERG. From this parish there have gone to
Carolina, etc.

1

Johannes Bachofen, glazier, aged 22 years.
His pregnant wife was left behind.
The departure took place September 18, 1734. On the way he changed his
mind and entered the French military service, in which he died, in the spring,
1735.

2

Felix Huber, glazier, aged 37 years.
Anna Müller, his wife, aged 39.
Children:
Catharina, aged 5.
The departure took place September 8, 1738. Nothing has been heard about
these since.

3

Jacob Schwenk, shoemaker, aged 46.
Catharina Belz, his wife, aged 42.
Children:
Anna, aged 5.
Elisabetha, aged 4.
Anna-Marja, aged 2.
With them there travelled also Esther Schwenk, the daughter of Johannes
Schwenk, the tailor, aged 17 years. The departure occurred April 4, 1741.
Concerning these, their arrival in London and prospective sailing for Pennsyl-
vania, but beyond this nothing has been heard, except that recently, without
good foundation it was reported that they had arrived in Pennsylvania, and that
one of the children had died.
Total of those that left—10.
Attested by JOH. JACOB WOLFF, *Pastor in Regensperg.*
March 31, 1744.

No. 68. EXTRACT FROM PASTOR AND CHAMBERLAIN VOGLER'S
COMMUNICATION FROM RICHTERSSCHWEIL

As far as concerns those who left for West India, there left here for Pennsylvania about thirty years ago several by the name of Höhn and Wisz, who
wrote once or twice without much exaltation, and part of them have died.
Rodolph Bachman, son of Rodolf, is said to have gone to Carolina about
five years ago, but we know nothing of him.
In the week following Whitsuntide there also went thither two by the name
of Huber, and one Tanner, with wife and children. The latter has six children,
five sons and one daughter, among them an infant three weeks old, and the oldest
twelve years.
Several times the magistrate and myself spoke to him earnestly, whereupon
he replied: He could not ward off bankruptcy, that he wanted to sell his possessions and if anything remained, to stay at home, which, however, he did not
keep, and said: "He could now not do otherwise."
The carpenter Huber has taken eight children with him together with his
wife, among them seven sons, the oldest 14, the youngest ½ year old. His
brother Jacob Huber has left with his wife and three children, did not ask leave,
his boy is 10, one daughter 4, the other 1 year old. They are people who could
no longer sustain themselves with their work, and nothing could be done with

them, whatever you might say, their reply always remained: They had to work here day and night and even then could not get their daily bread, and were therefore forced to seek it elsewhere.

Still another Bachman is said to have gone to Pennsylvania before the war, and to have died there.

Richtenschweil, May 15, 1744.   Attested, JOH. FELIX VOGLER, *Pastor.*

No. 69. RORBASS

From this parish there went to Carolina in the year 1738, the following parties:

Hans Conradt Rietiker, mower, aged 49.
Verena Hiltibrand, his wife, aged 46.
And their children:
> Hans Jacob, aged 16.
> Jacobli, aged 10.
> Caspar, aged 6.
> The same year:

Jacob Rietiker, tailor, aged 47.
Barbel Dünki, aged 41.
And their little daughter:
> Margareth, aged 9.
> > The same year:

Heinrich Rietiker, sexton, aged 38.
Rägula Landert, aged 36.
And their children:
> Heinrich, aged 7.
> Catharina, aged 3.
> Barbara, aged ½.
> > Furthermore there left anno 1738 at the end of August, from Rorbasz to Carolina:

Conradt Fritschi, weaver from Freyenstein, aged 38.
Rägel Hiltibrand, his wife, aged 33.
And their children:
> Heinrich, aged 9.
> Babeli, aged 7.
> Heirechli, aged 5.
> Elsbeethli, aged 2.
> Rodolf, aged 3 months.
> > The same year:

Conradt Dünki, called Alpen-Baur, aged 60.   Widower.
And his children:
> Heinrich, aged 25.
> Anna, aged 22.
> Total of all who in 1738 left for Carolina: 23.

Furthermore in the spring 1743, from Rorbasz for Carolina, the following parties left:

Jacob Dünki, the above alpine farmer's son, aged 36.
Anna Dandert, his wife, aged 34.
And their children:
> Heinrich, aged 5.
> Jacobli, aged 4.
> Cathari, aged 2.
> > The same year:

Hans Jacob Schurter, son of Kräuszli Hans, unmarried, aged 25.

The same year:

Heinrich Fritschi, son of the old castle-farmer from Teüffen, aged 41.

Anna Brändli, his wife, aged 39.

And their children:

Clephee Babli, aged 14.

Vreeneli, aged 12.

Anneli, aged 7.

The total of all those persons gone away in 1743—11.

Grand total of all who left with my knowledge but against my will, and against my earnest protests: 34. Of all of those not a word has been heard since their departure. The Gracious Dean need not fear an exodus this time.

Rorbass, March 27, 1744.   Pastor WOLFF.

No. 70.   RÜMLANG

From this parish there went to Carolina in the year 1734:

Rudolff Weidmann, a tailor, born 1699.

Anna Maria Wäber, from Zurich, his wife, born 1711.

Children:

Judith, born 1732.

This was a poor family, the husband did not understand his trade, and there was the greatest anxiety that they might become a burden to the authorities.

Anno 1735

These wanted to go to Carolina:

Heinrich Meyer, a mason, born 1703.

Elisabetha Schmid, his wife, born 1700.

Children:

Heinrich, born 1729.

Hans Heinrich, born 1731.

This household, however, got only as far as Kreuzach in the Margravate of Baden, where they settled, and thank God live happily, and in the year 1738 were increased with a son Tobias. The reason why they left their fatherland was hard times and debts.

Anno 1736

Left for the new country:

Jacob Gering, born 1700.

Anna Cappeler, his wife, born 1698.

Children:

Catharina, born 1725.

Heinrich, born 1731.

This family was also very poor and the father was almost blind.

They took with them their oldest son Johannes, born 1725. The two younger sons Hans Conrad, born 1727, and Heinrich, born 1729, they left at home. But after this man, like a real good-for-nothing, had spent all his money, that he had intended for the trip to Carolina, consisting of about 150 florins, and got to Frankfurt, he went to Berlin, according to reliable reports, and lives now upon a Royal Prussian colony. The son Conrad left not before 1743 with a party for Carolina. The younger, good-for-nothing in body and soul, is bound in service for twenty years in the governmental hospital.

Anno 1743

There left for Carolina, with permission of the most revered governors:

Caspar Hinnen, born 1709.

Elsbeth Widmer, his wife, born 1707.

Children:
    Caspar, born 1736.
    Anna Barbara, born 1738.
    With these there also left:
Heinrich Hinnen, the unmarried brother of the above, born 1714.
Rudolff Schmid, the deceased Fridlis' son, born 1722.
Also the above-mentioned Conrad Haszler.
    There left also, without anyone's knowledge:
Caspar Wäber, a table-maker by trade, born 1705.
Margareth Gering, his wife, born 1705.
Son: Johannes, born 1734.

    This family was compelled to leave on account of poverty into which they got through their own indolence and dissoluteness. They are settled, it is said, on Würtemberg lands.

    Attested by most humbly HANS HEINRICH VOLLENWEIDER, *Pastor.*
April 4, 1744.

No. 71. THERE LEFT FOR CAROLINA OUT OF THE PARISH RUSSICON

Hansz Ulrich Ringger.
Margreth Boszhardt, his wife.
Children:
    Jacob, baptized September 8, 1737.
    Hans Jaco, baptized, September 27, 1739.

    Attested, as per circular: FEL. NÜSCH, *Dec.*

No. 72. SCHLIEREN. (SEE PLATES 3–7)

Most Honorable, Learned and Most Revered Dean:

    Because I have the honor, as a humble member of the chapter of Zürich, to be remembered with the circular, but as far as mandates and decrees are concerned cannot follow them, being under the jurisdiction of the County of Baden,—so that many times, though being so near the city, and so near to me the authoritative mandates are read, I am at a loss what to do in regard to this or that command; whereas a list of those of the parish in war service, as also of those who have gone to North America, who have gone either with permission, or at least with passes from the governor of Baden, in opposition to my public and private repeated warnings and arguments well founded, is asked for by the circular, I have thought it to be of some service to prepare a list of those who since ten years have gone to Carolina and Pennsylvania as into another land, "cut off from the righteous," [4] with wife and children.

  I. Anno 1735, Conrad Rütschi, aged 37, with his wife Barbara Lips, aged 38, and two children, the oldest 11 years, the other 9 years old. Concerning this family the most Rev. Dean has read the letter that has come to me.

 II. April 7, 1736, there left the sometime commissioner Caspar Müller, aged 50, together with his wife, Margareth Zimmerli, born in Arburg, with three young children. A son and daughter remained behind.

III. May 15, 1743, there left here amid pitiable lamentations of several mothers, accompanied by a large crowd of people as far as Fährli, the following families:

    [4] This quotation appears in Hebrew in the original manuscript, photographs of which are herein reproduced (Plates 3–7).

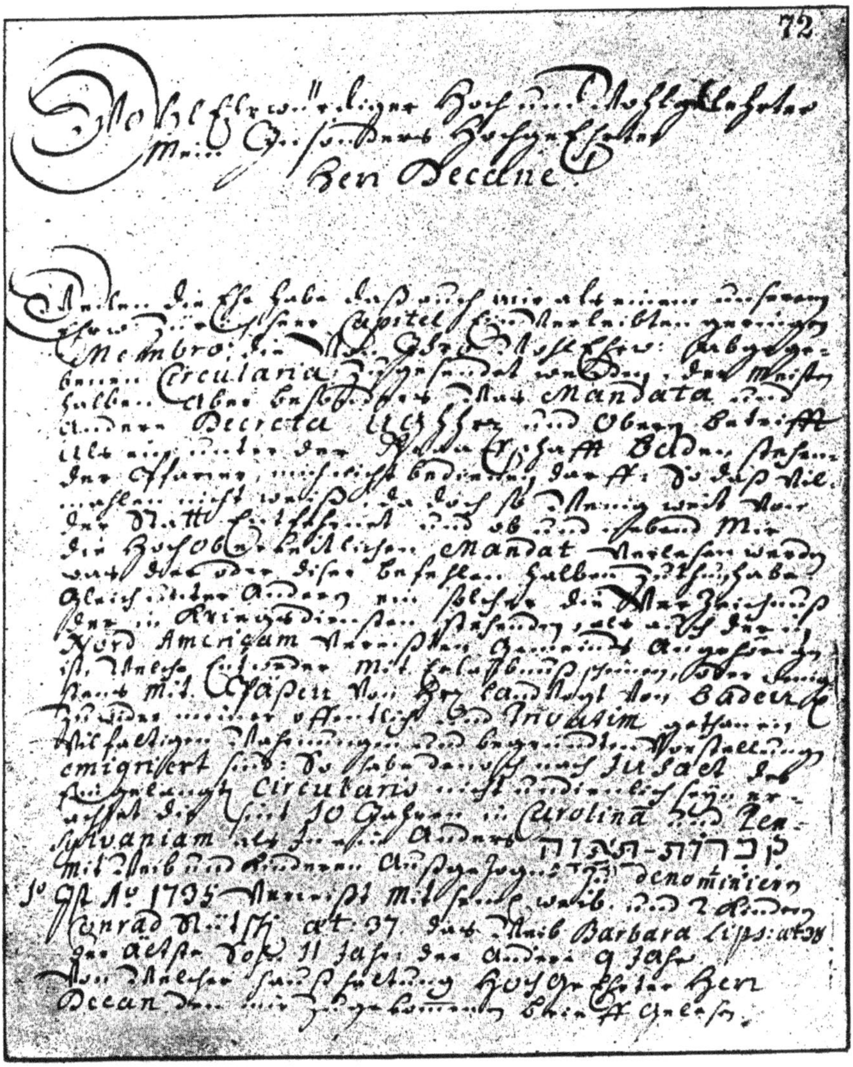

Plate 3

72

REPRODUCTION OF THE ORIGINAL LIST No. 72, SCHLIEREN, APRIL 3, 1744

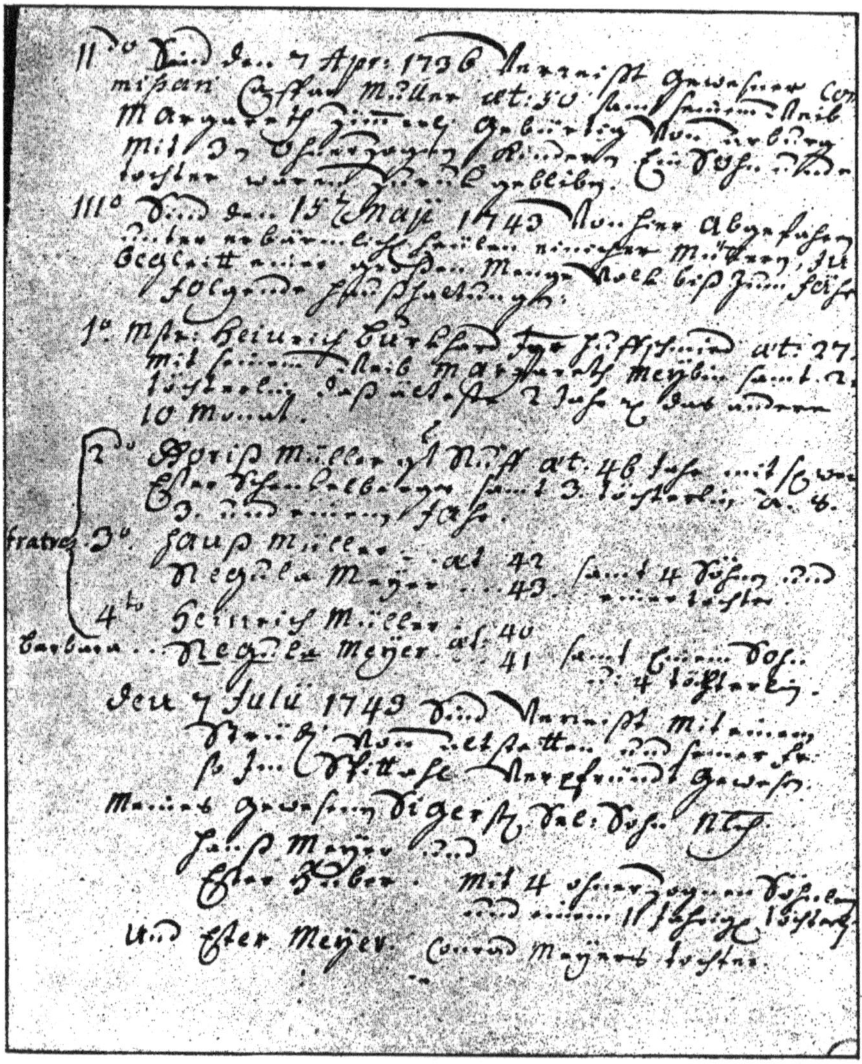

Plate 4

PAGE 2 OF LIST NO. 72

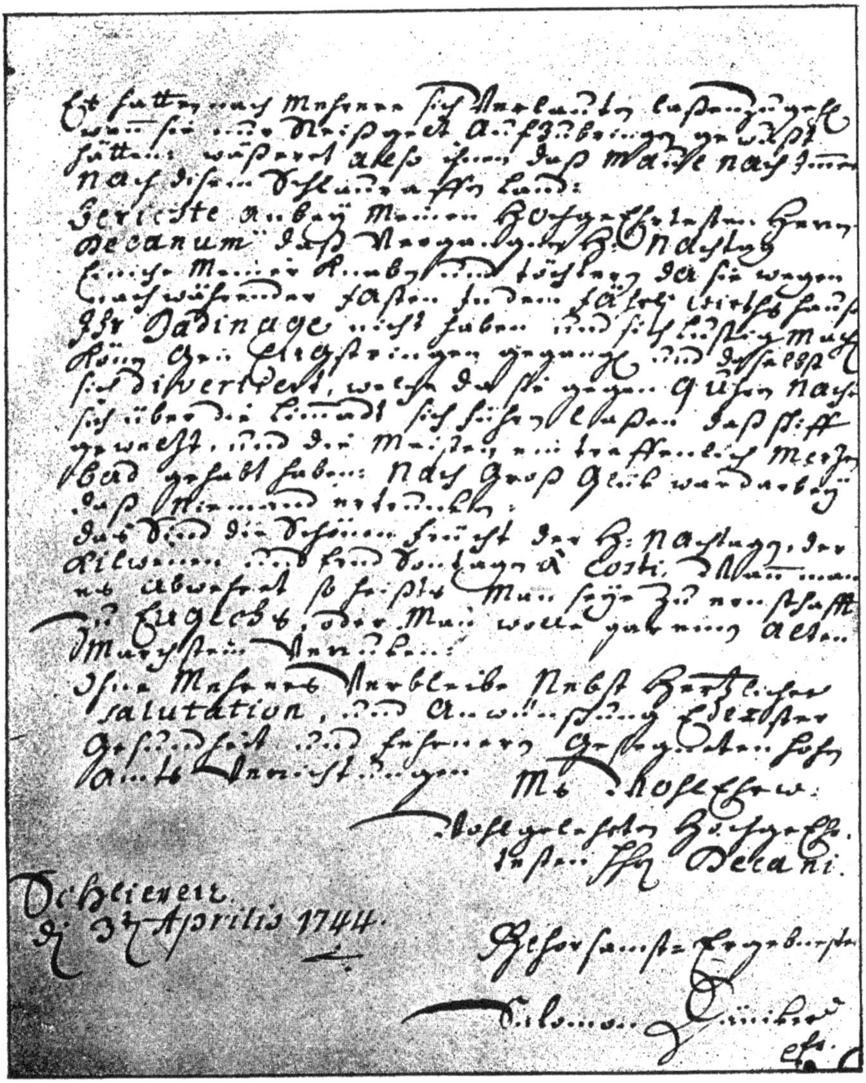

Plate 5

Plate 6

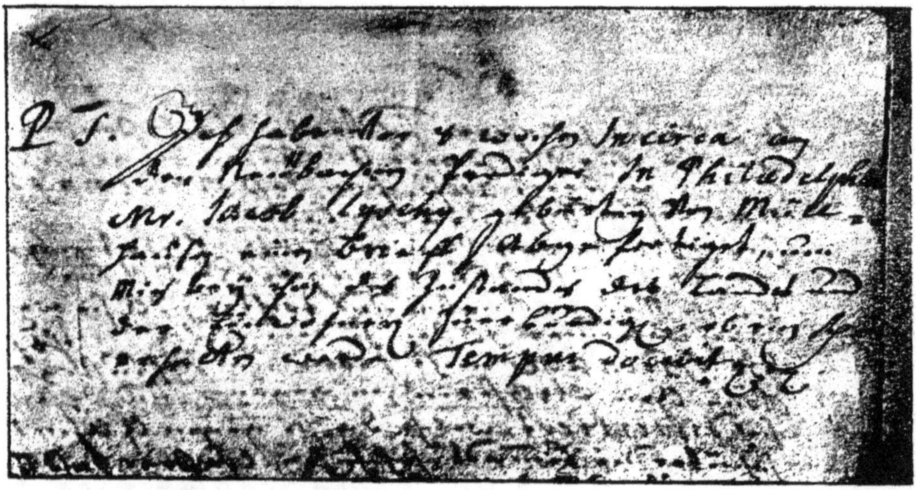

PAGE 4 OF LIST NO. 72

Plate 7

No.72.

Wohlehrwürdiger,hoch und wohlgelehrter mein Jnsonders höchgeehrter
Herr Devane.

Weilen die Ehr habe,daß auch mir als einem unserem Ehrw.Zürichseer
Capitel einverleibten geringen Membro,die von Ihro Wohlehrw.abgege-
benen Circularis zugesendet werden,der meisten halben aber besonders
was Mandata und andere Decreta UGHHren und Oberen betrifft,als ein
unter der Graaffschafft Baden stehender Pfarrer mich nicht bedienen
darff; So daß vilmahlen nicht weiß,da doch so wenig weit von der
Statt entfehrnet und ob und nebend mit die hochoberkeitlichen Man-
dat verlesen werden,was der oder diser befehlen halben zu thun habe.
Gleich unter anderen ein soelcher die Verzeichnuß der in Kriegsdien-
sten stehenden,als auch der in Nord Americam Verreißten Gemeinds An-
gehörigen ist,welche entweder mit Erlaubnußscheinen,oder wenigstens
mit Paßen von Herren Landvogt von Baden,zuwider meiner offentlich
und privatim gethanen vilfaltigen Wahrnungen und begründten Vorstel-
lungen emigriert sind: So habe dennoch nach Jnhalt des eingelangten
Circularis nicht undienlich seyn erachtet,die sint 10 Jahren in Ca-
rolin und Pensylvaniam als in ein anders [. . . . .] .mit Weib
und Kinderen Außgezogne zu denominieren.
I°.Ist Ao.1735 verreißt mit seinem Weib und 2 Kindern,der älteste
Sohn 11 Jahr,der andere 9 Jahr. Von welcher Haußhaltung hoch-
ehrter Herr Decan den mir zugekommenen Brieff gelesen.
II°.Sind den 7.Apr.1736 verreißt gewesner Commißari Caspar Müller,
aet.50,samt seinem Weib Margareth Zimmerlj,gebürtig von Arburg,
mit 3 ohnerzognen Kindern,ein Sohn und ein Tochter waren zurück-
geblieben.
III°.Sind den 15ten Maji 1743 von hier abgefahren unter erbärmlichen
heülen einicher Müttern,in begleitt einer großen Menge Volk biß
zum Fährlj folgende Haußhaltungen:
1°.Mstr.Heinrich Burkhard,Tyrhuffschmied,aet.29. Mit seinem Weib
Margareth Meylin,samt 2 Töchterlin,daß älteste 2 Jahr und das
andere 10 Monat.

Fratres {
2°.Goriß Müller gt.Ruff,aet.46 Jahr,mit seinem Weib
Ester Schenkelberger,samt 3 Töchterlin,& 8,3 und einem Jahr.
3°.Hans Müller,aet.42 | samt 4 Söhnen und einer
Regula Meyer,aet.43. } Tochter.
4.Heinrich Müller,aet.40. samt Einem Sohn und
Barbara Regula Meyer,aet.41. 4 Töchterlin.
}

Den 7.Julii sind verreißt mit einem Ströbj von Altstetten und seiner Fr.so im Spittahl verpfründt gewesen.

Meines gewesenen Sigersten sel.Sohn Nloh.
Hans Meyer und Mit 4 ohnerzognen Söhnlein und einem 11
Ester Huber. jährigen Töchterlj.

Und Ester Meyer,Conrad Meyers Tochter.

Es hatten nach Mehrere sich verlauten laßen,zu gehen,wann sie nur
Reißgelt aufzubringen gewußt hätten:wäßeret also ihnen daß Maul nach
immer nach disem Schlavraffen Land:
Berichte anbey meinen Hochgeehrtesten Herren Decanum,daß vergangne
H:Nachtrag einiche meiner Knaben und Töchteren,da sie wegen nach
währender Fasten in dem Fährlj Wirthshauß Ihr Badinage nicht haben
und sich lustig machen könen gen Engstringen gegangen und daselbst
sich divertiert,welche da sie gegen 9 Uhr Nachts sich über die Limmat sich führen laßen,daß schiff gewelzt und die meisten ein tref-
fenlich Merzen Bad gehabt haben: Nach Gross Glük war darbey,dass
niemand ertrunken.
Das sind die schönen Frücht der H.Nachtagen,der Kilwenen und End
Sonntagen a costi. Wann man es abwehret,so heißts,man seye zu enrst-
hafft,zu Engers,oder man wolle gar einen alten Marchstein verucken.
Ohne Mehrers verbleibe nebst hertzlicher Salutation und Anwünschung
Edlester Gesundheit und fehrneren gesegneten hohen Amts-Verrichtun-
gen
Me:Wohlerw.,wohlgelehrten,
Hochgeehrtester HHren.Decani
Gehorsamst Ergehenster
Salomon Däniker,Pfr.

Schlieren,den 3ten Aprilis
1744

Plate 8

P.S. Ich habe vor 8 wochen in circa an der Neübachen Prediger in
Philadelphia-M.Jacob Lyschy,gebürtig von Müllhausen,einen Brieff
abgefertiget,um mich bey ihm des Zustandes des Landes und der Ein-
wohnern zu erkundigen,*t im A[...]] erhalten werde: tempus docebit.

No.73.

Verzeichnus derjenigen,welche auß der Pfarr Schäfflistorf seit 1734
weggereißet,willens in Amerisa.

			Getaufft.
1738,den 28ten Augst- monat von Schäfflistorf.	Hans Merkj	)Copuliert	11.Febr.1683.
	Lisabeth Kaüffeler	)den 5.Xbris 1702.	16.7br.1677.
	Kinder:		
	Barbara		10.Febr.1715.
	Margaretha		19.Xbr.1717.
Ihr erstgebohrner Sohn.	Heinrich Merkj) Cop.11.Jan.		28.Jan.17äß.
	Verena Bucher) 1729.		8.Febr.1705.
	Kinder:		
	Jacob		26.Jun.1729.
	Rudolff		29.Jul.1731.
	Anna		1.8br.1733.
	Regula		7.Aug.1735.
	Verena		1.Jan.1738.
Von Oberweningen.	Susanna,Hans Surbers sel.Toch- ter.		30.Jul.1713.
Von Schlyniken.	Heinrich,Hans Heinrich,Rummens sel.Sohn.		17.Maj 1716.
1741,18.April. Von Oberweningen.	Caspar Surber)copuliert auf die		5.Martii 171?
	Barbara Merkj)abreis 14.Merts 1741.		7.April 1715
	Hans,Jacob Duttweiler-s Sohn.		11.7br.1718.
	Hans,Hans Meyers Sohn.		12.8br.1721.
1743,21.April. Auch von Oberweningen.	Heinrich Surber,Jacobs Sohn.		17.Maj 1723.
	Hans,Jacob Zöbelis Sohn.		22.9br.1722.
	Catharina,Ehegaumer Duttweilers sel.Tochter.		28.Jul.1726.
Ab dem Klupf.	Jacob Zöbelj)Hans Zöbelis sel.		23.Febr1716.
	Hans) Sohn.		6.8bris 1722.

Summa:22.

Bescheint Hans Jacob Karodj,den 26ten Merts 1744.

No.74.

Verzeichnuß derjennigen Persohnen,so auß der Gemeind Schwersenbach in
Carolinam abgereiset sind.

1. Jacob Diethrich,Wilhelm Diethrichs Sohn,gebohren den 19.Julij 1716.
Verreisete im Augusto 1738.

2. Ferner Hans Ulrich Blatmann,geb.den 22.Maij 1703 und sein Eheweib
Elsbeth Hoffmann von Uster,alt.43 jahr. Verreiseten den 2.Maij 1743
mit 5 Söhnen:
   1. Christophel,getaufft den 22.Apr.1725.
   2. Rudolff, - 5.Xum. 1733.
   3. Christoffel, - 25. Weinm. 1739.(1)
   4. Jacob, - den 4.Hornung 1738.
   5. Hans Heinrich, - den 18.Harstm.1740.

REPRODUCTION FROM THE TRANSCRIPTS OF LISTS NO. 73, 74

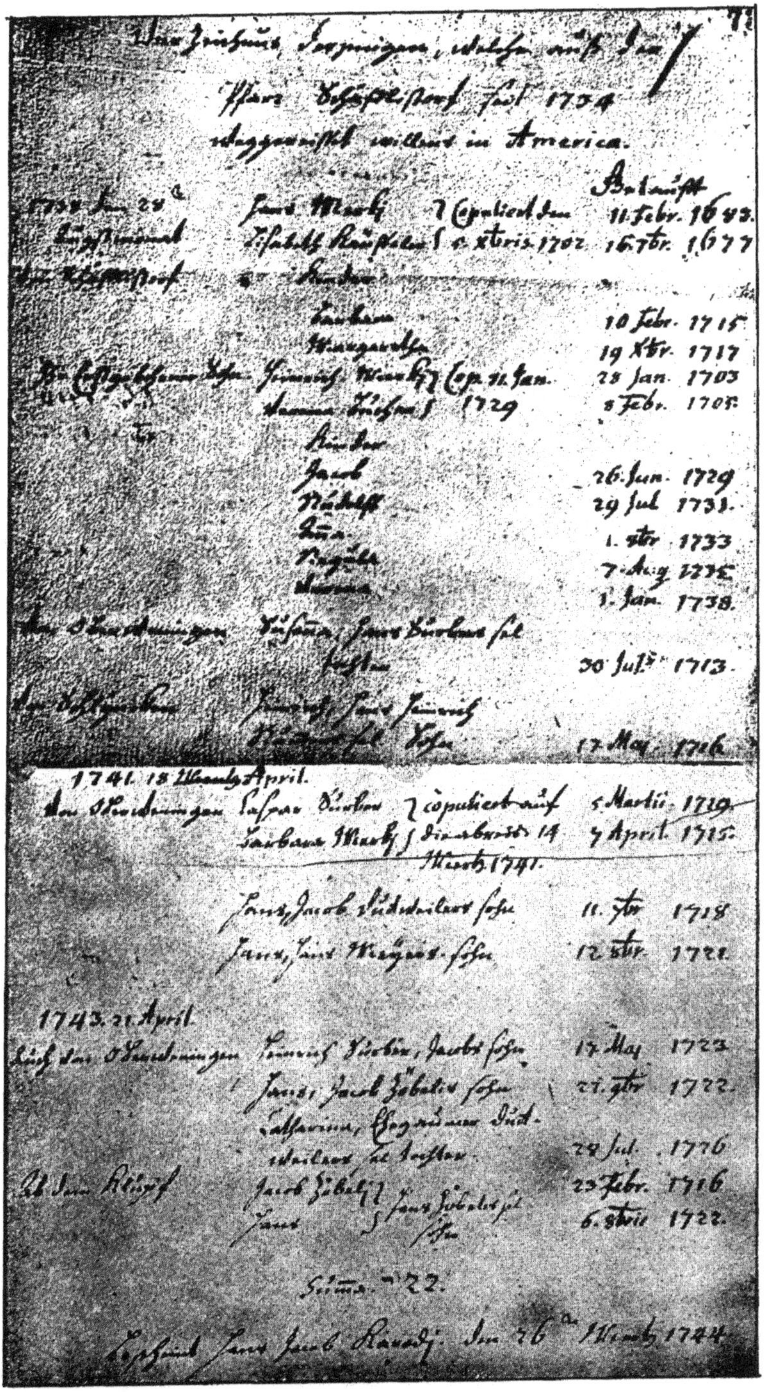
Weggezogen ... Pfarr Schäfflistorf seit 1734 ... in America.

Getauft

11. Febr. 1683.
16. 7br. 1677

10 Febr. 1715
19 Xbr. 1717
28 Jan. 1703
8 Febr. 1705

Kinder
Jacob 26. Jun. 1729
29 Jul 1731.
1. 8br 1733
7. Aug 1735
1. Jan. 1738.

30 Jul. 1713.

17 May 1716

1741. 18 ... April.
5 Martii 1719
7 April 1715
... Martz 1741.

11. 7br 1718
12. 8br 1721.

1743. 21. April
17 May 1723
21. 9br 1722.
28 Jul. 1726
23 Febr. 1716
6. 8bris 1722.

Summa 22.

... den 26 ... 1744.

REPRODUCTION OF THE ORIGINAL LIST NO. 73, "PARISH SCHÄFFLISTORF, SINCE 1734"

1. Master Heinrich Burkhard, blacksmith, aged 27, and his wife Margareth
    Meylin, and two daughters, the oldest two years and the other 10 months.
2. Goriss Müller, called Ruff, aged 46, with his wife Ester Schenkelberger, and
    three daughters, at 8, 3 and 1 years.
3. Hans Müller, aged 42.   } With 4 sons and 1 daughter.
    Regula Müller, aged 43.
4. Heinrich Müller, aged 40.   } With 1 son and 4 daughters.
    Barbara Regula Meyer, aged 41.

July 7, 1743, there left with a certain Strübj from Altstetten and his wife,
who had been a serf at the hospital, my deceased sexton's son, Hansz Meye. and
Ester Huber with four infant sons, and a daughter 11 years old. And Ester
Meyer, Conrad Meyer's daughter.

Several others had spoken of going, if they had only had the money to
travel with, their mouths evidently water for the land of indolence and plenty.
(Schlaraffenland.)

I beg also to report to the Most Rev. Dean that several of my young men
and women, since they could not during Lent have their sport and enjoy themselves in the inn at Fährli, went to Engstringen and diverted themselves there,
and about 9 o'clock at night since they had to be ferried across the river Limmat,
rocked the boat and most of them had an excellent March bath; it was a great
piece of good fortune that no one was drowned.

These are the beautiful fruits of the Holy Week, of church and Sunday
festivals. If you try to prevent it, they say that you are too serious, too narrow,
or that you wish to remove ancient boundary-stones.

Without more to say, I remain with heartfelt salutation and wishes for the
best of health and blessed execution of your high offices,

Your etc. etc.,
Most obedient,

Schlieren, April 3, 1744.   SALOMON DÄNIKER, *Pastor.*

P.S.   About eight weeks ago I completed a letter to Mr. Jacob Lyschy,[5]
preacher in Philadelphia, born in Müllhaüsen, in order to inquire of him as to the
condition of the land and its inhabitants.   Whether an answer will be received,
time will tell.

No. 73. List of those who left the Parish Schäfflistorf since 1734, with the Intention of Going to America (See Plates 8, 9)

			Baptized.
August 28, 1738	Hans Merkj } Married	{ February 11, 1683
From Schäfflistorf.	Lisabeth Kaüffeler } Dec. 5, 1702	{ September 16, 1677
Children:		
Barbara..February 10, 1715
Margaretha..December 19, 1717
The first born son:	Heinrich Merkj } Married	{ January 28, 1703
	Verena Bucher } Jan. 11, 1729	{ February 8, 1705
Children:		
Jacob..June 26, 1729
Rudolff..July 29, 1731
Anna..October 1, 1733
Regula..August 7, 1735
Verena..January 1, 1738

[5] The Rev. Jacob Lischy is mentioned a number of times in *Hallesche Nach-
richten*, Vol. I.   He was a minister of the Reformed Church, with friendly leanings
toward the Moravians.   A.B.F.

From Oberwenigen.	Susanna, daughter of the deceased		
	Hans Surber................July	30, 1713
From Schlyniken.	Heinrich, son of deceased Hans		
	Heinrich Rummen............May	17, 1716
April 18, 1741	Caspar Surber ⎤ Married before ⎧ March	5, 1719
From Oberwenigen.	Barbara Merkj ⎬ leaving, Mar.⎨ April	7, 1715
	⎦ 14, 1741. ⎩	
	Hans, Jacob Duttweiler's son.....September 11, 1718
	Hans, Hans Meyer's son.........October 12, 1721
April 21, 1743	Heinrich Surber, Jacob's son......May	17, 1723
Also from Oberwenigen.	Hans, Jacob Zöbelis' son.........November 22, 1722
	Catharina, the deceased Ehe-		
	gaumer Duttweiler's daughter...July	28, 1726
From Klupf.	Jacob Zöbeli ⎤ Deceased Hans ⎧ February 23, 1716
	Hans ⎦ Zöbeli's sons ⎩ October 6, 1722
Total: 22.		

Attested, HANS JACOB KAROD:, March 26, 1744.

No. 74. List of those Persons who left the Parish Schwerzenbach to go to Carolina

1. Jacob Diethrich, Wilhelm Diethrich's son, born July 19, 1716. Left in August, 1738.
2. Also Hansz Ulrich Blatmann, born May 22, 1703, and his wife Elsbeth Hoffmann from Uster, aged 43 years. Left May 2, 1743, with five sons:
   1. Christophel,   baptized April   22, 1725.
   2. Rudolff,   "   July   5, 1733.
   3. Christoffel,   "   October   25, 1739(?)
   4. Jacob,   "   February 4, 1738.
   5. Hans Heinrich, "   September 18, 1740.

No. 75. Oberwinterthur, April 12, 1744. Emigrants from the Parish Seen

1734

Hans Wysz, aged 45.
Els. Hofman, his wife, aged 35.
Children:
  Babelj, aged 18.
  Betelj,   "   16.
  Vre.   "   13.
  Anna,   "   11.
  Els.   "   9.

1742

Heinrich Bauer, aged 45.
Barbara Müller,   33.
Children:
  Heinrich, aged 5
  Anna,   2
Urech Jeglj,   39
Vre Brunner,   36
Children:
  Hans Urech,   10
  Babelj,   9

Elsbeth Huggenberger, aged 18, unmarried.

Anna Ehrensperger, 26.
  Childless widow.
Regula Müller, left without her
  husband,   36
Hans Jucker,   36
  his wife
    Maria Müller, 31

Plate 10

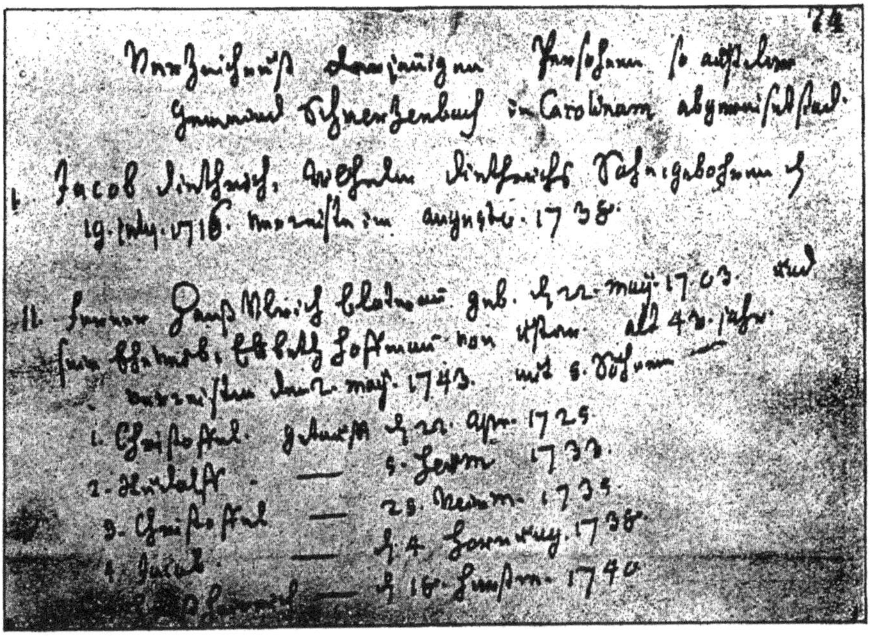

REPRODUCTION OF THE ORIGINAL LIST NO. 74, PARISH SCHWERZENBACH

Jacob,   6
Hans Urich Jeglj, aged 24
    his wife Els. Rösej,   19
Jac. Rüegg, aged 43
Barb.. Büchj,   39
Children:
    Heinrich, 30.
    Jacob,   24.
    Ulrich,   12.
    Konr,   11.
    Caspar,   7.

Children:
    Babelj,   5
    Anna,   2

No. 76. LIST OF THOSE PERSONS, WHO SINCE 1734 LEFT THE PARISH STADEL FOR CAROLINA AND PENNSYLVANIA, taken out of the registers kept by the parishes, by Hans Heinrich Goss-weiler, Pastor.

Whole
Families   Persons
                    Anno 1734 there left from Windlach
1. Hans Ulrich Auer, baptized December 5, 1699.
   Verena Eberhardt, his wife, baptized September 25, 1701.
   Children:
       Verena,   baptized January 29, 1725.
       Felix,   "   January 5, 1727.
       Hans Ulrich,   "   January 10, 1729.
       Margretha,   "   March   5, 1730.........................6
                        1738 from Stadel
2. Hans Heinrich Lang, Büljorgen, the father, baptized December 13, 1674. Jung Hans, son, baptized April 9, 1705. Son's wife, Margareth Maag, baptized October 7, 1704.
   Children:
       Anna, baptized May 8, 1731.
       Regula, baptized May 25, 1733.
       Johannes, baptized February 19, 1736.
       Verena, baptized March 25, 1738...............................7
3. Felix Huser, glazier, baptized December 5, 1706.
   His wife, Barbara Örtli, baptized April 25, 1707.
   Children:
       Anna, baptized February 1, 1733.
       Hans Jacob, baptized October 2, 1735.......................4
   Heinrich Albrächt, called Kümin, baptized August 24, 1710.............1
   Jacob Lang, carpenter, baptized September 28, 1710..................1
   Jacob Herzog, shoemaker, deceased Heinrich's son, baptized May 28, 1717..1
   Jacob Albrächt, Rather's, baptized September 18, 1721................1
   Verena Huser, daughter of the mason Hans, baptized May 25, 1704.......1
   Jacob Wüst, son of deceased Leonhardt, baptized September 4, 1712......1
4. Felix Albrächt, drummer, baptized May 3, 1691.
   His wife, Anna Huber, baptized August 5, 1683.......................2
   Hans Huser, Leonhardt's son, baptized August 11, 1715...............1
5. Hans Heinrich Albrächt, indoor weaver, baptized August 8, 1709.
   His wife, Anna Merki, baptized April 29, 1714.......................2

Hans Ulrich Albrächt, Hans' son, baptized September 17, 1719...........1
Hans Jacob Albrächt, captain, Joggeli's son, baptized January 24, 1717....1

6. Felix Albrächt, Balz's son, baptized September 18, 1707.
His wife, Anna Schmid, baptized January 31, 1708.
His sister, Barbara, baptized September 18, 1712......................3

7. Heinrich Huser, wagon-maker, baptized January 21, 1707.
His wife Verena Huser, baptized, September 8, 1709.
Children:
    Hans Jacob, baptized October 22, 1733.
    Heinrich, baptized May 15, 1735.
    Rägula, baptized February 10, 1737.........................5

8. Hans Albrächt, glazier, baptized August 9, 1696.
His wife, Anna Dübendorffer, baptized January 21, 1696.
Children:
    Heinrich, baptized, March 5, 1724.
    Verena, July 26, 1732...4

From Windlach

9. Felix Lang, called Stoffel Felix, baptized April 12, 1710.
His wife, Rägula Müller, baptized July 31, 1703.
Children:
    Hans, baptized July 3, 1735.
    Barbara, baptized January 30, 1737.........................4

10. Heinrich Schmid, Schmid's son, baptized March 28, 1706.
His wife, Verena Weidmann, baptized 1705.
Child:
    Hans Conradt, baptized March 19, 1737.........................3

11. Hans Heinrich Lang, mason, baptized October 31, 1698.
His wife, Anna Vogel, baptized December 4, 1703.
Children:
    Anna, baptized April 4, 1728.
    Anna Barbara, baptized February 27, 1735.
    Barbara, baptized February 16, 1738.........................5
Hans Auer, Hans' son, baptized April 13, 1716.......................1

From Schüpfen

Jung Hans Huber, Ehgaumer's son, baptized October 14, 1708.
His sister, Vronegg, baptized May 5, 1715.........................2
Rudolph Weidmann, deceased Joggli's son, baptized January 14, 1716.....1

January 24, 1740.   *From Stadel*

Abraham Schmid, Heinrich's son, baptized February 4, 1720............1
Margareth Schmid, Joggli's daughter, baptized May 29, 1707...........1
Anna Müller, Jung Hans' daughter, baptized May 26, 1715.............1
Elisabeth Land, deceased Heinrich's daughter, baptized September 27
   1713...1

From Windlach

12. Hans Ulrich Schleher, baptized October 5, 1710.
His wife Barbara Müller, baptized March 24, 1705.
Children:
    Heinrich, baptized December 6, 1733.
    Johannes, baptized February 19, 1736.........................4

13. Heinrich Lang, baptized September 1, 1694.
His wife, Maria Mayer, baptized February 14, 1712.

Children:
    Hans, baptized November 16, 1726.
    Barbara, baptized May 18, 1739.................................4
14. Felix Huser, baptized November 22, 1707.
    Barbara Mayer, his wife, baptized December 8, 1709...................2

From Rath

15. Hans Lang, baptized November 28, 1686.
    His wife, Anna Meyer, baptized May 13, 1697.
    Children:
        Esther, baptized January 15, 1721.
        Felix, baptized March 14, 1724.
        Anna, baptized July 31, 1729.
        Jacob, baptized December 1, 1737.............................6
16. Hans Cunz, Peter Heiri, baptized July 14, 1695.
    His wife, Veronica Lang, baptized May 21, 1693.
    Children:
        Anna, baptized May 22, 1729.
        Hans Jacob, baptized December 21, 1730........................4
17. Jung Hans Cunz, baptized February 5, 1697.
    His wife, Elszbeth Lang, baptized December 19, 1697.
    Children:
        Rägula, December 19, 1720.
        Veronica, baptized May 2, 1734.
        Elisabeth, baptized March 29, 1739...........................5

April 25, 1743.   *From Stadel*

18. Vronegg Auer, Felix Lange's widow, baptized December 11, 1708.
    Children:
        Johannes, baptized August 22, 1734.
        Margaretha, baptized September 1, 1737.......................3
19. Jacob Schmid, carpenter, baptized January 24, 1688.
    His wife, Elisabeth Duttweiler, baptized November 15, 1696.
    Children:
        Barbara, baptized April 25, 1723.
        Jacob, baptized August 19, 1732.
        Hartmann, baptized July 20, 1735............................5

From Windlach

20. Heinrich Köchli, baptized May 4, 1704.
    Elszbeth Meyerhoffer, his wife, December 20, 1699.
    Children:
        Verena, baptized September 22, 1726.
        Cleophea, baptized July 11, 1728.
        Anna Maria, baptized August 16, 1733.
        Hans Jacob, baptized August 11, 1737.
        Barbara, baptized March 19, 1741............................7

From Rath

21. Hans Rudolff Meyerhoffer, baptized August 18, 1689.
    His wife Margaretha Bersinger, baptized 1695.
    Children:
        Hans Rudolff, baptized June 1, 1721.
        Johannes, baptized April 25, 1723.

Hans Ulrich, baptized December 9, 1731.
Anna, baptized May 8, 1729.
Abraham, baptized May 8, 1735. 7
22. Hans Meyerhoffer, baptized August 27, 1694.
Children:
Hans, baptized February 12, 1726.
Anna, baptized July 19, 1733.
Margaretha, baptized February 22, 1735. 4
23. Heinrich Moor, baptized February 17, 1711.
His wife, Barbara Lang, baptized July 12, 1711.
Children:
Felix, baptized September 13, 1739.
Hans Jacob, baptized November 27, 1740.
Heinrich, baptized December 2, 1742. 5
Jung Hans Lang, Deker's son, baptized July 25, 1686. 1
24. Heinrich Huser, baptized December 5, 1697.
His wife, Rägula Mayer, baptized July 24, 1698.
Children:
Rägula, baptized March 23, 1725.
Anna Barbara, baptized July 13, 1726.
Johannes, baptized August 27, 1730.
Christoph, baptized October 18, 1733.
Caspar, baptized May 22, 1735. 7
25. Felix Mayer, so-called Hospel, baptized December 30, 1703.
His wife, Veronica Schmid, baptized May 29, 1707.
Children:
Jacob, baptized January 30, 1729.
Hans Ulrich, baptized December 16, 1731.
Johannes, baptized April 2, 1733.
Anna, baptized February 20, 1735.
Veronica, baptized October 3, 1736.
Johannes, baptized September 26, 1739.
Verena, baptized March 26, 1741. 9
Suszanna Kämpf, daughter of Hans deceased, baptized August 7, 1719. 1
Anna Mayer, Hans Koch's housewife, baptized January 10, 1691. 1

March 27, 1744.   *From Stadel*

Margaretha Albrächt, daughter of deceased Felix, baptized October 24,
1723.
Total of all who left from the whole parish, 138.
Total 25 families.

No. 77. From the Parish Steinmur from 1734–1744 there left for Carolina

1734.   *From Obersteinmur*

1. Hans Müller, baptized September 25, 1707.
Anna Weidmann, baptized March 16, 1704.
Children:
Anna Maria, baptized July 23, 1730.
Hansz, baptized February 15, 1733.
His brother:
Heinrich Müller, baptized May 29, 1712.
2. Heinrich Surber, wagon-maker, baptized March 20, 1683.
Anna Hinnen, baptized January 24, 1685.

Children:
>Hans Caspar, baptized November 29, 1707.
>Hans Heinrich, baptized January 8, 1719.
>Verena, baptized June 5, 1729.

1738 in August

3. Caspar Koch, smith, baptized August 4, 1700.
Verena Müller, baptized September 1, 1700.
Children:
>Verena, baptized October 8, 1724.
>Rodolff, baptized March 14, 1728.
>Anna, baptized June 18, 1730.
>Barbara, baptized November 16, 1732.
>Beat., baptized March 26, 1735.
>Caspar, baptized March 24, 1737.

4. Heinrich Meyer, Tisen, baptized September 1, 1695.
Anna Trub, baptized July 26, 1711.
Children:
>Hans Jacob, baptized October 13, 1720.
>Verena, baptized May 15, 1729.
>Lienhart, baptized August 28, 1735.
>Margreth, baptized December 1, 1737.

1741, in March.   *From Obersteinmur*

5. Hansz Surber, baptized November 23, 1690.
Verena Surber, baptized October 9, 1675.

6. Heinrich Weiszmüller, baptized February 26, 1706.
Barbara Schmid, baptized October 9, 1690.

7. Hans Koch, Michel's son, baptized August 14, 1681.
Verena Meyer, baptized June 6, 1686.
Children:
>Cleophee, baptized August 2, 1716.
>Cathrj, baptized February 18, 1720.
>Regula, baptized November 5, 1724.

Son:
>Joseph, baptized March 1, 1713.
>Kljannj Meyer, baptized June 10, 1715.

Child:
>Maria, baptized January 8, 1741.

8. Heinrich Köchlj, joiner, baptized November 20, 1707.
Margreth Vogler, baptized June 27, 1716.
Children:
>Johannes, baptized February 27, 1738.
>Felix, baptized January 29, 1741.

9. Heinrich Huber, cabinet-maker, baptized January 10, 1686.
Barbara Bleüler, baptized September 26, 1706.
Children:
>Anna Magdalena, baptized January 1, 1736.
>Barbara, baptized February 24, 1737.
>Anna, baptized April 23, 1741.
>N.B.   Has also with him his wife Barbara, baptized January 31, 1734.
>He is living at Friedrichsthal in the Margravate-Baden-Durlach.

1743 in May.   *From Obersteinmur*

10. Hansz Koch, sergeant, baptized January 31, 1708.
Verena Müller, baptized September 2, 1703.

Children:
> Anna, baptized April 29, 1731.
> Hans, baptized April 26, 1733.
> Kljannelj, baptized April, 1735.
> Regula, baptized October 5, 1738.
> Johannes, baptized April 16, 1741.

1738, August.   *From Nidersteinmur*

1. Hans Meyer, baptized January 11, 1691.
   Kljvree Huber, baptized January 14, 1690.
   Children:
   > Verena, baptized October 25, 1716.
   > Verena, baptized September 9, 1723.
   > Barbara, baptized December 8, 1726.
   > Regula, baptized June 6, 1728.
   > Jacob, baptized June 11, 1730.
   > Anna Margreth, baptized May 11, 1734.
2. Caspar Lips, baptized June 25, 1695.
   Regula Näff, baptized November 5, 1693.
   Children:
   > Heinrich, baptized July 28, 1726.
   > Anna, baptized May 6, 1728.
   > Hans Caspar, baptized January 7, 1731.
   > Felix, baptized May 16, 1734.

1741, April.   *Also from Nidersteinmur*

3. Hans Heirj Frölj, baptized March 28, 1700.
   Anna Huber, baptized October 1, 1702.
   Children:
   > Heirj, baptized July 6, 1732.
   > Hans Jacob, baptized April 4, 1734.
   > Anna, baptized November 11, 1736.
   > John Baptista, baptized December 11, 1740.

   N.B.   This man is said to have taken with him over one hundred pounds, but after he had squandered this sum, returned with his whole household.   The women and children wander about as beggars.   He serves for a time in a place, but not too long.   But at Nidersteinmur he is no longer tolerated.
4. Hans Jacob Trub, baptized February 28, 1717.   Jacob's the mender's son.

1738, August.   *From Sünnicken*

1. Two brothers:
   Heinrich Zweidler, baptized May 31, 1716. } Hans Heiri's sons.
   Mathys Zweidler, baptized December 25, 1723. }
2. Two brothers:
   Heinrich Volkhart, baptized November 17, 1712. } The deceased Jacob Volk-
   Hans Heinrich Volkhart, baptized July 4, 1717. } hart's sons.
3. Heirj Bräm, baptized June 17, 1712.   Deceased Felix Bräm's son.

1741, March

4. Hans Huber, glazier, baptized February 7, 1688.
5. Hans Ulrich Huber, carpenter, baptized March 20, 1698.
   Margreth Weidmann, baptized March 11, 1697.
   Child:
   > Lienhard, baptized October 3, 1730.

Mother of the above Huber:
    Anna Zweidler, baptized April 20, 1671.
Sister-in-law:
    Regula Weidmann, baptized December 22, 1709.

1741. *Also from Sünnicken*

6. Heinrich Weidman, mender, baptized November 4, 1703.
Anna Zweidler, baptized March 28, 1709.
Children:
    Heinrich, baptized February 1735.
    Hans Jacob, baptized June 22, 1738.
    Anna, baptized June 12, 1740.

1738. *From Neerach*

1. Heinrich Huszer, baptized June 13, 1697.
Anna Bucher, baptized January 25, 1691.
Son:
    Felix, baptized September 6, 1722.

1743

2. Johannes Albrecht, wagon-maker, baptized February 13, 1701
Magreth Moor, baptized January 23, 1707.
Children:
    1. Verena, baptized March 25, 1728.
    2. Hans Jacob, baptized November 6, 1729.
    3. Jacob, baptized February 11, 1731.
    4. Felix, baptized March 14, 1734.
    5. Annelj, baptized February 7, 1740.
    6. Regina, baptized July 22, 1742.

1743, May

3. Annelj Kuenz, baptized October 5, 1710.   Daughter of the deceased magistrate (Vogt) Heiri.

1741

4. Barbara Kuenz, baptized March 12, 1719. Johannes', the carpenter's daughter.

1738

5. Melchior Meyer, baptized August 3, 1710.
Anna Barbara Meyer, baptized August 20, 1713.
6. Anna Müller, baptized September 15, 1700.
Illegitimate child of Melcher Streiff, tailor's help-mate from Glarus.
Hans Jacob, baptized September 24, 1729.

1743, May

7. Barbara Albrecht (spinner), baptized July 21, 1720.   ⎫ Jacob Albrecht's
Margreth Albrecht (spinner), baptized February 15, 1722. ⎬ (called Wägeli)
Regula Albrecht, baptized August 31, 1723.   ⎭ daughters.
8. Margreth Kuenz, baptized October 5, 1721. Heinrich Kuenz's (called "Engelheinrich") daughter.

1738, August. *From Rieth*

1. Cathrj Kuenz, baptized April 14, 1715.   ⎫ Three brothers and sisters,
Heirj Kuenz, baptized July 6, 1719.   ⎬ children of the deceased
Annelj Kuenz, baptized February 15, 1722. ⎭ Hans Kuenz.

2. Jacob Kuenz, baptized October 6, 1715. Deceased Hans Heinrich Kuenz's son.

3. Heinrich Schellenberg, baptized December 20, 1716. Felix's son.

No. 78. From the Parish Sternenberg there left on April 16, 1743, the Following Families

(a) Hansz Rügg, 43 years, and his wife Elsbetha Ott 35 years of age, with their five children, the oldest of which was 12 years and the youngest 10 weeks old.

(b) Felix Rebsamen, 45 and his wife Regula Graff 39 years old, with 6 children, the oldest of which was 15 years and the youngest 1 year old.

After selling his house and goods, and paying the emigration tax on the total, each of these men took away with him about 300 florins in money.

Attested ex-officio, Heinrich Sprüngli, Pastor.

Sternenberg, May 5, 1744.

No. 79. Anno 1738, there left Töss, from the Estate Tetnau, Two Families for Carolina

1. Parents:	Children:		
Jacob Meyer, born 1695.	Heinrich, born April	28, 1725.	
Elisabeth Hofmann, from Ober-Schotti-	Elsabeth	December	9, 1726.
ken.	Anna Barbara	December 18, 1729.	
	Catharina	January	1, 1735.
	Jacob	September 12, 1737.	
2. Hans Heinrich, born 1709.	Hans Jacob	April	14, 1733.
Barbara Keller, from Jsliken.	Elsbeth	October	23, 1735.
	Hans Geörg	April	7, 1738.

Note: Concerning these two families I have not been able to learn up to the present, in spite of frequent inquiries, where they got to.

Anno July 31, 1743

Has gone from Tosz to Pennsylvania with wife and child:

Parents:	Child:
Hans Caspar Siber, born June 12, 1717.	Anna, October 25, 1739.
Elsbetha Klaüe, born September 8, 1707.	

Note: Concerning this family the report was circulated in the first four weeks, that the father and the child has died at Basel.[6] But since then nothing has been heard, whether this rumor be true or whether they travelled farther.

No. 80. Trüllikon

From this parish and all four sections of it, since 1734 there was no one with the intention of going to the new-found-land, except:

Conrad Wieland, from Trutikon, who faithlessly left his wife, on account of bad management, at the end of the year 1732, and I do not know whither he has gone.

1. Anna Engeler, his wife, born July 1, 1693, with four children: (1) Lisab., born March 23, 1718. (2) Hans Rud., October 6, 1720. (3) Urss., August 25, 1723. (4) Hans Conrad, May 10, 1731.

[6] The same sold her house and goods in October, and after she missed getting away the first time, and I in the meantime had spoken to the magistrate of Toggenburg about these people, she left with the rest of her means and children. Where they got to, God knows!

2. Elsbeth Hablüzel from Trüllikon, who however first married Herman Gyger from the parish Diebolzau in Rhynthal, February 26, 1734. He is said to have taken away from his father, etc., according to an understanding with him, about 800 pounds.

From their destination the man wrote to his poor brother-in-law and relatives, as I have seen and read in the letter, that he was getting along well, he had plenty of food, and if they wished, they should come to him. Enough to eat and also to work they would find with him; if they could only provide for themselves as far as England, he would from there on pay their passage, but with the provision, that they would pay back the outlay with work. But on my advice they remained, but had not the old sister-in-law died, and if poverty did not hold them back, I do not know what they would do.

Hans Ulrich Vogeler and his wife Elsbeth Peyer from Trüllikon with two children, who are overloaded with debts and would make more if they could, are also anxious to go, but poverty holds them back. But they have stirred up another neighbor, who has no children and an infirm wife, that he should sell his property and go along, etc.

But he wished that he and his wife and his surplus 200 pounds be put under the care of the hospital, before their property should grow less. I started negotiations for them, but was told that for a married couple there was no room.

Therefore I proposed another plan to His Honor the Governor, which was feasible in case these people would desire more assistance. I tell you this, so that you may see what efforts are necessary, and that Christian care with its seriousness is very much needed.

Martj Zehender, a young unmarried man, petitioned his older brother Hans Ulrich, he should give him 18 pounds, so that he might on Easter Monday go forth with those from Andelfingen to Carolina, and he would no longer then as before come to him in bad clothes and be a burden to him, and would also make no further claim to his inheritance. On that he would give a written pledge.

I said, that if he wished to give up his citizen's rights, he could apply at the proper place, but if not, his honest brother should not spend money as for the interest, and let the good-for-nothing waste it. After squandering it, he would come back, and then he would have to support him again.

This report I am glad to furnish, so that our poor people be spared needless governmental expenses. If the saving were only carried through in all things, particularly as concerns widows and orphans. For if despair once adopts another road, conditions would really be very bad, because God's severe judgment is to be feared.

April 25, 1744.   Pastor CASPAR BRUNNER.

No. 81.   From the Parish Turbenthal the Following have gone to Carolina

February 1743.   Catharina Rüegg, legitimate daughter of Hans Heinrich Rüegg, from the Ramsberg. Baptized November 15, 1711.

March   1743.   Johannes Büchj, Postumous, legitimate son of Rudolph Büchj, deceased, from Neubrunn. Baptized December 14, 1721.

Turbenthal, April 23, 1744.

Attested, Pastor SCHEÜCHZER.

No. 82.   Uhwisen

Very Revered, Learned, Honored Minister and Dean:

In reply to your gracious command, etc., etc., I report as follows: About three years ago, four heads of families, possessed of many children, announced themselves to me and truly sought counsel as to whether they should go to Carolina, but on my representations they yielded at once, so that up to date, God be thanked, no one is known to have gone thither out of my parish. Those that are in military service were specified a year ago and sent to the high authorities; for their glory was but half as great as the seducers claimed. With a well provided Divine service, I should be pleased to care for 40 families or more. With salutations etc.,

Uhwisen, April 6, 1744.   JOH. HEINRICH HEITZ, *Pastor.*

P.S.   What happened at the visitation of BANKEN, will undoubtedly have been reported by his Honor Chamberlain Wirth, etc., etc.

No. 83.   URDORFF

To go to Carolina and lands about there, since 1734, no one left this parish of Nider-Urdorff, nor the middle or lower Räbstal, but two unmarried boys:

Jacob Grob, son of Hans Grob, 37 years old, and

Felix Huber, son of the deceased Jacob Huber, aged 35 years, who up to this served under peasants at other places, and on the 16th of July, 1743, without permission of the authorities, and without a certificate of baptism left the country. But because the latter left behind a woman with a child, to whom he was betrothed, named Verena Lips, daughter of the deceased Melcher Lips, from this place, who suspecting his departure, followed him to Basel, but could neither overtake him nor find out anything about him, the matter was brought before the marriage court, November 5, 1743, the promise of marriage nullified, the child declared legitimate and with the right of inheritance, and its bringing up put in charge in the meantime of his brothers Caspar and Heinrich Huber. This is a pattern of what fruits the emigration-fever grows and leaves.

Urdorff, April 3, 1744.   Attested, JOHANN JACOB ULRICH, *Pastor.*

No. 84.   LIST OF THOSE PERSONS WHO LEFT THE PARISH USTER FOR CAROLINA

Jacob Frey, sergeant, son of the deceased Heinrich Frey, from Sultzbach, baptized 1695, December 1, aged 48 years and 11 months, left for Carolina September 5, 1736, with his wife Regula Appert,* baptized January 8, 1699, aged 45 years and 3 months, with three children: Anna Barbara, baptized December 17, 1724, aged 19 years and 3 months; Elsbetha, baptized January 30, 1725, aged 18 years, 3 months; Heinrich baptized October 24, 1728, aged 15 years, 10 months.

With him there has gone to Carolina also Hans Jacob Homberger, from Sultzbach, a boy of 17 years, 2 months. Has neither wife nor child, brothers nor sisters.

Hans Wolfensperger, sergeant, son of the deceased Hans Wolfensperger, from Kirch-Uster, baptized August 26, 1706, aged 37 years, 7 months, also went to Carolina in 1743, in September, with his wife Anna Regina Huber, baptized January 10, 1711, aged 33 years and 3 months, with four children: Regula, baptized March 1, 1731, aged 13 years, 1 month; Elisabeth, baptized January 1, 1735, aged 9 years, 3 months; Anna, baptized October 28, 1737, aged 7 years, 5 months; Cleophea, baptized March 26, 1739, aged 5 years.

Attested, JOHANNES SCHWYTZER, *Vicar at Uster.*

* Note: He is not in Carolina, but in the Spanish service, his wife and children with Hans.

No. 85.   Fehraltorff

Ulrich Stutz, baptized May 27, 1688.
Elisabeth Ochsner, from Zimikon, the parish Volkenschweyl.
> Married here September 4, 1731. After selling all their property, which netted 200 pounds, left here for Carolina, August 29, 1738.

Children of the above:
> Heinrich, baptized, May 28, 1732.
> Caspar, baptized November 20, 1735.
> Barbara, baptized July 14, 1737.
> For their children's sake they took with them:

Hans Wolgemuth, Hans' posthumous son, a very poor boy, baptized April 2, 1719.
> Concerning these no certain report has been obtainable. In the meantime there was a rumor, that they suffered shipwreck, and with a great number wretchedly went to their doom.
> Just at the same time there went away from here, to go to Carolina:

Hans Jacob Bachofen, baptized November 25, 1703.
Cleophela Wolgemuth, baptized August 16, 1707.
> Married couple wedded here December 13, 1735.
> At Basel they were dissuaded from their purpose. The woman came back, the man, however, sought a livelihood elsewhere, and found it with a charcoal-burner in Alsace, where he remains in a wretched condition.
> This honest and pitiable man might have very well earned his bread here with weaving woolen fabric. But his wife in her evil ways not only deprived him of his food and household goods, but even abstracted some of the wool-yarn, so that he could not return the full weight, and finally lost him employment, which reduced him to this sad extremity. The above mentioned woman has now become vagrant, so that in spite of all inquiries, I do not know where she may be.
> Margreth Gut, from the Senscheür, a fief depending upon Kyburg, baptized October 14, 1718, married here May 23, 1742, to Rodolff Brüngger, a carpenter by trade. She could not get along with her husband and father-in-law, departed from here without taking leave, June 28, 1743, to join those from Dägerlen reported to be going to Carolina. She went with a woman who was following her husband, a smith, who had journeyed thither in order to help support his children on wages promised him.
> For the rest I am quite sure, that now no one else in the parish has a leaning toward the so-called New-found-land.
> Fehraltorff, April 2, 1744.   Thus testifies Hans Jacob Wirtz, *p.l.*

No. 86.   List of those who since 1734 left the Parish Volket-schweiler to go to Carolina

Born 1698, Heinrich Hegetschweiler,   February 20. ⎫ These left in the pre-
    1697, Barbara Buchmann, his wife, September 26. ⎭   ceding year, 1742.
Children: Margaretha, born 1719, in October; Anna, March, 1720; Susanna, September, 1722; Anna Barbara, May, 1724; Heinrich, August, 1726; Hans Heinrich, August, 1728; Beat. Rudolff, August, 1731; Jacob, — 1739; Verena, April, 1736.
> Total 4 sons and 5 daughters.

From Zimickon

1694, Caspar Hesz, and   ⎫ These also in the 42nd year (1742).
1706, Anna Knecht, his wife. ⎭
Child: Hans Rudolff, born April 1739.
> Margretha Knecht, sister of the above Anna, unmarried, born May, 1708.

1699, Hansz Ochsner, April 29, and ⎫
    Anna Zuricher, October 22. ⎬ These left 3 years ago.
Child: Hans Jacoblj, born November, 1737.
    Volketschweil, attested April 2, 1744.   J. H. FREY, *Pastor.*

NO. 87. WÄDESCHWEIL. (SEE PLATE 11)

Highly Revered, etc., Dean! I have the honor, in reply to the circular received, to inform the Highborn, etc., Dean that no more, as far as we can learn, have left Wädeschweil for Carolina, than,

1. Johannes Theiler, baptized October 8, 1690 and his wife,
Margretha Meyer, baptized, September 8, 1698.
    Also their son with his family, to wit:
2. Hans Jacob Theiler, baptized December 3, 1713.
Magdalena Belon, from the Dauphiné, baptized September 15, 1737.
    Children: Hans Rudolff, baptized September 15, 1737.
            Elisabeth, baptized January 12, 1739.
    Joining them and leaving his wife, Anna Tobler, behind:
3. Hans Heinrich Baumann, baptized March 23, 1673.

This departure took place in April, 1739. It was rumored that old Theiler, the father of Johannes, died on the way. Hans Jacob, as much as two years ago, sent back a letter in which he praises his good fortune and the new land. Other than these, thank Heaven, I know of none from my parish, who were possessed by the desire to emigrate.

           . . . . .Obedient Servant,
           JOS. CASPAR HOFMEISTER, *Pastor.*
    Wädeschweilen, April 10, 1744.

FROM THE PARISH SCHÖNENBERG NO ONE WAS SO PERVERSE AS TO GO

NO. 88. LIST OF PERSONS FROM THE PARISH WALLISSELLEN, WHO SINCE THE YEAR 1734 LEFT FOR CAROLINA

	Married people.	Left October 5, 1734.	Baptized.	
1.	I. Hans Heinrich Merki	. . . . .June	3,	1688
2.	Elsbeth Wezstein, wife	. . . . .May	30,	1693
	Children:			
3.	Heinrich	. . . . .February	23,	1716
4.	Kilian	. . . . .November	22,	1719
5.	Hans	. . . . .October	26,	1722
6.	Hans Conrad	. . . . .September	21,	1727
7.	II. Konrad Näff	. . . . .July	11,	1680
8.	Ana Barb. Däppeler, wife	. . . . .May	2,	1686
	Children:			
9.	Anna	. . . . .June	23,	1715
10.	Hans Jacob	. . . . .January	20,	1726
11.	Hans Jacob (same name)	. . . . .January	25,	1728
12.	III. Jacob Näff	. . . . .February	17,	1692
13.	Lisabeth Kuhn, wife	. . . . .December	15,	1695
	Children:			
14.	Anna	. . . . .July	28,	1720
15.	Lisabeth	. . . . .March	18,	1725
16.	IV. Hans Conrad Keller, carpenter	. . . . .March	14,	1706
17.	Barbara Blaar, wife	. . . . .December	9,	1703

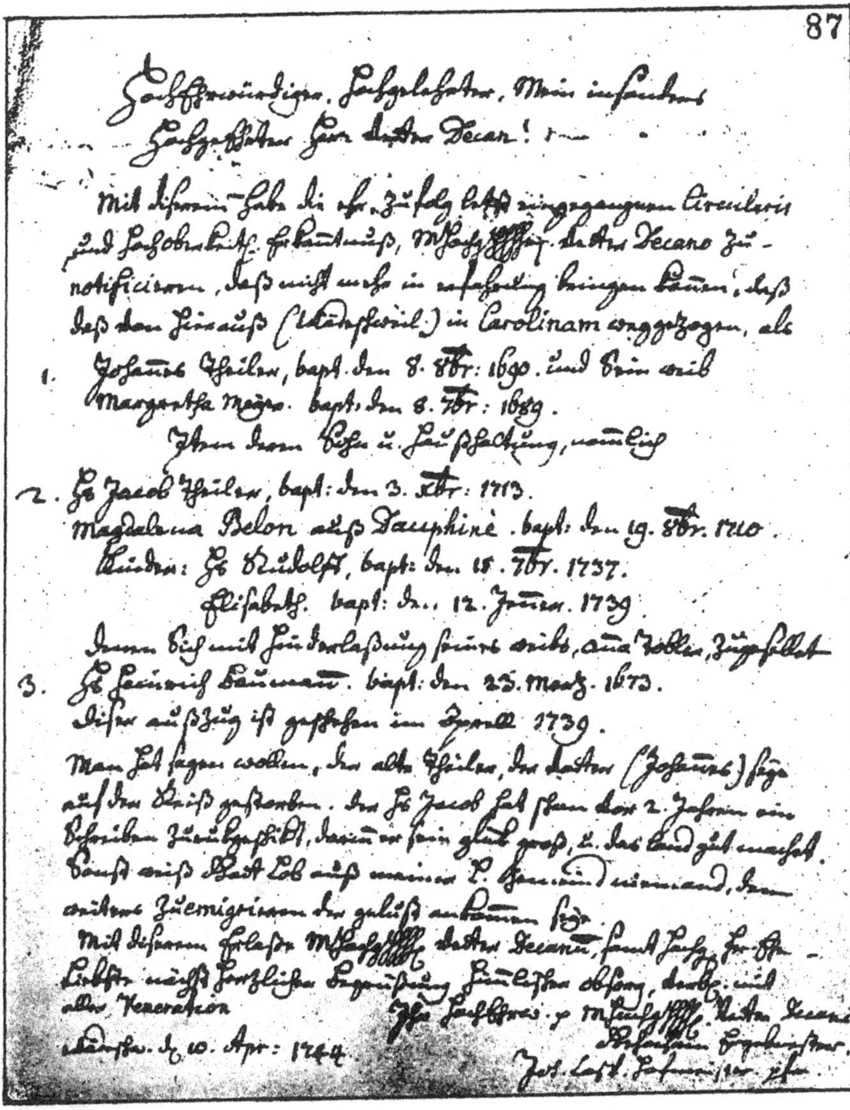

Plate II

REPRODUCTION OF THE ORIGINAL LIST No. 87, WÄDESCHWEIL

Child:

18.	Matheus	July	25, 1734
19.	V. Martin Schellenberg	November	29, 1706
20.	Verena Benz, wife	April	13, 1713
21.	VI. Jacob Näff, above Conrad Näff's son	December	1, 1710
22.	Elsbeth Haller, wife	May	24, 1711

Unmarried people.

23.	Barbara Haller, daughter of Hans Geörg	October	7, 1708
24.	Hans Conrad Näff, deceased Ulrich's son	April	30, 1713
25.	Ursula Schellenberg, above Hans Martin's sister	July	4, 1711
26.	Hans Jacob Rathgeb, son of Jacob deceased	July	29, 1708
27.	Jacob Wüest, son of Hans Heinrich	March	18, 1714
28.	Hans Rudolf Aeberli, son of Jacob deceased	September	11, 1712
29.	Hans Ludwig Lienhardt, son of Heinrich	July	26, 1712

Left on May 6, 1743

Married.

1.	I. Hans Heinrich Keller, carpenter	October	27, 1672
2.	Jacob Keller, his son, also a carpenter	May	1, 1702
3.	Anna Näff, wife	March	2, 1702

Children of Jacob Keller:

4.	Rudolf	June	29, 1727
5.	Jacob	April	17, 1729
6.	Anna	July	19, 1733
7.	Lisabeth	September	16, 1736
8.	Magdalena	January	4, 1739
9.	Susanna	November	20, 1740
10.	II. Rudolff Näff	May	25, 1679
11.	Hans Näff, his son, the above Hans Heinrich Keller's son-in-law	February	9, 1710
12.	Susanna Keller, wife	October	29, 1713

There left on May 8, 1743

Married.

1.	I. Hans Heinrich Näff	March	29, 1692
	Lisabeth Winsch, wife	January	7, 1703

Children:

2.	Hans Heinrich	September	21, 1727
3.	Hans Jacob	September	23, 1731
4.	Verena	August	8, 1734
5.	Elsbeth	December	16, 1736
6.	Beat	January	8, 1741
7.	Barbara	March	17, 1743
9.	II. Hans Jacob Näff, brother of the above	November	14, 1697
10.	Barbara Kuhn, wife	February	5, 1699

Children:

11.	Elsbeth	August	20, 1730
12.	Balthasar	May	2, 1734
13.	Jacob	February	17, 1743
14.	III. Ulrich Näff, brother of the above	March	18, 1703
15.	Elsbeth Weber	July	18, 1706

Children:

16.	Anna	April	28, 1726
17.	Regula	February	20, 1729
18.	Heinrich	February	20, 1735

Unmarried.

19.   Anna Barbara Näff, daughter of Hanz Näff, schoolmaster......................................December 12, 1717
20.   Esther Näff, her sister....................June   11, 1719
Total: 61 persons.

No. 89. List of Persons, who from 1734–1744 foolishly left the Parish Wyach to go to other strange Countries

Anno 1734	Born
Heinrich Meyerhofer, Rudolf Meyerhofer's son	1703
Hans Heinrich Meyerhofer, Rudolf Meyerhofer's son	1709

Anno 1738	
Andreas Baumgartner, tiler	1687
Barbara Meyer	1697
Children:	
Rudolf	1720
Anna	1724
Anna Barbara	1726
Andreas	1728
Christofell	1731
Heinrich Baumgartner	1687
Barbara Griesser	1688
Children:	
Verena	1720
Heinrich	1727
Anna	1730
Maria Baumgartner, widow	1679
Children:	
Andreas	1713
Veronica Kempf, his wife	1715
Anna	1718
Heinrich	1723
Hans Meyerhofer	1689
Elsbetha Albrächt	1682
Children:	
Hansz	1726
Catharina	1730
Rudolf Meyerhofer	1673
Elsabetha Baumgartner	1673
Mathias Baumgartner	1708
Susanna Meyerhofer	1705

Anno 1743	
Heinrich Baumgartner	1695
Margretha Bersinger	1694
Children:	
Barbara	1724
Cleophea	1727
Barbara Baumgartner, this man's sister	1691
Regula Balthasar, widow of Felix Bersinger	1695
Child:	
Andreas	1728

Anno 1744

Rudolf Baumgartner 1698
Barbara Meyerhofer 1688

N.B.   Margretha Albrecht, from Stadell, who served with this Baumgartner, and is said to be with child by him.

Total: 36.   WOLF.

April 14, 1744.

No. 90.   LIST OF PERSONS WHO LEFT THE PARISH WENNINGEN
FOR PENNSYLVANIA AND CAROLINA

1

1734 Hansz Caspar Meyer,
      Margaretha Buecher.
      Children:
          Hansz Rudolff,
          Anna,
          Hansz Jacob.
              Unmarried:
      Heinrich Schmid, ⎱ Brothers.
      Jacob Schmid,   ⎰
1738 Caspar Buecher,
      Margreth Häuser,
      Children:
          Heinrich,
          Verena,
          Hans Heinrich.
              Unmarried:
      Heinrich Schyblin,
      Hansz Schyblin,
      Lisabeth Schyblin,
      Heinrich Wirth,
      Anna Klayslin,
      Hansz Jacob Duttweiler,
      Jacob Meyer,
      Barbara Meyer(in),
          Total: 32 persons.

1743 Hans Jacob Scheür Meyer,
      Anna Eberhardt.
      Child:
          Anna.
                        2
      Hansz Bucher,
      Anna Lang.
      Children:
          Hansz,
          Anna.
              Unmarried:
      Hans Jacob Meyer,
      Margaretha Scheur Meyer,
      Heinrich Jägli,
      Heinrich Surber, ⎱ Brothers.
      Jacob Surber,   ⎰

No. 91.   FROM THE PARISH WETZIKON THERE LEFT FOR CAROLINA
IN MAY 1743

Heinrich Furrer, from Stägen, who really belongs to the Gossau district, born November 13, 1691. He has with him his wife Susanna Baumann, born January 24, 1692 and the following children:

Felix, April 1, 1720.
Hans Jacob, October 4, 1722.
Susanna, December 31, 1724.
Hans Felix, July 12, 1729.
Anna Maria, October 8, 1731.
Barbara, May 15, 1735.

A son Hans, born October 10, 1717, is in the Dutch service, the father wrote to him from Rotterdam that he should also make the journey with them, but he did not go.   About two weeks after Whitsuntide 1743, there also travelled thither Felix Schmid from Kempten, born January 6, 1695, who was later declared a bankrupt.   Attested, JOHANNES ULRICH, *Pastor*

No. 92. From Wangen there went to Carolina the Following Two Boys

1. Caspar Gut, baptized November 14, 1713. Went there after the death of both his parents, anno 1734.
2. Felix Hürrlimann, baptized November 26, 1719. Also betook himself thither after the death of his parents, anno 1743.
   Both had no more means to take along than about 10 pounds, and could in no way be got away from their purpose. It happened with the knowledge of the authorities.
   March 31, 1744.   Felix Weyss, *Pastor*.

No. 93. List of Persons who since 1734 and up to 1744 left the Parish Weisslingen to go to the New World in Pennsylvania

Anno 1734

1. Anna Juker, from Neschweil, daughter of Ulj Juker, 20 years old: Went first to Brabant to a relative, and from there she got an opportunity to go to Pennsylvania. She is also said to be married there.

Anno 1736

2. Left here, Heinrich Keller, from Theilingen, the deceased Caspar Keller's son, born February 1716, unmarried youth.
3. Left with the above, Christophel Jsler, from Theilingen, the deceased Hans Jszler's unmarried son, born January 11, 1712.

Anno 1742

4. Ludwig Koblet, from Neschweil, 25 years old, unmarried.
5. Jacob Spörri, from Neschweil, the deceased Jacob Spörri's unmarried son: Of these four persons there has been no news until now.
6. Caspar Spörri, from Neschweil, the above deceased Jacob Sporri's son, 20 years old. The latter took with him
   Anna Meilj, from Dettenried, and they are said to have been united in marriage at Basel, or on the ship.

Anno 1743

Left here, Heinrich Meilj from Lendiken:
> Regula Homberger, his wife.
> Children:
>> Verena, aged 3 years.
>> Jacob, aged 1 year.
and with him Heinrich Meilj, his half-brother, aged 16.
   The latter had been in the Dutch service since about 10 years under Captain Werdmüller, and declared that he was going to Holland again. No news has been received, as to whether he remained in Holland or went to Carolina.
                                       Felix Nüscheler, *Pastor*.

No. 94. Wisendangen

Very Revered, Learned and Esteemed Dean!
   In response to the command of the authorities, I am sending a list of those who emigrated from their fatherland between 1734–1744 and were destined for the New World.

Anno November 12, 1734

Johannes Wurman, baptized February 6, 1698. } Married January, 1627.
Elsbeth Boszhart, baptized May 31, 1696.

With their children:

    Anna, baptized October 31, 1728.

    Elsbeth, baptized August 27, 1730.

Hans Heiri Wurmann, baptized, March 17, 1696. } Married November 1, 1728.
Magdalena Goszweiler, baptized March 15, 1707.

With their children:

    Rudolf, baptized August 2, 1729.

    Barbara, November 12, 1730.

    Ursula, January 8, 1732.

    Hans Heinrich, October 18, 1733.

Jacob Widmer, baptized August 28, 1681. } Married June 17, 1721.
Margretha Deebrunner, January 8, 1793.

With their children:

    Jacob, August 25, 1722.

    Margr., January 21, 1725.

    Elsbeth, December 5, 1728.

    Suszanna, June 10, 1731.

    Anna, March 2, 1734.

Andreas Widmer, baptized August 11, 1696. } Married February 3, 1728.
Susanna Hiltzinger, April 12, 1696.

June 21, 1743

Rudolf Hegj, baptized December 6, 1698. } Married March 3, 1723.
Barbara Brandenberger, baptized April 20, 1696.

With their children:

    Suszanna, April 2, 1724.

    Rudolf, February 13, 1729.

    Hans Jacob, June 1, 1732.

    Jacob, April 3, 1738.

Hans Conrad Süsztrunk, baptized February 7, 1712. } Married November 30, 1734.
Anna Bühlmann, February 26, 1713.

With their children:

    Jacob, November 13, 1735.

    Hans Conrad, January 1, 1737.

    Magdalena, February 15, 1739.

    Ulrich, February 5, 1741.

    Othmar, September 30, 1742.

    With the wish for true well-being and most reverent respect, I consign my most devoutly honored Dean to the protection of Heaven.

    Wisendangen, April 10, 1744.

I am His most deeply indebted servant,
HANS JACOB BERGER, *Pastor.*

No. 95. From the Parish Wyla, a year ago after Whitsuntide, the Following Persons went to Carolina

Hans Jacob Ott, from Ottenhuò, aged 48.
Lisabeth Keller,   " 35.
Children:

    Elsbeth,   aged 14.

    Magdalena,   " 12.

    Margaretha,   " 8.

    Barbara,   " 3.

Hans Heinrich Ott, the deceased Hans Rudolff Ott's (from Ottenhub) surviving son, aged 26.

Hans Ulrich Ott, Hans Jacob Ott's son, aged 19.

Barbara Frey, Hans Jacob Frey's daughter (from the Auw), aged 24.

April 28, 1744.   Written by BEAT KITT, *Pastor at Wyla.*

No. 96. From the Parish Wildberg there went to Carolina in the Year 1734

Jacob Steinman, tenant on a fief at Wildberg, otherwise from the parish Schlatt, aged 55.

Children:

> Hansz Jacob, aged 33.
> Magdalena,   "   30.
> Heinrich,   "   29.
> Hans Ulrich, "   25.
> Beatrix,   "   22.
> David,   "   20.
> Susanna,   "   18.
> Salomon,   "   15.
> Anna,   "   13.

This Steinmann, however, and his children are said not to have got further than the Palatinate, where they are said to have settled.

Hansz Kübler, aged about 50, from Wildberg, his wife and two children.

Hansz Jacob Jszler, aged 40, with wife and three children.

Hansz Heinrich Boszhart, from Töszegg, aged 22.

1743. Kli Jogg Meylj, from Erikon, aged 61.

His son: Jacob Meilj, aged 29.

Rägula Keller, Gotthard Keller's (the suicide's) surviving daughter from Schalchen, aged 30.

Attested by WASER, *Vicar of Wildberg.*

No. 97. Wyla

List of all those persons who since 1734, against all warnings, went out of the land, leaving homes and fatherland. Anno 1734, September 4, there left for Carolina—

Michel Keller, from Wasterkingen, with his wife, born in Rorbas, and a child.

Jacob Nükom, from Wyl, soldier, who lately committed adultery with Anna Nükomm.

Elsbeth Witenberger, a young pretty unmarried girl, who allowed herself to be persuaded by this soldier, they wish to be united in marriage on the way.

It has not been possible to get any information about them.

Anno 1741 in the spring there left for Carolina:

Hansz Rutschmann, from Hüntwangen with his wife, born in Bachs, and a child.

Heinrich Mejer with his wife, both from Hüntwangen, no children.

Bachschlj Demuth, smith, from Hüntwangen, with his wife and a child.

Of the first two parties nothing has been ascertainable, but the smith succeeded in getting to Carolina with his wife and child, and has been able to send a letter brought by a man from Glarus, the contents of which were, that he is strong and can work well, can finally sustain himself (in the new country), that whoever is at home in his fatherland, should remain there, he wished that he had done so.

Anno 1744, March 31, there left for Pennsylvania:

Heinrich Keller, a young schoolmaster from Hüntwangen, with his wife born in Eglisau, together with his little son, called Samuel, who according to her opinion is to become a prophet ("der nach ihrer Meinung ein Prophet werden soll").

This young schoolmaster, and the shop-keeper Bersinger from Weyach, have been agitators for many years already, and all the emigrants in the district Eglisau, and many also in Kleggau they have seduced with falsified letters and booklets. Because everything was given out to them to be so good, these people finally left their homes.

Hans Sigerist, called Müllerhanseli from Hoff Buchenlo, 60 years of age, has left his old wife malitiously.

Hans Sigerist, his son, with his wife, born in Rafz, with two little children.

Heinrich Sigerist, also from Buchenlo with his wife from Rafz and a daughter 10 years old, who can read and pray very well indeed.

Magdalena Mejer, born in Hüntwangen, malitiously left her husband Heinrich Nükomm of Wyl, and through the seduction of the above-named schoolmaster, also left with him.

N.B. The most of these emigrants could still very well have got along and supported themselves in the fatherland.

Total of all persons who left the parish WYL from 1734 to date is 26.

The truth of this statement is attested by,

April 1, 1744.   MARX THOMANN, *Pastor at Wyla.*

No. 98. FROM THE PARISH ZELL, AGAINST ALL WARNINGS AND ADMONITIONS, THERE LEFT FOR THE PURPOSE OF GOING TO PENNSYLVANIA, CAROLINA, ETC., THE FOLLOWING PERSONS:

August 29, 1734

Hans Ott, Rudi's son, from Under-Langenhard, unmarried help-mate.

Jacob Weckerli, schoolmaster's son, unmarried.

Boy from Zell.

Oberlangenhardt.

Hans Conradt Zuppinger.

Babelj Meyer, March 19, 1689.

Children:

Margetlj, July 12, 1718.

Hans Uerech, September 20, 1722.

Heinrich, February 19, 1730.

Hans Caspar, December 21, 1732.

Abraham Weckerling.

Catrj Meylj, April 13, 1705.

Children:

Verena, January 7, 1731.

Wilpert.

Hans Ulrich Nüszlj, April 5, 1705.

A man who with his wife Margreth Boszhardt led a wicked life, and from vexation left with the above.

Zell.

Hans Ulrich Näff, July 25, 1709.

Hans Ulrich's son, unmarried.

Hans Rudj Ramp, Jacob's son, baptized February 14, 1717, unmarried.

September 8, 1734

Lisabeth Ott, deceased Rudi's daughter from Kollbrunnen, baptized December 20, 1726.

Heinrich Hoffman, March 7, 1697.

Susanna Meyer, April 26, 1705.

Children:

1. Verena, December 18, 1719.
2. Anna Babelj, January 26, 1721.
3. Hans Urech, August 8, 1723.
4. Adelheit, November 4, 1725.
5. Rudj, June 12, 1731.
6. Susanelj, November 4, 1733.

Bernhardt Furer, September 19, 1697.

Babelj Zuppinger, August 8, 1697.

Children:

1. Heinrich, July 6, 1631.
2. Hans Rudolff, January 27, 1737.

Married July 17, 1722 { Caspar Peter, October 27, 1698.
{ Maria Zuppinger, February 28, 1699.

Children:

1. Hans Jacob, March 4, 1723.
2. Caspar, August 13, 1724.
3. Rudolf, December 25, 1728.
4. Margeth, September 9, 1734.
5. Anna, January 19, 1738.

Married August 20, 1737 { Hans Ulrich Müller, June 9, 1715.
{ Barbara Jsler, July 8, 1710.

Child:

Heinrich, October 27, 1737.

Maria Müller, Hans Urech's sister, baptized February 5, 1719. She went with him, but because she regretted it, she returned after a few days; is now in service in Zürich.

In May, 1743

Heirj Ott, Hans Rudi's (from Underlangenhardt) son, unmarried.

Jacob Ott, Hans Heinrich Ott's legitimate son, unmarried.

Magdalena Haffner, from Zell.

Heinrich Haffner's daughter, November 13, 1717.

Maria Ott, deceased Rudi's (from Underlangenhardt) daughter, March 16, 1721.

February 28, 1743 { Hans Conradt Winkler, from Obl.
{ Hans Jagelj Winkler's son, baptized.

May 13, 1743 { Ulrich Furer, Ulrich Furrer's son, baptized August 18, 1720.
{ Heirj Ott, tenant's son, unmarried.

Total: 44.

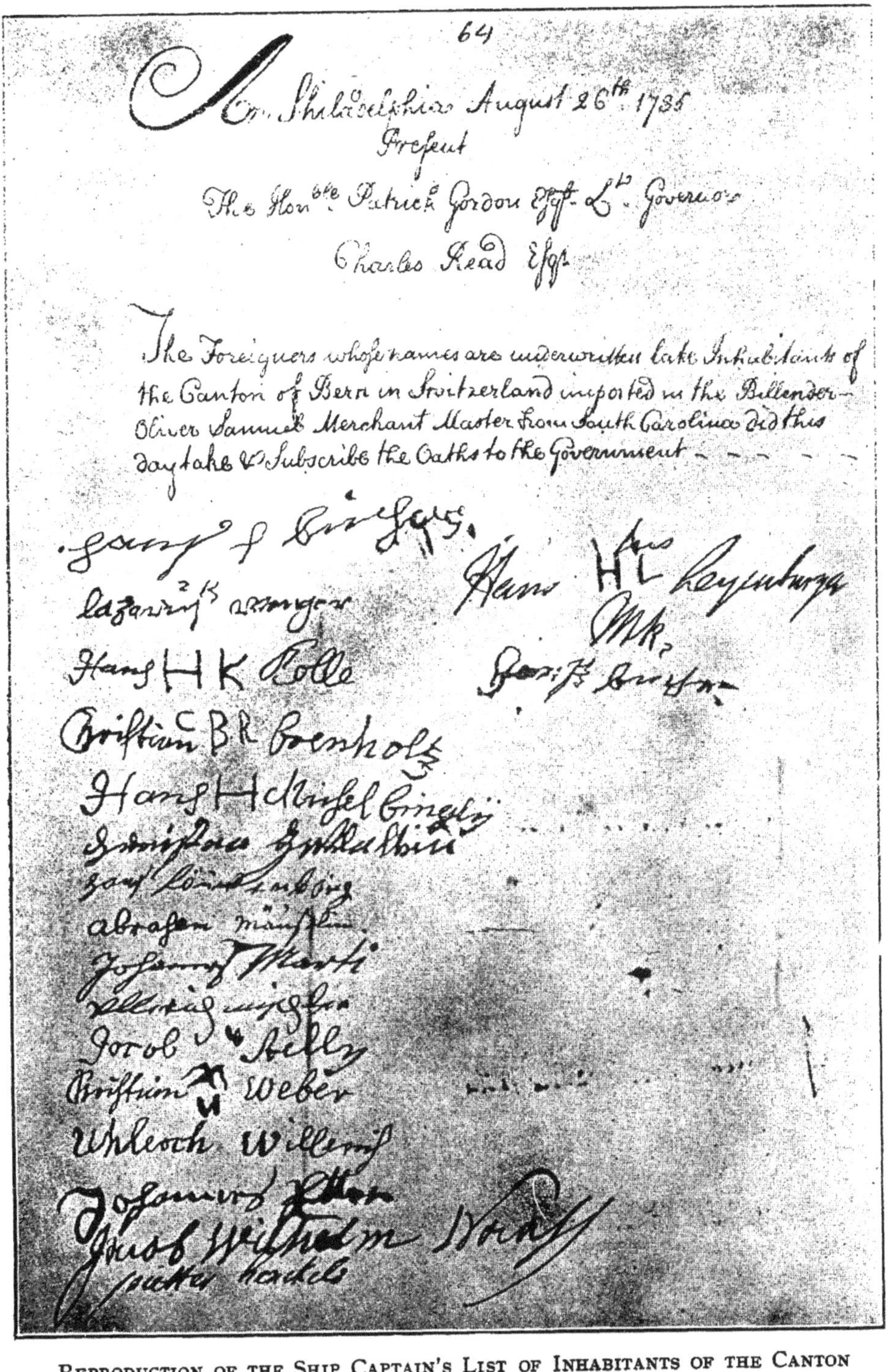
64

In Philadelphia August 26th 1735
Present
The Honble Patrick Gordon Esqr Lt Governor
Charles Read Esqr

The Foreigners whose names are underwritten late Inhabitants of the Canton of Bern in Switzerland imported in the Billender Oliver Samuel Merchant Master from South Carolina did this day take & Subscribe the Oaths to the Government

REPRODUCTION OF THE SHIP CAPTAIN'S LIST OF INHABITANTS OF THE CANTON OF BERN, IMPORTED FROM SOUTH CAROLINA, PHILADELPHIA, AUGUST 26, 1735

Plate 13

Mens Names	Ages	Womans Names	Ages
Hans Booker	54	Cristana Booker	52
John Booker	20	Ann Winger	56
Lazerus Winger	19	Ann Winger	18
Hans Koller	40	Susannah Kollad	35
Christian Brenholts	39	Ame Brenholts	40
Hans Pinkley	23	Lizarbeth Lyinburged	45
Christian Swaller	24	Lizarbeth Lyinburged	20
Hans Lyinburged	50	Barbery Lyinburged	14
Hans Lyinburged	25	Lizarbeth Messed	25
Abram Meeseley	43	Ann Wewer	25
Hans Marty	44	Ann Wewer	20
Uldrick Messer	30	Barbry Yelin	25
Jacob Starley	20	Barbry Yelin	45
Cristan Wewer	28	Cristan Yelin	20
Uldrick Yelin	27	Maddling Spring	23
~~Maddling Spring~~		Margat Allesten	20
Johannes Attesley	40	Applency Greeno	60
William Haws	39	Marry Haws	38
Peter Henkler	21		

Childrens Names	Ages
Benjaman Booked	13
Cristian Booked	10
Jacob Collad	9
Peter Lyinburged	8
Hannah Lyinburged	3
Ann Messer	13
Hans Wewed	7
Cristan Wewed	3

Aug 26 1735

A true List

Sam: Marchant

PAGE 2 OF SHIP CAPTAIN'S LIST OF AUGUST 26, 1735

MOVEMENTS OF SWISS EMIGRANTS IN THE AMERICAN COLONIES

Supplemental to the preceding records, and to the statements on page 1 of this volume, it was my pleasure to find in *Minutes of the Provincial Council* (Pennsylvania), Vol. 3, p. 607, this record:[1] At the Courthouse of Philadia, August 26th, 1735.

Present:

The Honble Patrick Gordon, Esqr., Lieut. Governor with some ᴜ₁ the Magistrates.

Eighteen Switzers, who, with their families, making in all forty-five Persons, were imported in the Billinder Oliver, Samuel Merchant, Master, from South Carolina, were this day Qualified as usual, and their names are hereunto subjoined.

Bucher, Hans,	Meysler, Ulrich,
Wanger, Lazarus,	Stelly, Jacob,
Koller, Hans,	Weber, Christian,
Brenholtze, Christian,	Willem, Ulrich,
Pingly, Hans Michel,	Otter, Johannes,
Swalher, Christian,	Haross, Jacob Wilhelm,
Lyinburger, Hans,	Henckels, Pieter,
Mauslin, Abraham,	Lyinburger, Hans, junr.,
Marti, Johannes,	Bucher, Hans, junr.

PENNSYLVANIA STATE LIBRARY,
HARRISBURG, PA.

Nov. 28, 1919.

[1] Surname placed first for easy reference

MEMORANDA REFERRING TO THE ARRIVAL INTO PHILADELPHIA OF SWISS FROM CAROLINA.

The Division of Public Records has the original Oath of Allegiance list and also the Ship Captain's list of the Arrivals in Philadelphia from South Carolina referred to in Volume Three, page 607, Colonial Records. These lists are also published in Rupp, p. 100, and in the Seventeenth Volume of Second Series, pages 119 and 120. The Seventeenth Volume of Second Series was taken from the Ship Captain's list and contains the names of the women and children, as well as of the men.

I have made a careful examination of all the lists from 1734 to 1744 and find no other lists of Immigrants coming to Philadelphia from South Carolina.

H. H. Shenk,
Custodian of the Public Records

Correspondence with Dr. Thomas L. Montgomery, State Librarian, Harrisburg, Pa., resulted in receiving from him photographs of the original records connected with the foregoing emigration of Swiss from South Carolina, and they are reproduced (see Plates 12, 13, 14) together with the memoranda from Mr. H. H. Shenk, Custodian of the Public Records.

Search in North Carolina, South Carolina, New York, Maryland, Pennsylvania, Louisiana, etc., and in the Library of Congress has yet failed to disclose any other document bearing upon this subject.

The extensive Swiss settlements in Louisiana seem to have been wholly distinct from the emigration into the Atlantic colonies. There may later be discovered records of land migration from the Carolinas other than the known movements northward into Virginia and Pennsylvania, and from Pennsylvania southward.

Gaius M. Brumbaugh

Washington, D. C., April 12, 1920

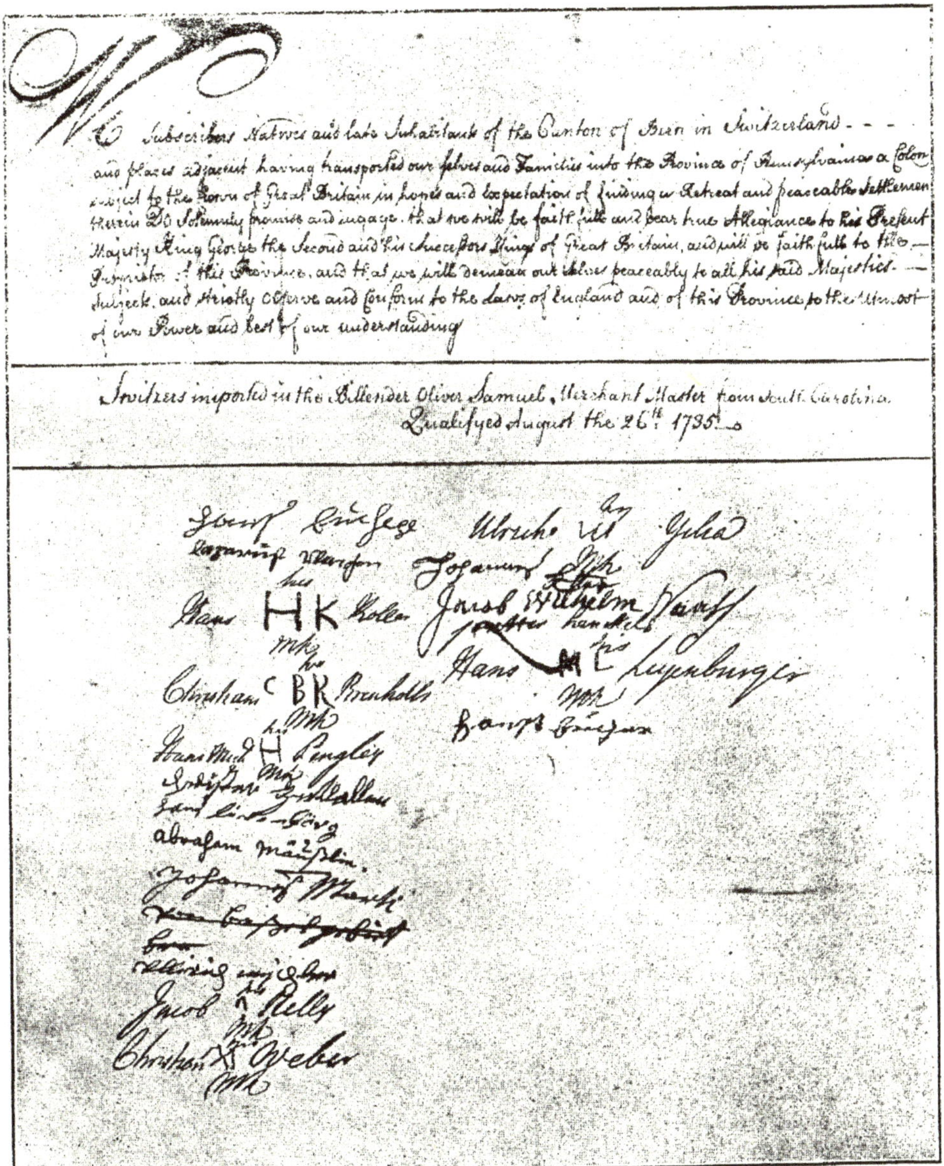

Plate 14

REPRODUCTION OF THE ORIGINAL OATH OF ALLEGIANCE LIST OF INHABITANTS OF THE CANTON OF BERN, IMPORTED FROM SOUTH CAROLINA, PHILADELPHIA, AUGUST 26, 1735

INDEX [1]

[1] Except where names are given, references to wife and children are omitted. Figures in parenthesis (3) mean that the name occurs that number of times on the indicated page.

Minor variations in spelling occur where different persons make the reports, as: Alt-stätten, Alttstätten, Ringger, Ringer, etc., but the Index presents the material variations.

The indefiniteness of knowledge of destination should cause the reader to carefully scrutinize all the "Lists" for names being sought.

The managing editor will appreciate word of any error discovered in the index, which he has carefully prepared.   G. M. B.

LISTS OF

SWISS EMIGRANTS IN THE EIGHTEENTH CENTURY

TO THE
AMERICAN COLONIES

VOLUME II

From the State Archives of
Bern and Basel
Switzerland

Compiled and Edited
by
ALBERT BERNHARDT FAUST, A.B., PH.D.
AND
GAIUS MARCUS BRUMBAUGH, M.S., M.D.

PUBLISHED BY
THE NATIONAL GENEALOGICAL SOCIETY
GAIUS M. BRUMBAUGH, *Managing Editor*
WASHINGTON, D. C.
1925

Lists of Swiss Emigrants in the Eighteenth Century to the American Colonies

BERN, 1706–1795; BASEL, 1734–1794.

I

PREFACE

THE publication of Volume One of the LISTS OF SWISS EMIGRANTS IN THE EIGHTEENTH CENTURY TO THE AMERICAN COLONIES aroused keen interest among genealogists and the large number of persons who were thereby aided in tracing their family history, also those who appreciated the deeper insight which the Zürich manuscript afforded them into the human side of the immigration problem during the colonial period. The hope was frequently expressed that another volume might soon follow the first, extending the scope of investigation at least to the two other great centers of Swiss emigration, Bern, the largest and most populous canton in the eighteenth century, and Basel, the great natural gateway, through which most of the emigrants had to pass.

But the fulfillment of the wish proved to be by no means an easy task. In the state archives of Bern and Basel there was not to be found one single manuscript, as that discovered in the state archive of Zürich, which gave an approximately accurate list of all emigrants to the American colonies from the canton of Zürich during the period of greatest emigration. Such information, if attainable at all, had now to be searched for in hidden places, thousands of pages in various classes of record books had to be carefully examined, and all references needed verification, before accurate lists could be constructed of persons who had beyond a doubt left for the American colonies. This painstaking search could only be carried on by men of skill and experience in archive work, and they were frequently compelled to interrupt their investigations because of other duties. Thus more than a twelve-month was consumed before the results obtained in Bern and Basel could be put together for presentation.

The investigations in the city of BERN were made under the
direction and supervision of the state archivist, Mr. G. Kurz, who
employed assistants to work out the details. Without Mr. Kurz's
masterful control of his archive materials and his unselfish devotion
to the laborious task, the work at Bern is inconceivable. Under his
expert guidance, the harvest surpassed all expectations. Materials
were derived from many sources, as *e.g.*: the Minute-books of the
Governing Council of Bern (Ratsmanuale, R.M.), the Lists of Citi-
zenships Withdrawn (Rodel Weggezogener Mannrechte), Records
of Withdrawals of Property (Mittelwegziehungsprotokolle), Account-books of Those Absent from the Country (Etat der Landesabwesenden), Expense Account-books of the Governors (Amtsrechnungen der Landvögte), Record Books of Sundry Districts (Ämterbücher). The materials discovered have been divided into three
groups:

  I. Special investigations, five in number, contributed by the
       state archivist of Bern, Mr. G. Kurz.
      (*a*) The First Bernese Emigrants to America.
      (*b*) The Bernese Colonists of New Bern.
      (*c*) Bernese Soldiers in America.
      (*d*) From the Years of the "Rabies Carolinae."
      (*e*) Newspaper Reports, 1735.
 II. Lists of Emigrants from Various Districts.
III. Names of about 200 Emigrant Families, with numerous items
       of information concerning them.
       Seven photographs of representative documents, mostly bear-
           ing on these family names, are added, to testify to the
           genuineness of the materials.

The Bern investigations, prepared and received in the German
language, were carefully translated into English by Mrs. Van
Dyck Hespelt (Ph.D. Cornell), with the coöperation of the editor.
The family names appear in the spelling of the present day in the
headings, but in the descriptive matter also in older forms. The
references to sources have been left untranslated, as Ratsmanuale
(R.M.), Ämterbücher, etc., thereby facilitating further inquiries
or researches in the archives. German words of a local or technical
meaning have frequently been left untranslated, or an attempted
translation has been placed by the side of the German, as: Landvogt
(governor), Manumission (liberation from serfdom), Gemeinde
(commune), Landrecht (certain special rights of the Swiss citizen),
Mannrecht (citizenship), Amt (district), etc.

The BASEL archive researches are more entirely the work of one man, experienced in archive investigations, Dr. Adolph Gerber, who spent the greater part of a year in Basel, Liestal and environs, making an exhaustive study of the eighteenth century emigration from the canton of Basel. The state archivist of Basel, Dr. August Huber, and the state archivist at Liestal, Mr. Florian Meng, and their assistants responded readily when Dr. Gerber called for aid, and he desires to express his indebtedness to them, however, the planning of the work and the carrying out of every detail were done by himself. To Dr. Gerber therefore belongs the entire credit for the excellent results he has achieved, not less in amount or importance than the splendid materials extracted from the archive of Bern. There is an admirable unity in Dr. Gerber's contribution, and it is easy to see that his heart was in his work. He has himself explained his methods and sources fully in a Preface and Introduction, and it is therefore only necessary to add that he himself translated his materials into the English language as he went along. Dr. Gerber has spent the greater part of his life in the United States, and only recently has been living abroad as professor emeritus.

The editor feels confident that Volume Two of the LISTS OF SWISS EMIGRANTS IN THE EIGHTEENTH CENTURY TO THE AMERICAN COLONIES surpasses Volume One in the quantity and variety of genealogical and historical materials gathered together, and that in human interest it does not fall behind. He wishes to state in conclusion that the person who called this second volume into being was the editor of the *National Genealogical Society Quarterly*, and the managing editor of these volumes, Dr. Gaius M. Brumbaugh, whose zeal and faith in this enterprise never failed and has been justified by the enthusiastic reception of the volumes.

CORNELL UNIVERSITY,
ITHACA, N. Y.,
April 15, 1925.

A. B. Faust

TABLE OF CONTENTS

ILLUSTRATIONS

STATE ARCHIVES OF BERN

SPECIAL INVESTIGATIONS BY STATE ARCHIVIST
G. KURZ

(a) THE FIRST BERNESE EMIGRANTS TO AMERICA

DURING the first half of the seventeenth century, Switzerland, almost untouched by the horrors of the Thirty Years' War, enjoyed peace and prosperity and had a good market for her excess products. In the second half of the seventeenth century a social reaction set in, which was made more acute by political and religious confusion. Since there were good opportunities for new settlers in depopulated Germany, many people left the canton of Bern during this period and journeyed northward into foreign parts. This emigration to the "lowland" (Niederland), as the destination of the emigrants used to be called, lasted into the eighteenth century and was much more numerous than the emigration to America, which ran parallel to it.

Of the Bernese emigrants who went to Alsace, the Palatinate, and other parts of Germany, many may later have had reason to journey on to the other side of the ocean.

At least one such case is definitely known, which extends back into the seventeenth century. In the year 1653, in the cantons of Bern, Luzern, Solothurn and Basel the peasants revolted against the authorities, chiefly for social reasons. With the help of the other cantons the authorities succeeded in quelling the dangerous uprising after hot fighting. One of the most obstinate nests of rebels was the commune (Gemeinde) of Melchnau (District of Aarwangen) on the boundary between Bern and Luzern. In this district of hills and forests many outlawed rebels hid for months until an opportunity came for them to escape out of the country. Among other people who could expect no mercy to be shown them, were the brothers Hans and Friederich *Leibundgut* of Melchnau, where the family still flourishes to-day. They both escaped into Alsace, where definite reference is made to them in the church registers of Schalkendorf from the year 1655. An American, Mr. *Livingood*, after careful research in the archives, has been able to prove that he was certainly descended from this same Hans Leibundgut. This case has been discussed in the work of a reliable Bernese historian, P. Kasser: "*Geschichte des Amtes und des Schlosses Aarwangen*," p. 259.

But let us now turn to the eighteenth century! Even before the founding of New Bern in North Carolina (1710) individual Bernese people, women among them, had sought their fortunes in the New World. In the founding of this colony the leader, Christoph von Graffenried, was assisted by Franz Ludwig *Michel*, who, to be sure, because of his rough and violent nature, caused his colleague some great disappointments. Michel, who came from a patrician family in Bern, had already made two trips to America before his journey to establish New Bern, the first in 1701, the second in 1703. Both times he had stayed over there for some time. The reports, letters and documents of Michel which refer to these two journeys have been published by J. H. Graf in the *Neues Berner Taschenbuch 1898*, pages 59–144.[1] In these writings a great number of Bernese and Swiss people are mentioned whom Michel met over there. The above-named publisher only partially attempted their identification, therefore some additions and corrections may be mentioned here.

In the vicinity of Gloucester, Michel, to his astonishment, met "the four *Lerber* sisters" (p. 83) whose mother had died soon after their arrival in America and who were not very well off. The facts concerning the emigration of these women are as follows:

In the Bernese Staatsrechnung (account-book) of 1700 there is an entry stating that Mrs. Captain Lerber received on September 8 as a viaticum "in order to travel to Florida" a subsidy of 200 Bernese pounds (*see Plate 1*). (Florida was then one of the many designations which were used in Switzerland to refer to the East coast of North America.)

The matter had actually been taken up on August 29th by the Great Council (Grosser Rat), from which at all events it is to be concluded that it had created a great stir in the city of Bern. We learn that this was a case in the city's *chronique scandaleuse*. The above-mentioned Board decided, therefore, to give to Mrs. Captain Lerber and her daughters pecuniary aid to the amount of

---

[1] A translation of Michel's journal into English by Professor William J. Hinke appeared in the *Virginia Magazine of History*, beginning in January, 1916. See also Faust: *Guide to the Materials for American History in Swiss and Austrian Archives*, p. 72.

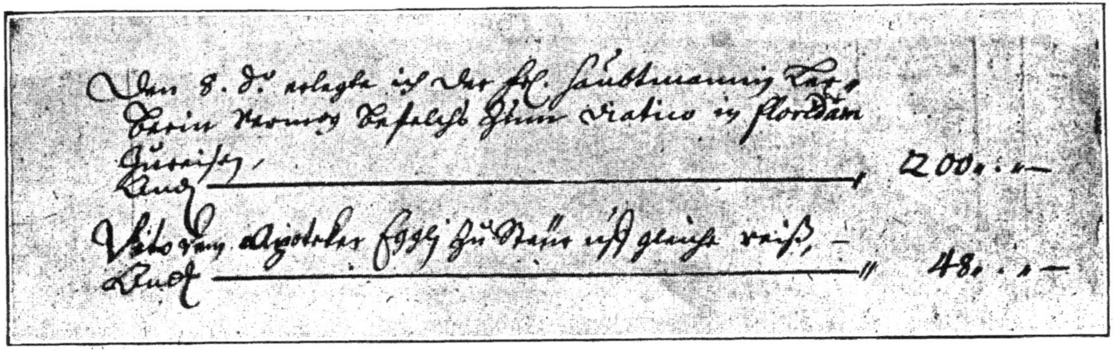

Plate 1

VIATICUM OF 200 POUNDS PAID TO THE WIDOW OF CAPTAIN LERBER. (See page 2.)
From: Account Book of the Canton of Bern, 1700.

200 pounds or 50 thalers and also to release them from a debt of 600 pounds with which their house was encumbered, all on the condition that these women should never return.   At the same time the Great Council asked the corporation zu Gerbern (subdivision of the city commune) also to make a contribution in order to send away this family.   The latter had, in fact, been supported by this corporation for years.   The opportunity should now be seized to spend a little more and get rid of them.   (R. M. 273, 459/60.)

Since the Lerber family could now sell their house without the mortgage and since they doubtless were assisted not only by the corporation but also by their patrician relatives, they were not obliged to approach the strange country destitute.

The head of this family was Mrs. Maria Elisabeth Lerber, née Bourgeois, widow of Captain Daniel Lerber, who commanded a Bernese company stationed in Strassburg about the year 1678 and later held the same rank at home in the fire-brigade and in the militia.   Lerber distinguished himself during the defense of Strassburg against the French.   He died about 1689, not yet 50 years old, to the great misfortune of his family.   (The exact date of his death has not been determined.)

Reference is made in the church records of the city of Bern to three daughters by this marriage:

Johanna Margreth, baptized May 9, 1673,

Maria Elisabetha, baptized January 29, 1675,

Martha, baptized June 3, 1681.

A little son, Franz Daniel, baptized July 26, 1687, must have died early, since there is a notice saying that the father died without male issue.   (Stammregister, p. 239.)

The oldest daughter, who was not yet 20 years old, began to be talked of as leading a frivolous life and had to be warned by the Council on Morals (Sittenbehörde).   But she did not reform; on the contrary, she continued to carry on various love affairs.   She became the mother of an illegitimate child which first saw the light at the beginning of August, 1698.   It was a girl whose name has not been recorded.

Since the Captain's wife, because of her lack of means and because of her oldest daughter's loss of honor, could no longer hope to provide favorable marriages for either this daughter or the two others, she probably decided to emigrate to America.   For just at this time the emigration fever began to break out in Bernese territory.

On the same day on which the Captain's wife and her daughters received from the authorities the subsidy for their journey to

Florida, the Bernese apothecary *Eggli* also obtained a viaticum of 48 pounds for the same destination.   Because of the summary way in which the old church records were kept, it has not been possible to identify this man with certainty.   Reference is indeed made to an apothecary named Hans Jakob Eggli, who, however, would have been about 68 years old at the time of the emigration in 1700.   At all events, this apothecary, according to a contemporary list, did not have an establishment of his own in Bern.   He is not mentioned in Michel's writings, although in all probability he accompanied the Lerber family to America.

When Michel reported, however, that he had met four Lerber sisters, whereas the church records make reference to only three, he perhaps thought that the little illegitimate daughter of Johanna Margreth was her younger sister.   The child was about four years old at that time.   Since Michel had been away from home in foreign military service for some time before his journeys to America, he probably did not know all the gossip of the city of Bern.   However, this attempt at an explanation does not claim to be authentic.

Michel also met on his second journey in the vicinity of Germantown,[2] among other acquaintances, " Landvogt *Mattheys* of Heimenhausen and the sons of the armorer *Bundeli*" who had recently settled there and had acquired an estate of 100 acres (p. 135). Unfortunately this report is not very definite, since it is not clear whether reference is made to two sons of this Bernese citizen or to several.

Heimenhausen is an estate in the commune of Kirchlindach in the vicinity of Bern, and belonged to Hans Conrad Matthey.   He had been Landvogt of Wangen from 1674–80.   In addition to several daughters he had three sons:

> Rudolf, baptized October 4, 1660,
> Hans Conrad, baptized July 22, 1670,
> Conrad, baptized December 21, 1682.

Probably the large number of children in this family made it seem advisable for one, or possibly all, of the sons to emigrate.   The family is extinct in the city of Bern.   It ceases to appear in the baptismal records from 1700 on.

On the other hand, the manuals of the Chorgericht and of the Council (Rat) show that the family affairs of David Bundeli (Bondeli), the armorer, were in a state of complete confusion.

---

[2] In 1720 a petition was sent from Germantown to the Evangelical cantons asking their aid in installing Divine service there. Because of the remoteness of the locality the petition was not given consideration. (Evang. Abschiede T, 384.)

Bundeli had been married a second time.   By his first marriage with Elisabeth Dick he had three sons:

Abraham, baptized February 16, 1676,

David, baptized November 18, 1677,

Hans Rudolf, baptized January 20, 1684.

The son last mentioned is later referred to as the father of a numerous family in Bern, so that probably the colonists were only the two older sons, or possibly one of them.

In Mattabaney Michel found among the Swiss people there one of his comrades in arms named *Willion* who came from Bex in the Waadtland (p. 83).   He and a *man from Neuenstadt* (either Villeneuve on Lake Geneva or Neuveville on the Lake of Bienne) had come to the country in 1700.   The leader of the colony, who was rather severe with the people dependent upon him, was a Major *Borel*, probably from Neuenburg (Neuchâtel), which was at that time a principality and is now a canton (p. 86).

In Manigkinton our traveller was entertained by an *Aargauer* (p. 91), he also visited the French Swiss, *Nicon* and *Detoit*, or *Dutoit*, as well as the village magistrate *Chaltin*, who had formerly been a surgeon in Yverdon (Waadtland).   Michel gives no information concerning the origin of the village pastor *Dujaux* (p. 92).   He tried to continue his journey into Pennsylvania in order to visit his countryman *Charriere* from Cossonay (Waadtland) who had settled there, but he was unable to do so (p. 103).   This was a member of an important family of the nobility in the Waadtland (Canton de Vaud).

To this account of the earliest emigration from Bern in the eighteenth century must be added the cases of Samuel *Güldi* [3] of Bern (1710), the pietistic theologian, of the miller, Joseph *Anken* of Därstetten (1706), and of the *Widmer* father and sons, peasants from Heimiswil (1709).   In the separate extracts has been given all the definite information regarding these cases which can be gathered from the materials in the state archives.   Further investigation might be carried on in the archives of the individual communes.

---

[3] Güldi did not emigrate to America in 1703, but in 1710.   A copy of his account of his journey is in the library of the city of Bern (Mss. Hist. Helv. III, 243, and III, 166/3) and the greater part of it has been printed in Ernst Stachelin: *Schweizer Theologen im Dienste der reformierten Kirche in den Vereinigten Staaten* (Schweizerische Theolog. Zeitschrift, 1919, Hefte 4/6).   He left at the beginning of July, 1710, from England in the same fleet with Graffenried's Bernese colonists, but with a different ship.   He landed September 24, in Philadelphia, and settled in Roxboro as a planter.   He died New Year's Eve, 1745.

(b) The Bernese Colonists of New Bern

The founding of the colony of New Bern in North Carolina in the year 1710 has been discussed by Albert B. Faust in the October number of the *American Historical Review* for 1916. Faust has also published the writings and plans of the founder of the colony, the Bernese patrician, Christoph *von Graffenried*, in the *German American Annals*, New Series, Vol. 11, Nos. 5 and 6, and Vol. 12, Nos. 2–5, with references to other literature on this undertaking.

For the present complementary discussion, therefore, it is sufficient to mention only the main facts concerning the founding of the colony.

When Christoph von Graffenried undertook to found his colony, he chose as his first colonists 600 "Pfälzer," *i.e.*, people from the Palatinate (Pfalz), from other parts of Germany and from Switzerland, who had just come to England to look for a new home. To discover the names and the exact origin of these so-called "Pfälzer" is a problem in itself, which shall not further concern us here. This first group of colonists left England in January, 1710, had a hard journey and soon met an adverse fate.

The leader, von Graffenried, remained in England, waiting for a second, smaller group of colonists which came from the canton of Bern. For the establishment of the colony, von Graffenried, together with other business men in Bern, had formed a stock company whose chief purpose was to recruit emigrants and to arrange for their equipment and transportation.

The government of Bern gave money for the support of the undertaking, since the people interested were chiefly from the poorer families. At the same time it wished to take advantage of the opportunity to force about 50 Anabaptists to go to America. These Anabaptists, under police guard, actually did embark in Bern with the other emigrants on March 18, 1710, to be sent by the water-route, Aare-Rhine, first to Holland. But about half of them, who were sickly old people, had to be left behind in Mannheim, whereas the other half were set at liberty in Holland, by members of their faith there. These Bernese Anabaptists, therefore, did not reach North Carolina, but their companions, who did not belong to this sect, did arrive there.

Unfortunately the *List of Emigrants recruited by the Firm Ritter & Cie and supported by the Government* has not been preserved. It is, therefore, the purpose of our investigation to reconstruct this list as far as is possible from different sources and to give what information we can concerning the origin of the people there represented.

The number of the voluntary emigrants can be determined as follows:

(a) On March 11th the Bernese government petitioned the Imperial ambassador as well as the French ambassador for a free pass for about 50 Anabaptists, 12 guards and about 120 other emigrants (D. Miss. 41, 397).

(b) On March 17th, the day before their departure, a subsidy of 2120 Bernese pounds was paid out to the voluntary emigrants according to the Staatsrechnung (Official Account-book). Since 4 such pounds were the equivalent of 1 Reichstaler, this amounts to 530 Reichstaler, and since on March 2d the amount for every person, large or small, was fixed at 5 Reichstaler, one finds the number of subsidized emigrants to have been 106. Some individuals, who had more means, were given less or nothing at all, so the number of 120 recruited colonists, given above, is confirmed.

(c) According to the letters from the colonists published in the G. A. Annals, Vol. 11, pages 285/302, several people died on the tedious journey from Bern to England and two people stayed behind in London (p. 292). On the other hand, none of the 100 emigrants suffered death on the journey across the Atlantic (p. 287); in fact there was even an increase in their number by the birth on the ship of the little son of Bendicht *Kupferschmied* (pp. 290 and 298).

So then we have to account for about 120 colonists who set out from Bern and for about 100 who landed in America. Whether their leader, Christoph von Graffenried, his 19-year-old son with the same name, and the servants of these two gentlemen were included in this number, may remain an open question.

In order to obtain definite information concerning many of these individuals, we must consult the entries referring to them in the protocols (Manualen) of the Bernese government (R. M.), the letters from colonists, just mentioned, and finally the contemporary plan of the colony (G. A. Annals, Vol. 12, p. 104).

INFORMATION FROM THE RATSMANUALEN

1710, March 11.   R. M. 41, 280.

Anna *Griess* of Reutigen, whose property amounts to only 40 crowns, wishes to go to America with the emigrants who are prepared to depart. The government excuses her from paying the emigration tax and the Landvogt of Wimmis is informed of this fact. Anna Griess receives a passport.

(Reutigen is a village in the district of Nieder-Simmenthal.)

2

A passport is also issued to Christen *Küntzli*, who wishes to emigrate to America with his wife and six children. The family is granted 10 thaler as a viaticum. On the following day Küntzli is also excused from paying the emigration tax on his property of 60 crowns. It is evident from the entries that this man was a tanner and that he came from Biglen in the district of Konolfingen (41, 284). Küntzli's farm appears on the plan of the colony.

1710, March 13/15.   R. M. 41, 288/310.

The government gives instructions to the Committee in charge of the matter of emigration to talk with Mr. Ritter and see whether a woman named *Bärtschi*, who is at present in custody, cannot be sent along with the company. She has often caused the authorities trouble. Since Mr. Ritter is willing, the Chief of Police is ordered to pay a viaticum of 22 thaler for this good-for-nothing person, so that they may be rid of this burden. Her given name is not recorded. She is usually referred to by the nickname "Bärtscheli."

In the records of the Divorce Court of this period there are numerous references to this person. Her name was Johanna Magdalena Bärtschi and she came from a middle-class family in the city of Bern.

(At about the same time the government had a number of good-for-nothing young fellows seized and sent away into foreign military service.)

1710, March 14/17.   R. M. 41, 295.

The widow of Pastor Johannes *Lüti* (Lüthi) wishes to take advantage of this occasion to seek her fortune across the sea, with her two children. She is advised to obtain the consent of her relatives and of the commune of Signau, which has been acting as guardian.

After this has been done, a passport for Virginia is made out to this family, consisting of the mother, a son and a daughter.

Pastor Johannes Lüti, who was last active in Dürrenroth in the Emmen valley, was dismissed from there in 1703, because of bankruptcy, and died some time afterward. His wife Johanna Salome, née May, came from a patrician family in the city of Bern. She was baptized on November 24, 1664, and was therefore in her 46th year at the time of the emigration. Out of the ruins of their fortune a little property had been saved for her and this was administered by her husband's native commune, Signau, in the district of that name. The mother and the daughter gave up their land-right and received their share of the property, but the son, who went with them, retained his land-right and had to leave his share in the country.

1710, March 17.   R. M. 41, 322/23.

The government instructs the Landvogt of Lausanne to give to the *Real* brothers and to a certain *des Ruines* the permission to emigrate to Pennsylvania for which they have petitioned. It is probable, but by no means certain, that these people later joined the colonists who left on March 18th.

Total, 16 Persons

INFORMATION FROM LETTERS OF THE COLONISTS

We shall examine these letters in the order in which they appear in the *German American Annals*, New Series, Vol. 11, 285–302, and shall refer to them by the numbers 1–10.

1st Letter

The author of the letter, Hans *Rüegsegger*, states that his son, who bore his name, has died in the colony and that his daughter, the wife of Bendicht *Kupferschmied*, bore a son on the way over. No mention is made of the mother Rüegsegger, but the "household" is spoken of. Since the father and son-in-law have two farms a half mile distant from each other, it is to be assumed that the former, after the death of his son, had at least his wife with him.

Rüegsegger's farm as well as Kupferschmied's appears on the plan of the colony.

Both of these names would indicate that these people came originally from the Emmen valley, as would also the names of the persons in their old home mentioned in the letter. The locality, Niederey, which is also mentioned in the letter, is situated in the commune of Röthenbach, where the Rüegsegger family still has home rights. Kupferschmied probably came from the nearby commune of Eggiwil.

Since the writer of the letter sends friendly greetings to the pastor of his native village, he was probably not secretly an Anabaptist, although one might conclude this from the religious tone in which he concludes his letter. The merciless treatment which the Baptists received at the hands of the Bernese authorities and which Rüegsegger witnessed, evidently so outraged this simple man of the people that he prizes most highly the religious freedom which he found in America.

(About 6 Persons.)

2d Letter

The writers of the letter are Samuel Jacob *Gabley* and his wife Margareth *Pfund*, whom he had married since leaving home and who came from Zweisimmen. The husband, too, is surely from the same neighborhood (District of Ober-Simmenthal) where there are still many members of the *Gobeli* family, as the name is commonly written to-day, in the three communes of Boltigen, St. Stephan and Zweisimmen. On the plan of the colony the property of the young married couple appears under the name Gobeli.

(2 Persons.)

3d Letter

The writer of the letter, Jakob *Währen*, says himself that he comes from Zweisimmen and that his brother has not been able to find time to write. The name is now written *Werren*. The adjoining farms of the two brothers appear on the plan of the colony.

In addition to this, a tailor, named *Graf*, who has married in the colony a woman named *Monzua*, is mentioned in the letter in an ironical tone. The latter, at least, seems to be known to the person to whom the letter is addressed, probably the tailor also. The Graf family is represented in the commune of Lenk not far from Zweisimmen, and elsewhere. The Monzua woman, however, can not be identified. There are people by the name of Munz in various parts of the Unterland.

(4 Persons.)

4th Letter

This letter, which is only partly legible, was written by a widow, Anna Eva *Zautin*. Her husband, Johannes Zaut (the correct spelling is *Zaugg*), has died on the journey and also her little daughter Katharina. Her relatives live in Eriswil in the Vogtei 'of Trachselwald, where the family still flourishes.

(3 Persons.)

5th Letter

This letter is one of the most difficult in the whole collection, because the names of various places and people are badly garbled in it. It is certain that the letter, which petitions for the payment of a legacy, was attested by the Landgraf Christoph *von Graffenried* and by the clerk (Landschreiber) Johann Jacob *Götschi*. Götschi, whose farm appears on the plan of the colony, probably came from the Aargau or from the vicinity of Murten; he doubtless did not attain the position of clerk and captain until he came to Carolina.

The relationships of the family in question seem to be as follows:

Bendicht *Simon* and his wife, whose maiden name was Schetele (the correct spelling is Schädeli), emigrated with 5 children, namely Katharina, Madlena, Anna Margaretha, Johann and Maria Magdalena.

The parents have since died, as has also the daughter Katharina.

The daughter Madlena, née Simon, has married Joseph *Stern* of Riggisberg (District of Seftigen) and has by this marriage a son, Johannes Stern. Her second husband's name is Jacob *Himler* (?) and he is from Madiswil (District of Aarwangen).

A third daughter, Anna Margaretha, née Simon, has married in the colony Andreas *Beinmann* or *Weinmann*, who comes from Mentzingen (Menziken in the canton of Aargau).

The son Johann Simon resides in the colony.

The fourth daughter, Maria Magdalena, née Simon, stayed behind in London with her husband, Johann Heinrich *Hans* (?) of Buchse.

The Simon and Schädeli families have home rights in the neighborhood northwest of the city of Bern. The family Krächig in the old home (the name should be spelled Kräuchi), which is mentioned in the letter, also have home rights in that vicinity.

(Counting the Landgraf and the clerk [Landschreiber] at least 14 emigrants. The clerk, who has a farm, probably also has his family with him, so that one may set this number still higher.)

6th Letter

The writer of the letter, Bendicht *Zionien* (correctly written Ziörjen), gives very little information concerning his personal affairs. The Ziörjen family comes from Zweisimmen in Ober-Simmenthal.

On the plan of the colony two farms are indicated of which one belongs to the Ziörjen brothers and the other to Jakob Ziörjen. One cannot tell whether Bendicht resided on the first of these farms, since he makes no mention of a brother in the colony.

(1 Person.)

7th Letter

The writer of this letter must be designated as *Anonymus*, since he has addressed it to Hans Wichtermann in Gutenbrunnen (District of Seftigen) but has signed no name. He has left at home in the commune of Toffen (in the same district) a capital of 45 crowns. He emigrated with his old father, his wife and four children, two of whom, Maria and Hansli, died in Rotterdam on the way. Anna

Wäll of Rümligen, who is mentioned in the postscript and who accompanied them on their journey, comes from same neighborhood. This name is now written *Wühl*.

(8 Persons.)

8th Letter

The writers of this letter are Mr. and Mrs. *Ziörjen*. The husband's first name is not given. The wife's name is Salome, née *von Mühlenen*, from Boltigen in Ober-Simmenthal.

The remarks concerning the 6th letter should be noted. In the letter with which we are dealing at present it is stated that this man named Ziörjen has amicably separated from his brothers. There are, therefore, at least three men of this name in the colony, a fact which must be borne in mind when reckoning the number of the colonists. We shall assume that one of the three brothers has been counted in the 6th letter.

(3 Persons.)

9th Letter

The writer of the letter is Christen *Engel*, who has several people living with him. His wife, Anni, or a daughter with this name, has apparently died on the journey. At his house or near him there is working a man named *Dietrich*, whom the people at home also know. People and places mentioned in the letter clearly indicate Eggiwil as Engel's home commune. (District of Signau.) Dietrich, however, who understood smithing, probably originally came from the Oberland from the vicinity of the Lake of Thun.

Engel's farm is indicated.

(About 4–6 Persons.)

10th Letter

The letter is from Christen *Janz*, whose name appears on the plan of the colony as *Janssi*. Both forms of the name, Janz and Janzi, are still found in the communes of Boltigen, Zweisimmen and St. Stephan in Ober-Simmenthal.

Janz emigrated with his wife and two daughters (perhaps more children). Mrs. Janz died in England. The one daughter married Peter *Reutiger* (Boltigen), the other is still living with her father. Her name is Dichtli (Benedicta). The farms of Reutiger, of Janz and of Zioria (the Ziörjen brothers) adjoin one another, according to the plan of the colony, and, according to the letter, are already in a much more flourishing condition than neighboring English settlements.

Janz has married as his second wife the widow Christina *Christeler* of Saanen. It is her third marriage. Her first husband was a certain *Plösch* (correctly written *Blösch*) from Mörigen (District of Nidau). A 13-year-old son by this marriage is still at home. This Christina emigrated with either her first or her second husband (whose name is not indicated) and three children and lost her husband and children on the journey.

A shoemaker, *Maritz* from Simmenthal, is mentioned as a fellow-colonist. This is perhaps only his given name. This man, whom the receiver of the letter knew, has died.

In addition to this, mention is made of Christen *Walker* of Saanen. Both he and his wife have died in the colony. These people, whose farm is indicated on the plan, have left eight children. (At least 21 Persons.)

Total, at least 66 Persons

Information from the Plan of the Colony

In the plan of the colony von Graffenried entered only the names of the owners of such farms as were occupied by Swiss colonists. In the preceding paragraphs mention has been made of such entries referring to the following families: Künzli, Rüegsegger, Kupferschmied, Gobeli, Werren, Götschi, Ziörjen, Engel, Janz, Reutiger and Walker.

In addition to these we find indicated the names of the Swiss owners of 13 other farms. Of these, the *Müller's*, *Nussbaum's* and *Buhlmann's* (Peter), who are still widely represented in Bernese territory, may come from many different communes. *Kistler* (Rudy) should probably be traced to Aargau rather than to the little city of Aarberg or to the commune of Hasle near Burgdorf. The *Hopf* family may have come from the little cities of Erlach or Thun, the *Haberstich* family probably from Aargau. *Z'öbrist* (now written *Zobrist* (Caspar) suggests the communes of Frutigen and Brienz, *Heimberger* (now written *Heimberg*) Oberwil in Simmenthal or Radelfingen near Aarberg. *Huntziger* (now written *Hunziker*) (Rudi and Samuel, each with a farm) is a family which is common in Oberaargau and Aargau. The *Raubly's*, the *Wyssmer's* (Johann) and the *Werger's* are still to be accounted for. No facts which would help in determining their origin have come to light.

The plan also contains the statement that 20 families have settled in the little city of New Bern. We may assume that not only "Pfälzer," but also Bernese resided in the little town, since pains were taken to enlist artisans when the Bernese colonists were being recruited.

If we therefore add only 10 Bernese families living in the town to the 13 farmer families just mentioned, and reckon the number of individuals in each family as 3, the information obtained from the plan of the colony would give us as a

Total, 69 Persons

From our references to the Ratsmanualen (Government protocols), the colonists' letters and the plan of the colony, therefore, we obtain as a result $16 + 66 + 69 = 151$ *persons*, that is, more than the 120 who left Bern and the 100 who arrived in Carolina. This is clearly to be explained by the fact that there were also Swiss among the first group of colonists, the so-called "Pfälzer."

On the other hand, it may be concluded from this discussion that it is possible to reconstruct with some accuracy the missing list of the people from Bern who left on March 18, 1710, for the New World.

(c) Bernese Soldiers in America

In the course of centuries more than 90 members of the Bernese family *von Erlach*, which is as flourishing to-day as it was in the fourteenth century, have held positions as officers in the service of the Empire, of France, of Holland, of Sweden, etc. Among them must also be mentioned a *Diebold von Erlach*, who perished in 1562 in Florida as a Captain in the French service [4] (Schweizerisches Geschlechterbuch I/104).

In general, however, the Swiss, who were very much sought after as mercenary soldiers, showed no great desire to sell themselves for service on the other side of the ocean. When foreign princes wanted to obtain Swiss soldiers, they had to reckon with the inland native's distrust of the sea.

In a report dated October 23, 1665, which the French ambassador to the Confederacy, François Mouslier, sent from Solothurn to the Minister of Finances and of the Navy, Colbert, he states that there is a large surplus population in the Reformed cantons and that France could get mercenary troops from there. However, the condition is made that these troops shall not be destined for the "islands of America" since they did not like to go to a land so entirely unknown to them and they did not like to cross the ocean. (Ed. Rodt, *Histoire de la représentation diplomatique de la France auprès des cantons suisses*, VII/56.)

---

[4] This seems to have happened during the Huguenot expedition sent out by Admiral Coligny, but this must be made the subject of further research.

When an attempt was made in 1720 to recruit soldiers in Bernese territory for the *Karrer Regiment*, which was to be sent to Mississippi, the government and the Commission on Enlistments (Rekrutenkammer), which was in charge of the official recruiting service, took action against this unwelcome competition. The following citations give information on this subject:

1720, Jan. 15.   Fremder Kriegsdienst, Generalia 7, 208.

The Commission on Enlistments conducts an investigation against a certain Steinegger who is convicted of having recruited men for military service "for the Mississippi in America" without permission. He was acting for "the occidental Company in France, for which company a certain Mr. Karrer, a native of Alsace, had undertaken to hire several battalions."

The agent Steinegger was forced to take service himself in a recognized regiment in France.

The officer in question was not a native of Alsace, but of Solothurn, and was named Franz Adam Karrer. Karrer, who had been active in the French service since 1680, undertook on his own responsibility in 1719 to raise a Swiss corps for the colonial service. The regiment, named after him and assigned to the navy, had as its headquarters the harbor of Rochefort and served the crown of France on water and on land in Louisiana, on Martinique and Santo Domingo.

1720, May 22.   Ibid., 7, 247.

The Landvogt of Yverdon is instructed by the Commission on Enlistments to give careful heed to the activities of "N. Merveilleux, Captain of 200 men recruited for Mississippi." It has been reported that Bernese citizens have been enticed to the border and forced into this service.

Nearby officials are also asked to be on the watch.

(This Captain Merveilleux carried on his traffic in human beings from the principality of Neuenburg. He was Charles-Frédéric de Merveilleux, a typical adventurer of that time. He personally took part in the campaigns of 1734–36 in Louisiana, then fought again on European battlefields and died a Catholic in Paris in 1749.)

1720, Sept. 18.   Ibid., 8, 7.

In the company for Mississippi or Louisiana for which N. Merveilleux of Neuenburg is enlisting recruits, there are in the first place criminals sentenced to be sent there, in the second place volunteers, and in the third place people who have been captured for this purpose either by treachery or by force.

So it happened that the Bernese citizen Daniel *Müller* of Steffisburg, while he was working in Neuenburg, was enticed to Valangin and dragged away to this service with his two minor sons.

The Commission on Enlistments requests the government to make a complaint in Neuenburg because of this event and to proscribe Merveilleux and his agents.

(This was done. To the protest of Bern the government of Neuenburg [Neuchâtel] answered that in spite of strenuous investigations they had not been able to obtain any definite information concerning the Müller case. R. M. 85, 577.)

1721, Dec. 1.   Ibid., 8, 25.

Frédéric *Vannaz*, of Gingins in the Vogtei Bonmont in Vaud, together with others was pressed into military service for Mississippi. He was able to escape, however, before they embarked, and is now to give information concerning the whole matter to the Landvogt in the presence of the Commission on Enlistments.

1722, Jan. 9.   Ibid., 8, 26.

It turns out that Vannaz had volunteered and had then run away. The Commission on Enlistments sends him word that he really ought to be sent to prison as punishment. Because he is not very intelligent, however, they will let him go free.

In another case from the year 1720 the Bernese government sought by diplomatic means to free one of the men recruited for Mississippi. The facts in the case were as follows:

Pierre *Sales*, the son of the stocking-maker of Lausanne of the same name, travelled to St. Laurent near Nîmes some months ago to visit some relatives. There he and some other persons, entirely unsuspecting, were arrested while at a prayer meeting; after several months' imprisonment he was put in chains on June 11, 1720, and transported to Brittany to be sent to the Mississippi. The first intercession of the home government with the French ambassador in his behalf was successful to the extent that at least young Sales' chains were removed in Rochelles. On September 26 the government directed a second letter to the ambassador requesting entire freedom for the prisoner. The ambassador on October 2d expressed his willingness to use his influence in Paris to this end. Since the documents are not complete, it is impossible to say whether Sales actually was set at liberty. (Frankreich-Buch BB, 445 ff.)

In addition to recruiting and impressing people for military service, the agents of Captain Merveilleux enticed also whole families, mostly poor people, to emigrate to Mississippi, while about 1725 the firm Pury et Cie., also of Neuenburg, was seeking settlers for Carolina.   (Erlach Buch C, 661 and 669.)

Both of these movements were confined for the most part to the Bernese territory in the vicinity of Neuenburg (Neuchâtel).   But in the other Landvogteien of the canton of Bern some emigration overseas was in progress during the 20's, as the cases *Bucher*, *Egger*, *Gurtner*, *Scherz*, *Schwarz*, *Stauffer*, and *Thomi*, discussed in the separate records, show.   The last three families belonged to the Emmen valley, the others to the Oberland, mountainous regions from which the superfluous population emigrates even to-day.

In a large list of Bernese officers who returned home from foreign service in the course of the 18th century only very few appear who have borne arms across the sea.   These are as follows:

Beat Ludwig *Braun* of Bern took part in all the expeditions in the West Indies from 1739 to 1744 under Admiral Vernon, and from 1750–57 he was in Surinam (Dutch Guiana, South America).

Georges du *Fes* of Moudon (Vaud) took part in five campaigns in America in the English service from 1756–60.

Abraham *Bonjour* of Avenches (Vaud) was in the same service from 1757–75 and fought in the East Indies as well as in the Philippines.   (*Wehrwesen* bis 1798, Nr. 242, 2, 79, 87.)

Concerning General Friederich *Haldimand* and his comrade Henri *Bouquet*, compare the separate records.   In the work by P. de Valliere, *Treue und Ehre. Geschichte der Schweizer in fremden Diensten*, the military exploits of Bouquet are described on pages 445/50. In the same place the following Swiss captains under the command of Bouquet are mentioned: the above-named *du Fes* (Fez), also Simon *Ecuyer* of Neuenburg, *Steiner* of Zurich, *Vulliamoz* of Lausanne, *Burnaud* of Moudon, Jean-Auguste and Marc *Prévost* of Geneva, all of whom distinguished themselves in the Indian War.

(d) FROM THE YEARS OF THE "RABIES CAROLINAE"

In the fourth decade of the eighteenth century, emigration overseas from the canton of Bern increased greatly, for the firm Pury et Cie., in English employ, was carrying on lively propaganda in Neuenburg (Neuchâtel) by means of numerous pamphlets and agents.   Colonel Jean Pierre de Pury founded the colony of Purrysburgh in South Carolina in 1732.   The movement reached its height in the years 1734 and 1735.   It had at that time assumed

such proportions that it can really be called an "emigration fever."
A Bernese official of the time coined for it the fitting expression
"Rabies Carolinae."

The authorities of the canton of Bern tried to restrain this emigration as much as possible, but they were at a loss to know how to
counteract the urge of whole classes of people toward better living
conditions.   The decisions of the government and of the Great
Council (Grosser Rat) in regard to the matter were therefore not
consistent, as the following examples will show:

1734, July 5/8.   R. M. 144, 92 and 123.

The government grants to Ludwig *Tschiffeli*, clerk of chancery
and of the archives, an honorarium of 100 thaler for translating
the Bernese Synodus (theological doctrine) into the French language.
In case he really intends "to seek his fortune abroad" he is to apply
to the mayor (Schultheiss) for permission to emigrate.

After this has been done he is granted a subsidy of 100 thaler
more in consideration of his services in chancery and for other
reasons.

From the Staatsrechnung (official account-book) of 1734, pages 90
and 98, we learn that Tschiffeli's goal was Carolina.   He received
also a modest compensation for his work in the record office of the
archives.   According to Gruner's Genealogies (Stadtbibliothek,
Bern), his wife, Johanna Catharina, née Herbort, went with him to
Carolina, but came back again.   In these meager notes nothing is
said of the reasons which led this man and wife from patrician
circles to turn their backs on their fatherland.   Religious beliefs
may have entered into the question, since Pietism had been accepted
by the Tschiffeli family.

1734, October/December.   R. M. 145, 1/284.

Hans Georg *Striker*, an armorer of Graubünden, who lives in
Steffisburg, is suspected of recruiting people to emigrate to Carolina.
He is watched and on December 11 he is ordered to leave Bernese
territory within a month.   Not long before this, people eager to
emigrate have gone to see him at his house.

On December 23, the government gives Striker permission to stay
in the country until spring.   He is strictly forbidden, however, to
encourage people to emigrate or to give them information concerning
Carolina.

1734, Nov. 26.   R. M. 145, 165.

Jacques *Bernhardet*, a proselyte, born in Burgundy, wishes to
emigrate to Carolina with his wife and two children.   The govern-
·ment has a viaticum of two thalers apiece paid to these people.

1734, Dec. 16. R. M. 145, 311.

Hans *Anken* of Wimmis, Christian *Rubiner* and Josua *Schoch* from Appenzell, who, however, reside in the Vogtei of Wimmis, and Abraham *Turian* of Därstetten wish to emigrate to Carolina. They are brought before the Landvogt. Because it is still midwinter, the government makes no decisions in regard to the matter for the time being.

On December 21, on the other hand, it refuses to issue any passport to Carolina to Daniel *Wüetrich*, a shoemaker living in Bollingen near Bern. The whole matter is being investigated (145, 335).

Although the government had been carefully advised by a Special Commission, which had studied reports from London and statements of officials concerning the matter, it came to no decision until shortly before the beginning of spring, *i.e.*, of the travel season. Then things took the following course:

After the Great Council had decided on February 23 because of the rapidly increasing emigration to Carolina to grant no more passes thither for the time being and to allow no emigrant ship to sail, the people who were thus hindered from departing submitted a petition for reconsideration. The Great Council consented to this and on March 2d gave permission to no less than 322 persons to set sail in four ships (R. M. 146, 215 ff. and 266, and Mand. Buch 15, 66). Unfortunately the list of people in question has not been preserved. According to the opinion of the government, the matter, after this one swoop, was to come to an end.

On March 13 it refused the petition of the cooper, Johann Jakob *Maser* of the city of Bern, who had decided to emigrate and asked for a subsidy (146, 337).

Among the people who announced their intention of emigrating there was a man from the district of Schwarzenburg, named *Bucher*. Since he was skilled in the healing of broken legs and similar cures, the government wished to dissuade him from his project and even commissioned the mayor (Schultheiss), that is, the chief magistrate of the state, to talk with him and to give him certain assurances (146, 354). Bucher, however, emigrated in spite of this, as will shortly appear.

The emigration for which permission had been given on March 2d did not immediately follow, since the matter, of course, had first to be published; it took place about two weeks later. On March 17th the government decided to return to the emigrants the tax which they had paid, providing they could produce receipts from the magistrates. At the same time those emigrants who had begun to hesitate were given assurances of different kinds if they would remain in the country (146, 368 ff.).

It turned out that *Striker*, the armorer, had been the leader of the crowd, a fact which angered the government not a little.

According to the Staatsrechnung of 1735, page 76, the emigration tax was paid back to the following people when they departed for Carolina:

Hans *Bucher* of Schwarzenburg	54	Kr.	18	Bz.	3	Kreuzer.			
Hans *Wänger* of Guggisberg	15	"							
Ulli *Gilgen* of Schwarzenburg	11	"							
Christian *Wäber*	"		7	"	12	"	2		"
Jakob *Stähli*	"		1	"					
Ulli *Mischler*	"		2	"					
Christian *Zwahlen*	"		1	"	12	"	2		"
Hans *Stüdler* of Oberhasle	31	"	2	"	2	"			
Christian *Meiden* and Hans *Egger* of Oberhasle,	13	"							
Madle *Rubi* of Oberhasle	13	"	20	"	1		"		
Simon *Zänger*	"		10	"					
Heinrich *Horger*	"		50	"					
Hans *im Aebnit* of Interlaken	27	"							

On the other hand, to those emigrants who let themselves be persuaded to remain in the country there was paid out for travelling expenses back to their homes the sum of 226 pounds, 13 shillings, 4 pence.

This list agrees in the main with the accounts taken from the Amtsrechnungen (official account-books) of Schwarzenburg (Grasburg) and Oberhasle.

In so far as the emigrants from the district of Schwarzenburg are concerned, we find them and other fellow countrymen again on the lists of passengers of the two ships and in the official document of the Provincial Council, all of which are dated August 26, 1735, and were made out in Philadelphia. They were published at the end of Volume I of the *Lists of Swiss Emigrants*.

With the help of these different references from their old home and their new one, it is now possible to give a good deal of exact information concerning several of the emigrant families in question and to quote correctly almost all of the names which were garbled in part. The entire work, however, is a beautiful example of the advantages of coöperation between friends of historical investigation on both sides of the Atlantic and has been a source of especial pleasure to the author of the present article. Thus, the following facts have been definitely established:

Bucher Family.   Came originally from Würzershaus near Schwarzenburg (commune [Kirchgemeinde] of Wahlern).   The head of the
family is Hans Bucher, 54 years old, a peasant and a self-taught
surgeon, whom the Bernese government would have liked to retain
in the country.   Since Bucher possesses considerable property and
is plainly the richest and most able man in the whole company, he
is looked upon as its leader and his name appears at the head of the
lists.   His wife's name is Christina Bucher and she is 35 years old.
The couple have two sons: Benjamin, 13 years old, and Christian,
10 years old.   A man who is probably a younger relative of the
head of the family is also named Hans Bucher and is 20 years old.

Wenger Family.   The family comes originally from the Ey estate
in the commune (Kirchgemeinde) of Guggisberg, south of Schwarzenburg.   The father, Hans Wenger, who was among the emigrants
from Bern, evidently died on the way, for his name does not appear
in the lists made out in Philadelphia.   The mother, Anna Wenger,
is 56 years old, the son Lazarus 19 and the daughter Anna 18.
They are people of means.

(The Wenger family, which has been divided into many branches,
can be traced back as far as the fourteenth century in the materials
of the State Archives of Bern.)

Kohli Family (not Koller).   This family is also widely represented
in the district of Schwarzenburg.   The father, Hans Kohli, is 40,
the wife Susanna 35, and the son Jacob 9 years old.

Brünnisholz Family (not Brenholtz).   According to the separate
report concerning this family, it comes originally from the commune
(Kirchgemeinde) of Wahlern, where some of its relatives reside in
the hamlet of Ried.   The husband, Christen Brünnisholz, is 39
years old, the wife, Anna, 40.   These people later, *i.e.*, in 1763,
settled in Cocalico township (as did Hiltbrand *Inäbnit*, who did not
emigrate until 1738 or 1742) and they seem to have been or to have
become people of some means.

Hans Binggeli, from a family common in this vicinity, is a young
man of 23 years.   The middle name, Michel, which was written by
a strange hand on two of the American lists, seems to me to be
questionable.   The strange scribe probably simply wrote Michel
for the difficult name Binggeli, and then the lad himself, who could
only write with difficulty, scrawled bingly after it.   The spelling Hans
Pinkley which appears on one of the lists is more nearly correct.

Christen Zwahlen, who also comes from a family common in this
vicinity, is a young man of 24 years, who has some money but who
can only write his name with difficulty.   The foreign scribes made
Swalher and Swaller of it.

Leuenberger Family. Members of this family reside in numerous communes in the canton of Bern, especially in the Emmen valley and the Upper Aargau. The family has produced two distinguished men—in the seventeenth century *Niklaus Leuenberger*, the leader of the Swiss peasants during the revolt of 1653, and in the nineteenth century the jurist and historian, Professor Dr. *Johann Jakob Leuenberger.* The family referred to here consists of the father, Hans Leuenberger, 50 years old, the mother Elisabeth 45 years old, the sons Hans 25 and Peter 8, and the daughters Elisabeth 20, Barbara 14, and Hanna 3 years old. (This is the most probable relationship between them.)

Abraham Mäusslin, a man of 43 years, wrote his name on two lists in firm, legible handwriting. The name was immediately Americanized by a foreign scribe into Abram Meeseley. The home of the Mäusli's, as the name is written to-day, is in the district of Seftigen, and at that time was also in the city of Bern. The handwriting would indicate that the man was probably from the city of Bern.

Johannes Marti, a man 44 years old, also knew how to write his name clearly and unmistakably. There are a great number of families with this name in Bernese communes and in the district of Schwarzenburg.

Mischler Family. This family also comes from the district of Schwarzenburg and possesses some property of its own. The man's name is Ulrich Mischler (Mesler, Meysler); he is a shoemaker by trade and 30 years old. His wife, or perhaps sister, is called Elisabeth and is 25 years old. A younger sister (probably) of the man is called Anna Mischler and is 13 years old. In the separate report concerning this family which refers to payment of property in 1751, another sister, Barbara Mischler, is mentioned.

Jakob Stähli, who comes from the same place, is a lad of 20 years with very little money. (Stelly, Staeley.)

Weber Family. These people come from the hamlet near the granary (Scheuer) in Schwarzenburg and have a little property. The husband's name is Christen Weber and he is 28 years old; the wife's name is Anna and she is 25 years old. A little three-year-old boy, Christen Weber, is probably her child, whereas a second Anna Weber, 20 years old, is presumably the sister of her husband and a boy, Hans Weber, 7 years old, his brother.

Gilgien or Gilgen Family. Considering the relationship between the sounds g and j and the singing intonation of these mountaineers, it is not surprising that the American scribes wrote the name of this family as Yelin and Yelia and that through further confusion it finally even became Willem. These people of modest means came from the village of Schwarzenburg. Ulrich Gilgien, a baker by trade, is 27 years old, his wife Barbara 25 years old. A second Barbara Gilgien, 45 years old, is either the mother or some other relative of the baker's. By mistake a lad 20 years old, Christen Gilgien, was entered on the list of the ship's passengers (Plate 13) in the women's column. According to the separate report concerning this family, the above-mentioned Christen Gilgien later sent considerable sums of money from Pennsylvania to his relatives in his old home. He died about 1750.

Magdalena Spring (separately reported) is 23 years old. She comes from the little village of Sädel near Gerzensee (District of Seftigen). She later married a certain Wüthrich in Lancaster.

Although these references are not quite complete, they do give reliable information concerning the group of people whom the ship which landed in Philadelphia on August 26, 1735, brought to a new home.

On the other hand, the most devoted efforts to determine the names of the other six persons which appear on the more detailed of the two passenger lists and in part also on the other lists have been utterly vain. The cases in question and the various ways in which the names are given are as follows:

Johannes *Etter*—Otter—Atterley, a man, 40 years old. There is actually an Etter family which has home rights in the neighborhood west of the city of Bern. The name of the woman who is apparently the wife of this man, and who is of the same age as he, is given as Mirgat Otlersin (??).[5]

Jakob Heinrich *Naath* (?)—Haross—Naws, a man 39 years old, has a wife 38 years old whose given name is Marie.

Apploney *Greeno* (?), 60 years old, might be an Appollonia Grünig from the district of Seftigen.

Pieter *Henckels*—Hankler, a lad 21 years old, may perhaps be identified with a Peter Kunkler from the same district.

With regard to the other people from the districts of Oberhasle and Interlaken listed above (Staatsrechnung 1735) we find information in the separate reports only concerning the *Horger* and *Inäbnit* families. The *Meiden's* or *Möuden's* have become extinct in the homeland. The *Rubi's* or *Rubin's* still have home rights in the district of Interlaken, but no longer have them in Oberhasle. The

---

[5] In the separate report concerning the Kurt family a Daniel Etter is mentioned who was in Pennsylvania in 1749.

Zänger's now write their name *Zenger*. The *Steudler's* (this is the present spelling) are the most distinguished of these families even to-day in the old home. Two men bearing this name attained the dignity of Landammann in Oberhasle in the eighteenth century. The district of Oberhasle was not governed by a patrician Landvogt, as were all the other Bernese districts, but by a highly respected native citizen—the Landammann.

In addition to the people mentioned in these statements, the following families or single persons emigrated to America in the thirties, according to the accounts given in the separate records: *Augspurger* (see Spycher), *Aebi, Bartlome, Berret, Burkhalter, Christen, Dällenbach, Frydig, Gohl, Gurtner, Hänni, Hubler, Huggler, Kislig, Künzi, Maurer, Nidegger, Sollinger, Spycher, Sterchi* (Oberburg), *Tanner, Tschanz, Valloton*. In some other cases the date is not certain, and many people emigrated without the knowledge of the authorities.

According to the letter from Esther Werndtlin in Philadelphia, Hans Georg *Striker*, the armorer, the leader of the large group in 1735, died in Philadelphia in the autumn of 1736, leaving a widow and a little son. According to the statements of the writer of the letter, he was not born in Graubünden, but in the Rhine valley in St. Gall (Wartau). (*American Historical Review*, Vol. 22/125.)

Finally, special mention must be made of the case of the *Consul* family which emigrated in 1735. These people came originally from Northern Italy, they were Protestant refugees and they emigrated to America by the round-about way of Geneva and Bern. The facts of the case are as follows:

In April 1730 Protestant refugees from Pragelas, a commune in the Alps west of Turin, 258 in number, arrived in the western part of Switzerland, and in July, 65 more followed them. Most of them found shelter in the French Landvogteien of Bern. A part of the fugitives sought refuge also in Hessen-Cassel, Holland and Great Britain. The States-General of Holland paid a subsidy of 50,000 Dutch gulden to the Protestant cantons for the support and care of these Pragelans and other Piedmontese, and the cantons themselves contributed to a common fund. The leader of the fugitives was the Sieur Consul, who travelled widely in the interests of these people. At the beginning of the year 1735 he was again in Bern and declared his intention of emigrating to Carolina with his step-brother and step-sister, probably with the purpose of founding a colony.

The Bernese government approved of his plan and granted the Consul family a viaticum of 150 thaler for the journey to Carolina.

(R. M. 145, 508.) On February 24, 1735, a passport was made out to them, sealed with the great State Seal, and issued to Antoine, Jean and Catherine Consul. (R. M. 146, 217. Also Eidg. Absch. 7, Abt. 1 in numerous passages.)

(e) NEWSPAPER REPORTS CONCERNING THE EMIGRANTS TO CAROLINA IN THE YEAR 1735

Concerning the fate of the Bernese who emigrated to Carolina at this time and the warnings which were given to those who were eager to emigrate, the "Bernische Avis-Blättlein" of the year 1735 gives further information.

No. 12. March 19. For the good of those who have no scruples against leaving their fatherland and going to a strange country, the following extract from a letter from a citizen of Bern residing in London is here inserted.

London, February 4, 1735.

"There have arrived here 340 Swiss who have no money left to pay for their passage to Carolina and who are in the direst need because of Mr. Pury's little book in which Carolina is represented as much better than it is and no mention is made of the difficulties, expenses, nor of how to plan for the journey, so that they are forced to accept any conditions, however hard they may be, in order to reach Carolina. Finally they have all departed in a little ship in which twice as many were placed as it will probably hold, so that in all probability many of them will die on the way. I am writing about this only from pity of these poor people, in order that they may not be led on to their destruction; for not only are they taken to the hottest part and to the borderlands of Carolina, but Mr. Pury requires of them a threefold ground-rent, and as I have said, makes them agree to pay over a sixth of the produce of the land to him. I have also heard that Mr. Pury treats the German Swiss very badly; he makes them work for him a half year before he assigns their land to them; he also sells rum to those who like to drink, in return for which they must work his land for him, and so Mr. Oglethorp who is a member of Parliament (Parlaments-Herr) and trustee of Georgia, had the bottoms of all the casks broken, since it is a practise very harmful to the people to sell them this liquor; so that when the people complained, this gentleman, when he was in that country, put them under the supervision of a German, in order that Mr. Pury should no longer have control over them."

This is therefore in brief the report, anyone who wishes to know more particulars from this letter can call at the Bureau of Information (Berichthaus) where he will be shown where to obtain them.

No. 22. June 4. Reliable account of the people from Bern who recently set out in three ships for the English colony of Carolina. After they left here they were 53 days on the way to Rotterdam because of bad weather and water, but contrary to expectation they passed the Rhine safely and without mishap, but with three times as much expense as they had expected, and on May 19th they arrived in Rotterdam, but those who wanted their money changed had to pay 7 per cent, the 21st of May they embarked there, 300 of them in one ship, in which a grown person had to pay 30 crowns for passage, in the hope that in seven weeks the journey might be ended, but doubtless in the belief that many of them by that time would have sailed for eternity. Although only three children, a lad of 18 years and the 82-year-old woman and the sailor Mosimann, who was usually vigorous, died on the way, probably most of them, alas! will scarcely see that Carolina which they have so desired and longed for, to say nothing of finding the earthly happiness and pleasure to which they have looked forward. Anyone who wishes to write to these people in Carolina about their affairs may address himself S. T. to Mr. Jacob Hoppen in Rotterdam.

No. 37. **September 10.** At the Bureau of Information (Berichthaus) here there is to be had: A Farewell Address which was delivered partly orally, partly in writing to those people from the Oberland (Oberländer) who longed to go to the famous Carolina and who departed thither in spite of all the difficulties lying in their way and of all the warnings and cautions which were given them, for their constant and sincere instruction as to how they shall conduct themselves, in all the adventures and adversities that may befall them, for the salvation of their souls.   Together with an account of the strange and previously unknown adventures which overtook these people on their journey from Bern to Rotterdam. With edifying reflections on the subject.   By Samuel *Lucius*, Pastor at Amsoltingen, in 8° 1735.   Price 2 Batzen each in albo.

No. 42. **October 15.** According to the Advis-Blatt of Zürich, a Pastor of Glarus, who is at present in London and very much respected there, has written the following in a letter to his father: With regard to the colonies in Carolina—I cannot advise anyone to go there! the land is good but it is entirely overgrown with forests.   The heat is very great there and those who go there suffer a great deal. I am in charge, under the Bishop of London, of ecclesiastical matters, not only in Carolina, but in all the West Indies, and I receive letters from both places. The last which I have had from Carolina, report that they have enough vegetables and garden truck, but neither meat nor grain.   Moreover, every one who goes there has to pay 5 pounds sterling passage money.   Several people from Zürich, Bern and Pündin have come here in the hope of obtaining free passage, but found things quite different from what they had expected, so that some have been obliged to beg, others to return home in great poverty and still others have died of poverty and disappointment.

No. 43. **October 22.** The letter from London contained in our recent issue concerning the journey to Carolina, agrees with the printed "Hinckenden Bott von Carolina" and with the descriptions of some soldiers who were formerly garrisoned at Namur, but who have now returned home, who cannot tell enough of the misery of the poor wandering Pilgrims to Carolina and who state that every man there considers it great good fortune to be able to enter military service.

All this is taken from the Avis-Blatt (or Advis-Blatt = *Intelligencer*) of Zürich.

III

LISTS OF EMIGRANTS FROM VARIOUS DISTRICTS

DISTRICT (LANDSCHAFT) OF OBERHASLE

1733/35.   Oberhasle, Amtsrechnung.

The following have emigrated to Carolina:

Heinrich *Horger* with wife and child.   Paid on 500 crowns an emigration tax of 166 pounds, 13 shillings, 4 pence.[1]

Simon *Zenger* with wife and child.   Paid on 100 crowns an emigration tax of 33 pounds, 6 sh., 8 d.

Peter *Egger* paid on 25 crowns an emigration tax of 8 pounds, 6 sh., 8 d.

The following also wished to emigrate to Carolina, but came back again from Bern:

Jacob *Ammacher* paid on 138 crowns, 2 Batzen, 2 Kreuzer, an emigration tax of 46 pounds,—8 pence.

Hans *Steüdler* paid on 311 crowns an emigration tax of 103 pounds, 13 sh., 4 d.

Christen *Möüden* paid on 100 crowns an emigration tax of 33 pounds, 6 sh., 8 d.

Hans *Egger* paid on 30 crowns an emigration tax of 10 pounds.

(Since neither in this account-book (Rechnung) nor in the next is it stated that this money was returned to the four would-be emigrants above mentioned, it is probable that they, too, finally emigrated.)

1744.   Oberhasle, Amtsrechnung.

On March 18th the emigration tax was paid by the following emigrants to Carolina:

Mosi *Schläppi*	23 pounds	6 sh.	8 d.			
Heinrich *Banholtzer*	11	"	2	"	—	
Madlena *von Bergen*	43	"	6	"	8	"
Barbara *Nägeli*	63	"	6	"	8	"
Melcher *Oth*	39	"	13	"	4	"
Jacob *am Acher*	6	"	13	"	4	"

(The district of Oberhasle, from which all these people came, is in the territory of the highest Bernese Alps.   The names of the cantons of this district are Gadmen, Guttannen, Hasleberg, Innertkirchen, Meiringen, the principal community, Schattenhalb.   Many members of the families mentioned in these two lists are still living

[1] Since the emigration tax amounted to ten percent, it is evident from the Bernese calculations above that the Swiss crown was estimated at about three times the value of the Swiss pound (lb.).   20 shillings were equivalent to one pound, and twelve pence to one shilling; 15 batzen were equal to one gulden or florin.   The equivalents in American money have been most variously estimated, for the crown, from 75 cents to three dollars; for the Swiss pound from 30 cents to one dollar; for the gulden (fl.) 45–50 cents (the batzen about 3 cents); the Carolina pound was worth about three dollars.   The currency fluctuated, and the purchasing power of money varied still more.

in this district, with the exception of the Möüden family. The spelling of the family names is almost identical throughout, except that we now write Amacher and Banholzer.)

EMIGRANTS FROM THE LANDVOGTEI OF GRASBURG (SCHWARZENBURG)

1734/35.   Schwarzenburg, Amtsrechnung.

The following men from the district (Amt) of Schwarzenburg have emigrated to Carolina and have paid the emigration tax of the property which they took with them as follows:

	Property	Tax
1. Christen *Wäber*, bei der Scheuer........	150 crowns	15 crowns.
2. Jacob *Stähli* of Schwarzenburg.........	20 "	2 "
3. Christen *Zwahlen*.....................	30 "	10 pounds.
4. Hans *Mischler*, the shoemaker..........	40 "	4 crowns.
5. Hans *Bucher* of Würtzershaus..........1099	"	109 cr. 22 Btz. 2 Kr.
6. Ulli *Gilgien*, the baker of Schwarzenburg..	220 "	22 crowns.
7. Hans *Wenger*, in der Ey..............	300 "	100 pounds.

Of the 7 emigrants above mentioned those numbered 1, 2, 3, 5 and 6 appear on the lists of immigrants made in Philadelphia on August 26, 1735 (*Lists of Swiss Emigrants* 1, 101 ff.). On these lists some of the names are misspelled, viz., Zwahlen (Swaller, Zwallen) and Gilgien (Yelin, Yilia). Most of the other people who appear on the lists of the 26th of August, 1735, are from the same neighborhood as the five who have been identified (Winger—Wenger; Brenholtz—Brünnisholz; Pinkley—Binggeli; Lyinburger—Leuenberger; Meeseley—Mäusli; Messler—Mischler).

EMIGRANTS FROM THE LANDVOGTEI OF INTERLAKEN

1744.   Interlaken, Amtsrechnung.

On March 9 I have received from the following people departing for Carolina the emigration tax as follows:

1. From Hans *Bläüwer* (now written Bleuer), father and son, of Grindelwald, on 1200 pounds withdrawn @ 10%...120 pounds.				
2. From Peter *Roth* on 600 pounds.................. 60	"			
3. From Andres *Schlegel* on 400 pounds.............. 40	"			
4. From Heinrich *Burgener* on 300 pounds............ 30	"			
5. From Hans *Egger* on 20 crowns................... 6	"	13 sh. 4 d.		
6. From Walthard *Kauffmann* on 200 crowns.......... 66	"	13 " 4 "		
7. From Hans *Müller* on 500 pounds................. 50	"			
8. From Walthard *Brawand* on 20 crowns............. 6	"	13 " 4 "		
9. From Peter in Aebnit in the name of Hiltbrand *in Aebnit* on 1000 pounds.........................100	"			
(This Peter is also designated as a "Carolinian" (Caroliner) by the Landvogt on January 29.)				
10. From Hans *Aebiger*, of Wilderswil, on 50 crowns..... 16	"	13 " 4 "		
11. From Hans *Perret*, of Ringgenberg, on 100 crowns.... 33	"	6 " 8 "		

Total 530 " — —

(These people came from Grindelwald or other communes in the present district of Interlaken. The families are still to be found in these communes, except that there are no longer Perret's in Ringgenberg on the Lake of Brienz, but Bernet's in Grindelwald.)

EMIGRANTS FROM THE LANDVOGTEI OF MOUDON

This Landvogtei in the French-speaking territory belonged to the canton of Bern until 1796; since then it forms a part of the canton of Waadt (Vaud).

1782.   Etat der Landesabwesenden, S. 167/71.

The Landvogt of Moudon reports to the government that many people from his district (Vogtei) have settled abroad. In America there are:

N. N. *Guidroz,*
Samuel *Cholet,* son of Gabriel,
Abraham *Cholet,*
Constantin *Cholet,*
Louis *Faucherre,*
Jean *Fabri*

> all from the city of Moudon itself. Constantin Cholet emigrated only a few years ago. The other five have been gone a long time (p. 167).

François *Ehinguer* from the commune of Lucens (p. 168).
Jacques David *Estopey* from the commune of Trey. Absent 10 years (p. 169).
Michel *Cornu* from the commune of Villars-Mendraz, residing in Quebec (p. 170).
Jacob *Perroud* with his family from the commune of Combremont-le-Petit, residing in Quebec (p. 171).

EMIGRANTS FROM THE LANDVOGTEI OF ERGUEL

This Landvogtei was formerly a part of the bishopric of Basel and since 1815 forms the district of Courtelary in the canton of Bern. Part of the emigrants spoke French and were of the Reformed faith, part spoke German and were Anabaptists. The latter did not originally come from the district (Landschaft) of Erguel but from the German part of the old canton of Bern, where the Anabaptists were at that time being persecuted. They or their ancestors had fled to Erguel, where neither they nor the members of the Reformed church were annoyed on account of their faith, although the ruler of the country was a Catholic prince.

1754, June 27.   B. 116 (Ab-und Freizug).

Communication from the Bishop to the Vogt in Erguel

We have learned that some people from Erguel, namely Anabaptists, have now actually emigrated to America. When the steward (Schaffner) of Biel was in Pruntrut (*i.e.,* in the capital) recently and was asked why he brought so little money with him, he gave as the reason the fact that the Anabaptists before they left had collected all the money due them, so that the peasants had little cash at their disposal.   When the steward (Schaffner) was asked whether he had not received any emigration tax from these emigrants, he answered that the Landvogt had probably collected it.

The Landvogt is now asked for information concerning the collection of this emigration tax.

The Landvogt's answer has not been preserved; but it is evident from the records that most of the emigrants were poor and could pay little or no tax money.

It is to be noted that the administration of the Landvogtei of Erguel was in the hands of both the Landvogt in Courtelary and the steward (Schaffner) in Biel, so that the emigration tax moneys finally do appear in the steward's accounts (Schaffnerrechnungen). In the following extracts the amounts which the individual emigrants were obliged to pay were, for the most part, not given, because the account would otherwise have become too voluminous.

The German family names suggest Anabaptists: Brechbühler, Burckhalter, Gouman (Gäumann), Liechti, Moser, Neuenschwander, Neukommet (Neukomm), Schanz (Tschanz), Schönauer, Schwarz, Stauffer, Wenger.

1754.   Bielische Schaffnerei-Rechnung.

The following have paid the tax before emigrating to America:

Hans *Schwarz*
Jost *Schönauer*
Isaac *Neuenschwander*
Niclaus *Moser*

Magdalena *Stauffer*
Ulrich *Neukommet*
Bäbi *Burckhalter*

All people from the mountains near Corgémont; most of them very poor.

Jean Pierre *Cuguet* took 380 crowns with him.
Jean Pierre *Raiguel* "   120   "   "   "
Abraham *Raiguel*   "   60   "   "
Jean Pierre *Voisin*   "   100   "   "   "

These four people from Corgémont pay no tax. They declared that they only wished to take a trip to America. However, in case they remain in America they will pay the tax later.

(Adam *Maire* of Tramelan goes, without his wife, only as far as Holland.)
Hans *Schanz* from la Chaux d'Abelle.
Christen *Neukommet* of Cormoret.
The widow J. *Huguelet* from Vaufelin possesses absolutely nothing.
Jean-Jacques *Raiguel* from Corgémont.
David *Trotier* from Corgémont.
Jean-Jacques *Pic* from Tramelan, poor.
Jos. *Wenger* from la Hutte.
Peter *Schwarz*
Joh. *Gouman*
Christen *Schwarz*
None of these three pay a tax. They took with them only what they had received from the canton of Bern.
Jean Pierre *Estienne* from Tramelan.
David *Estienne*
Jean Jacques *Guenin*
Marianne *Guenin*
All three are from Tramelan and form one household.

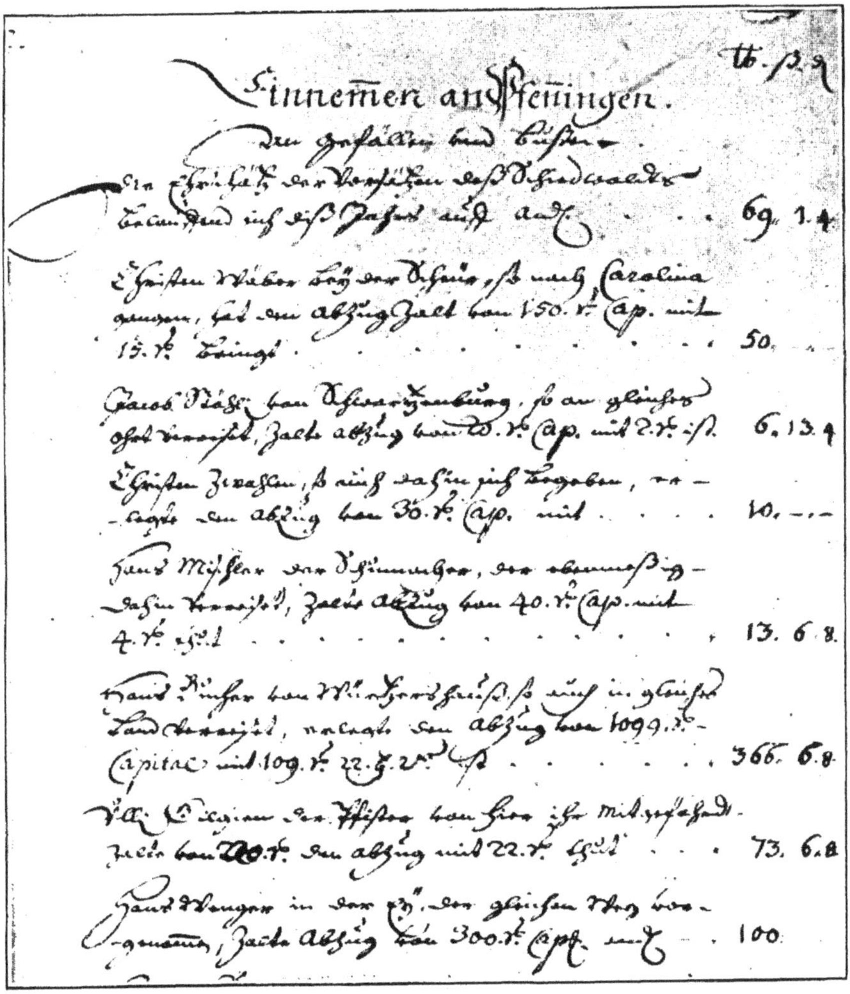

Plate 2

SINNEMMEN TO PFENNINGEN: ACCOUNTING OF EMIGRATION TAXES, 1734–35.
(See p. 28.)

Friederich *Lingme* from Cormoret, poor.

The widow Madeleine *Monin* from Tramelan, with five children. (She paid 200 pounds tax, more than twice as much as all the people previously mentioned.)

Adam de *Gomois* of Tramelan and his wife. (Pays 234 pounds emigration tax.)

Abraham *Brechbühler* and family } Very poor Anabaptists, who could hardly pay
Ulrich *Liechti* and family   } their rent (Hintersassengeld).

Jean Jacques *Villard* of Frinvillier and family.

David *Marchand* from Sonvilier. (The commune and the hospital gave him his travelling expenses. He started for America with 3 louis d'or.)

There are to-day in the district of Courtelary members of the families with French names appearing in these lists, with the exception of the Trotier family. The name Pic is still found in the neighboring district of Delémont. Some of the names are now written differently: Cuquet, Etienne, Liengme, Monnin, Degoumois, Villars.

N.B. The well-known book by E. Miller: "*Geschichte der bernischen Täufer*" (Frauenfeld, J. Hubers Verlag, 1895), gives detailed information concerning the condition of the Anabaptists in the bishopric of Basel (pp. 233–252). The fact that many Anabaptists emigrated from Erguel in 1754 is to be traced to lively propaganda on the part of emigration agents as well as to certain social conditions. Since the Anabaptists were skillful farmers and prosperous, they aroused the envy of the poorer native population. These tried to drive out the Baptists. Moreover, from about 1750 until 1850 a continuous migration of Anabaptists from the former bishopric of Basel to America was taking place. This was due to the fact that the industrious and temperate Anabaptist or Mennonite families throve and increased, whereas their goods and their land did not grow in the same proportion in the country which had been so long under cultivation. The excess population had to emigrate, but these people always kept in touch by letters with those related to them by blood and by faith in their old home.

Citizens of Bern in America toward the End of the Eighteenth Century

The following data are found in the archival section entitled WEHRWESEN bis 1798, Nr. 273–281.

At the annual arms-inspection held in the city of Bern, every able-bodied member of those civic organizations that had succeeded the proscribed guilds, was obliged to furnish proof of owning a rifle as prescribed by law. Unfortunately only the records of the years 1780–1797 have survived. In these the names of absentees are also given, including some who had gone to America, as follows:

1780.   Eyen, Friedrich, merchant (Schmieden).
        Wild, Franz, son of the deceased foreman (Affen).
1781.   Flügel, Wilhelm, born 1733, baker, in Brazil (Pfistern).
        Fueter, Ludwig Anton, born 1746 } Pfistern.
        Fueter, Daniel Emanuel, born 1747 }
          These Fueter brothers were sons of the goldsmith Daniel Fueter, who
        in 1749 had taken part in the conspiracy of Samuel Henzi for the over-
        throw of aristocratic rule.   Daniel Fueter got away safely in time, and
        was condemned to death in contumacium.   Not before 1779 was he
        pardoned and permitted, a feeble old man, to return to his native city,
        where he was taken care of by younger relatives of the above-named
        brothers.
                        Another son,
        Fueter, Sigmund Emanuel, born 1749, appears on the lists since 1785,
            with the remark that he is in America.
          In the records of the nineties it is stated that the brothers Daniel
        Emanuel and Sigmund Emanuel are occupied as goldsmiths in New
        York.   Ludwig Anton disappears from the lists in 1794, and presumably
        died in his new homeland.
        Stuber, Samuel, born 1737, son of the baker and fireman (Pfistern).
            From 1794–1797 he is said to have resided in Guadeloupe.
1782.   Rätzer, Johann Bernhard, born 1726, a goldsmith, in the English service
            as engineer-captain of artillery in Jamaica (Metzgern).
1784.   Haller, Albrecht Emanuel, born 1765, son of the clerk-of-the-court
            Gottlieb Emanuel Haller, therefore grandson of the famous poet and
            naturalist Albrecht Haller (Ober Gerwern).   This Albrecht Emanuel
            H. was active as a merchant, and returned to Europe.   In 1793 he
            was in Marseille, the following year again in Bern, where he entered
            the service of the state.
1785.   von Bergen, Karl Daniel Emanuel, born 1743, son of the tax commissioner
            (Pfistern).   He is said to have resided first in East India, then in
            America.
1789.   Roder, Johann Ludwig, born 1770, son of the tin manufacturer.   He is
            designated as a ship's clerk.   His residence is given as America, and
            also East India.   (He had visited the higher schools of Bern, but
            had not made good progress.)
1793.   Blauner, Johann Samuel, born 1773 baker (Pfistern).
          Most of these people appear year after year on the lists as emigrants, and
        probably remained in the foreign country, or otherwise have been lost track of.
          For several years, 1783–1795, there is named in the lists also:
            von Graffenried, Tscharner (Pfistern).   He was born in America, and is
            the grandson of the founder of Newbern, N. C.

IV

FAMILY NAMES, BERN

AEBI

1734, May 18.   R. M. 143, 336.

Communication from the Government to the Landvogt of Burgdorf

Hans and Christian *Aebi* from Heimismatt, parish of Heimiswil, are granted permission to emigrate to Pennsylvania. They must give up their land-right and pay an emigration tax of 10 percent on their property. They are to take with them their mother, an Anabaptist. Or else they must arrange with the commune for her support.

(Heimiswil is a commune [Gemeinde] in the district of Burgdorf.)

AEGERTER

1749, March 3.   R. M. 201, 9/11.

Communication from the Government to the Landvogt of Zweisimmen

Johannes *Aegerter* from Boltigen emigrated to Pennsylvania when a young man. His property in this country, amounting to 176 crowns, is being administered by his relative, District Treasurer Johan Aegerter. By a proxy, dated November 24, 1748, J. Aegerter commissions Johan Jacob *Walder* from Knonau in the territory of Zürich, who has, however, settled in Philadelphia, to withdraw his property in return for the surrender of his land-right.

Moreover, a teamster (*i.e.*, a man who transports goods with horses), Hans *Zmos*, of Boltigen also emigrated to Pennsylvania and has died there, leaving a considerable property. Here Zmos had left behind him a little daughter and debts.

The proxy, Walder, is instructed to renounce his claim to the 176 crowns in the possession of the Treasurer Aegerter in favor of the daughter of Zmos and the latter's creditors, in return for an assignation of the same value of 176 crowns on the estate of Zmos, deceased in America.

The Government approves this transfer and authorizes the Mayor to carry out the matter in this manner, if the Commune is agreed.

(Boltigen is a commune in the district of Ober-Simmenthal.)

AELLEN

1749, March 3.   R. M. 201, 11.

Communication from the Government to the Landvogt of Saanen

Ulrich *Aellen* of Saanen, residing in Pennsylvania, has commissioned Johann Jakob *Walder* from Philadelphia to withdraw his property in this country amounting to 260 crowns. As in the cases of Aegerter and Jaggi (cf. these!), Aellen's property shall remain in the country and be credited to the little daughter of Hans *Zmos* who died in Pennsylvania. In return an assignation of 260 crowns shall be made out to Walder on the estate of this Zmos. The government gives its sanction to this and sends Ulrich Aellen a letter regarding the surrender of his citizenship (Mannrecht).

1751.   Saanen, Amtsrechnung.

To Ulrich *Aellen* and Johannes Christoph *Hausmann* of Saanen, who have
been living in Pennsylvania for some years, the Government grants permission
to withdraw their property, amounting to 258 crowns, 18 btz., 2 kreuzer, through
their proxy, Johann *Kuhnrad*. The Landvogt receives the emigration tax of 10
percent, which amounts to 25 crowns, 21 btz., 3 kr.

(This Kuhnrad—also written Conrad or Konrad—likewise came
from the canton of Bern. See Konrad.)

1751, April 22.   R. M. 210, 21.

Communication from the Government to the Landvogt of Saanen

Ulrich *Aellen* and Johann Christoph *Hausman*, both of Saanen, emigrated to
Pennsylvania some years ago. In return for the surrender of their land-right,
they now desire, through their proxy, Johann *Conrad*, to withdraw the property
which they have in this country. The Government commissions the Landvogt
to relinquish the property after deducting 10 percent, unless some legitimate
opposition shall be made. Conrad's power of attorney is to be deposited in the
Commune as surety.

(Saanen is a small district in the Bernese Oberland.)

1759, Feb./March.   Saanen-Buch F, 713/17.

Ulrich *Aellen* of Saanen emigrated to America about 10 years ago and is
residing in Philadelphia. He gave up his land-right and withdrew his property
according to permission granted March 3, 1749. He is still credited annually
with 14 crowns income from a usufrucht in this country. This interest now
amounts to 140 crowns. Aellen commissions Christian *Fuhrer* of Langnau, who
also resides in Philadelphia, to withdraw this money and, in fact, without paying
a tax on it, since it is only the interest on a usufruct. In order not to delay the
proxy, Fuhrer, who wishes to leave the country soon, the Landvogt gives him
permission to withdraw the money without tax and reports to the government
concerning his action. In case the tax should have been paid, it is to be deducted
from the future interest. The government explains to the Landvogt that the
tax of 10 percent is to be required only in case the interest is on property belonging
to Ulr. Aellen.

ALLENBACH

1767, March/April.   Frutigen-Buch D, 1091/1103.

Elisabeth *Allenbach* of Adelboden, who was engaged to Gilgian *Rösti*, emigrated
in 1750 to Nova Scotia, against the will of her parents. Elisabeth was the daughter of David Allenbach of Adelboden and she left behind her in this country four
brothers and a sister: Abraham, David, Peter, Steffen and Susanna Allenbach.
They now request the government to allow them the usufruct of the interest on
Elisabeth's inheritance of 222 crowns, and their request is granted.

According to oral reports Elisabeth Allenbach died during the journey at sea.

It is not clear from the documents whether this Giglian Rösti also emigrated,
as may be assumed. It is possible, however, that Elisabeth Allenbach left because
she did not wish to marry this man.

(There are still many members of the Allenbach and Rösti families
living in the district of Frutigen.)

AMACHER

1742, Feb. 2.   Oberhasle, Amtsrechnung.

To Hans *am Acher*, who emigrated to Carolina, have been sent the proceeds
from the sale of his little house, 16 crowns less 5 pounds, 6 shillings, 8 pence
emigration tax.   This money Peter *Huber* will personally deliver to am Acher.

(Amacher is still a common family name in the district of Oberhasle.)

AMMANN

1752, July 17.   R. M. 213, 387.

The brothers Durs (Urs) and Philipp *Ammann* of Roggwil emigrated to Pennsylvania some years ago.   Durs has come home in order to take over their
inheritance of 425 gulden.   The government gives him permission to withdraw
the capital after paying the 10 percent emigration tax and surrendering their
citizenship (Mannrecht).   The Landvogt of Aarwangen is instructed to take
care that Durs does not entice anyone to emigrate and that he haštens his
departure.

The property which he has come to collect came from the grandfather of the
two brothers.   A tax of 85 pounds was paid.

(Roggwil is a large village in the district of Aarwangen.)

ANKEN

1706, Oct. 22.   R. M. 25, 371.

Communication from the Government to the Landvogt of Wimmis

Joseph *Anken* of Därstetten, a miller, wishes to emigrate to Pennsylvania and
asks for release from his land-right.   The Government grants him permission to
emigrate and authorizes the Landvogt of Wimmis to deduct the tax from the
property of Anken which amounts to 90 crowns and to have the surrender of his
land-right duly recorded.

(Därstetten is a commune in the district of Nieder-Simmenthal.)

BARTLOME

1733, March 19.   R. M. 138, 591/92.

Johannes *Bartlome* of Münchenbuchsee emigrated to America and has settled
in Philadelphia.   The government gives him permission to withdraw his maternal
inheritance, amounting to 140-150 Thaler.   The Landvogt of Münchenbuchsee
is instructed to deduct the customary emigration tax and to record Bartlome's
surrender of his land-right.

He had made a similar petition three years previously, but had
at that time been refused (126, 3).

(Münchenbuchsee is a large village in the district of Frau-
brunnen.)

According to the Amtsrechnung of Buchsee, the emigration tax
on 600 Bernese pounds (150 thaler) was paid at 5 percent,—30
pounds.

BERGER

1750, Feb. 4.   R. M. 204, 513/14.

The Anabaptists Christen and Hans *Berger* and their sisters Madle (Magdalena) and Anna Berger from the parish of Signau have settled in Pennsylvania. Their property in this country amounts to about 90 crowns.   Upon presentation of satisfactory warrants of authority the brothers are given permission to withdraw their property, but the sisters may do so only on condition that the commune (Gemeinde) gives its consent.   The Landvogt of Signau is to deduct the emigration tax and record the surrender of their citizenship (Mannrecht).

This case is noted in the Amtsrechnung of Signau. Christen Berger appeared before the Landvogt in person and paid the tax, but only on 80 crowns.

(Signau is a district in the Emmen valley.)

1750, March 10/21.   Büren, Amtsrechnung.

Bendicht *Berger* of Wengi in the district of Büren wishes to emigrate to Pennsylvania with all his family.   The government instructs the Landvogt of Büren to hold up to the emigrants all the dangers and difficulties of the journey and of colonization.   In case not all of Bendicht's children go with him, the share of the property due to those who remain shall be withheld.   Those who leave must renounce their land-right and pay the emigration tax of 10 percent on 79 crowns capital (R. M. 205, 208/9).

In the account book (Amtsrechnung) for the following year it is further stated that when Bendicht Berger departed he had received 60 crowns from his father-in-law, Gerichtsässe (Member of the Court) Schlupp, auf der Holen, who has since died. After his death the affair was discovered from his papers and the heirs had subsequently to pay the tax of 10 percent on these 60 crowns. Nova Scotia is here given as the destination of the Bergers.

(Wengi is a commune of considerable importance in the district of Büren.)

BERNHARD

1751, May 24.   R. M. 210, 281.

Christian *Bernhard*, the nail-maker, of Wiedlisbach, has no property, but has only debts, besides a wife and child.   The government has no objection to the emigration of this family; it commissions the Landvogt of Bipp, however, to inquire from the man who promised him to pay his way as far as the sea.   (Bernhard's home is also given as Attiswil.)

It is discovered that the following agents from the canton of Basel are involved in the matter: Bratteler, Joner and Tschudi. These were proscribed June 26 (210, 540/41).

Wiedlisbach and Attiswil are in the district of Wangen, as is also Seeberg, where the Bernhard family still has home-rights; this is no longer true of the other localities.

BERRET

1731/33.   Oberhasle, Amtsrechnung.

Heinrich *Berret* has emigrated to Carolina and has paid an emigration tax of 46 pounds, 13 shillings, 4 pence.

(The Berret family is extinct in the district of Oberhasle.)

1732, Jan. 28.   R. M. 134, 61/62.

Heinrich *Berret* of the parish of Guttannen (District of Oberhasle) requests permission to emigrate to Pennsylvania and to take with him his property of 140 crowns without paying the emigration tax. The latter request is not granted because of the orders prohibiting it. The Landammann of Oberhasle is instructed to let Berret go after he has paid the emigration tax and surrendered his landright. The government grants him for travelling expenses (Reisegeld) 14 crowns, *i.e.*, the emigration tax is returned to him in this form.

(In the district of Oberhasle, which enjoyed greater freedom, the representative of the government was called the Landammann.)

BOUQUET

A. de Montet in the *Dictionnaire biographique des Genevois et des Vaudois* reports as follows concerning this general who became famous in America:

Henri-Louis *Bouquet*, born about 1715 in Rolle (a little city in the Waadtland), served first in a Swiss regiment in Holland, then in Sardinia, where he became Captain.

In 1754 Bouquet entered the English service and undertook the problem of organizing the artillery and engineers corps of the Royal American regiment. In 1754, during the great war against the Mingos on the banks of the Ohio, Bouquet was given command of the troops sent out against these Indians. He was victorious over the tribe in several battles and finally conquered them to the last man near Bushy-Run, August 5 and 6, 1763.

Thereupon the English king appointed Bouquet Governor of the southern territory of English-America. General Bouquet died in 1765 in Pensacola.

BRAWAND—BRAWENDT

1764, January.   Interlaken-Buch K, 745/65.

In the year 1743 Walthard *Brawendt* of Grindelwald travelled with his wife and children from England to Pennsylvania. David *Roht* and Hans *Egger*, both also of Grindelwald, went in the same ship. According to the latter's story (Egger wrote from France in 1750 to the pastor of Grindelwald concerning the matter), the ship was seized by Spaniards. The men were then forced into military service. Since Brawendt was not able to undertake this, he and his family died of hunger and other privations. For the food supplies were not sufficient to provide for people who were incapable of military service. Roth himself helped throw the bodies overboard. The brothers Peter and Bartholome Brawendt and their sister Barbara, as well as other relatives, request the government for permission to divide between them the property of Walthard in his country. A certain Heinrich Brawendt, a brother of Walthard, also disappeared abroad 20 years ago. The property in question amounts to 500 pounds

Since the death of the Brawendt brothers was not conclusively proved, the request was refused.

(Compare the list of emigrants from Interlaken of 1744. According to this, the emigration did not take place until this year.)

BRÜNNISHOLZ

1763. Dec. 29.   Schwarzenburg-Buch O, 851/57.

Christen *Brünnisholz* of the parish of Wahlern emigrated to Pennsylvania in the year 1735 and seems to have settled in the same neighborhood as Hiltbrand *in Aebnit* of Grindelwald, who emigrated in 1738. These two had made an agreement whereby Chr. Brünnisholz paid in Aebnit 400 crowns. In return, the latter was to have the same sum paid out of his property in this country to the brothers Jacob and Peter Brünnisholz, auf dem Ried, in the parish of Wahlern. The request of the Brünnisholz brothers for the payment of the 400 crowns is refused, because, according to an order of April 26, 1742, and a decree of the government of May 17, 1763, in Aebnit's property in this country is at the disposal of the authorities and is to be administered by a guardian.

Ulrich *Brunner* from the canton of Zürich acted as the proxy of the two emigrants. He was himself also a resident of Pennsylvania.

(Wahlern, where the Brünnisholz family is still represented, is a commune in the district of Schwarzenburg.)

BUCHER

1724, Nov. 23.   R. M. 98, 616.

Peter *Bucher* of Uttigen requests permission to emigrate to Pennsylvania and to take his property with him. The government grants both requests in return for the surrender of his land-right and the payment of the emigration tax on his property. The Landvogt of Thun is also instructed to give Buchner a viaticum of 2 Thaler.

(Uttigen is a village in the vicinity of the city of Thun and in the district of Seftigen.)

BURGENER

1742.   Interlaken, Amtsrechnung.

On February 24 I have received from Peter *Burgener* of Grindelwald, who left for Carolina or somewhere else abroad, 100 pounds from the 1000 pounds which he had withdrawn.

(Grindelwald is a commune in the district of Interlaken.)

BURKHALTER

1735, Nov. 3.   Brandis, Amtsrechnung.

Hans Knobel of Schaufelbühl in the commune of Lützelflüh in the district (Amt) of Brandis has bought the homestead of Michael *Burckhalter*, who is believed to have emigrated secretly to Carolina, and still owes him a sum of 90 crowns. Since Burckhalter emigrated without permission and paid no emigration tax, these 90 crowns are confiscated by the Landvogt for the use of the government.

(Lützelflüh now belongs to the district of Trachselwald.)

CART. CANTINE

[Cf. Montet, *Dictionnaire biographique des Genevois et des Vaudois*, p. 128; *Revue historique vaudoise*, 1915, p. 77.]

1769 and 1793.

Jean-Jacques *Cart* (1747–1813), a politician from the Waadtland, was twice in America. He came from the little city of Morges on Lake Geneva, studied law in the Academy at Lausanne and then became tutor to the son of General Wood. Cart accompanied the latter to America and was in Boston 1769–1773. He returned to his native city and took up the practice of law. The outbreak of the French Revolution brought him into the political arena. Cart disseminated the revolutionary ideas in his fatherland and attacked the aristocratic form of government to which the German and the French territory in the canton of Bern were subjugated. He tried to separate the French-speaking Waadtland from the canton of Bern and to bring it under a French protectorate.

As a result of these activities Cart had to flee to France in 1791, where he became connected with the Girondists. The Minister of Naval Affairs, Monge, sent him to America in March 1793, in order that he might make purchases there for the French State. After the fall of the Girondists, Cart lost his official character. He became a planter; however he returned home in 1798 when the French had conquered Switzerland and had made a "Border State (Randstaat)" of it. A separate canton was then formed of the Waadtland, in which Cart played the rôle of political leader until his death.

In Ithaca, in the center of New York State, there still live direct descendants of this Vaudois revolutionary. One of them has in his possession letters from the period of 1794–1827. They are communications from Switzerland which Cart, his wife, her son and other relatives and acquaintances, as well as the executors of his will and the administrators of Cart's estate—Muret, Grivel and Berdez—sent to America to Jacqueline or Jenny *Cantine*, a daughter of J. J. Cart, who had married in America an American named John Cantine.

Cart, as has been said, emigrated to America in 1793 with his two sons and his daughter Jenny, leaving his wife behind in Switzerland. After a stay of two years in New York, he settled in 1795 in Rosendale in the Hudson valley where, with the help of some Swiss and of numerous slaves, he worked a large farm. Jenny, who was about 12 years old when she came to America, adapted herself quickly to the new circumstances, soon learned English and was on terms of intimacy with the other young girls of the Swiss colony, *e.g.*, the *Rossier's*, *Roulet's*, etc.

Near the estate in Rosendale there lived a General, named Cantine, who had taken part in the American War of Independence. He came from a Huguenot family of Bordeaux (Cantin or Quantin) which had been obliged to leave France as a result of the revocation of the Edict of Nantes. Jenny made the acquaintance of the son of this General, John Cantine, who later became a "member of the State Legislature," and she married him against the will of her father. The latter is said to have become so enraged at this act of his daughter's that he wanted to shoot them both. Later he grew calmer again, but he went back to Switzerland broken-hearted.

The young couple did not stay long on the General's estate in the Hudson valley, but moved over toward the center of New York State, where soldiers in the American Revolution could receive land from the State. On the banks of a little stream, which is now called Six Mile Creek, they took up their abode. At that time the country round about was still a wilderness in which one could find only a few poor huts. To-day it is the site of a fine village, surrounded by fertile fields, which is called Brookton. Here in this lonely place the young Vaudois woman spent 20 years of her life at the side of her husband, whom she bore 9 children. Here she received the letters from home (Lausanne, Morges, etc.); from her mother, from her father, who had become reconciled with her, as well as from other relatives and friends. These letters contain nothing unusual. Political events are scarcely mentioned in them.

About 1826 Jenny Cantine moved to Ithaca, where she died about 1858.

CHRISTEN

1735, March 29.   R. M. 146, 434.

The government is informed that certain Bernese subjects who wish to emigrate to Carolina are in London in great need and would like to return home. The government establishes a credit with the commission in charge of emigration, so that these people can be sent home again. On the other hand, the widow of Johannes *Christen* of Aarburg and her children shall be encouraged to continue their journey. The widow and the children shall each receive a guinea.

This Christen had been a proselyte. He came from Matzendorf in the canton of Solothurn and was brought before the Bernese Proselytenkammer (Commission on Proselytes) on September 26, 1710, as a member of the Reformed Church. He lived at that time in Oftringen, not far from Aarburg; both are localities in the present canton of Aargau. (Kirchenwesen 2, 122).

COTTIER

1781, May/June.   Saanen-Buch J, 585/99.

Pierre *Cottier* of Rougemont, a student of theology in the academy of Bern, emigrated to America about 30 years ago. According to private information, he is said to have died 24 years ago on an unknown plantation on the island of Jamaica. Pastor Nöthiger of Ringgenberg, Cottier's half-brother on his mother's side, requests the government that there be ceded to him the property of the missing man which was left behind with the commune of Rougemont. Since neither the commune nor the other relatives of Cottier protest against this, the government grants permission for the property to be ceded to Pastor Nöthiger. The claims of other relatives who might be legal heirs are reserved.

(Rougemont is now in the canton of Waadt (Vaud). Cottier— whose name is also written Gauthier—came from a respected peasant family, he studied hard and conducted himself with propriety. Because he was of peasant stock he was looked down upon by his fellow-students. The government, to be sure, definitely stated on April 3, 1753, that he would be admitted to the clergy after the conclusion of his studies. Cottier, however, preferred to emigrate. R. M. 217, 535.)

DÄLLENBACH

1732, May 12.   Trachselwald, Amtsrechnung.

Martin *Dällenbach* of Lauperswil has emigrated to America and resides in Schaggarill. He commissions his brother, Johannes Dällenbach, who has settled in Zweibrücken, to withdraw the property which he has in this country, amounting to 13 crowns, 10 btz., from which 10 percent emigration tax is deducted.

(The Dällenbach family is widely represented in the district of Trachselbach. The name is sometimes written Tellenbach.)

DEDIE

1754.   Münstertal, Schaffnereirechnung.

Abraham *Dedie* of Corcelles, who has emigrated to Pennsylvania, has paid on property amounting to 245 pounds, 10 shillings, an emigration tax of 10 percent, 24 pounds, 11 shillings, 3 pence.

(Corcelles is a little commune in the district of Moutier or Münster in the French-speaking territory. This neighborhood belonged in 1754 to the bishopric of Basel. The Dedie family has home-rights only in this one commune.)

DYSLI

1784.   Verzeichnis der Geistlichkeit.

In the spring of this year, the German pastor of Vivis (French Vevey, in the canton of Waadt), Heinrich *Dysslin*, because of debts and other misunderstandings, withdrew from his pastorate. Since he has not been seen again, the Government discharged him. Later it was reported that he had emigrated to America and had become pastor in St. Johnsville (New York).

Dysslin, born in 1752, came originally from the city of Burgdorf (canton of Bern), attended the higher schools in Bern and was ordained minister in 1777.   In 1778 he received the above-mentioned pastorate in Vivis.   He is said to have died in America in 1798.

EGGER

1762, October 21.   Frutigen-Buch D, 797/802.

Peter *Egger* from the commune (Gemeinde) of Frutigen, with his wife Verena (née Gillmann of Reichenbach) and his children, emigrated to Carolina more than 40 years ago and has not been heard from since.   His brother, Gilgian Egger, who died in the commune of Frutigen, left Peter a legacy of 1100 pounds.   The government grants permission to the relatives of the missing Egger to divide this legacy between them.   They must, however, give security to the commune.

(The large village of Frutigen is the most important community in the district of that name.)

EGGLER

1752, March 23.   R. M. 213, 333/34.

Ulrich *Eggler*, the former treasurer of Aarmühle, emigrated to Pennsylvania two years ago with two of his children and has settled in Lancaster.   He has now come home to take his wife and the other children, as well as his property of about 10,000 pounds, over with him.   In order to obtain the necessary permission he applied personally to the government, stating the reasons for his departure. The government grants him permission to take with him his family and also his property, from which the emigration tax of 10 percent is to be deducted as well as from the 66 new doubloons which he took with him when he first went over. The departure of the whole family is to take place before the first of May.   In addition to this, it is stipulated that Eggler shall not carry on any propaganda for emigration in this country,and shall not entice any one away.   Otherwise, the Landvogt of Interlaken is instructed to hold back his property.

1752.   Interlaken, Amtsrechnung.

On May 9, the former treasurer, Ullrich *Eggler*, who has moved to America, paid the usual 10 percent emigration tax on the property which he took out of the country with him with the permission of the authorities; his means amount to 3779 crowns.   Hence the tax was 377 crowns, 23 btz.

(This emigrant came from the neighborhood of Interlaken; he was a much respected man, who had held the office of treasurer of the district of Interlaken.)

ERHARD

1754, May 9.   Quodlibet 3, 983/990.

Franz *Erhard* from the city of Bern emigrated to Carolina, with two sisters. The sisters have married there and do not expect to return.   Franz has now come back in order to take over the property left by the mother of the three. This is being administered by the corporation of carpenters.

Franz Erhard is empowered to receive the share of the property belonging to his sisters and to send it to them after paying the tax.   He himself does not wish to return to Carolina, but wants to learn watch-making in Vivis (Vevey). He is also paid his share and retains his citizenship.

Exactly 100 years before this, an ancestor of this family had been granted home-right (Einwohnerrecht) in Bern. This was the cabinet-maker, Samuel Erhard (Erard), who came from Morges, *i.e.*, from the French part of the former canton of Bern.

This family has long since died out in the city of Bern.

FIESS

1772, March 21.   England-Buch D, 493/96.

Christen and Peter *Fiess* of Nieder-Wichtrach have emigrated to Pennsylvania and have settled in and near Philadelphia. Christen is a farmer and Peter a harness-maker. They have been left an inheritance of about 140 crowns by their uncle, Ulrich Fiess, and his widow, and also by Elisabeth Tschanz; this capital is being administered by a guardian in the commune of Nieder-Wichtrach. Through their proxy, Daniel *Kahn*, the two Fiess's request permission to withdraw their inheritance, and the request is granted both by the government and the commune. The emigration tax of 10 percent must, however, be deducted.

(Wichtrach is a commune in the district of Konolfingen.)

FRIEDLI

1751, April 21.   R. M. 210, 5.

Andreas *Friedli* and Hans *Schneeberger*, both of the Landvogtei of Wangen, and several Oberländer (inhabitants of the Oberland) wish to emigrate to Pennsylvania with their wives and children. There are also some people here from over there with warrants of authority, who wish to collect the property in this country of some who have already emigrated. All these matters are referred by the government to a special commission for investigation.

1751, April 22.   R. M. 210, 22/23.

Andreas *Fridli* of Wäckerschwend emigrates with his wife to Pennsylvania. They must leave their minor child in this country. The maternal inheritance is to remain here for this child and also a part of the father's property. The Landvogt of Wangen is instructed to make the division of the property, to deduct the emigration tax of 10 percent from the capital withdrawn and to record the surrender of the land-right.

(Wäckerschwend is a locality in the large commune (Kirchgemeinde) of Herzogenbuchsee in the district of Wangen.)

1751, May 29.   Wangen, Amtsrechnung.

Andreas *Fridli* of Wäckerschwend leaves with his wife for Pennsylvania. They take with them a capital of 185 crowns and pay 10 percent emigration tax on it—61 pounds, 13 shillings, 4 pence.

In 1758, according to the account-book (Amtsrechnung) of that year, Fridli fell heir to a legacy of 335 crowns from his daughter Barbara, who had remained at home. He has to pay on it a tax of 10 percent—111 pounds, 13 shillings, and 4 pence.

(Wäckerschwend is a hamlet in the commune of Ochlenberg in the district of Wangen.)

The above-mentioned Schneeberger also emigrated.

FRYDIG

1750, Dec. 26.   R. M. 208, 352.

Hans *Freydig* of Frutigen emigrated to America in 1735. No further news of him seems to have reached this country. He falls heir to a legacy of 75 crowns and his relatives here request that this property be given to them, since Freydig had said that he would give up his right to the legacy. The government, however, refuses this request on the grounds that the family circumstances of the emigrant are not known and that sufficient time has not elapsed for him to be declared missing. The interest on the capital, however, may be divided annually among the relatives.

(This family name, which is common in the district of Frutigen, is officially written Frydig. There are also Freydig's who have home-rights in Lenk in the district of Ober-Simmenthal.)

FUHRER

1754, May 18.   R. M. 223, 45/46.

The brothers *Fuhrer* of Langnau have emigrated to Pennsylvania. Born in the district (Amt) of Trachselwald, they possessed an estate named Löhren near Mett in the district of Nidau. The Landvogt of Trachselwald is instructed to place a steward (Vogt) in charge of the property which the Fuhrer's left behind, especially of the estate, Löhren, which was left unprovided for. The Landvogt of Nidau is instructed to make inquiries in the neighboring district (Landschaft) of Erguel, because so many former Bernese who were residing there have emigrated to Pennsylvania.

(Langnau is now in the district of Signau, Mett in the district of Biel.)

1757, Aug. 8.   Trachselwald, Amtsrechnung.

In 1754 Christen *Fuhrer* and his brother(s) and sister(s) from the district (Amt) of Trachselwald emigrated to Pennsylvania and settled in Lancaster. At that time they took 600 crowns with them. Now, with the permission of the government, they are taking over the remainder—1866 crowns. They pay the emigration tax of 10 percent, 246 crowns, 16 btz., 2 kreuzer, in all.

(The commune of Langnau now belongs to the district of Signau. The Fuhrer family is still to be found there.)

1757, Aug. 29.   Nidau, Amtsrechnung.

Christen, Daniel and Christina *Fuhrer*, who emigrated to Pennsylvania, have settled in Lancaster. The estate Löhren in the district (Amt) of Nidau, which belonged to them, has been sold, with the permission of the government, for 9733 pounds, 6 sh., 8 pence. The Landvogt receives the 10 percent emigration tax on this amount, 973 pounds.

GABI

1751, April 22. R. M. 210, 20.

Ulrich and Maria *Gabi* of Oberbipp have settled in Pennsylvania. Their proxy Johann *Conrad* (see Konrad) receives 400 gulden for the above-mentioned emigrants, under the usual conditions.

(Gabi and Conrad came from the present district of Wangen.)

GARRAUX

1768, May 3. B. 116. (Ab- und Freizug)

Communication from the Stadtholder of the Münster Valley, Bajol, from Delsberg to the Bishop

David *Garraux* of Malleray has a brother in Lancaster (Pennsylvania) named Jacob. Since their father, Jean-Jacques Garraux, has died, David would like to send his brother Jacob the portion of the paternal estate due him. He therefore requests permission to deliver this inheritance to his brother's proxies, Adam *le Roy* or Daniel *Kahn*, both of whom have also settled in Lancaster.

The answer is found in the "Cameral Bescheid-Buch," dated May 5, 1768, and runs in the same tone. David Garraux is granted permission to send to his brother Jacob in America 430 pounds, Basel currency; the legal emigration tax of 10 percent, however, is to remain in the country.

(Garraux and le Roy came from the French-speaking part of the bishopric of Basel, the former from Malleray in the present district of Moutier or Münster, the latter from Sonceboz in the present district of Courtelary, which was formerly called Erguel.)

GÄUMANN

1794, Jan. 21. Mittelwegziehungs-Prot. (Record of withdrawal of property) 3, 661/62.

Communication from the Government to the Mayor of Signau

Anna Schönauer, the widow of Christian Gäumann from the neighborhood of Zäziwil, parish of Höchstetten, has settled in Pennsylvania with the two sons which she bore Gäumann. In return for the surrender of the land-right for herself and her two sons she requests permission to withdraw her property which is at present being administered by the commune of Oberthal. Since there are many objections to the relinquishment of this, the proxy of the widow Schönauer, Notary Witschi of Signau, was refused his request.

(Grosshöchstetten, Zäziwil and Oberthal are in the district of Konolfingen.)

GERBER

1770, May. Wangen, Amtsrechnung.

About 17 years ago Felix and Barbara *Gerber* of Herzogenbuchsee emigrated to North America. The government gives them permission to take over their capital of 265 crowns, 19 batzen, which they had left at home. The Landvogt of

Wangen receives the tax of 10 percent—26 crowns, 14 btz. and 2 kreuzer, together with an extra charge of 1 crown, 10 btz., since the property is really larger than this.

According to the record in R. M. 300, 417, this Barbara Gerber married Andreas *Lanz* of Rohrbach. These people live in Pennsylvania and have commissioned Daniel *Kahn* of Lancaster to look after their affairs. The latter can prove that his principals are still members of the Evangelical Church and that they give up their home-right in this country.

(Herzogenbuchsee and Rohrbach are two large villages in the Oberaargau.)

GILGIEN

1750, Dec. 26.   Schwarzenburg, Amtsrechnung and
                                         R. M. 208, 352/53.

Christen *Gilgien* from the district (Amt) of Schwarzenburg has died in Carolina. To his heirs there is sent their property in this country, amounting to 572 crowns, 15 btz. A tax of 5 percent was charged. Urs Stöckli from Wallenried in the commune of Wahlern (Schwarzenburg) represented the Gilgien heirs.

Only a 5 percent tax was charged because Chr. Gilgien had sent considerable money over to this country from America. The Bernese government acts in this matter in conjunction with the government of Freiburg. The neighborhood in question, which is to-day Bernese, at that time was administered jointly by the two above-named cantons

GOHL

1735.   Aarberg, Amtsrechnung.

Jakob *Gohl* of Aarberg has emigrated to New Georgia. His possessions were sold at auction for 176 crowns, on which a tax of 17 crowns, 15 batzen was paid.

On April 1, 1735, the government discusses the case of the brother and sister, Rudolf and Katharina Gohl, who wished to emigrate to Carolina and had already paid the emigration tax. Then they repented. They each now receive a subsidy of 10 thaler from the government. The Landvogt is also instructed to return the emigration tax to them.

(Aarberg is a small city and the principal community in the district of the same name.)

VON GRAFFENRIED

1792, April 19.   Mittelwegziehungs-Prot. 3, 548/50.

*Communication from the Government to the Orphans' Court of the
City of Bern*

Mr. Christoph von *Graffenried*, who emigrated to Carolina, married in Charlestown in 1714 Barbara Tempest, née Needham. The issue of this marriage was an only son, Mr. Tscharner v. Graffenried, born Nov. 28, 1722, in Williamsbourg in Virginia. He is now residing in Lünebourg in Virginia and requests through his proxy, H. Simeon Busigny de Chavannes, that there be delivered to him the property which his father inherited in the year 1735, which according to the last official reckoning amounts to 28,122 crowns, 19 btz., 3 kreutzer.   The Government decrees: As long as Mr. Tscharner v. Graffenried has not renounced his citizenship, only the increase which this property has accumulated since 1735 may be remitted to him and that without any deduction.   The original capital of 22,000 pounds, however, must remain here until his renunciation of his citizenship.   In any event, Mr. von Graffenried can draw the annual interest from it.   In case the entire property is withdrawn, the Government reserves its right to the emigration tax.

(Christoph von Graffenried, born 1691, was the oldest son of the founder of Newbern and bore his name; Tscharner von Graffenried the latter's grandson.)

GRÜNIG

1780, June 9.   Mittelwegziehungsprotokoll, 1, 478.

Fifty years ago, Abraham *Grünig*, of Burgistein, emigrated to America.   His property still remaining in the country under the administration of the commune will now be turned over to the relatives.

(Burgistein is a parish in the district of Seftigen.)

GÜLDI

Samuel *Güldi* studied theology in Bern.   With three other like-minded fellow-students he was attracted to Pietism which was just coming into vogue.   Their inclination toward this new conception of religion and of the duties of a pastor was strengthened still more by travel abroad, so that they finally came forward in Bern as the first representatives of Pietism in the church.   Their attempts to meet the spiritual needs of the common people in their instruction and intercourse brought great numbers to their churches and attracted the attention of the council (Konvent) to them.   But then the persecution of the representatives of this new doctrine began.

At first the ecclesiastical and educational council (Kirchen- und Schulrat) was favorably inclined toward the Pietists, so Güldi received in 1692 the pastorate of Stettlen near Bern and at the end of 1696 was even called to Bern as Assistant.   But the opposition of the orthodox clergy won the upper hand.   So in 1698 a "special commission against Quakerism, illicit gatherings, and schisms in doctrine" was appointed to take action against the Pietistic preachers.   Güldi was dismissed from his position as Assistant, and his friends experienced a similar fate.   The government introduced the so-called Oath of Association (Assoziationseid) which even the preachers were obliged to take.

Güldi's trial took place December 5, 1698.   After his conviction and dismissal Güldi retired to private life in Muri (near Bern).

But besieged by his relatives and friends, he finally took the Oath of Association and was thereupon appointed to the pastorate of Boltigen in the Simmen valley. Here he preached with ardent zeal; but his conscience troubled him and so he begged the government to release him from his oath. He was dismissed and told to leave the country.

He stayed for some time with his friend, Beat Ludwig, of Muralt in Rüfenacht, and then emigrated to North Germany. From there he probably went to America and settled in Philadelphia in 1710. In 1719 there were published there his defense and apology, *i.e.*, his answer to the attacks of the commission on religion (Religionskommission). Güldi lived on for a long time in Philadelphia and was able to enjoy his religion in peace without being troubled by the authorities. He found in abundance in the New World that which the Old World had denied him. (Cf. W. Hadorn, *Geschichte des Pietismus in der Schweiz; d. reformierten Kirchen.* History of Pietism in Switzerland; reformed churches.)

According to the Taufbuch (Record of Baptisms) 11, of the city of Bern, Pastor Samuel *Güldi* and his wife Maria Magdalena, née Malacrida, have had the following children baptized:

Samuel	on November 10, 1693.
Maria Catharina	on January 8, 1696,
Christoffel	on July 17, 1697,
Emanuel Fridenrich	on March 13, 1699.

The above-mentioned Samuel junior is the same man whose will, from the year 1773, is mentioned in the Regest of February 23, 1790. In Samuel Senior's report of their journey in 1710, he says that on the way from England to Philadelphia no one of all the family was sea sick, "neither I, nor Susanna, nor any of my children." It is still to be discovered who this Susanna was. Nothing definite is known concerning the family circumstances of the Güldi's in the period from 1703 to 1710.

1748, Nov. 20.   R. M. 199, 446.

Emanuel Friedrich Güldi of Bern, who has settled in America, desires to renounce his citizenship in this country and withdraw his property. The government empowers the corporation at Metzgern, where the property was left in trust, to arrange the matter as they think best, and in case the permission is granted, to pay the emigration tax to the warehouse.

(The warehouse [Kaufhaus] in Bern was a store-house and custom-house. Its manager was entrusted with the collection of the emigration tax for the township. The Güldi family is extinct in the city of Bern.)

1790, Feb. 23.   Mittelwegziehungs-Prot. 3, 299/303.

Communication from the Government to the Corporation at Metzgern
(Subdivision of the City Commune of Bern)

Samuel Güldi, a citizen of Bern, emigrated to Pennsylvania in the year 1710. In his will, drawn up in 1773, he appointed as executors his 3 sons, Samuel, Johannes and Daniel. Besides these there are in existence a fourth son, Friedrich, and three daughters, the latter all married. The three brothers first named reside in Oley in Berks county in Pennsylvania. Through their friend and proxy, Martin *Gaul* from Philadelphia, they request the corporation of Metzgern to deliver to them their property of 6258 crowns which is still in Bern in return for the surrender of their citizenship and land-right. In regard to the latter matter, however, the proxy has no credentials with him.

The Government empowers the corporation of Metzgern to deliver $\frac{2}{3}$ of said property to the proxy. The remainder shall not be paid until the Güldi brothers have made the declarations necessary for the surrender of their citizenship and land-right. From this third, then, the legal emigration tax is also to be paid.

According to the Abzug-Rechnung of 1791/1, Captain Walther, as guardian of the brothers Güldi who are in America, paid on July 10, 1791, the emigration tax of 10 percent on the rest of their property here, 6258 crowns, with 625 crowns, 20 batzen.

The property, then, had been at home under the care of a guardian for almost 90 years. Samuel Güldi emigrated to America with his family in 1710. (Stadtbibl. Bern, Mss. Hist. Helv. III, 243 and III, 166/3.) His writings in his defense appeared in 1718, not in 1719.

1791, May 25.   Mittelwegziehungs-Prot. 3, 442/45.

Communication from the Government to the Corporation at Metzgern
in Bern

Martin *Gaul* of Philadelphia, the proxy of the Güldi brothers, now brings the necessary credentials from his employers for the surrender of their citizenship and land-right and the withdrawal of the remainder of the property. The corporation of Metzgern is authorized to pay over the capital after deducting the 10 percent tax.

Of the Güldi brothers, Samuel died unmarried. Johann and Daniel live in Oley in Berks county in Pennsylvania. Friedrich Güldi is also dead and left three sons, Samuel, Johann and Jakob, who reside in Montgomery county, Maryland. The sisters are married.

GURTNER

1774, April 19.   Mittelwegziehungs-Prot. 1, 76/77.

Communication from the Government to the Landvogt of Wimmis

Peter *Gurtner* of Oberwil emigrated to Virginia about 50 years ago. For 30 years no word has come of him or of his family. Fourteen years ago Gurtner's children inherited a legacy of 124 crowns from Rudolf Zeller, which now, with the consent of the Government, is to be divided among the nearest heirs.

(Oberwil in the Simmen valley is a village of some importance in the district of Niedersimmenthal.)

HALDIMAND

1782.   Etat der Landesabwesenden, p. 105.

The Landvogt of Yverdon informs the Government that Mr. *Haldimand*, the General and Governor of Canada, has been naturalized in England.

(Yverdon, a little city on Lake Neuchâtel, is in the canton of Vaud.)

The reference is to Friedrich Haldimand, concerning whom A. de Montet in the "Dictionnaire biographique des Genevois et des Vaudois," on page 411, writes:

Friedrich Haldimand was born in Yverdon about 1725. He began his career as a soldier in the Sardinian service and took part in the campaigns of 1743, 1744, 1745 and 1746 against France and Spain as an ensign. From 1747–1750 he was in the Prussian service, which he left to join the Swiss Guard of the Stadtholder of the Netherlands as lieutenant-colonel. In 1754 he left Holland to enter the English service as colonel of the newly formed Royal-American regiment. He was sent by the Government to Canada where he soon found opportunity to prove his courage in the war against the French. He distinguished himself especially at the storming of the fortifications at Ticonderoga on July 8, 1758, at the defence of Oswego, where he forced the besieging army to withdraw, and finally at the siege of Montreal. In 1764 he was appointed Brigadier-General and recalled to England by King George III. In 1776 the monarch promoted him to the rank of Lieutenant-General. In the following year he was obliged to return to Canada and in 1780 was appointed Governor of that country. Later he was entrusted with the duties of Inspector-General of the West India garrisons, in which position he remained until 1783. On October 15, 1785, he was decorated with the order of Bath, shortly after which he retired to his home in Yverdon, where he died June 5, 1791.

HÄNI

1733, Feb. 5.   R. M. 138, 342.

Bendicht *Häni* of Leuzigen, 50 years old and unmarried, a linen-weaver by profession, who resided during most of his life in Landau (Palatinate), emigrates to Pennsylvania. He pays the emigration tax due on his property of 100 crowns— that portion of it that is still in the canton of Bern—and surrenders his land-right.

(Leuzigen is a village in the district of Büren—see Plate 3.)

HASLER

1781, Feb./March.   Herrschaftsherren-Buch H, 158 b/160 b.

According to the reports of some members of the same commune, there emigrated to America in April 1750 from Oberhünigen, in the parish of Wyl: Jakob *Hasler* with his wife and his daughter Susanna, his son Abraham Hasler with his wife and a certain *Scheurer* from the same commune. The latter wrote to his

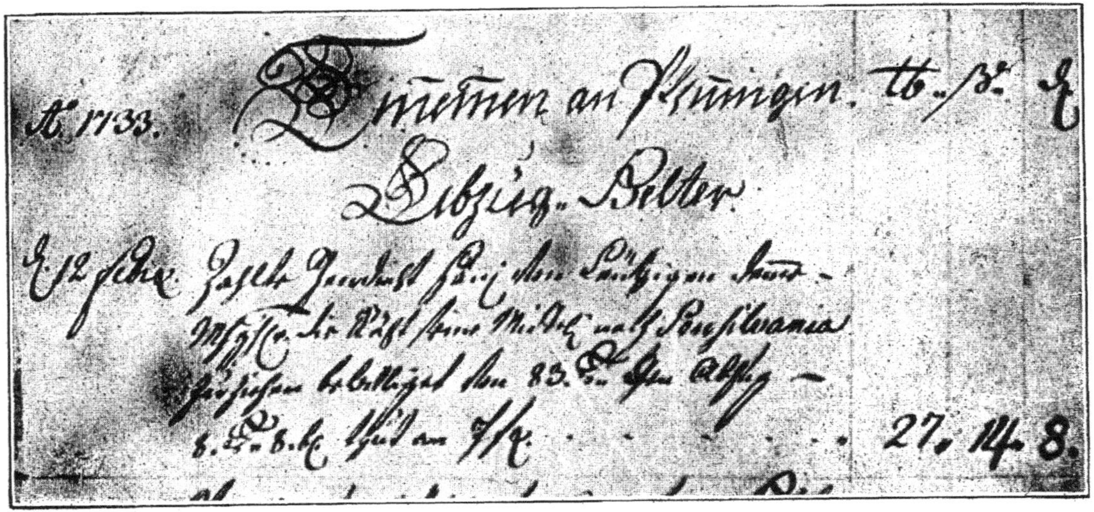

Plate 3

Büren = Amtsrechnung, 1733.

PAYMENT OF EMIGRANT TAX BY BENEDICHT HÄNI, FEBR. 5, 1733

(see p. 50).

father, Peter Scheurer, on June 1, 1750, from Rotterdam, saying that they had arrived there safely and would sail for America on June 3.

There is still credited here to Susanna Hasler a property amounting to 41 crowns, 8 btz.   Since no word from her has ever reached this country since her departure, her brother, Heinrich Hasler, and her brother-in-law, Niklaus Zimmermann, both of whom remained at home, request that this money be given them in return for security.   The government grants their petition.

HAUSER

1755, April 28.   Abzug—Rechnungen.

The Freiweibel of Münsingen is instructed to collect the emigration tax of 10 percent on 250 crowns which Christen *Hauser* is taking away to Pennsylvania.

(Münsingen is a large village in the district of Konolfingen.   The Freiweibel was an official with duties in the department of Justice, in the police and in the militia.)

1763, May/June.   Thun-Buch J, 259/70.

Christian *Hauser* of Münsingen emigrated to Pennsylvania some time ago with his daughter Anna and is now residing in Lancaster.   Anna has married a certain Theophilus *Hortmann* there.   Through his proxy, Johannes *Christe* from the canton of Basel, who also resides in Lancaster, Hauser requests permission to withdraw his property of 50 louis d'or in this country.   This money was left in the care of Hauser's nephew, Abraham Linder of Lueg in the commune of Steffisburg.   The government permits the withdrawal of the money in return for the surrender of the land-right and the payment of the emigration tax of 10 percent.   Christe's warrant of authority is to be left with the commune as security.

It is stated that Hauser is a very aged man.   It is to be supposed, then, that he had already been in America a long time.   The warrant made out to J. Christe is dated August 17, 1762.   It is only mentioned in the documents; no copy of it has been preserved.

(Münsingen is a large village in the district of Konolfingen.)

HEGISWYLER

1765/72.   England-Buch D, 587/88.

According to the statements of Daniel *Kahn* of Lancaster, Pennsylvania, who was born in the canton of Zürich, a certain Jacob *Plüss* of Ryken, a former soldier in the fortress Aarburg, emigrated to Pennsylvania in 1765, but died on the way, after leaving Rotterdam.   His belongings were taken in charge by a Johannes *Hegiswyler* of Lancaster.

The relatives of Jacob Plüss in Ryken and Vordemwald request the government in Bern for assistance in procuring the property in question.   The government took up the matter in 1772.   What the result was is not to be gathered from the documents.   (R. M. 312/81.)

(Plüss came from the present canton of Aargau; Hegiswyler seems also to have been from the same neighborhood.)

HENNER

1792, April 14.   Mittelwegziehungs-Prot. 3, 531/32.

Communication from the Government to the Landvogt of Trachselwald

Hans *Henner* of Bretzwyl in the territory of Basel married Magdalena *Geiss-bühler* of Rüderswil. Both emigrated to Pennsylvania about 25 years ago. By his formal proxy, Hans Oppliger of the district of Signau, Henner now requests that he may be given the property of 149 crowns of his deceased wife. Since no one raises any objections the Government allows the withdrawal of the capital.

(Rüderswil is a large commune in the district of Trachselwald.)

HOFER

1778, Feb. 3.   Mittelwegziehungs-Prot. 1, 279.

Communication from the Government to the Landvogt of Aarburg

Elisabeth *Hofer* from the commune of Brittnau emigrated to Pennsylvania more than 30 years ago. Her legal heir, Samuel Stirnemann, of Gränichen, requests that he be given the property which she left behind, 167 gulden. The request is granted by the Government. However, Stirnemann is to give legal security to the commune.

(Brittnau is a village in the present canton of Aargau, in the district of Zofingen.)

HORGER

1742, Jan./Feb.   Hasle-Buch D, 323/27.

Heinrich *Horger* of Oberhasle emigrated to Carolina with his wife and children some years ago. His daughter Barbara remained in this country and entered service as a maid in the canton of Zürich. She has now had an illegitimate child and wishes to go to her father in Carolina with it. Barbara requests permission to emigrate and to take with her her property of 90 crowns. The government puts no obstacles in her way and instructs the Amtmann to deduct the tax due from the capital. Moreover, he is to pay strict heed that no other people be enticed to emigrate.

1742, Feb. 21.   Oberhasle, Amtsrechnung.

Ulrich Berger, as guardian of Barbara *Horger* who has emigrated to Carolina, pays the usual emigration tax on 108 crowns with 10 crowns, 20 batzen.

(The Horger family originally came from the canton of Zürich. It still has home-rights (is "heimatberechtigt") in the district of Oberhasle in the commune of Guttannen. This is the highest commune in the canton of Bern.)

HUBLER

1770, Feb./March.   Niday-Buch 3, 897/921.

Hans Jacob *Hubler* of Twann, born about 1710, had learned the shoemaker's trade and had gone to Holland as a journeyman, from whence he emigrated to Pennsylvania. There he settled in Plainfield in Northampton county (3 miles from Nazareth). Of his numerous children 7 sons and 4 daughters were still living. His first letter from America to a friend in Twann was dated in the year 1739. Hubler now requests, through his proxy, permission to withdraw his property of 300 crowns. This proxy is Jacob *Schaffner* of Lausen who is established as an inn-keeper in Pennsylvania in Lancaster County in the city of Lebanon. The government refuses the request on the grounds that it is not certain whether or not some of the children are still minors and does not know to what religion they belong.

A letter has been preserved from the Clerk of the Court (Gerichtsschreiber) Jacob Engel, a notary of Twann, to his friend Hubler, which is addressed as follows: "To Mr. James Hubler at Blenfield in Northampton shire 3 Meiles from Nazareth in Pensilvania, to rendre at Mr. Christoff *Sauer*, Bookseller in Germantown in Pensilvania." This letter was an answer to a letter from Hubler in the year 1763.

The proxy Schaffner evidently brought this letter of Engel's back as a means of identification.

(Schaffner came from the canton of Basel, in which the village of Lausen is situated.)

1782.   Etat der Landesabwesenden, p. 207.

The Landvogt of Nidau informs the Government that Jacob Hubler of Twann with his numerous family has emigrated to America. The property which he leaves at home is administered by a guardian.

(Twann on the Lake of Bienne is a village of wine-growers in the district of Nidau.)

1793, June/October.   Nidau-Buch 6, 1/10.

Johann Jakob *Hubler* of Twann emigrated to America almost 50 years ago and settled there in Plainfield in Northampton County. Before his death in 1789 (1792?) he willed his property of 400 crowns in this country to his oldest son, Jakob Hubler, on the grounds that the other numerous children were sufficiently provided for by the property which he had accumulated in America. Jakob Hubler, through his proxy, Marc Voulaire, the teacher at Montmirail (Canton of Neuenburg [Neuchâtel]), now requests permission to withdraw this capital in return for the surrender of his citizenship (Mannrecht). A copy of the will in favor of Jakob Hubler, attested by a notary, is submitted. The commune (Gemeinde) of Twann wishes to oppose the withdrawal; but the government relies on the copy of the will which has been produced and grants the payment of the 400 crowns after the tax of 10 percent has been deducted and the land-right surrendered. The copy of the will and Jakob Hubler's renunciation of his land-right shall be delivered to the commune for its security.

The identification papers (Ausweisschriften) were confirmed on October 1, 1792, by the notary John *Hasse* in Bethlehem, Northampton County.   He said that he was thoroughly acquainted with both the English and the German languages.

HUG

1742.   Interlaken, Amtsrechnung.

On the 14th of February I have received from the 55 crowns which have been sent to Peter *Hug* of Aarmühle, who is now in Carolina, the emigration tax of 10 percent—18 pounds 6 sh. 8 d.

(Aarmühle was formerly the name of Interlaken.)

HURNI

1780, December 2.   Mittelwegziehungsprotokoll, 1, 505.

Thirty years ago Bendicht *Hurni*, and his son of the same name, left Lattrigen for Pennsylvania.   They have never since sent any message to their home.   The property still remaining of these two emigrants, amounting to 200 crowns, will now be turned over to their relatives.

(Lattrigen together with Utz forms a parish in the district Nidau. The family is still spread over that area and also over the districts of Aarberg and Laupen.)

HUGGLER

1735, March 16.   R. M. 146, 353/54.

Hans *Huggler*, a tanner from the district of Hasle, goes to Carolina with his wife and five children.   Two sons, Hans and Peter Huggler, are already abroad, but probably not in America.   Huggler surrenders his land-right and pays the 10 percent emigration tax.   The land-right for the absent sons remains intact and their share of the paternal property must remain in the country.   Huggler receives from the district a subsidy of 50 crowns.

(There are still many members of the Huggler family living in the district of Oberhasle.)

IMBODEN

1744.   Unterseen, Amtsrechnung.

Received on March 14 from Jaggi (Jakob) *im Boden*, who has left for Carolina, 7 crowns, the tax on 70 crowns.

(The former district of Unterseen now forms a part of the district of Interlaken.)

INÄBNIT

1735.   Interlaken, Amtsrechnung.

On March 13 Hans *in Aebnith* of Wärgistal in Grindelwald paid the emigration tax of 10 percent on the 900 pounds which he is taking with him to Carolina, viz. 27 crowns.

(Wärgistal is a subdivision of the large commune Grindelwald in the district of Interlaken.)

1744.   Interlaken, Amtsrechnung.

On January 29 I have received the emigration tax of 10 percent on the 40 crowns which have been sent to Bern to the Carolinian Peter *in Aebnit*, viz. 4 crowns.

INÄBNIT [1]

1763, April/May.   Interlaken-Buch K, 717/27.

Johannse *Christe*, who was born in the canton of Basel, but who has been living for many years in Pennsylvania (Lancaster), appeared before the Landvogt of Interlaken in order to take possession of the property of Hiltbrand *in Aebnit* which is still in this country.   The latter is also residing in Pennsylvania.   He is a linen-weaver by profession.   The property amounts to 1200 crowns.   From it are to be paid 620 crowns to the relatives of a certain *Brünnisholz*, who live in Wahlern in the district (Amt) of Schwarzenburg.   Hiltbrand gave Brünnisholz, who also lives in Pennsylvania, a note for that amount.   The remainder the proxy, Christe, is to take back with him.

The Landvogt first inquires whether Christe is trying to persuade people to emigrate, but discovers nothing incriminating.   However, he forces him to return immediately to Basel.   The commune of Grindelwald protests against the surrender of the property.

According to the warrant of authority to be found among the documents, Hiltbrand in Aebnit resides in "Cocalico taunship" (township).   His father's name was Peter, his mother's Anna, née Brawand.   As witnesses to the drawing up of the warrant Fred. *Stone* and John *Barr* are mentioned.   The warrant was attested by the mayor of Lancaster, James *Bickham*.

On May 17, 1763, the government decided to refuse all these requests and to continue to have the property of 1200 crowns administered by the commune.   For, according to the decree of April 26, 1742, in Aebnit had no further claim to the property. (R. M. 265, 355.)

It is still to be mentioned that according to the documents Hiltbrand was in good circumstances and had children—how many and what their names were is not stated.

1777, Feb. 1.   Mittelwegziehungs-Prot. 1, 221/22.

Communication from the Government to the Landvogt of Interlaken

In the year 1742 Hans *Müller* with his wife, Catharina *in Aebnit*, and her unmarried brother Hiltbrand *in Aebnit* emigrated from the district of Interlaken to Pennsylvania.   The Müllers seem to have died childless.   Hiltbrand in Aebnit is also dead, but from a report, dated Nov. 14, 1764, from Cuculeyo (Cocalico), he is said to have left three minor children.   Their guardian now lays claim to the property which was left at home.   But since neither the necessary documents

[1] For the name Inäbnit see also Vol. 1, *Lists of Swiss Emigrants in the Eighteenth Century*, pp. 16–20, etc.

concerning the marriage of Hiltbrand in Aebnit, nor baptismal certificates for his children were presented, the property is not yet to be delivered to them.

Since no further claims arrived from America, the Government, on the 21st of June, 1782, permitted the property of the brother and sister Hiltbrand and Catharina in Aebnit which was still in the country to be divided among their relatives here named in Aebnit and Born (650/52). The heirs, however, are to give security to the commune of Grindelwald.

1783, Jan. 30.   Mittelwegziehungs-Prot. 2, 49/52.

Communication from the Government to the Landvögte of Interlaken and Unterseen

(The latter locality, a small city, at present also belongs to the district of Interlaken.)

The matter concerning the property in this country of Hiltbrand *Inäbnit* has again been brought before the Government. A second investigation of the affair has given the following results:

Hiltbrand Inäbnit emigrated in 1742. (His emigration tax was not paid until 1744.) Hans *Müller*, the husband of Hiltbrand's sister Catharina Inäbnit, left at the same time. (This Hans Müller seems to have had his home-right in Unterseen.) Anna *Schlegel*, probably from Grindelwald, also went to America at that time. She then married Hiltbrand Inäbnit. From this marriage were born several children, of whom the oldest son is said to be now 35 years old. The last letter from the Inäbnit-Schlegel couple to reach home was written from Pennsylvania August 8, 1762.

A brother of Anna Schlegel, named Hans, is still living at home. He is now called upon to give more exact information concerning these circumstances, by which it is shown that the statement that conditions warrant the division of the property of the Inäbnit brother and sister is incorrect.

The Government therefore recalls its permission of June 21, 1782, and decrees that the property in question shall continue to be administered by the communes of Grindelwald and Unterseen until more certain information from America is at hand.

INGOLD

1766, May 12.   Wangen, Amtsrechnung.

Maria *Ingold* of Herzogenbuchsee has settled in Pennsylvania. In 1753 a capital of 800 pounds was sent over to her. Her brother, Andreas Ingold, is now subsequently paying the emigration tax of 10 percent with 80 pounds.

(Herzogenbuchsee is a village in the district of Wangen.)

JAGGI

1749, March 3.   R. M. 201, 12.

Communication from the Government to the Landvogt of Zweisimmen

Christen *Jaggi* of St. Stephan is in Pennsylvania and would like to withdraw his property of 59 crowns which is still at home. The Government, however, is using this property to bring up the little daughter of Hans Zmos who died in

Philadelphia, and to satisfy his creditors here.   In its place Jaggi receives an assignment of 50 crowns which he can collect from the estate of Hans Zmos.

(St. Stephan is a commune in the district of Ober-Simmenthal).

KALLEN

1769, April 13.   Frutigen-Buch D, 1147/53.

Elisabeth *Kallen*, the daughter of Hans and Anna Kallen of Schwanden in the parish of Frutigen, emigrated to Pennsylvania many years ago, and married there a Jakob *Beyeler* of Guggisberg.   The latter resides in Bern Township in Berks County.   Hans Kallen, the father, died 20 years ago and his wife three years ago.   Through a proxy of July 13, 1768, made out to a Michael *Keller* of Lancaster, Elisabeth petitions to withdraw her inheritance from her parents, which amounts to 300 crowns, upon giving up her land-right.   The government instructs the Landvogt of Frutigen to pay the property over to the proxy, after deducting the tax of 10 percent, unless the commune (Gemeinde) protests. (See Plate 4.)

(There are still many members of the Kallen family in the district of Frutigen, and of the Beyeler family in the district of Schwarzenburg where Guggisberg is situated.   The documents do not show where Keller came from.)

KAUFMANN

1776, June 11.   Mittelwegziehungsprotokoll, 1, 183.

In the year 1744 Walther *Kaufmann* of Grindelwald emigrated to America. (See the lists of emigrants from the magistracy of Interlaken, 1744.)   His mother also emigrated and died there in 1762.   In the old home there still remain two grandchildren, and also some property of said Walther Kaufmann.   This property, of about 150 crowns, is hereby given over to the grandchildren.

KERNEN

1744.   Unterseen, Amtsrechnung.

Received March 14 from Jaggi (Jakob) *Kernen*, who left with 4 children for Carolina, the emigration tax on 70 crowns of 7 crowns.

(The former district of Unterseen now forms a part of the district of Interlaken.)

KISLIG

1738, March 12.   R. M. 157, 370.

According to a report from the Freiweibel (Assistant Stadtholder) of Seftigen, Daniel *Kisslig* wishes to emigrate to Carolina.   Other cases are also known.   The government has an inquiry made by the Burgerkammer (a board for the protection of the poor and of wards) as to ways of combatting emigration.

(The Kissligs have home-rights in the communes of Riggisberg, Rüeggisberg, Seftigen and Wattenwil in the district of Seftigen.)

KISTLER

1779, March 28.   Mittelwegziehungs-Prot. 1, 380.

Communication from the Government to the Landvogt of Wildenstein

Hans *Kistler* from the commune of Bötzen emigrated to Pennsylvania with his wife and children 30 years ago. His relatives here ask that they be given his property, amounting to about 596 gulden, but the Government refuses the request. The property is to continue to be administered by the commune.

Bötzen is a commune in the present canton of Aargau, in the district of Brugg.)

KONRAD

1751, April 22.   R. M. 210, 19/20.

Jonannes *Conrad* of Walliswil emigrated to Pennsylvania some years ago, with his parents and his brothers and sisters. The government gives him permission to withdraw a sum of money amounting to 1955 gulden which belongs to the family. The Landvogt of Wangen is to deduct the 10 percent emigration tax and have the surrender of the land-right recorded. Conrad's proxy is to be left with the commune.

(Walliswil is a little village in the district of Wangen. The name is written Konrad now and is still to be found in the vicinity.)

KRAZER

1775, Jan. 11.   Mittelwegziehungs-Prot. 1, 111/12.

Communication from the Government to the Landvogt of Frutigen

Johann Heinrich *Krazer* of Aeschi emigrated to Pennsylvania in his youth. Since no information is available concerning him or his descendants, his relatives here request permission to divide among themselves his inheritance from his father and grandfather. Since it is still possible that there are heirs living in America, this permission is refused for the present. The property in question is to continue to remain under guardianship.

(Aeschi is a large commune in the district of Frutigen.)

KÜNZI

1734, Jan. 21.   R. M. 142, 95.

Christen Küntzi of Honegg wishes to emigrate to Pennsylvania. The government is agreed to this and gives the commune of Thierachern instructions to let Küntzi have as much of his property as he needs for the journey.

The place referred to is the hamlet, Honegg in the commune of Uebeschi, which belongs to the parish of Thierachern and to the district of Thun. There are still representatives of this family in their old home.

KÜNZLI

1774, April/May.   England-Buch D, 551/65.

Anna Barbara *Künzli* of Strengelbach married Michael *Schmidt*, a butcher, in the city of Roxborough in Pennsylvania. Through her proxy, Johan Jacob

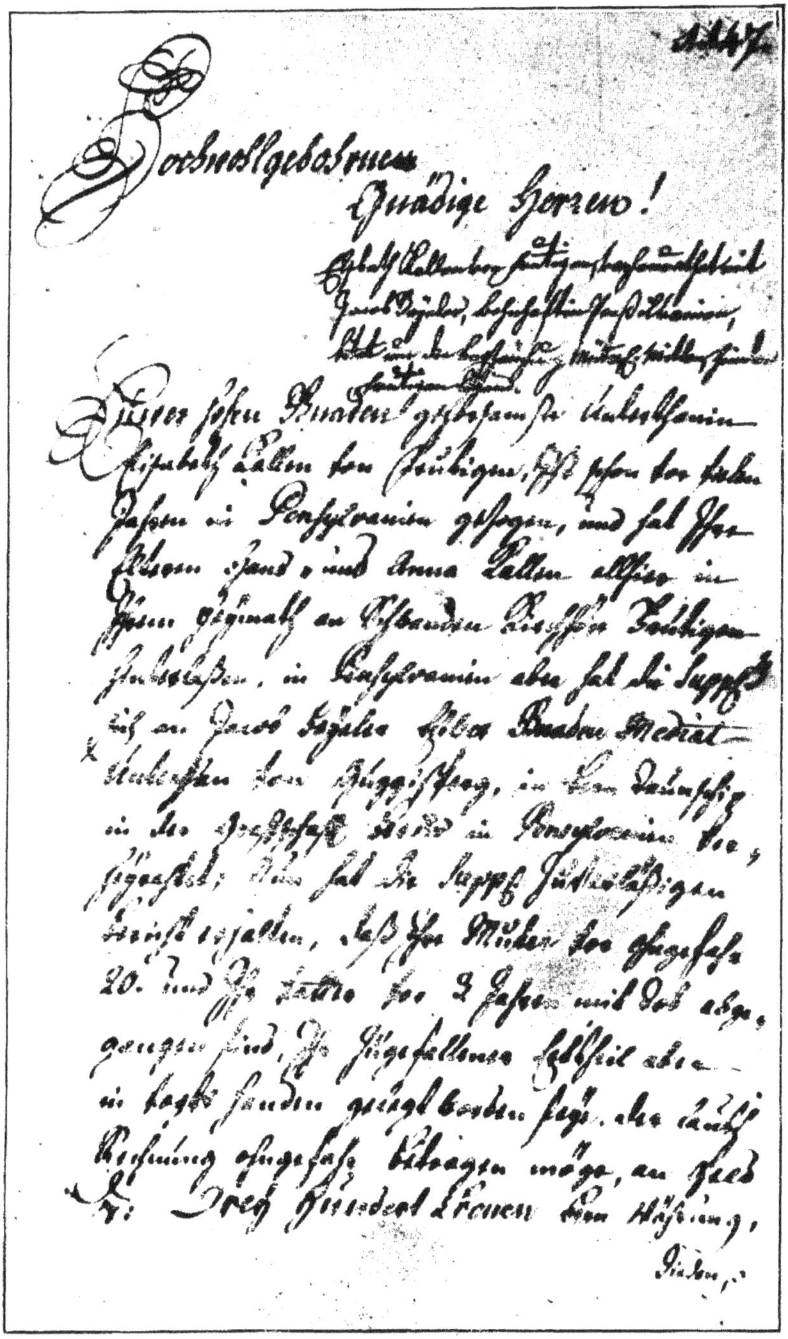

Plate 4

PETITION OF ELIZABETH KALLEN FOR HER INHERITANCE OF 300 CROWNS.
(1769—see page 57.)

Pfister, a master butcher in the city of Reading, she wishes to take her inheritance in this country over to America.   Anna Barbara is a daughter of Conrad Künzli, who died in America in 1769, by his first wife who bore him 2 children.   He had three children by a second wife who died in 1750 on the way to Pennsylvania. In 1753 Künzli came back home for a short time and told about his circumstances. Since it is not known where the other children are, or whether they are still living, the government only allows one fifth of the property of 937 gulden to be withdrawn.   The emigration tax of 10 percent is deducted.

Among the documents there is a statement made out by Pastor A. *Helffenstein* on December 10, 1773, in Germantown, saying that the Schmidt-Künzli couple are members of the Reformed Church; there is also the original of the warrant of authority of Dec. 9, 1773, for Joh. Jak. Pfister.   A form printed in the German language was used for this warrant.   Peter *Miller*, Esquire, royal judge of the city and county of Philadelphia, acted as notary, and Benjamin Miller and Abraham Schoemaker as witnesses

1774, May 3.   Mittelwegziehungs-Prot. 1, 79.

Communication from the Government to the Landvogt of Aarburg

Anna Barbara *Künzlin* of Strengelbach married Michael Schmid, a butcher, in Roxborough near Philadelphia in Pennsylvania.   Her father Conrad Künzlin left a capital of 937 gulden, and one fifth of this, after deduction of the emigration tax of 10 percent, is to be sent to Anna Barbara.

The name of her representative in this country is Johann Jakob Pfister.

(Strengelbach is a village in the present canton of Aargau in the district of Zofingen.)

1776, April/June.   England-Buch D, 591/609.

Elisabeth *Künzli*, a second daughter of the before mentioned Conrad Künzli of Strengelbach, has married Abraham *Fischer* of Abington in Pennsylvania.   She, too, and her unmarried sisters Maria and Hanna request permission through their proxy, Christoph *Lochner*, a printer and merchant from Philadelphia, to withdraw their property which still remains at home.   With the consent of the government, these three sisters are given their share of the inheritance by the commune of Strengelbach, but the share of the fifth sister Anna, who has married an Englishman named Isaak *Walfart*, a cooper by trade, is held back.   The lega emigration tax is deducted and the three sisters renounce their land-right in this country.

The proxy (Lochner) gives as references for his honesty the Messrs. Sarasin in Basel.   The marriage between Isaak Walfart and Anna Künzli took place about 20 years ago.   This couple live far away in another part of the country.

1776, June 14.   Mittelwegziehungs-Prot. 1, 187/88.

Communication from the Government to the Landvogt of Aarburg

Elisabeth Künzli of Strengelbach married Abraham *Fischer*, a resident of Abington, Philadelphia County in Pennsylvania.   Her sister Maria lives in the same locality, whereas her second sister Hanna resides in Philadelphia.   A fourth sister, Anna Künzli, is married and living somewhere else.   The commune of Strengelbach is empowered to send to the three sisters in America ¾ of their property which amounts to 857 gulden 9 btz. 2 kreutzer, after deducting the tax of 10 percent.   The fourth part is to continue to be administered by a guardian for Anna Künzli.

(Strengelbach is in the present canton of Aargau in the district of Zofingen.)

KURT (CHURT, CURT)

1749, April 11.   R. M. 201, 234.

Hans *Churt* of Wallisweil in the parish of Wangen and his wife, two of his sons with their wives and children, 11–12 members of the family in all, wish to emigrate to Pennsylvania.   They therefore address to the government a petition for permission to emigrate.   The government would like to prevent them from doing so and gives the Landvogt of Wangen instructions to inquire whether the people are not acting too hastily and will later regret their decision.   Then he shall summon them to him and shall bring forward every possible argument to dissuade them from their project.   He shall also hold up to them the dangers and difficulties of settling in Pennsylvania.   If, however, he should not succeed in keeping them from their undertaking, he is to inquire whether anyone had urged them to emigrate and how much property they expected to take with them?

April 21.   Ibid. 309/12.

In spite of the Landvogt's warnings the family of Hans Churt (also written Curt) of Wallisweil insisted upon emigrating to Pennsylvania.   Only one unmarried son and two daughters are willing to remain at home.   The father Churt with his wife and three children, the oldest son with his wife and two children and a third illegitimate child, 10 persons in all, are determined to emigrate and receive permission to do so.   From their property of 6000 pounds they are allowed to take with them, after paying the tax of 10 percent, only 2000 pounds.   The remaining 4000 pounds is to be left in care of the commune.   The emigrants need never count on receiving these 4000 pounds.

A certain Hans Jacob *Walter*, the son of the Untervogt of Knonau in the canton of Zürich, is known to be an instigator of emigration to Pennsylvania.   The Landvogt of Wangen is to have him arrested as soon as he comes into Bernese territory.

From the letter of a certain Daniel *Etter* of Pennsylvania it is seen that he advises the emigrants not to pay for their own passage, but to give their money to this Walter.   The Landvogt is instructed to warn the people against the questionable counsels of this man.

The government of Bern also sends a communication to the government of Zürich asking that Walter be warned against carrying on his propaganda in the canton of Bern.   In case he ever again steps upon Bernese territory, he will be arrested.   (D. Miss. 70, 105.)

The emigration of the Churt family brings the question up before the government whether it would not be better to raise the emigration tax from 10 percent to 20 percent in order to check emigration in this way.   The Vennerkammer (Financial Board, Finanzbehörde) is instructed to examine into the matter.

According to the Amtsrechnung of Wangen, this family was really only permitted to take with them 2000 pounds of their property, minus the emigration tax of 10 percent.

LANGEL—ENGEL

1754.   Münstertal, Schaffnereirechnung.

Ulrich *Engel*, of Sonceboz, who has gone to Pennsylvania, has paid an emigration tax of 67 pounds, 13 shillings, 3 pence.

(In the case of this man who comes from the French-speaking territory, it is very probable that the German accountant translated the French family name Langel as Engel. Sonceboz is in the present district of Courtelary, the principal community of which bears the same name, where the Langels still have home-rights. In 1754 the locality belonged to the bishopric of Basel.)

LANGENEGGER

1748, April 8.   R. M. 197, 466/67.

Ulrich *Langenegger* of Langnau emigrated to Pennsylvania with three sons. Jakob Huber, the son-in-law of Ulrich, asks the government to remit to him the sum of 30 crowns which the father Langenegger and his sons had made over to him; they also surrender their land-right. The government instructs the Landvogt of Trachselwald to deduct the emigration tax and to record the surrender of the land-right.

This Jakob Huber did not live in Pennsylvania, but in Lenzweiler in the territory of Pfalz-Zweibrücken.

(Langnau, formerly a part of the district (Landvogtei) of Trachselwald, is now the most important community in the district of Signau.)

LANZ

1751, April 22.   R. M. 210, 22/23.

Andreas *Lanz* of the district (Amt) of Wangen, unmarried, receives permission to emigrate to Pennsylvania. He must surrender his land-right and pay the Landvogt an emigration tax of 10 percent on his property.

(There are many people with the family name of Lanz in the districts of Wangen and Aarwangen, *i.e.*, the so-called Oberaargau.)

LE ROY

1754, March 11.   B. 116 (Ab- und Freizug).

The Vogt of Erguel, David Imuer, informs the bishop that in the coming spring a large number of the inhabitants of Erguel intend to emigrate to America. The greater part of these are Anabaptists and, with exception of the two *le Roy* brothers from Sonceboz, poor people. He will make further inquiries concerning the tax to be paid by the emigrants.

1754, March 22. The bishop answers that no tax is to be required of the *le Roy* brothers, since they have declared that they are only taking as much of their property with them as is necessary for the journey.

1762.   Biel, Schaffnerei-Rechnungen.

Jacques-Henri le Roy of Sonceboz, steward of the clockmaker Abraham *le Roy*, pays the tax on 2931 crowns, 1½ batzen, 3 kreutzer, which the latter at two different times had taken with him to America.. The 10 percent amounts to 293 crowns.   This Abraham le Roy was therefore a very wealthy man.

1756/1817.   Journal du Jura, 1817, 78.

In the year 1756 Lydia *Le Roy*, the daughter of Jean-Jacques, emigrated to America.   Her relatives in this country, the brothers Adam and David Le Roy, of Sonceboz and Sombeval, begin legal proceedings in the year 1817 in order to obtain possession of the property which Lydia left at home.

(Sonceboz and Sombeval are in the district of Courtelary.)

1769, March 2.   B. 116 (Ab- und Freizug).

From David le Roy of Sonceboz to the Bishop

Since 1765 I have been the steward of the dyer, Jean-Jacques *le Roy*, who emigrated to America in 1754.   He himself, who had intended to practise his trade in America, was attacked by the savages shortly after his arrival there, robbed and killed.   Two of his children were carried off by the savages, but later returned to their relatives in Lancaster.

In order to carry on the business of this Jean-Jacques le Roy who was murdered, Adam le Roy, who had emigrated with Jean-Jacques in 1754 and had subsequently married his daughter, decided to make a journey to their old home.   He came to Sonceboz (1768) provided with the necessary warrants of authority from his brothers-in-law and sisters-in-law, in order to fetch whatever property still belonged to them.

As steward of Jean-Jacques le Roy, I made over to him 1378 crowns, 12 Btz. 2 kreutzer.   With a part of this money he bought merchandise (among other things cheese) which he took with him when he returned to America, so that he exported only 479 crowns, 14 btz. 3 kr. in cash.   David le Roy now requests the bishop not to require the tax on these 479 kr.

(The district of Erguel in the former bishopric of Basel corresponds to the present district of Courtelary.   These different le Roys spoke French and probably were not Anabaptists, but enterprising business people.)

Maillardet—Michaud

1751, April 29.   B. 116 (Ab- und Freizug).

The following wish to emigrate to America (Pennsylvania) from Orvin:
  1. *Maillardet*, Jean-Henri, with wife and one child.
  2. *Maillardet*, Elisabeth, a sister of Jean-Henri.
  3. *Michaud*, Jean-Jacques, with wife and five children.

The Landvogt of Orvin, François de Chemyleret, asks the bishop in their name for permission to emigrate and for remission of the customary emigration tax, since the families in question are poor.

On the 5th of May, 1751, the bishop grants the request and gives the Landvogt to understand at the same time that people of means are to be discouraged from emigration as much as is possible.

(Orvin or in German Ilfingen is now in the district of Courtelary. French is spoken in Orvin.   At the time of this emigration Orvin belonged to the bishopric of Basel.)

Kund und zu wissen sey

hiermit jedermänniglich, daß ich *[handwritten text]*

[handwritten text]

Habe eingesetzet, gemacht und verordnet, und thue hierbey Krafft dieses, einsetzen, machen und verordnen *~~meinen~~* wehrten Freund *[handwritten]*

[handwritten] Postmaster *[handwritten]*

[handwritten] *~~mein~~* wahrer und rechtmäßiger Bevollmächtiger und Sach=Verwalter zu seyn, vor *~~mich~~* und in *~~meinem~~* Namen, statt *~~meiner~~* und zu *~~meinem~~* Gebrauch, zu begehren, einzufordern und gerichtlicher weise zu erhalten, und einzunehmen alle solche Summa oder Summen Geldes, Intressen, Güter, Waaren oder einig ander Gut, welches auf einigerley weise an *~~mich~~* gehöret von einiger Person, wer es auch seyn möchte. *[handwritten lines]*

[handwritten lines]

[handwritten lines]

[handwritten lines]

[handwritten] gehaltenen Interesse — — — — — —

Und *~~ich~~* gebe und übergebe hierbey *~~meinem~~* ermelten Bevollmächtigten *[handwritten]* *~~meine~~* gäntzliche Macht, Vollmacht und Autorität in allen ermeldten Stücken, sich aller und jeder rechtmäßigen Wege und Mittel in *~~meinem~~* *[handwritten]* Namen, vor die Erhaltung *~~meines~~* ermelten Geldes und Güter zu gebrauchen, und nach empfang dessen in *~~meinem~~* Namen volle und gnügsame Quitanz darüber zu ertheilen. Und überhaupt hierinnen alles andere und jedes in *~~meinem~~* Namen so wohl völlig zu thun als ob *~~ich~~* selbst Persönlich gegenwärtig wäre, auch so die Sache etwa mehr Autorität erfordern solte, noch einen oder mehr Bevollmächtiger unter Ihm in dieser Sache zu setzen und nach gefallen wieder zu revociren. Und *~~ich~~* Ratificire und bestättige hierbey alles und jedes, was *~~mein~~* ermelter Bevollmächtiger hierinnen dieserwegen rechtmäßiger weise Krafft dieses thun wird. In Zeugnuß hiervon habe *~~ich~~* *~~meine~~* Hand und Siegel hierzu gesetzt den *Ersten Tag* Septembris — — — — —

im *[handwritten]* Jahr seiner Britannischen Majestät

Regierung. Anno Domini 1755 *[handwritten]*

Besiegelt und überliefert
in Gegenwart unserer

[signature] Wm Edwards

[signature] Abraham Büninger

[signature] Thomas Tschoop

[signatures]

MANN

1761, March/Aug.   Oberhofen-Buch A, 681/739.

Anna *Mann* of Schoren emigrated to Pennsylvania many years ago and married there a weaver, Thomas *Schaaf* of Bethlehem in Northampton County. She died, leaving a little daughter, Anna, as whose guardians the Orphans' Court of Easton appointed Mattheus *Schropp* and Andreas Anthoni *Lawatsch*. Throughout her lifetime Anna Mann had tried in vain to have her small inheritance brought over to America. In the name of Anna Schaaf, her guardians now request the delivery of this inheritance.

In 1755 Anna Mann had written a letter to her brother Hans Peter Mann and had made out a proxy to Postmaster Fischer in Bern in order to withdraw the legacy. These measures did not have the desired result. Now the father and the two guardians, with the help of David Futer, a grocer in Bern, are striving for the same end.

The warrant of authority made out to Postmaster Fischer in Bern on September 1, 1755, in German and in English is among the documents. (See Plate 6.) It is certified on the reverse side by the Justice of the Peace, W. Parsons.

From the other documents referring to this matter, it is evident that Anna Mann emigrated with her aunt, Madlena Stucki of Wimmis. This aunt died unmarried in America.

After the commune and the relatives had declared themselves agreed, the government gave permission on August 25th, 1761, for the legacy to be relinquished. According to the official account-book (Amtsrechnung) of Oberhofen, the latter, after payment of the costs, amounted to 133 crowns, 9 batzen.

(The commune from which Anna Mann came is now called Strät-ligen and forms a suburb of the city of Thun. Wimmis is the principal community in the district of Nieder-Simmenthal.)

1759/61.   Oberhofen-Buch A, 697/98.

Among the documents referring to the legacy of Anna *Schaaf*, whose mother was Anna *Mann* of Schoren near Thun, are found the originals of the following certificates:

At an Orphans Court held at Easton in and for the County of Northampton in the Province of Pennsylvania the fourth day of August in the Year of our Lord one thousand seven hundred and fifty nine, before James *Martin*, Timothy *Horsfield* and Conrad *Hess* esquires Justices of the said Court.

It is ordered, on the Petition of Thomas Schaaf, in Behalf of his Infant Child Anna, aged two years, that Andreas Anton *Lawatsch* and Matthew *Schropp*, be Guardians of the said Infant Child and they are accordingly appointed.

CHARLES SWAINE, *Register.*

On the reverse side is written (in French):

The undersigned minister of his Britannic Majesty in the presence of the Honorable Swiss Council (Corps) declares and certifies to all whom it may concern that the seal affixed to the document on the other side is indeed that of the city of Easton in Pennsylvania, one of the English colonies in America: And also that the said document on the other side is an Act of the Court of Orphans of the said colony of Pennsylvania situated in the said city of Easton, by which the Judges of this court have authorised André Antoine *Lawatsch* and Mathieu *Schropp* to be guardians of Anne *Schaaf*, a minor child, daughter of Thomas Schaaf of the said colony, who agrees to the said nomination in his capacity as father. In assurance of which the undersigned minister has caused the seal of his arms to be affixed to these presents and has signed them with his hand.

A. DE VILLETTES.

Berne, March 26, 1761.   By order of the Minister, J. G. CATT.

MAURER

1764, Sept. 18.   Twingherren-Buch D, 157/60.

Albrecht and Barbara *Maurer* from the commune of Gysenstein in the district of Konolfingen emigrated to Carolina more than 30 years ago and since then they have not been heard from. A legacy of 63 crowns, 17 btz. has been left them by a relative who died in Strassburg, and their own property which they left here amounts to 36 crowns, 1 kreuzer.

Their relatives, most of whom are also abroad, request the government to deliver this capital to them, and their request is granted.

MEYER

1753.   Interlaken, Amtsrechnung.

On March 20 Geörg *Meyer* of Grindelwald paid on 90 crowns which he gave last year to his son who went to Pennsylvania, as has only just been discovered, the regular tax of 10 percent, 30 pounds.

1780, Feb. 14.   Mittelwegziehungs-Prot. 1, 440/41.

Communication from the Government to the Landvogt of Interlaken

Georg *Meyer* of Grindelwald emigrated to Carolina about 30 years ago and has not been heard of since. His legal heirs here are granted permission to divide his property of 400 crowns; they must, however, give security to the commune.

(Grindelwald is a large commune in the district of Interlaken in the neighborhood of the most beautiful mountains of the Bernese Alps.)

MINNIG

1758.   Pferdezucht 12.

At the end of this year Captain *Minnig*, who had accumulated a large estate in America, made an offer to the Bernese Commission on Horse-breeding to import 6–8 good breeding stallions from England. He had become an English citizen and this would facilitate his project. He expected to go to England soon on business. The

Commission which brought its own horses from Holstein and Oldenburg declined the offer with thanks (6, 36).

It seems that this Minnig had attained the rank of Captain abroad.

As is evident from numerous entries in the protocols of the government and of the Oberehegericht (Divorce Court) during the period from December 1760 to May 1764, the person referred to is Christian Minnig of Latterbach in the parish of Erlenbach (District of Nieder-Simmenthal). According to statements contained in these records, Minnig really possessed considerable property. He was involved in a paternity suit with Maria Koch, the daughter of a respectable family in the city of Thun. A child had been born to them. The mother petitioned for marriage and subsequent divorce, concerning which, through the mediation of the authorities, a compromise was effected. While the affair was going on, Minnig, who had acquired an estate in Gwatt, near Thun, converted his property into money and disappeared. He probably went back to America.

MISCHLER

1751, April 22.   R. M. 210, 21/22.

Anna and Barbara *Mischler* of Schwarzenburg emigrated to America many years ago and request permission to withdraw their paternal inheritance. The government agrees to this and instructs the Landvogt to pay over the capital to the proxy of the petitioners, who is not named, after the emigration tax of 10 percent has been deducted.

(Schwarzenburg is the principal community in the district of the same name, which at the time of this emigration was called Grasburg and was administered jointly by the cantons of Bern and Freiburg.)

1751, April 22.   Schwarzenburg, Amtsrechnung.

Jacob *Joner* from the canton of Basel, as proxy of the sisters Anna and Barbara *Mischler* who have settled in Pennsylvania, takes over their property here amounting to 483 crowns, 18 btz. 1 kr. The emigration tax of 10 percent is paid.

MOSER—RITSCHARD

1756, Jan. 20/24.   R. M. 229, 455/481.

Hans *Moser* and Heinrich *Ritschard* are arrested by the Landvogt of Interlaken and brought to trial for having recruited people to go to Carolina. Both have come back to their old home from Basel and have aroused the well-founded suspicion that they have had a part in the great increase of emigration to Carolina. The government threatens them with extreme measures, if they do not desist from their activities.

MUTACH

1785, April 26.   D. Miss. 95, 199.

In the year 1772, Christoph Samuel *Mutach*, a member of an aristocratic family of Bern, was appointed Secretary of a special Commission of the Council (Ratskommission). His uncle, Johann Rudolf Mutach, had filled the important office of Secretary of State (Staatsschreiber).

But the nephew leads a dissolute life and is disowned by his family because of his extravagance. In 1777 he goes out into the world, apparently first to the East Indies (Pondicherry). Later, under the name of Baron von Grünenberg, he comes to New York, either as a passenger or a prisoner of war, and there he becomes indebted to a Mrs. Peters, née Brand, to the amount of 150 pounds for board and room. Her husband was chef at the court of Hessen-Cassel in 1785. Mutach, in the meantime, has gone to Paris and died there.

The chef Peters tries to collect from Cassel the New York bill in Bern, but he is refused, because Mutach's relatives had already renounced all claim to his estate through judicial proceedings in 1784. The government of Hessen-Cassel is officially informed of this fact. (Cf. Spruchbuch des Stadtgerichts 1c, 38.)

NÄGELI

1742, May 20.   Oberhasle, Amtsrechnung.

Lieutenant Caspar *Nägeli* paid in the name of the widow and children of Balthasar Nägeli, who went to Carolina, 40 crowns, the customary tax on 400 crowns.

(The district Oberhasle, from which this family came, has only a few villages.)

1776, October 14.   Mittelwegziehungsprotokoll, 1, 201.

In the year 1742, the five brothers and sisters, Peter, Heinrich, Belthasar, Barbara, and Margaretha *Nägeli*, of Oberhasle, emigrated to America. Their property still left in the country, amounting to about 449 crowns, will be awarded to their nearest relatives.

(The family Nägeli is spread over almost all the parishes of the district of Oberhasle.)

NIDEGGER

1731/32.   Schwarzenburg, Amtsrechnung.

Stiny (Christine) *Nidegger* from the district of Schwarzenburg has settled in America. She is taking over her property here of 40 crowns and pays the 10 percent emigration tax.

(There are still many members of the Nidegger family living in the district of Schwarzenburg.)

PFISTER

1774, April 19.   Mittelwegziehungs-Prot. 1, 75/76.

Communication from the Government to the Landvogt of Wangen

Durs *Pfister*, a citizen of Walliswil, and his wife Elisabeth Born of Thunstetten emigrated to America and have settled there in Reading in Pennsylvania and have become citizens. They are permitted to take over their capital of 150 crowns after payment of the tax of 10 percent.

(Walliswil-Wangen is a little village in the district of Wangen on the right bank of the river Aare. Thunstetten is a commune of some size in the district of Aarwangen.)

According to the Amtsrechnung of Wangen, the property in this country amounted to 192 crowns, 14 batzen, on which the emigration tax of 10 percent was paid by the son of Durs (Urs) Pfister named Jakob. It is not clear from the entries whether this Jakob still lived in this country or whether he had come over from America (Reading, Pa.).

PIEREN

1763, June 8.   Frutigen-Buch D, 809/13.

Steffen Pieren from Adelboden went abroad 60 years ago and embraced the Catholic faith. His brother Jacob *Pieren* emigrated to Carolina about 30 years ago. Their relatives in this country request the government to deliver to them the property of these two brothers which was left in the care of the commune of Adelboden. 190 crowns belong to Steffen Pieren and 80 crowns to Jacob. The government orders that from the property of Steffen 120 crowns shall be paid to the relatives, whereas 70 crowns shall fall to the government.

As regards the property of Jacob Pieren, the request is refused.

(The Pieren family from the district of Frutigen spoke German, although the form of the name seems to be French.)

RITSCHARD

1750, April.   Oberhofen-Buch A, 677/80.

According to a report from the Landvogt of Oberhofen, Christen *Ritschard*, of Oberhofen, in spite of all warnings and in spite of his vows, has emigrated to America (Pennsylvania). His family consisted of his wife, 5 children, and his 80 year old mother-in-law. Joseph *Gyger* of Hilterfingen, Ritschard's brother-in-law, with his wife and one child, left the country with him. They left secretly, by night, and went to Basel, in order to take ship there. They were pursued by the Landvogt as runaways, and orders were given that they should be transported back. Ritschard had secretly sold his small property. The present owner is to pay over the emigration tax for this Ritschard, according to the valuation of the property.

This case is a typical example of how people of little means were obliged to use every possible device in order to leave the country which could not support them.

(Oberhofen and Hilterfingen are two beautiful villages on the Lake of Thun, in the present district of Thun.)

1751, Jan. 30.   Oberhofen, Amtsrechnung, 1750 and
                                              R. M. 209, 52/53.

Christen *Ritschard* of Oberhofen emigrated to Carolina some time ago and took away secretly 670 crowns, without paying the emigration tax. His brothers

Jacob and Johannes, who live here, were obliged to pay it. Since then Christen has fallen heir to an inheritance of 800 pounds. His brothers above named ask that they be reimbursed the 67 crowns tax which they paid from this sum and request that the rest of the legacy be delivered to them in return for security.

The government grants the reimbursement of the tax, but the rest of the property, in accordance with the decree of 1742, is to be left in charge of the commune.

1752, March 23.   R. M. 213, 333/34.

Michel *Ritschard*, 50 years old, from the district (Amt) of Interlaken, who has been a servant of the former treasurer Ulrich Eggler (see Egger) for 28 years, goes with the latter to Pennsylvania. He, too, is obliged to pay the emigration tax of 10 percent.

(There are many members of the Ritschard family living in Interlaken and the vicinity. The people are German despite the foreign sound of their name.)

ROTHENBÜHLER

1764, March 27.   R. M. 269, 158/59.

In a letter from America there is found an unfavorable report concerning Philadelphia, which is signed by Pastor *Rothenbühler*. The government wishes to have this report published, but first would like to make certain that the signature is genuine. This is to be decided by the brother of Pastor Rothenbühler who is living at home.

The person in question is Friedrich Samuel Rothenbühler from Münsingen, who passed his theological examination in 1752 and became chaplain in a Piedmontese regiment of Swiss troops. This was unfortunate for him. He was obliged to give up the position in 1755. He returned home and took charge of various vicarships; but his conduct gave cause for complaint.

Moreover, he became involved in different law-suits, (R. M. 246, 441/63, and 247, 29/35). On August 14, 1759, he was dismissed by the government from the service of the church. However, the ecclesiastical council (Kirchenkonvent) on December 16 of the same year gave him a certificate stating that he had passed the theological examination and that he had been ordained. Rothenbühler stated that he had a position on a ship in prospect. He went immediately to America and is said to have become pastor of the German Reformed Church in Philadelphia. The above-mentioned brother of Rothenbühler, Viktor Anton, was also a member of the clergy and was at that time engaged as assistant librarian in Bern.

(Münsingen is a large village in the district of Konolfingen.)

The letter itself has, unfortunately, not been preserved among the documents.

SCHAAD

1780, March 14.   Mittelwegziehungs-Prot. 1, 450/51.

Communication from the Government to the Landvogt of Bipp.

In 1750 four members of the Schaad family (brothers and sisters) emigrated from Walliswil to America.

The petition of some of their relatives here for the relinquishment of their property of 4221 crowns, 14 btz. is denied for the present.   All the relatives who are legally entitled to inherit from them must first be accounted for.

(Walliswil-Bipp is a little village in the district of Wangen on the left bank of the river Aare.)

SCHERZ (SCHERTZ)

1725.   Frutingen, Amtsrechnung.

Jacob *Schertz* of Scharnachthal, to whom your Honors gave permission to take his property with him on the journey to Pennsylvania which he is planning, has paid the tax, not on 800 pounds which he thought he had, but, because of a debt of 200 pounds on his land, only on 600 pounds, namely 60 pounds.

(Scharnachthal is a village in the district of Frutigen.)

1725, Nov. 26.   R. M. 104, 18.

Jacob *Schertz* of Scharnachthal receives permission from the government to emigrate to Pennsylvania.   He must pay the usual emigration tax on his property of 800 pounds and he is to surrender his land-right.

The government commissions the Ausburgerkammer (Board of Charities [Armenbehörde]) to prepare a report on the emigration question, since it is reported that still more people intend to emigrate to Pennsylvania.—This report unfortunately has not been preserved.

(Scharnachthal is a subdivision of the commune Reichenbach in the district of Frutigen.)

SCHLÄPPI

1774, October 31.   Mittelwegziehungsprotokoll, 1,96.

Many years ago Georg *Schleppig* of Oberhasle left for America.   His sister Christina lives in Berlin as the widow of the silk-weaver Laport.   According to the statements of this sister, George has disappeared without ever having given a report of himself.   She wishes the award of one-half of the property still remaining in Oberhasle belonging to George, amounting to 185 crowns.   The government demands first the proofs that George died without natural heirs.

(The Schläppi family is spread over almost all parishes of the district Oberhasle.)

SCHNEEBERGER
1751, April 22.   R. M. 210, 22/23.

Hans *Schneeberger* of Ochlenberg receives permission to emigrate to Pennsylvania with his wife and his two sons who are of age.   His minor children, however, because of the dangers of the journey, are to remain in this country under guardianship.   A part of the property must be left here for the education of the children.   The rest Schneeberger can take with him after paying the emigration tax of 10 percent and giving up his land-right.

According to the Amtsrechnung of Wangen, Hans Schneeberger and his two sons were allowed to take with them a share of the property amounting to 370 crowns, less 10 percent emigration tax, when they emigrated in the spring of 1751.

1753, Feb. 17/20.   R. M. 217, 172/201.

In the year 1751 Hans *Schneeberger* of Ochlenberg in the district of Wangen emigrated to Pennsylvania with his wife and their two oldest children.   The little children, 3 sons and a daughter, and their share of the property, had to be left behind, by order of the government.   Schneeberger now asks personally that these children be permitted to emigrate.

His request is refused on the grounds that he is suspected of being a religious fanatic and that it is to be feared that he may bring up his children to share his opinions.   They are recommended to the special care and instruction of the pastor.

The father Schneeberger is ordered to leave Bernese territory within 8 days and never to enter it again.

On May 1, 1753, the government orders the Landvogt in the Oberland and the Landvogt of Wangen to institute a search for this Hans Schneeberger, who, in spite of having been expelled from the country, is lingering around and trying to entice people to emigrate (217, 282).

1774, Nov. 25.   Mittelwegziehungs-Prot. 1, 99.

Communication from the Government to the Landvogt of Wangen

The three brothers Hans, Ulrich and Andreas *Schneeberger* and their two sisters Anna and Maria from the commune of Ochlenberg have settled in America, in Maryland.   In return for the surrender of their citizenship and land-right they are permitted to take their property of 1220 crowns with them after the tax of 10 percent has been deducted.

Later upon protest from the commune this decision was altered, March 15, 1775, so that only Andreas, Anna and Maria Schneeberger receive their shares of the property.   Hans and Ulrich took their property out of the country in 1751 at the same time as their parents took theirs, and they have no further claims.

Two other sons, Joseph and Jakob, belong to the family of whom nothing is said.   Their shares of the property are to continue to be administered by the commune (p. 147/48).

(Ochlenberg is a commune in the district of Wangen.)

1782.   Etat der Landesabwesenden p. 335.

The Landvogt of Wangen reports to the Government that the brothers Jakob and Joseph *Schneeberger* of Ochlenberg, commune of Bollodingen, emigrated to Pennsylvania in 1752.   They have not yet surrendered their home-right.

1783, Feb. 6.   Mittelwegziehungs-Prot. 2/56.

Communication from the Government to the Landvogt of Wangen

Hans *Schneeberger* of Ochlenberg is said to have secretly taken two minor children with him to America, more than 30 years ago.   The property of these children which is still in this country amounts to about 600 crowns.

The Uebersax, Mühlethaler, Jost and König families, their nearest relatives, petition for the relinquishment of this property, to which the government consents.

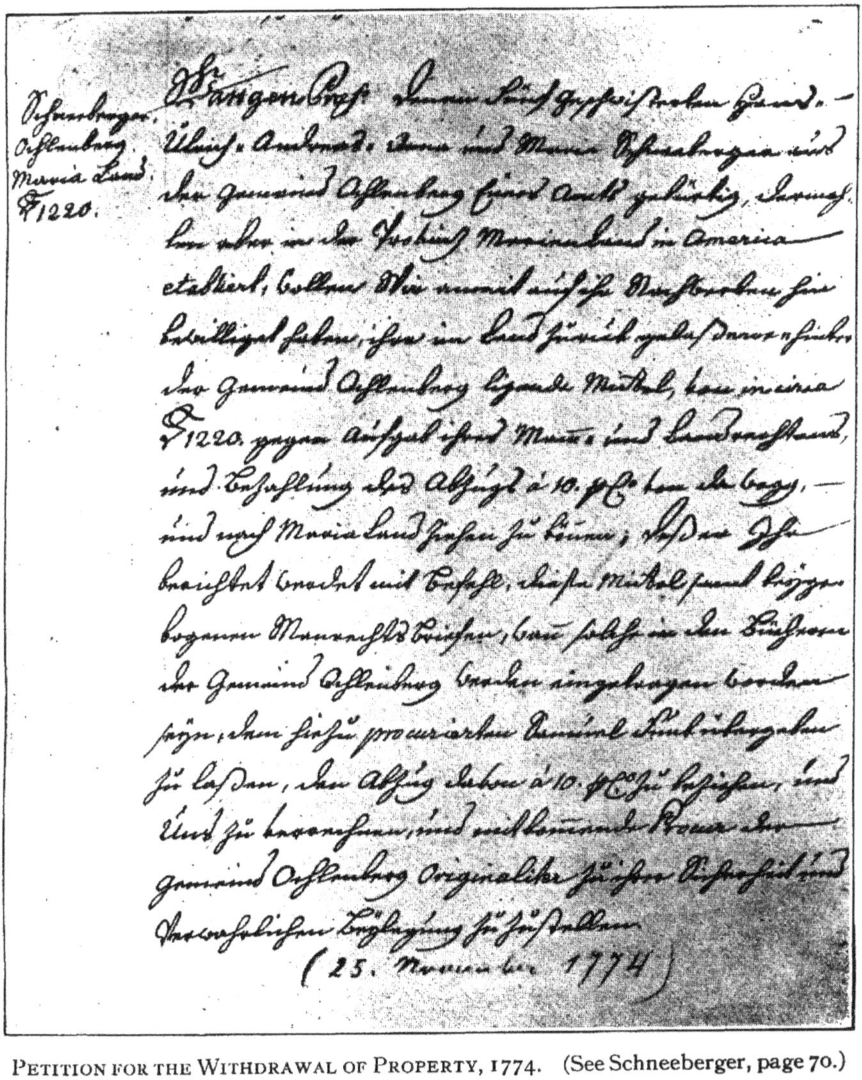

Plate 6

(25. November 1774)

PETITION FOR THE WITHDRAWAL OF PROPERTY, 1774.   (See Schneeberger, page 70.)

SCHRANZ

1759, May 31.   Frutigen-Buch C, 1167/75.

Hans *Schranz* of Adelboden emigrated to America in 1749 without the permission of the government and has settled in Philadelphia, in Canastoga. His property in this country amounts to 100 thaler and has been confiscated. Now his relatives here ask that this capital be given over to them. In accordance with the order of April 26, 1742, Hans Schranz's land-right was taken away from him and his property placed at the disposition of the government. The petition of his relatives is answered thus: they shall be able to enjoy the interest on the capital, but the capital itself shall continue in the charge of the commune.

(Adelboden is a commune in the district of Frutigen in the territory of the Alps.)

1766, Dec. 9.   Frutigen-Buch D, 1061/72.

Hans *Schranz*, a son of Gilgian Schranz (by his first marriage) of Adelboden, emigrated to Carolina in 1749, settled in Canastoga and is said to have become a rich man, according to the reports of a certain *Ritschart*. The latter, some years ago, was commissioned by Hans Schranz to bring over 20 Spanish doubloons for his father Gilgian.

Elisabeth, Hans Schranz's own sister, and his half-brothers and sisters, four in number, request the government to pay over to them the paternal and maternal inheritance of Hans, 200 crowns in all. The government grants the sister Elisabeth the usufruct of the property in question.

SCHÜPBACH

1725.   Schweiz. Theol. Zeitschrift, 1919, p. 164.

About this time the Hessian schoolmaster, Johann Philipp *Boehm*, organized in Pennsylvania the little German Reformed parishes in Falckner Swamp, Schippach and White Marsch. Inasmuch as the locality Schippach is called by the name of one of the first settlers, it is very probable that this was a Bernese, for the Schüpbach or Schüppach family is very widely represented in Bernese territory, especially in the Emmen valley. There are also many members of the family in the district between Thun and Burgdorf.

SCHWARZ

1729, March 24.   R. M. 121, 291/92.

The brothers Niclaus and Daniel *Schwarz* of Langnau petition to withdraw their property and give up their land-right in order to emigrate to Pennsylvania. The sons of Niclaus Schwarz: Christen, Jacob, Johannes and Mathys, are going with them. The government is opposed to the surrender of their land-right before the people have become citizens elsewhere, but does not wish to make trouble about it, if the emigrants' commune (Gemeinde) is agreed to their withdrawal. The emigration tax of 10 percent is to be deducted from the 55 and 19 crowns which the brothers possess. These emigrants, then, were almost without means.

(Langnau is the most important community in the district of Signau and the principal village in the Emmen valley.)

6

SOLLINGER

1734, Nov. 27.   R. M. 145, 172/73.

Bartlome *Sollinger*, a shoemaker from St. Stephan, wishes to emigrate to Carolina in spite of the objections that have been made to this. The government grants him permission to depart and to take his property with him under the usual conditions.

(St. Stephan is a village in the district of Ober-Simmenthal; the family is no longer represented there.)

SPYCHER

1750, January.   Twingherren-Buch B, 183/99.

Catharina *Zaugg* of Röthenbach married Franz *Spycher* of Gerzensee and both emigrated to Carolina with Samuel *Augspurger*, whose servant Spycher had been. According to a statement by Samuel Augsburger, dated June 9, 1741, Franz Spycher died in Purisburg, South Carolina, in the year 1734, and his wife, Catharina Zaugg, in the same place, in the year 1736. They left a little daughter, Anna Spycher, who in 1739 was still living in the home of a Captain *Holtzendorf* in Purisburg.

The above-mentioned Augsburger was in Muri, in the vicinity of Bern, in 1741, either for a visit, or as a returned emigrant. The relatives of Catharina Zaugg ask that the property belonging to her here be delivered to them. Their petition is not granted because the statement of Augsburger is not officially certified and because the space of 30 years has not yet elapsed since the emigration of Catharina. (Röthenbach is in the district of Signau, Gerzensee in the district of Seftigen.)

STAUB

1774, Nov. 25.   Mittelwegziehungs-Prot. 1, 98/99.

Communication from the Government to the Landvogt of Wangen

Andreas *Staub* of Wynigshaus, commune of Ochlenberg, has emigrated to America and settled in Maryland. In return for the surrender of his citizenship and land-right permission is given him to take over his property of 835 crowns, which is still in this country, after the tax of 10 percent has been deducted.

A certain Samuel *Funk* is acting as proxy for the petitioner.

(Wynigshaus and Ochlenberg are localities in the district of Wangen in the neighborhood of the large village Herzogenbuchsee.)

STAUFFER

1727, March 4.   R. M. 111, 267/68.

Communication from the Government to the Landvogt of Signau

Christen Stauffer from the parish of Signau is the guardian of the family of his Anabaptist brother, Ulli *Stauffer*. The latter seems to have emigrated. His wife

Lucia Stauffer, née Ramseyer, and their six children through their guardian request permission to emigrate to Pennsylvania and to take with them their property of 1900 pounds.

The Government grants their petition, but requires the usual emigration tax. Mrs. Stauffer, née Ramseyer, and her children resided in the commune Grosshöchstetten (District of Konolfingen).

1727/57.   Signau, Amtsrechnungen.

In the account-book of 1727 it is written that Lucia *Stauffer*, née Ramseyer, the wife of the Anabaptist Ulrich Stauffer, has emigrated to Pennsylvania with her children and has paid the emigration tax on 550 crowns.

Thirty years later the property amounting to 178 crowns, which was left behind in this country, is sent over to the children of this Ulrich Stauffer who are living in America, through the agency of Christen Fuhrer. The Landvogt of Signau deducts the tax of 59 pounds, 6 shillings and 8 pence therefrom.

1757, Aug. 31.   Signau-Buch 3, 500/2.

In 1727 Ulrich *Stauffer* and his wife Lucia, née Ramseyer, emigrated to Pennsylvania. They gave up their land-right and citizenship (Mannrecht) and took 1900 pounds with them. In 1742 Lucia Stauffer fell heir to a legacy of 962 pounds, which is intended for her children. The children of the couple, Hans, Madle and Barbara Stauffer, through their proxy, Christen *Fuhrer* of Pennsylvania, petition to withdraw this property and the government grants their request. Hans Stauffer renounces his land-right and the Landvogt of Signau deducts the usual emigration tax.

Since Ulrich Stauffer in his day had not satisfied all his creditors, a certain part of the property is to be used for that purpose.

STERCHI

1734, July 6.   R. M. 144, 110.

Peter *Sterchi* of Oberburg has gone to Carolina with his daughter. The latter had borne an illegitimate child whose father was Johannes Benedikt of Bern. When the Sterchi's went away they left this child behind. The government arranges for it to be cared for temporarily and requests a statement from the Board of Charities (Ausburger-Kammer) as to who is responsible for its bringing up.

(Oberburg is a commune in Emmental, in the district of Burgdorf.)

1752, May 29.   R. M. 214, 269/70.

The increase of emigration to America from the district of Interlaken troubles the government and they discuss what measures can be taken against it.

The Landvogt of Interlaken reports that the former Landsvenner *Sterchi* has probably emigrated to America and has enticed many people to go with him. His son-in-law has confessed that Sterchi took away about 3000 pounds. He is ready to pay the emigration tax for his father-in-law. The government instructs the Landvogt to receive the tax and to have the people warned against emigration, from the pulpits. Those who disregard the warning will incur the ill-will of the authorities.

1752.   Interlaken, Amtsrechnung.

On June 6th Jacob von Bergen of Oberried, in the name of his brother-in-law, Ullrich *Sterchi* of Aarmühle, the Landsvenner (color bearer), who went incognito to Pennsylvania, paid the emigration tax of 10 percent, in this case 90 crowns, on the property, amounting to 900 crowns, which the latter took with him, according to his formally executed oath.

(Aarmühle is the former name of the world-famous place, Interlaken. This Ullrich Sterchi was a respected man, since he had to carry the banner of the community in time of war. At the same time he was the mayor's deputy.)

1753, Feb. 19/20.   R. M. 217, 185.

The former Landsvenner (color bearer) *Sterchi* and the former treasurer (Landseckelmeister) *Eggler* have written letters from Pennsylvania to their old home, the neighborhood of Interlaken. These letters were delivered by Hans *Zurflüh* and Hans *Wyss* and invite people to emigrate.

Zurflüh comes from Oberried, Wyss from Isenfluh. Both must leave the country within 8 days (217, 202).

STOCKER

1752, April 29.   R. M. 214, 9.

Among the emigrants to Pennsylvania, there was the former banner-bearer (Landsvenner) *Stocker* of Ober-Simmenthal. He apparently wrote a disappointed letter to the stadtholder Martig of Zweisimmen. The government orders that this letter be seized and printed in the next calendar as a warning example against emigration.

(The Stocker family have home-rights [are " heimatberechtigt "] in the district of Obersimmenthal.)

TANNER

1734, April 16.   R. M. 143, 131/32.

Anna Kuhn, the widow of Hans *Tanner*, receives permission to emigrate to Carolina with her three children, Hans, Maria and Anna. Hans Tanner, the son, is married and takes his family with him, also. They cannot take away their property of 50 crowns unless their commune (Gemeinde) gives its consent and also recognizes the emigrants as its members. In case the commune will not permit the withdrawal of the property unless the Tanner family surrenders its land-right, the Landvogt of Zweisimmen is to report again to the government.

As a subsidy for their travelling expenses the government grants the Tanner family 20 thaler.

(The Tanner family came from the district of Ober-Simmenthal and from the commune of Zweisimmen.)

THOMI

1759, Jan. 24.   Signau-Buch 3, 520.

Catharina *Thomi* of the parish of Biglen is alleged to have emigrated to Pennsylvania in 1720 and since then has sent no word home. She has fallen heir to two legacies of 2700 pounds in all, and her relatives request the government that this property be delivered to them. In return for pledges of security given to the commune the government gives permission for the property to be divided.

(Biglen is a commune in the district of Konolfingen.)

TISSOT

1710, March 8.   D. Miss. 41, 391.

The Bernese government requests its ambassador in Holland, St. Saphorin, to make inquiries concerning the valuable estate of Abel *Tissot* from the vicinity of Mollens in the Waadtland, who died in Surinam.

According to an entry in R. M. 40, 213, the claimants of the estate were a widow Sigerat of Vuillerens and the sisters Elisabeth and Jaqueline Tissot.

(The materials concerning this matter are incomplete.)

TSCHANZ—KRAUS

1737, Feb. 9.   R. M. 153, 271/72.

Hans Georg *Kraus*, a saltpetre manufacturer of Blankenloch in Baden-Durlachischen, married the widow of Ulrich Tschanz from the vicinity of Thun. She brought him five children by her first husband. The Kraus family now wishes to emigrate to Pennsylvania. Mrs. Kraus would like to take with her her property which is still at home. Since the oldest son, Jacob Tschanz, is now of age, the government instructs the Schultheiss of Thun to keep the minor children's share of the property in the country. Mrs. Kraus and her son Jacob can withdraw their share after the tax of 10 percent has been deducted. Young Tschanz renounces his land-right.

(There are many members of the Tschanz family in the district of Thun.)

TSCHUMI

1750, April 8.   R. M. 205, 395/96.

Jacob *Tschumi* of Wangen wishes to emigrate to Pennsylvania with his wife and two unmarried daughters. Two sons remain at home. The Landvogt is instructed by the government to dissuade Tschumi from his undertaking. If this should not be successful, the Landvogt is to keep back the share in the property due to the two sons who remain here. The emigration tax is to be deducted from the exported capital; and the surrender of the land-right is to be recorded.

(Wangen, a small city, is the principal community in the district of the same name.)

1791/92.   Wangen-Buch O, 287/99.

Jakob *Tschumi* emigrated to America in 1750 with the permission of the government. Of his children, two daughters emigrated with him, whereas his sons, Jakob and Andreas, remained in this country, but later entered the Dutch military service. On his departure, Tschumi, the father, had left behind a property of 90 crowns for his sons.

Tschumi settled in America in Berkeley County, in the state of Virginia (now West Va.). Five miles from Mulenbury (?), Berkeley County, he owned one hundred acres of land. One of his daughters married a Daniel *Scheibli*, who was residing in the vicinity of Shepherdstown, also in the County of Berkeley. In addition to the 100 acres Tschumi owned some land in common with Scheibli.

The father Tschumi made out a will on November 19, 1782, in which his son-in-law Scheibli was made sole heir of his property in America after all claims had been settled. The second daughter had married a Michel *Close* and was named

Hannah. Scheibli was to pay her the sum of five shillings. The second piece of real property mentioned, Tschumi had formerly bought in common with the father of his son-in-law, the elder Daniel Scheibli; the purchase was registered in the courthouse of the Fredrick County Court.

The will was witnessed on March 18, 1783, at the courthouse of Berkeley County, and the copy was signed on the 19th of June, 1789, by the Clerk of the Court, Moses *Hunter*. As witnesses of the drawing-up of the will, Joseph *Thyle*, John *Thyle*, and John *Smith* are named. The name Scheibli is written *Schiveli* in the will.

In a letter to the Bernese government dated June 10, 1791, Daniel Scheibli requests permission to withdraw the 90 crowns which had remained in this country to the credit of the missing sons, Jakob and Andreas Tschumi. Scheibli had previously entrusted a certain Jacob *Michael* with the withdrawal of this capital, but had not obtained the desired result.

In his letter of June 10, 1791, Scheibli designates as his proxy a certain Johannes *Keller* from the canton of Basel and gives him a copy of the will. At the same time he requests that he be informed through the cooperation of the Recruiting Office (Rekrutenkammer) concerning the whereabouts and welfare of his brothers-in-law who entered the Dutch service.

His request is again refused on the grounds that it has not been shown whether or not any heirs of the two Tschumi brothers are still living. Moreover, Tschumi, the father, had no right to dispose of the property of his sons. This decision of the government was reached on January 3, 1792, and was to be forwarded to Daniel Scheibli through a certain Ziegler, a tradesman, who was evidently in touch with the proxy, Keller.

1792, Jan. 3.   Mittelwegziehungs-Prot. 3, 502.

Communication from the Government to the Landvogt of Wangen

Daniel *Scheibli* has settled near Schepertsthoun in Virginia (Shepherdstown, W. Va.). He asks for permission to withdraw the property of his deceased father-in-law, Jakob Tschumi of Wangen, which the latter left behind in this country. Scheibli's assertions that he was appointed sole heir by his father-in-law are disputed by the other relatives. The Government refuses to allow the property to be withdrawn until Scheibli has sufficiently proved his claim to the inheritance.

(Scheibli seems not to have been a Bernese.)

VALLOTON

1734, June 28.   R. M. 144, 43.

The Landvogt of Romainmotier writes to the government that three households of the *Valloton* family of Vallorbe wish to emigrate to Carolina, and inquires whether they are to be allowed to go without paying the emigration tax. The government refers the problem to the foreign (welsche) Vennerkammer (the finance commission of the Waadtland).

The commission is instructed also to investigate what precautionary measures should be taken, since Mr. Pury and others are urging the people to emigrate.

(Vallorbe is in the canton of Waadt [Vaud].)

VUILLE

1753.   Biel. Schaffnerei-Rechnungen.

Abraham *Vuille*, a goldsmith from the commune of des Montagnes, travelled to America. At the same time his brother Alexander also paid an emigration tax. It is not stated that the latter also went to America; but probably he accompanied his brother.

(This emigrant came from the bishopric of Basel and spoke French. The commune of des Montagnes is now called La Ferriere and lies in the district of Courtelary.)

WEBER—WÄBER

1749/50. Schwarzenburg, Amtsrechnung.

Anna *Wäber* from the district of Schwarzenburg has settled in Pennsylvania. Her inheritance here amounting to 132 crowns and 15 btz. has been paid over to a certain Urs Stöckli in exchange for a note. The agent of Anna Wäber must later pay the tax of 10 percent. This Stöckli did not live in America, but he looked after the emigrants' business affairs in their old home. (See Gilgien.)

WIDMER

1709, Sept. 4. R. M. 39, 44.

Caspar and Jost *Widmer* of Heimiswil wish to emigrate with their father to Florida. The government gives them permission to surrender their land-right and to withdraw their small property without paying the tax. The Landvogt of Burgdorf is instructed to communicate this decision to the home-commune of the emigrants.

(Heimiswil is a commune in the district of Burgdorf.)

1745, Aug. 16. R. M. 187, 34/35.

Oswald *Widmer*, born in Lützelflüh in the district of Brandis, a bachelor, in poor health, who can only walk with crutches, wishes, in spite of all this, to emigrate to Carolina. Widmer is at present in London and petitions from there for permission to withdraw his property of 200 gulden. The government grants him this permission in return for the surrender of his land-right and the payment of the emigration tax of 10 percent.

The Landvogt of Brandis is instructed to deliver the capital to the banker Gruner of this place, who will forward it to London to Commissioner von Diessbach to be paid to Widmer.

This commissioner had charge in London of the large sums of money which the Bernese government had invested in English securities.

(Lützelflüh now belongs to the district of Trachselwald.)

1761, May 1. Sumiswald-Buch A. 1701/13.

Isaac *Widmer*, of Sumiswald, emigrated to Pennsylvania about 9 years ago with his wife Anna, née Schneider, of Biglen, and has settled there in a Reformed parish. The couple has remained childless; they intend to stay permanently in Pennsylvania and since they have lost most of their possessions in a fire, they desire to withdraw their property at home. This consists of 602 pounds which Anna has inherited from her deceased father. Their proxy is an Ulrich *Brunner* from the canton of Zürich, who is also residing in Pennsylvania. The commune of Sumiswald [2] raises no objections to the withdrawal of the property, so the

---

[2] In the district of Trachselwald.

government grants the petition after the tax has been paid and the land-right surrendered.

According to the Amtsrechnung of Sumiswald, the property which Isaac Widmer and his wife Anna, née Schneider, took over with them amounted not to 602 pounds, but to 690 pounds, minus the tax of 10 percent.

WÜTHRICH

1772, March 21.   England-Buch D, 499/512.

Magdalena Spring, the daughter of Franz Spring, ab dem Sädel, in the commune of Gerzensee, emigrated to Pennsylvania more than 30 years ago, married a certain *Wüthrich* in the city of Lancaster, and is now a widow. Through her proxy, Daniel *Kahn* of Lancaster, she requests permission to withdraw her paternal inheritance of 222 crowns, 18 btz., 3 kreuzer. This property is being administered by the commune of Gerzensee. Since neither the government nor the commune raise any objection to the withdrawal of the capital, the money is paid over to the proxy Kahn after the emigration tax of 10 percent has been deducted. (See Plate 7.)

(Gerzensee, the home of this woman, is a commune in the district of Seftigen. The husband came from the Emmen valley where there are still many members of the Wüthrich family.)

ZINGRICH

1795, May 9.   Mittelwegziehungs-Prot. 3, 82.

Communication from the Government to the Landvogt of Interlaken

Peter *Zingri* of Saxeten emigrated to Pennsylvania more than 40 years ago. His parental estate, which remained in this country, amounts to about 500 crowns. The Government gives permission to the nearest relatives to divide this capital among themselves, if neither the commune nor any one else raises objections.

The name of this family is written Zingrich at home.

(Saxeten is in the district of Interlaken.)

ZMOOS

1749, March 26.   R. M. 201, 161, and U. Spr. LLL, 552/54.

Hans *Z'Moos* from the commune of Boltigen in Ober-Simmenthal, who emigrated to America, has died in Pennsylvania a wealthy man (apparently without heirs). His property has been left in charge of Emanuel *Zimmermann* of Wattenwil, who resides in Pennsylvania in Cannen-Stoben (Conestoga?). This Zimmermann bears the title: Justice or District Judge (Justus oder Lands-Richter).

When Hans Z'Moos emigrated, he left at home in Boltigen a little daughter, entirely unprovided for, since he could not even pay many of his debts. The child was brought up at the expense of the commune.

The commune of Boltigen now makes an attempt to take over the estate of Hans Z'Moos, and puts the matter in charge of Johann Jacob *Walder* from the canton of Zürich, a merchant, living in Philadelphia. This Walter is also given a Patent by the government in which the authorities of the province of Pennsylvania are asked for assistance.

(There are still members of the Zmoos family living in the commune of Boltigen in the district of Ober-Simmenthal.)

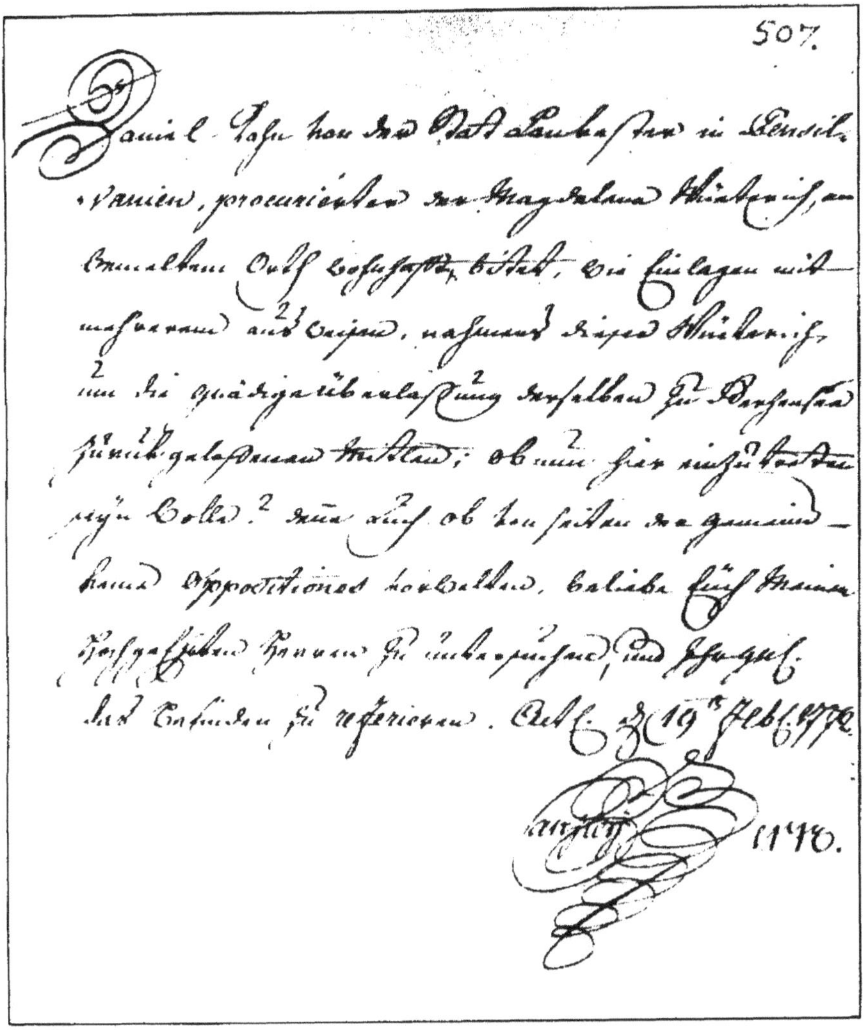

Plate 7

REQUEST FOR RELEASE OF PROPERTY (1772). (See Wüthrich, p. 78.)

ZULAUF

1782.   Etat der Landesabwesenden, p. 335.

The Landvogt of Wangen reports to the government that Lienhard *Zulauf* of Rohrbach emigrated to Newfoundland some years ago. He has not yet given up his home-right in Rohrbach.

(Rohrbach is now in the district of Aarwangen.)

ZURBUCHEN

1782.   Etat der Landesabwesenden, p. 117.

The Landvogt of Interlaken reports to the Government that Heinrich *zur Buchen* of Ringgenberg emigrated to Pennsylvania about 30 years ago. It is not known whether he or any of his descendants are still living.

(Ringgenberg on the Lake of Brienz is in the district of Interlaken.)

ZURFLÜH

1753, Feb. 20.   R. M. 217, 202/3.

Hans *Zur Flühe* of Oberried and Hans *Wyss* of Isenfluh, both in the district of Interlaken, emigrated a year ago to Pennsylvania. Both have come back and are trying to persuade their fellow-countrymen to emigrate by means of letters which they have brought with them from emigrants and by their own reports. The Landvogt is instructed to put both of these agents in prison for 24 hours and then to order them to leave the country forever within 8 days. Among the letters which they brought with them from Pennsylvania were some from the mountaineers (Oberländer) *Sterchi* and *Eggler* from the district of Interlaken (p. 185). In order to check emigration the government takes counsel whether it might not perhaps be advisable to deprive emigrants of their inheritance rights in this country.

1753, March 1.   R. M. 217, 281/82.

Hans *Zur Flühe* of Oberried, commune of Brienz, who has returned from Pennsylvania, requests the government for permission to settle again in his old home. The permission is granted him; but he is not to carry on any propaganda for emigration to America under threat of severe punishment.

V

STATE ARCHIVES OF BASEL

Special Investigations by Dr. Adolph Gerber

PREFACE

It is the purpose of this treatise to furnish as much general and individual information concerning the emigrants from Basel to the American Colonies in the eighteenth century, more especially between 1734 and 1794, as can be given in a limited space. The sources used are almost all manuscript sources and, with the exception of the majority of parish registers and part of the letters from emigrants in the Colonies to friends or relatives at home, are all found in the Staatsarchiv of Basel-Stadt. The principal ones are as follows, in the alphabetical order of the abbreviations by which they are cited:

AA = *Auswanderung A*, Emigration A, is a collection of documents relating mainly to emigration to the American Colonies, such as partial lists of emigrants, reports of commissions, letters of application on behalf of emigrants written by district officials, testimonials by pastors and others, letters from the Colonies, official examinations of returned emigrants, etc.

CAM = *Concepte Abgegangener Missiven*, drafts of official communications and informations sent out, a large volume for each year, containing also all instructions and orders issued to district officials in connection with emigration.

FAF = *Finanz-Acten F*, Revenue Records F, which contribute some itemized accounts of fees paid by emigrants.

GAV = *Gerichts-Archiv V*, Court-Archives V, a series of volumes with the proceedings of the 'Waisengericht,' Orphans' Court, to which all intricate and doubtful matters of inheritance, and requests to declare persons legally dead, were referred.

KA = *Kirchen-Archiv*, Church-Archives, records and documents relating to church matters.

KB = *Kirchenbücher*, Parish Registers, furnishing (apart from marriage and funeral dates) baptismal dates alone more frequently than both birth- and baptismal dates. The huge volumes of the city of Basel do not distinguish between the two and head their columns: 'Geburts-oder Tauftag.' Births and baptisms occurred sometimes on the same day and at least with very short intervals between. The parish registers of Basel-Land are now found mostly united in the Staatsarchiv of Liestal. Some registers, *e.g.* those of the parish of Waldenburg, Niederdorf and Oberdorf, are partly or entirely missing.

MP = *Manumissionsprotokoll*, Manumission Register, one volume only partly filled, intended to record all manumissions. It was begun in 1733 and discontinued in 1796, six years after the abolition of serfdom and manumission dues, the last years recording payments of taxes on emigrant property. There are no entries between July 7, 1736, and January 7, 1741, and for some other dates also a few are missing. The manumitted emigrants of 1736, 1749, 1771, 1772, 1788 and 1790, are given all together and also the emigrants of 1750 who were not manumitted are recorded.

RL = *Rechnungen der Landvögte*, accounts rendered by these officials at Oculi, four weeks before Easter, of each year.

RP = *Ratsprotokolle* or *Protokolle des Kleinen Rats*, Records of the Small Council, at first approximately and later on regularly a volume a year, averaging between 800 and 1000 pages, containing the minutes of the proceedings at all meetings of the Council. They are indexed, but not so fully as to make a page by page examination of important periods superfluous.

The letters from emigrants or contemporary copies of such which are not found in the Staatsarchiv of Basel-Stadt are in the University Library of Basel and in the Generallandesarchiv at Karlsruhe. Those from Hans Georg Gerster, which are repeatedly cited, are among the 'Briefe an Hieronymus d'Annone' at the former place.

The emigrants whose year of departure is definitely known, outnumber by far those concerning whom it is slightly or altogether uncertain. The former are given in their chronological order, year after year, and within each year in the alphabetical order of 'Aemter' (districts), villages and persons. The latter, who consist of a considerable part of the secret emigrants from the country and all but two of the comparatively few emigrants from the city (who are not recorded in MP because they needed no permission), are listed directly in the alphabetical order just explained.

An effort has been made to give with each emigrant, if possible, not only his bare name and financial status as found for most of them in MP or FAF, but also the names of his wife and children, mentioned in MP only in 1736 and a few other cases, dates of baptism, his occupation and other information concerning his conduct at home and his experiences in the Colonies.   The search for the names of the children and their baptismal dates has often been long and sometimes fruitless.   In some cases the home place was not their birth place, in others, and not infrequently, there were several fathers by the same name, and the right father and his children could only be determined if other sources furnished the name of the mother or that of his own father.   Also the habit of many parents of giving the names of deceased children once or more than once to children born later, complicated the matter. Ages instead of dates have not been controlled with the aid of KB, but are taken from other sources and will probably in most cases be found approximately correct.   Statements regarding the moral character of the emigrants cannot always be taken at their face value because those made by the pastors or other village officials not infrequently disagree with those of the 'Landvögte' (bailiffs). Upon the whole those of the former seem to deserve credence in preference to the latter, because they had a better individual knowledge of their people and were less inclined to wholesale disparagements.

With regard to destinations the sources also sometimes conflict or leave them uncertain, owing to the very hazy notions of American geography prevailing at the time.   In many cases it is simply stated that they went to the 'Neue Land' or the 'Neu gefundene Land,' the New-land or the Newly-found-land.   Also Carolina, which remained uppermost in the minds of some for quite a while, seems to have been used occasionally in the wider sense of America. After 1736, or possibly 1738, roughly speaking, the emigration from Basel was directed mainly to Pennsylvania, whence some proceeded to the colonies further South, very few to those further North. Destinations indicated in KB, even if incorrect, are, barring a few errors where a person deceased was designated as an emigrant, sure proof that the persons actually emigrated, just as, on the other hand, the records of baptisms of further children of supposed emigrants are proof that they did not go.   Persons who in MP or in the lists of 1738 and 1740, which take the place of MP, are recorded as emigrants and did not emigrate are marked with an asterisk. Some of them can be shown to have emigrated later.

As for the secret emigrants, it is impossible to find them all because there are any number of cases where persons are recorded as absent without any indication of where they had gone. Swiss people went all over the world as journeymen, into foreign military service or as emigrants and, though an emigration to America, if it proved successful, was apt to have been revealed sooner or later, there was perhaps no cause to make an official record of it. Also a majority of those who emigrated with permission never appear on the records again and disappear in the sea of oblivion as far as official Basel is concerned. The 'Verordnete zu den Landessachen,' the Commission which had especially to do with emigration, had in 1772 so little definite knowledge of the number of emigrants who had left within a few years, that it estimated them at about 500 or at most 600, a pretty large margin for an official statement.

A number of institutions and officials of the Canton of Basel of the eighteenth century have naturally nothing exactly corresponding to them in present-day America. They have been explained in our Introduction and are used throughout in their German form which leaves them their local coloring.

The spelling of the names varies greatly, not only between different sources, but also in the same source, sometimes even in KB. In the first place variations arise from doubling or not doubling of consonants where also changes between ck and k, tz and z belong; then the interchanges between b and p, especially sb and sp, d and t or dt, ff and ph or pf, f and v, ä and e or ö and e, with or without the addition of h, i, ie and y, or ü, üe and y; furthermore, the omission or nonomission of n after i in diminutives or otherwise, e.g. Küntzli, -lin, (-lein), Tschudi, Tschudy, Tschudin.

Besides there are the variations in the family names of women to which sometimes -in is added and mostly not, and in the Christian names owing to the use of familiar and dialectic forms by the side of the others. Most common is the change between Hans and Johannes and Joggi and Jacob, and Hans and Anna or sometimes prefixed to other Christian names, but now and then omitted. Then Baltzer or Baltz and Balthasar, Basche or Baschi and Sebastian, Christen and Christian, Claus and Niclaus, Elsbeth and Elisabeth, Frid, Fridlin and Fridrich, Heini, Heine, Heirech and Heinrich, Lienert, Lieni and Leonhard, Madle, Madalena and Magdalena, Rudi and Rudolf, Stoffel, Christoffel, and Christof,

Uhle, Uli and Ulrich, Ursel and Ursula, to which perhaps Urs and Durs should be added.

To note all these variations of spellings and forms throughout, which was originally our intention, would have unnecessarily encumbered this treatise. We give therefore the names simply in the spellings and forms of the leading source and add variants only where the former are faulty or unusual. Where h has the value of ch, we always write ch.

There are also not inconsiderable differences in the spelling of the names of some of the places. We have adhered to that of the sources where we reproduce them verbatim, but have used that of the *Geographisches Lexikon der Schweiz* in other cases.

With a few exceptions specially noted, all financial statements of this treatise are made in Basel pounds. The pound, libra, abbreviated lb. was not a coin, but a monetary unit which was divided into 20 'Schilling' (β) of 12 'Pfennig' or 'Denar' (ϑ). It was equal to 15 'Batzen' or 0.8 'Gulden,' florins, and corresponded in 1737 to 2/15 Pennsylvania pounds. It may however be assumed that some of the emigrants had at least a little more money at their disposal than they admitted.

The three figures which in the years 1749, 1771 and 1772 appear after the names of the emigrants are taken from MP and designate the number of men, women and children of whom the party consisted.

VI

INTRODUCTION

The Canton of Basel and the Conditions of its Inhabitants in the Country Districts

The Canton of Basel of the eighteenth century comprised both the present Canton of Basel-Stadt and the Canton of Basel-Land with the exception of a small strip of territory in the West. The main part was sloping down from the crest of the Jura Mountains to the Rhine and intersected by numerous valleys. Even to-day one third of Basel-Land is covered with forests. Fruit trees abound and vineyards still occupy one percent of the whole area, which is much less than they formerly occupied.

Administratively the Canton consisted of the city and seven country districts, called 'Aemter' or 'Vogteyen,' of very unequal size: Amt Riehen and Amt Kleinhüningen, both of them very small and to-day incorporated with Basel-Stadt, Amt München-stein, then mostly spelt Mönchenstein, Amt Liestal, formerly also Liechstal, Amt Homburg, and the two largest, Farnsburg, formerly Varnspurg, and Waldenburg, formerly also Wallenburg.

Ecclesiastically it was divided into the city and the three 'Capitul,' dioceses, of Liestal, Farnsburg and Waldenburg.

The city had control of the whole Canton and kept its subjects until 1790 in the state of serfdom in which it had acquired them from the bishop of Basel and other rulers. The executive power was vested in the 'Kleiner Rat,' Small Council, generally referred to as 'Meine (or Unsere) Gnädigen Herren,' often with the addition 'die Herren Häupter,' My Gracious Lords, etc.

The 'Aemter' or 'Vogteyen' were administrated by 'Landvögte' or 'Oberamtleute,' bailiffs or governors, who signed themselves as 'Obervögte' except that the administrator of Liestal was called 'Schultheiss.' The village magistrates were subordinate to them. In the larger places these were 'Geschworene' under the presidency of a 'Meyer' or an 'Untervogt,' in the smaller ones 'Geschworene' alone. Besides there were 'Amtspfleger in the districts of Farnsburg and Waldenburg, the 'Landschreiber' and some other officials whose functions need not be considered here.

The Church was the Reformed Church. It was in a measure under control of the government and upon the whole worked in harmony with the various secular authorities.   Matters of special importance came before the 'Conventus Ecclesiasticus,' composed of the four head pastors of the city, the three professors of Theology of the University and the four 'Deputaten,' a Church and School Board, which had also the administration of the poor relief in the country.   Matters of less consequence were transacted by the 'Sessiones,' meetings of the pastors of the Capitul, presided over by a 'Decanus.'   Internal parish affairs were in charge of the pastor and the 'Bann,' a kind of Board of Supervisors of Morals, selected by him from among his honorable parishioners.   Church discipline was very strict.   Wilful and continuous absence from public worship and persistent refusal to partake of the Lord's Supper together with the congregation, which was the case with some of the pietists who wished to worship in their own ways, could be punished by banishment.

Yet this restriction of religious liberty, which was by no means limited to Basel, was only one of several other restrictions and burdens of an irksome character.   To mention only the principal ones, the tithes and the extent to which they were exacted, the 'Fronungen,' statute-labors and their frequent occurrence, the inability to dispose of property, especially of real estate, which as a rule could only be done at a 'Gant,' a public sale, and with the consent of the government, and finally, if they wished to escape all these things, the obstacles put in the way of emigration.

For a number of reasons it had lately become more difficult for the subject population to find their sustenance.   The population had much increased, the best estates were being bought up by citizens of the city, the rate of interest was raised to no less than 5 percent and the peasants did not avail themselves as much of the help of the day-laborers as formerly on account of the hard times.

The Commission on Emigration says in its report of March 15, 1738, that the population of most villages had increased by one third or even by one half or more, during the last 30 or 40 years. The annual statistics published in the *Hoch-Obrigkeitlich begönstigtes Frag- und Anzeigungs-Blätlein von Basel*, the weekly paper of those days, show that in the five years just preceding the year 1736, when there was for the first time an emigration to the American Colonies of any consequence, the births had exceeded the deaths in the country districts by nearly 700.

As for the purchases of the best estates by citizens of the city, the Commission calls it in its report just cited the principal evil by which the subjects are deprived of their sustenance, because the

7

purchasers eventually made one estate, on which one or no subject could sustain himself, out of many, on which ten peasants might have found their sustenance.

The higher rate of interest was fixed by the mandate of Jan. 10, 1735, which renewed former ordinances, that had become obsolete in practice, and forbade any regard for the debtor. Nobody should lend money to a subject or 'Hindersäss,' tenant or subtenant, at a rate of interest of less than 5 percent nor take less under the pretext of a voluntary gift, nor refund the interest received to the debtor, nor do anything else by which the rate might become less than 5 percent. The transgressor should lose his capital, one fourth going to the denouncer, another fourth to the 'Oberamtmann' who brought the matter before the Council, and the remaining half to the 'Deputaten Amt' and the Churches under it. Officials of every rank were required by their oaths to be on the look-out in the matter. This draconic measure affected all, because all were carrying more or less heavy debts, but most of all the day-laborer because the peasants availed themselves less of his aid in order to meet as far as possible their higher expenses resulting from the mandate. Not a few turned to the trade of weaving and especially lace-making, but since the supply soon exceeded the demand, their wages were cut and no longer afforded them sufficient sustenance.

To these evils, which were beyond the control of the subjects, was added another for which they were responsible themselves and in which several of their superiors and also some of their pastors saw the principal reason for their not getting on, the excessive use of wine and especially of brandy. A report of the 'Oberamtleute,' read in Council Apr. 1, 1733 (RP 104) tells how particularly in winter time most people had begun to take brandy in place of a soup for breakfast, in the belief that it would keep them warmer in cold foggy and damp weather, besides being the cheapest and saving them the time and trouble of building a fire. May 3, 1738, the pastor of Bubendorf, to whose parish also Ziefen belonged, attached to a testimonial for some of his emigrants the request that measures might be taken to check the use of brandy, ruinous to people and country, which especially at Ziefen was so universal that it was served at perhaps 10 or 15 houses and particularly on Sundays before the sermon, so that many came to church filled with brandy. Although a few months later a mandate was issued which aimed to restrict the manufacture and sale of brandy and the excessive frequenting of inns and taverns, the pastor of Sissach writes in a private postscript, attached to his statements regarding two of his emigrants, to his Landvogt, March 3, 1749: "If a testimonial regarding their life and conduct is wanted, 'Herr Landvogt' surely knows as well as I do, if there were fewer taverns and vineyards in our country, people would also be more industrious and domestic and get along better." We have seen that there were also other reasons why people were not getting on, and many a testimonial will show us that the lack of industriousness, for which they were blamed by the pastor of Sissach and other superiors, was not applicable in all cases.

1734

While in Zürich about 300 emigrants left for America this year and a still larger number was getting ready in Bern to leave the next, we know of only one or perhaps two parties from Basel this year and 43 persons the next. The reason for this was not that the pamphlet on Carolina '*Der nunmehro in der neuen Welt vergnügt und ohne Heimweh lebende Schweitzer*,' etc., issued at Bern at the instigation of Mr. Pury, was not known in Basel. On the contrary, it had been advertised in the *Frag- und Anzeigungs-Blätlein von Basel*, July 13 and 20, and afterward. It could be purchased at the 'Berichthauss' and had even been carried around for sale in the country. Moreover, an account of the favorable passage under the command of Mr. Pury and a glowing description of Carolina had appeared in the same paper in October 1733. Furthermore the people saw the emigrants from Zürich pass their borders and their city. A large party, led by pastor Mauritz Göttschi, even had to make a forced stay among them while waiting for French passports. If we therefore seek for reasons why so few people emigrated from Basel this year and the next, it was probably the lack of leaders, such as Göttschi in Zürich and the gunsmith Striker or Strigger in Bern, and their closer acquaintance with the dangers arising from the warring parties of the French and the Austrians along the Rhine that restrained them. Restrictive governmental measures alone have never been able to stem a really strong tide of emigration.

BASEL

Hans Heinrich Breitenstein, son of Leonhard Br. and Anna Gisin, silk-weaver, born or baptized at Basel Febr. 6, 1681.
  According to RP 106, Oct. 23, he applied for a contribution toward his travelling expenses to Carolina and was granted 4 florins payable when he was aboard ship.

Jacob Müller (KB Hans Jacob), 'Informator.'
Catharina Elisabeth Weitnauer, his wife.
Their children:

1. Ester, born or bapt........................Apr. 26, 1729
2. Ludwig Friederich, born or bapt...............Oct. 21, 1732
3. Third child probably bapt. away from Basel.

His application for a contribution toward his travelling expenses was denied. He wished to emigrate to Carolina because he could not sustain himself at Basel, but we do not know whether he carried out his intention (RP 106, Nov. 17).

Daniel Hoch of Liestal, who emigrated to Carolina either in 1733 or 1734, will be found among the emigrants of uncertain date below.

1735

None of the seven families which received permission to emigrate this year is recorded in MP though two of them paid their manumission fees. We depend therefore on RP supplemented by FAF and for an emigrant not known to RP on letters of his own.

I. *Emigrants recorded in RP*

An entry of Apr. 23, 106, 389, says: "In the name of seven families . . . of the following fathers: Emanuel and Hans, the Giegelmanns of Bubendorf, Baltzer Strauman of Waldenburg, Heine Riggenbacher of Rüneberg, Heini Sälin and Hans Bitterlin of Zeglingen, and Wernet Buser of Oberdorf, which with wives and children comprise 42 souls, the communication was made that they had started down the Rhine to go to Carolina. Two of them, viz. Buser and Sälin, had paid for their manumission according to the decree, but all of them begged to be graciously released from the payment of it.

"Resolved that manumission dues and ten percent tax should be exacted from all and attention be given to the property which they possess or expect to inherit in this country."

It had not been an easy task for these families to secure their permission at first refused and finally reluctantly granted. Among other things an investigation had been instituted as to what or who had induced them to leave. Thus a report from Waldenburg, dated Dec. 11, 1734 (AA), states that the pamphlet on Carolina and an account of the real arrival and good reception of emigrants there, both of which we have mentioned above under 1734, had actuated the Giegelmann brothers, while a report from Farnsburg, dated Dec. 18 (AA), shows that Heini Riggenbacher was induced to go by conversations on this topic in city and country and besides especially by Emanuel Giegelmann, his brother in law.

AMT FARNSBURG

Rünenberg

Heine Riggenbacher, Heini.
Anna Bürgi from Bubendorf, his wife, bapt. or born Sept. 29, 1695, married Oct.

Heini Riggenbacher of Rünenberg is the only emigrant of this year of whom we still hear after 1736. In 1739 he sent through the agent Hans Spring a letter to his brother in which he asked for the release of some money and property of his. The government took great pains to get hold of the letter, but made no haste to settle the business, for this was not done till 1798, *i.e.*, nearly sixty years later, when the property was divided among the heirs in the Canton (GAV 21, 39, Sept. 24, 1798). According to GAV 17, 698, Heini Riggenbacher (father or son?) married Anna Till, presumably a daughter of Nicolaus whom we meet in 1736.

Zeglingen

Heini Sälin, KB Säli.

An entry in FAF, Saturday Apr. 23, 1735, says: 'From Heini Söhli of Zegligen, who has gone to Carolina,

For his own, his wife's and four children's manumission...40.—
Item ten percent tax on 200 pounds worth of property...20.—' 60.—

Maria von Arx, his wife.
Their children:

1. Anna Maria, bapt........................Nov. 11, 1721
2. Heini, bapt............................Oct. 10, 1723
3. Barbara, bapt..........................Jan. 4, 1725
4. Martin, bapt...........................May 12, 1730
5. Elsbeth, bapt..........................Febr. 1, 1733

Unless one of these five remained in the Canton, one of them must have died before emigrating. The death of a Heinrich Sälin is recorded in July, 1734, but without indication of age. The parish register is incomplete during these years as there are entered only five deaths from 1724 to 1728.

Zeglingen [or Rünenberg?]

Hans Bitterlin

KB of the parish of Kilchberg, which comprises also both Rünenberg and Zeglingen, knows of two Hans Bitterlins at this time, one married to Margreth Datz, without indication of the village, and another married to Barbara Möschinger or Möschiger, located at Rünenberg. The former has but one daughter, Anna Margreth, bapt. May 31, 1722, the latter five, Barbara, Elisabeth, Eva, Maria and Anna, baptized between Apr., 1720, and Aug., 1734. If the statement of RP is correct, the father of the one daughter may have been from Zeglingen and have emigrated; if not, it may have been the other who went abroad.

AMT WALDENBURG

Bubendorf

Emanuel Giegelmann.
Catharina Bürgi, his wife, married Febr. 28, 1719.
Their children:

1. Engel, bapt................................Febr. 18, 1720
2. Anna, bapt................................Apr. 27, 1721
3. Emanuel, bapt............................Dec.   3, 1724
4. Johannes, bapt...........................Dec. 12, 1728
5. Hans Rudolpf, bapt.......................July   1, 1731
   A sixth child, baptized together with its little cousin Magdalena
   below, did not live.

Hans Giegelmann, brother of Emanuel, married on the same day with him.
Barbara Rudin, Joggi's daughter, from Arboldswil, his wife.
Their children:

1. Barbara, bapt............................Oct. 15, 1719
2. Johannes, bapt..........................Oct. 21, 1721
3. Engel, bapt.............................Jan.   1, 1724
4. Jacob, bapt.............................July 20, 1727
5. Anna, bapt..............................Jan. 31, 1730
6. Magdalena, bapt........................Dec.   7, 1732

Oberdorf (or *Tenniken*)

Werner Buser.
An entry in FAF, Saturday, Apr. 23, 1735, says: 'Furthermore from Werner
Buser of Tennicken, who has gone to Carolina, for him, his wife and 3 children:
Manumission......................................35.—
Item ten percent tax on 50 pounds worth of property..... 5.—' 40.—

which makes his dues, if 50 pounds was all he possessed, four fifths of his property.
Barbara Suter, his wife.
Their children:

1. Jacob, bapt.....................Apr. 26, 1729 at Tenniken
2 and 3. Not recorded in Tenniken and therefore perhaps born and
   baptized in Oberdorf where RP locates the family.

Waldenburg

Balthasar Strauman, butcher.

Owing to the loss of KB nothing can be said about his wife and
the number of his children. He seems to have safely arrived in
Carolina, because in the following year the release of some property
of his, which he had left behind, came up in Council (RP 107,
Apr. 18, 1736).

II. *An Unrecorded Emigrant*

Pratteln (Amt Münchenstein)

Hans Martin, son of Lorenz Martin, butcher and later on innkeeper, and Catharina
Stachin, bapt. March 11, 1688.

Had three sisters, among them Maria, who also went to Pennsylvania, and a brother. Was married to Anna Hodel, who must

have died near the close of 1729 (RP 101, Jan. 11, 1730), leaving him two daughters, Anna Cathrina, bapt. Dec. 25, 1717, and Anna Maria, bapt. Apr. 5, 1722. They did not follow him to Pennsylvania in 1735.

Hans Martin is repeatedly mentioned in Prof. Wernle's work on Swiss Protestantism in the eighteenth century. It should, however, be observed that the long term of imprisonment at Bern recorded by Wernle, was not undergone by him, but by Jacob Martin, a silk-weaver of French extraction, and that it was also Jacob and not Hans Martin who reappeared at Hieronymus d'Annone's in Basel in 1746. Hans Martin's story is in short as follows: He was a small farmer with a few hundred pounds worth of property. Aroused by a dream he felt called upon to do religious work among his fellow villagers and others. He succeeded in influencing not a few to give up cursing and blaspheming and inducing them to lead better lives. His wife regarded him as an infallible divine teacher and also some others looked upon him as sent of God. His growing influence attracted however the attention of the church and the government, especially since he taught also that it was wrong to bear arms and to take an oath, while both military service and the oath of allegiance were fundamental requirements of the state. Since after a respite of two months, which the Conventus Ecclesiasticus had won for him, he would not make concessions on these points, he was solemnly banished July 19, 1719.

Then followed sixteen restless years on a fief in Baden, on another in Biel, in Neuchâtel, largely shared by his loyal wife, who was likewise banished, three years after him. In the meantime he made clandestine visits to his friends and adherents in the Canton of Basel. On the occasion of one of them, he was surprised and taken by village magistrates, yet not sent by them to Basel, but across the boundary. Hieronymus d'Annone, who on his journey through Switzerland received a visit from him Sept. 28, 1730, in Neuchâtel, says in his Diary of him that he moved him to pity by the narration of his tribulations and made him wish that liberty of conscience might be introduced everywhere as in Holland and Prussia and that it might not be possible for one man under the guise of religion to become a robber, murderer, wolf and Satan toward another.

Some years later, in 1735, while the government, which had heard rumors of his reappearance at Pratteln, sent out orders to arrest him because it was still anxious to keep him out of the country (CAM May 21), he was already on his way to Pennsylvania, at the instigation and with the financial support of Lucas Fattet and other pietistic friends. He went by way of Carolina, robbed and ill used by the people on board because he upbraided them for their dissolute conduct. After the lapse of two months he bought some uncleared land with the hundred Thalers he had left, and there in an empty log cabin wrote his letters home, copies and extracts of which are now in the Generallandesarchiv of Karlsruhe. The last information we receive concerning him comes through a letter of his sister Maria, a copy of which is also found at Karlsruhe, a year later and is rather disappointing. He had refused to keep her and her children longer than two weeks though she was coming from the burial of her husband in Philadelphia and still ill from the voyage herself and had hoped to find consolation and shelter with him. His mind seems to have become so much embittered that his heart could not readily respond to the appeals of sisterly love and charity. Perhaps he could not forgive her that she had finally submitted to the demands of Church and State for the sake of her family, while he had resisted to the bitter end.

There was much disappointment among the emigrants who came from Switzerland to Carolina in 1735. According to a letter of Strigger, dated Germantown, Pa., May 11, 1736, and printed in Neu-gefundenes Eden, 1737, also some from the Canton of Basel went from there to Pennsylvania.

1736

After the few sporadic cases of 1735 Basel experienced in 1736 for the first time an emigration movement which, at least from a distance, resembled those of Zürich in 1734 and Bern in 1735. Although the earliest petitions, among them that by Durs Thommen, the foremost emigrant of the year, were at first denied, applications multiplied so that the authorities found themselves obliged to give serious attention to the matter. In the absence of a standing Land Commission (which does not appear in the emigration records till 1740 and in the 'Neues Regiments-Büchlein oder Verzeichnuss der Vorgesetzten etc,' the directory of the officials still later) the 'Deputaten,' reinforced by some special deputies were instructed to call those desirous of emigration before them and examine their reasons. On February 15 their first report, followed by others in March and April, was read in Council. It covered 16 men, representing 80 souls, who were mostly poor.

These had alleged that their means only sufficed to pay their debts, that, as was generally known, the country was more than ever overcrowded with inhabitants and poor people. Moreover, in many places floods had carried away the good soil and left only the rocks. Day-laborers had no chance to earn anything. They could produce witnesses, that they had been hard-working and industrious all their lives, yet, though they had known nothing but pains and sweat, they could hardly sustain themselves. They hoped they would not be detained because through their emigration those remaining would be left in condition to sustain themselves more easily.

The remonstrances made to them regarding the uncertainties and difficulties of their undertaking had been of no avail. They had claimed to be so poor and miserable that nothing much worse could happen to them. They would manage to get to Holland and from there on they would find assistance according to the letter enclosed which they produced. Letters and reports from people who had been there assured them that they would be amply able to sustain themselves there and they trusted the good God would not forsake them in their troubles.

The 'Deputaten' and the other members of the Commission were impressed by these arguments and not being able to turn them from their purpose, did not see how they could be detained in the country. They recommended that the 'Obervögte' and pastors should make another attempt to dissuade them, and if they failed, the emigrants should be permitted to go. The Council acted accordingly and in the following month apparently all petitions were allowed until in view of the increasing stream of applicants it was decided on March 28 not to grant any more (RP 107, 382v).

Since there was a general claim for the reduction of dues or a complete release from them even on the part of some of the most able men, the Council complied also with this to some extent. E.g. in Pratteln, Amt Münchenstein, Hans Joner paid the tax on 1750 pounds instead of 2118.1.4, Fridlin Stohler on 250 instead of 374.19.—, Hans Buser on 110 instead of 170.5.10, etc. Moreover, those who after such reduction had less than 100 pounds left were allowed to go entirely free, and the children of all, whether able or poor, were released from the payment of manumission fees. Indeed even an application for a contribution toward their traveling expenses made by some ten of the poorest families was only nominally denied, in order to avoid a precedent, but virtually granted because they were allowed to apply to the 'Collect' station where poor travellers received support (RP 107, Apr. 30, 1736).

I. *Emigrants recorded in MP*

N.B.: Ages, dates, what follows after the financial statements and what is put in parentheses is taken from other sources.

AMT FARNSBURG
Ormalingen

Buess, Johannes, of Ormalingen.
Ester Breiting, his wife.
Their children: [N.B. These are not his children by Ester Breiting, whom he married only Jan. 10, 1736, but by Anna Buser, deceased Apr. 27, 1735.]
    1. Basche, bapt...............................Jan.   5, 1729
    2. Margret, bapt............................June   4, 1730
    3. Anna Maria, [KB Anna], bapt................Sept. 30, 1731
Children by the first marriage of Ester Breiting above [to N. N. Anisshäusslein]:
    1. Hans Jacob Anissh.   *2. Barbara Anissh.   3. Ursula Anissh.
    Gratis. Have no property.

Joh. Buess had been in England before.   Barbara Anisshäusslein postponed her emigration till 1740.

Schaub, Hans, of Ormalingen.
Anna Grieder, his wife.
Their children:
    1. Hans Jacob, bapt...........................Nov. 13, 1725
    2. Heini, bapt................................Apr. 20, 1728
    3. Hans, bapt.................................Oct. 16, 1729
    4. Martin, bapt...............................Dec. 3, 1730
    5. Catharina, bapt...........................Oct. 10, 1734
    Gratis. Has no property
Völmin, Martin, of Ormalingen.
Anna Weitnauerin from Oltingen, his wife.
Their children:
    1. Martin, bapt..............................Aug. 13, 1724
    2. Niclaus, bapt.............................March 10, 1726
    3. Elisabet, bapt............................May 23, 1728
    4. Barbel, bapt..............................Oct.   1, 1730
    5. Anna, bapt................................Febr. 14, 1734
    Gratis. Has no property.

Rickenbach

Handschin, Joggi, [Rothenfluher Marti's son] of Rickenbach, bapt. Dec. 25, 1704.
Catharine Thommen, his wife.
Their children:
    1. Ursel, bapt...............................Dec.   9, 1727
    2. Jacob, bapt...............................March 20, 1729
    3. Hans Jacob, bapt..........................March 11, 1731
    4. Catharina, bapt...........................Aug. 17, 1732
    Has 300 pounds worth of property.
    Pays: Ten percent tax..............................30.—
          Manumission for himself and his wife...........20.—   50.—

Handschin, Maria, [sister of Joggi above], an unmarried person of Riggenbach, bapt. March 14, 1706.
    Gratis. Has less than 100 pounds of property.

Rothenfluh[1]

Keller, Hans Jacob, [son of Geörg K. and Barbara Erb], of Rotennue, bapt. Nov.
14, 1706.
Elssbet im Hoff, [Imhoff], from Wintersingen, his wife.
Their children:

    1. Basche, bapt.................................March 27, 1729
    2. Hans Geörg, bapt..........................March 4, 1731
    3. Hans Jacob, bapt..........................Febr. 15, 1733
    Has 250 pounds worth of property.
    Pays: Ten percent tax.............................25.—
          Manumission................................20.—   45.—

There is a letter of Oct. 18, 1748, written by Durs Thommen
and signed by Keller, in which the latter commissions Jacob Joner
and Hans Adam Riggenbacher to collect an inheritance for him.

Martin, Hans Imbert, of Rothenflue.
Anna Schönenbergerin from Wintersingen, his wife.
    1. Hans Jacob, their son, bapt..................June 17, 1725
    Has 130 pounds worth of property.
    Pays: Ten percent tax.............................13.—
          Manumission................................20.—   33.—

Meyer, Hans, of Rotenflue.
Anna Weybel, his wife. Have no children.
    Pays: Ten percent tax on 200 pounds.................20.—
          Manumission................................20.—   40.—

Rünenberg

Grieder, Hans Joggi, of Rüneberg.
[N.] N. from the Frick Valley, his first wife.
    1. Fridlin and 2. Hans Martin, his children [by her].
Ursula, [KB Elsbeth], Häffelfinger from Dieckten, his second wife.
    1. Hans, their son, bapt......................Jan. 18, 1728.
Barbara Christen from Frenckendorf, his third still living wife. Barbara, her
    illegitimate daughter, has remained in the country.
    Has 170 pounds worth of property.
    Pays: Ten percent tax.............................17.—
          Manum. for himself and his wife...............20.—   37.—

Tecknau

Senn, Hans Jacob, of Tecknau.
Ursula Dörfflinger, his wife.
[Their children:]
    1. Martin, bapt. Jan. 17, 1717, who has pretended that he only
        wished to travel as a cooper-journeyman and therefore asked
        to reserve the landright for him.
    2. Margaret, bapt. Apr. 7, 1720.
    Gratis. Has no property.

[1] The modern spelling is used in the headings. The old spelling will frequently
appear below.

Senn, Heini, of Tecknau.
Madle Handschi, his wife.
Their children:

      1. Elssbet, bapt..............................March 3, 1726
      2. Verena, bapt..............................Nov. 16, 1727
      3. Martin, bapt..............................Nov. 13, 1729
    Gratis. Has no property.

Senn, Heini, of Tecknau.
Maria Tschudi, his wife.
Their children:

      1. Mattis, bapt..............................Sept. 2, 1730
      2. Elssbet, bapt..............................Apr. 20, 1732
      3. Anna, bapt..............................Jan. 19, 1734
    Gratis. Has no property.

Zeglingen

Thommen, Jacob, of Zegligen.
Barbara Bär, his wife.

    Elssbet, their child, bapt.......................Apr. 6, 1727
    Has 350 pounds worth of property.
    Pays: Ten percent tax.............................35.—
        Manumission for himself and his wife...........20.— 55.—

There is a letter by him written two months after his arrival in
Pennsylvania which he had reached in 4 months and 17 days—
Apr. 28 to Sept. 15—from Basel. It begins with a blessing and
closes with the words that whoever seeks religious liberty will
find it in Pennsylvania. Among other things he mentions the
absence of tithes. He settled at 'Kanastangen' (Conestoga).

Amt Homburg

Läufelfingen

Buser, Uli, of Leuffelfingen, 51 years of age.
Catharina Buess, his wife, aged 45.
Their children:

      1. Uhli, bapt..............................Apr. 16, 1719
      2. Anna, bapt..............................Febr. 15, 1722
      3. Elssbeth, bapt..............................Oct. 7, 1725

Gratis. Has only 24 pounds worth of property left.

Strub, Hans, 'Amptspfleger's son,' of Leuffelfingen, aged 48.
Anna Eglin, his wife, 36 years of age.
Their children:

      1. Anna.......................................12½ years old
      2. Sara.......................................11 years old
      3. Margret .... 5 years old
      4. Hans....................................... 3 years old
      5. Martin, bapt..............................March 13, 1735

Note: Has 3 more children by his first wife who remain in the country.
Gratis. Has less than 100 pounds worth of property left.

Thürnen

Gerster, Heini, of Thürnen, bapt. Jan. 15, 1688.
Anna Weissin, his wife, bapt. Oct. 20, 1695.
Their children:

    1. Barbara, bapt. ....March 20, 1718
    2. Anna, bapt................................Jan.   21, 1720
    3. Verena, bapt..............................June 13, 1724
    4. Heinrich, bapt............................Apr.   13, 1727
    Pays: Ten percent tax on 1300 pounds..............130.—
           Manumission.............................. 20.— 150.—

Keller, Mattis, of Thürnen, aged 31.
Elssbet Speiserin, his wife, aged 38.
Their children:

    1. Anna, bapt...............................July   29, 1731
    2. Verena, bapt.............................Dec. 14, 1732
    3. Hans Jacob, bapt........................Apr.   11, 1734
  Gratis.   Has less than 100 pounds worth of property.

Würtz, Joggi, of Thürnen, [called Miller Joggi, 'Lehenmüller'], aged 41.
Barbel Gisin, [Gysin], his wife, aged 39.
Their children:

    1. Heini, bapt..............................May   26, 1720
    2. Joggi, bapt..............................June 18, 1724
    3. Martin, bapt.............................June 10, 1727
    4. Elssbet, bapt......................March 29(?), 1729
    5. Eva, bapt................................Dec. 20, 1733
  Barbara remains in the country.
  Pays: Ten percent tax on 900 pounds.................90.—
          Manumission.............................20.— 110.—

The first four of the children were baptized in the parish of Rümlingen. KB says that Joggi, Martin and Elssbet came to Carolina.

Amt Liestal

Frenkendorf

Boni, Joggi, [Joggi's son], of Frenckendorff.
Eva Zeller, [from Gibenach], his wife.
Their children:

    1. Elssbet, bapt.............................Nov. 21, 1706
    2. Joggi, bapt.............................Oct.   7, 1708
    3. Verena, bapt.............................Nov.   3, 1720
    4. Anni, bapt...............................Oct. 11, 1722
    5. Barbara, bapt............................Nov. 26, 1724
    6. Michel, bapt.............................Apr. 27, 1728
    7. Weinbert, bapt...........................Oct.   7, 1731
  Pays: Ten percent tax on 600 pounds.................60.—
          Bondage.................................20.— 80.—

There are several more children in the long interval between Joggi and Verena. Some had died and at least one remained in the country. The others went to Carolina.

Lausen

Tschudi, Martin, of Lausen, [tailor].
Anna Balmer from Furlen, his wife.
Their children:

    1. Hans Jacob, bapt.......................... ?
    2. Anna, bapt......................Dec. 21, 1727
    3. Barbara, bapt....................March 16, 1732
    4. Elisabet, bapt...................May 16, 1734
    Pays: Ten percent tax on 120 pounds.................12.—
        Manumission...............................20.—   32.—

AMT MUENCHENSTEIN

Münchenstein

Bey, Rudolf, [KB Bay], of Mönchenstein, whose wife is deceased.
  Gratis. Has no property, and
Bey, Alexander, [KB], his son, of Mönchenstein.
Anna Brüderlin, his wife.
Their children:

    1. Rudi, KB Hans Rudolf, bapt...............Nov. 13, 1729
    2. Johannes, bapt........................... ?
    Gratis. Has only 67 pounds worth of property left.

Muttenz

Brüderlin, Jacob, son of Hans deceased, of Müttentz.
Barbara Schönenbergerin, his wife.
Their children:

    1. Anna, bapt...............................Nov. 16, 1721
    2. Margret, bapt...........................March 28, 1728
    Pays: Ten percent tax on 130 pounds.................13.—
        For bondage..............................20.—   33.—

KB adds to the entry of their marriage: 'Went to Pennsylvania 1736' and to the baptismal dates of their children similar notes.

Pratteln

Buser, Hans. of Brattelen, (tailor, linen-weaver), aged 38.
Babi Plapp, his wife.

    1. Jonas, their little son, bapt..................Nov. 5, 1726
    Pays: Ten percent tax on 110 pounds.................11.—
        Manumission.............................20.—   31.—

KB in connection with Jonas: 'in Carolina.' Stated in his examination Jan. 31 that he had often had to do statute-labour on a hungry stomach without having a piece of bread.

Johner, Hans, (correctly Joner), of Brattelen, bapt. Jan. 25, 1687.
Maria Martin, his wife, (sister of Hans, the emigrant of 1735), bapt. June 14, 1691.

Their children:

1. Jonas, bapt. . . . . Apr.   5, 1716
2. Jacob, bapt. . . . . Apr. 18, 1719
3. Niclaus, bapt. . . . . Oct.   4, 1722
Pays: Ten percent tax on 1750 pounds. . . . . 175.—
       Manumission. . . . . 20.—   195.—

KB adds to Jacob's date: 'in Pennsylvania' and to that of Niclaus: 'in Carolina.'

Hans Joner had perhaps not forgiven the authorities that they had laid a financial embargo upon him from Apr. 19, 1734, to Jan. 8, 1737, in order to break the resistance of his wife to the demands of Church and State in the matter of attendance upon the Lord's Supper. He found at least that it became more and more difficult for him to balance his accounts and he was eagerly looking forward to a better future in Pennsylvania. All the more tragic was his fate, for he was one of the few who died on the voyage and closed his eyes within sight of the promised land.

Maria Martin, his wife, is one of the most sympathetic characters among the emigrants, an earnest Christian and most devoted to her family. Her first husband, Simon Schwab, had been drowned in the Rhine and left her a baby son by the name of Johannes, who did not emigrate with the others. She was won for the pietistic movement by her brother Hans, bore exile and voluntary absence for her convictions' sake and made her submission only after five years, when her resistance to Church and State began seriously to imperil the welfare of her family. Yet as late as 1732 she was reported as being a rare attendant upon public services. In Pennsylvania we lose sight of her soon after her arrival. She seems to have bought property at 'Canastagen' (Conestoga). (See her own letters and one by Catharina Thommen in Karlsruhe and many entries and several documents in RP and KA.)

Jacob Joner, her third son, has occupied the authorities of Basel more than any other early emigrant because four times in four consecutive years he braved the perils of the sea, so serious in those days, to collect inheritances and to serve as a leader of departing emigrants down to the sea. Both Basel and Bern accused him, however, of soliciting subjects of theirs to emigrate, and, in spite of an intercession by the British ambassador at Bern with the authorities of Basel in his favor, both Basel and Bern banished him and declared that they would not release any inheritances to him any more. Since the last time, in 1752, he was the bearer of no less than twelve commissions and had probably bought part of the inheritances which he expected to collect, and since in addition to this he was robbed of a ship in which he was conducting emigrants to the sea, there is some likelihood that he was ruined and that the statement of Jacob Schaub that he lost money by going bail for him is true (RP 141, Dec. 28, 1768).—A personal description of him, of the year 1751, says that he measured 4½ feet, sported a silk neckcloth, Hamburg stockings and city shoes, a cane and a couteau.   Had a round sunburnt face, a large broad nose, dark eyes and dark curly hair and an 'aufgeworffenes grosses Maul' (up-turned large mouth).[1]

Schneider, Niclaus, of Brattelen, (linen-weaver), aged 34.
Elssbet Brogli, his wife.   Have no children.

Pays: Ten percent tax on 128 pounds...................12.—
Manumission....................................20.—   32.—

KB states that he went with his wife to Carolina.

Stohler, Fridlin, of Brattelen, (smith).
Anna Maria Heyd, his wife.
Their children:

1. Elssbet, bapt...............................Aug.   25, 1709
2. Anna Maria, bapt...........................Sept. 23, 1714
3. Anna, bapt.................................Oct.   9, 1718
4. Fridlin, bapt..............................Aug.   12, 1727
Pays: Ten percent tax on 250 pounds.............. ...25.—
Manumission....................................20.—   45.—

KB adds to the dates of the last two children: 'in Carolina.' He and especially his wife belonged also to the pietists of Pratteln, but came less into conflict with the pastor and the authorities than Maria Martin.

Till, Niclaus, of Brattelen, (linen-weaver and marksman), aged 41.
Anna Maria Düring, (from Lausen), his wife.
Their children:

1. Anna, bapt.................................Apr.   12, 1722
2. Hans Jacob, bapt...........................Sept. 21, 1723
3. Anna Maria, bapt...........................Febr. 12, 1725
4. Cathri, bapt..............................June   9, 1726
5. Niclaus, bapt.............................March 11, 1731
6. Johannes, bapt............................Jan.   24, 1735

Gratis.   Has only 85 pounds worth of property left.
KB: Anna Cathrina instead of Cathri, besides in connection with each of the children a note referring to Carolina.   A letter by Joh. Ulrich Giezendanner, a pietist who had sought religious toleration in Carolina, of Apr. 23, 1737 ('Briefe an d'Annone 244') contains the sad information that two of the children died on the voyage and the father himself ten days after arrival in Carolina.

[1] For the trial (Verhör) of Joner, and letters concerning him, printed verba, tim, see *Jahrbuch der Deutsch-Amerikanischer Historischen Gesellschaft von Illinois-*Jahrgang 1918-19: *Unpublished Documents on Emigration from the Archives of Switzerland*, by A. B. Faust, nos. 6, 7, 8, pp. 13-20.

AMT WALDENBURG

Bärenwil

Bidert, Hans Joggi, of Bärenwyl, (son of Hans deceased)._
Sara Mohlerin from Dieckten, his wife.
Their children:

    1. Joggi, bapt...............................Febr. 13, 1729
    2. Hans Martin, bapt........................Aug. 20, 1730
    3. Ursula, bapt.............................Nov. 25, 1731
    4. Sara, bapt..............................Jan. 8, 1736
    Has 170 pounds worth of property.
    Pays: Ten percent tax...........................17.—
          Manumission for himself and his wife.............20.— 37.—

Has led an honourable Christian life.

Bennwil

Spitteler, Hans, [KB Spittahler], of Bennwyl, (son of Hans deceased, day-labourer).
Catharina Schaffnerin from Eptingen, his wife.
Their children:

    1. Hans, bapt................................. ?
    2. Verena, bapt............................Nov. 3, 1720
    3. Jacob, bapt.............................Aug. 30, 1722
    4. Barbara, bapt...........................Apr. 4, 1728
    5. Hans Jacob, bapt........................May 12, 1732

Gratis. Has only 90 pounds worth of property left.
Confirmed the fact that the farmers were doing most of their work themselves and gave little employment to day-labourers. Lost his youngest son upon arrival at Philadelphia.

Höllstein

Thommen, Hans, of Höllstein, (Fridlin's son).
Veronica Flubacherin, his wife.
    Hans Jacob, their son, about ten years old.
    Gratis. Have no property.

Langenbruck

Heggendorn, Hans, (Heckendorn), of Langenbruck, (linen-weaver).
Margret Görien, (KB Jerien), from Neuenbrunnen, (his wife).
Their children:

    1. Hanss, bapt..............................Apr. 9, 1716
    2. Barbara, bapt............................Apr. 5, 1718
    3. Daniel, bapt.............................May 26, 1720
    4. Erhard, bapt.............................Aug. 11, 1726
    5. Magdalena, bapt.........................May 1, 1729
    6. Martin, bapt.............................Dec. 24, 1730
    7. Heini, bapt..............................Jan. 25, 1744

    Has 500 pounds worth of property.
    Pays: Ten percent tax...........................50.—
          Manumission for himself and his wife...........20.— 70.—

Has led an honourable Christian life Lost his youngest son on the voyage to Pennsylvania.

8

Niederdorf

Thommen, Durs, of Oberdorff (!).
Margret Rickenbacher from Rotenflue, his wife.
    1. Martin, their son.
Barbara Mohlerin from Eptingen, his wife.
Their children:
    2. Hans (son of Martin).
    3. Durss. 4. Hans Joggi. 5. Catharina. 6. Anna, (children of Durs
      above).
    Has 3100 pounds of property (RP even 3497.1).
    Pays: Ten percent tax.............................310.—
        Manumission for himself and his wife.......... 20.—   330.—

Durs Thommen's family had also been touched by the pietistic movement before leaving Switzerland. In 1732 his wife and his daughter Catharina had been taken to task for staying away from the Lord's Supper and, on applying for permission to emigrate, he himself had to answer a charge of 'Quakerism,' though the Conventus Ecclesiasticus declared him to be innocent of it.

In Pennsylvania his whole family except his sons Martin and Durs came under the influence of the Seventhday Baptists or Dunkards in their neighborhood. His son Hans Jacob and his daughters Catharina and Anna went to live with them at Ephrata, where the first two died as early as 1739 and 1742, followed by their mother before the close of the year (Briefe an d'Annone 921). Coming to Pennsylvania with a handsome sum of money, he had been able to buy a farm of 350 acres with two houses and barns at the price of £ 360 Pennsylvania or lb. 2700 Basel currency at 'Quitobihila' (Quitopahilla). In 1749 a sworn statement called him 'un homme fort riche et de Probité et de bonne Renommée, demeurant a Libanon.' In the meantime he had kept up connection with Basel by private and official correspondence.[1] The government had asked him for information as to how he had found things, and repeatedly countrymen who desired the release of inheritances had asked for his support of their petitions. In 1768 we shall meet with his son Martin and his grandson Johannes, called Hans above, who then made an attempt to resettle in the Canton of Basel.

Oberdorf

Schäublin, Christen, of Oberdorff, (smith).
Barbara Spitteler from Beenwyl, his wife.

[1] See his favorable letter of October 3, 1737, printed for the first time in the *American Historical Review* (1916), Vol. XXII, pp. 117–119, among the "Documents in Swiss Archives relating to Emigration to the American Colonies in the Eighteenth Century," contributed by A. B. Faust.

Their children:
1. Christen. 2. Uhli, 3. Barbara. 4. Catharina. 5. Anna. 6. Ursula. 7. Magdalena.

Has 1700 pounds worth of property which makes

Ten percent tax	170.—	
Bondage for him and his wife	20.—	190.—

He and his wife had also not remained untouched by the pietistic movement and early in 1722 Gmeli, who emigrated to Pennsylvania later on, had held a meeting at their smithy which caused much sensation. In 1736 he had to answer a charge of 'Quakerism.' In 1740 he was still living in Pennsylvania.

II. *Emigrants not recorded in MP*

BASEL

N. N., herdsman of the Aeschen Suburb.

Gerster says in his letter of 1737 that he came in the same ship with him and the other emigrants to Pennsylvania, but does not seem to have learned his name.

AMT FARNSBURG

Diegten

Margreth Eck, daughter of Fridlin, bapt. Nov. 24, 1709.
Had less than 100 pounds left. Emigrated because of lack of harmony with her step-mother, and found, as Gerster tells us, a husband in Pennsylvania during her first year. Her Obervogt had said of her that she was going to the "Island" of Carolina.

Gelterkinden

Hans Georg Gerster, son of Hans Georg Gerster, of Gelterkinden and Elsbeth Sparr from Herzogenbuchsee, Canton of Bern.

Hans Georg Gerster, to whose two long letters of 1737 and 1740 (Briefe an d'Annone 242 and 243) we owe so much valuable information concerning the fate of the Basel emigrants on their voyages and afterward, had the misfortune to be born illegitimate. His father repudiated his mother and believed that he had done his duty by allowing her a small consideration. Both the Canton of Basel where he was born and raised and the Canton of Bern, the home of his mother, refused to acknowledge him as a citizen. The courts of Bern declared that he belonged by his birth to Basel. Those of Basel maintained that through his mother he was entitled to citizenship in Bern. His amiable Christian character was of no avail to him. He had to emigrate to Pennsylvania in order to be admitted to citizenship. His old mother and his young bride, whom we shall meet below accompanied him.

After a favorable passage they settled in Germantown, Pa., yet even here fortune did not smile upon them. To be sure they had the joy of calling two sons their own, but he was seized with epileptic attacks which forbade him any kind of hard work and forced him to learn weaving and she suffered from violent rheumatism and a case of scurvy which long baffled all attempts to cure it. They bore however everything patiently and in a spirit that thanked God that he had chastised and also healed them again. They took affectionate care of his old mother while she was living and showed warm attachment to friends and relatives at home and in Pennsylvania where it was reciprocated by Christen Schäublin who had come over with them.

Elsbeth Sparr from Herzogenbuchsee, mother of the preceding.

Ormalingen

Ursula Schaub, wife of Hans Joggi Buser.

It is a singular coincidence that not only this Hans Joggi Buser, but also his namesake of Bennwil should see his wife join the emigrants without his knowledge and against his will. Ursula Schaub's departure from Basel is described in a report of the Obervogt (AA) as follows: 'At the departure of the Carolina people, which has lately taken place, Ursula Schaub, . . . pretending that she wished to accompany her son and daughter . . . to the ship, has secretly slipped aboard among the departing and has gone away with her children.'

But who were these children? An examination of KB of Gelter-kinden shows that she had first been married to Jacob Handschin of Rickenbach and that Joggi and Maria Handschin, whom we have met above, are her children. As moreover Joggi was accompanied by four children of his own, it is seen that it was not only her maternal affection, but also her attachment to her grandchildren that drew her away from her second husband and brought her to America.

Hans Joggi Thommen.
Margreth Apothecker, his wife.
Their children:

1. Anna Maria, bapt. . . . . .July   29, 1731
2. Barbara, bapt. . . . . .Jan.   1, 1733
3. Margreth, bapt. . . . . .July   11, 1734

He was one of the poorest among the emigrants, but since his name is on the final list of the Obervogt, it must be assumed that he somehow found the means to start on his journey.

Rothenfluh

Hans Rudi Erb, son of Hemmen Erb and Maria Itin, unmarried, bapt. Dec. 8, 1709.

He is not only mentioned by the Commission, but also on the final list of the Obervogt, where he is credited with a balance of 148 pounds in his favour.

Martin Gass, weaver.

His children by Barbara Schäublin from Gelterkinden, his former wife:

1. Verene, bapt..May   23, 1711
2. Anna Margreth, bapt........................Sept. 10, 1713
3. Barbara, bapt.................................Nov.   25, 1714
4. Martin, bapt..................................Febr. 20, 1718
5. Hans Jacob, bapt...........................Nov.   1, 1722

Sara Hassler, from Buus, his present wife.
His children by her:

1. Abraham, bapt...............................Febr. 23, 1727
2. Anna, bapt....................................Oct.   16, 1729
3. Catharina, bapt.............................Oct.   26, 1732

Martin Gass also figures not only on the last report of the Commission, but also on the final list of the Obervogt which says that he had only 68 pounds 9 sh. left, not enough to pay his debts. Evidently, however, he had made ready to leave and may have been among the ten, who received an indirect contribution toward their travelling expenses from the government (RP 107, Apr. 30, 1736).

As for a number of other parties of FARNSBURG Amt who had received permission to leave, it can be proved that several of them did not emigrate and that with the remaining there is no likelihood that they did.

Heinrich Weibel of Nusshof, with a wife, four daughters, baptized between 1726 and 1732, and a son, bapt. Nov. 7, 1734. He was fully expecting to go when he died in the midst of his preparations. KB of Wintersingen reports his death as follows: 'April 6. Heini Weibel . . . died at the time when he was '*in procinctu*' to go with others to Carolina.' It is not likely that his widow wanted or ventured to go alone with her little children.

Ulrich Schönenberger of Rothenfluh, married to Catharina Erb, a sister of Rudi, the emigrant, cannot have emigrated at this time because he had a daughter Anna, bapt. May 6, 1736, *i.e.*, just about the time of the departure of the others, and a son Fridrich, bapt. Aug. 30, 1739.

Hans Jacob Mundweiler, the lame knitter of Tenniken, had a son Hans Jacob, bapt. Aug. 7, 1736, and another, Jacob, bapt. March 1, 1739.

Adam Wörli, Hans Adam Wehrlin, the smith of Zeglingen, had another daughter, Maria, bapt. Apr. 14, 1737.

Regarding *Hans Thommen* of Ormalingen, *Heini Buser*, the carpenter of Sissach and *Jacob Oberer* of Tenniken, none of whom appears on the final list of the Obervogt, there is no evidence that they availed themselves of their permission.

AMT HOMBURG
Känerkinden

Matthis Eglin, linen-weaver.
Catharina Dürrenberger, from Lupsingen, his wife.
Their children:

1. Martin, bapt.................................July 18, 1730
2. Barbara, bapt...............................Aug.   3, 1732
3. Anna, bapt.................................Dec. 20, 1735

According to RP 107, 296, Jan. 28, 1736, he asked and received permission to go to Lorraine where he had a relative and according to RL 1736 he paid an emigration tax of lb. 15.— on 300 pounds. Yet, as KB notes in connection with each of the children that they went to Carolina, it must be assumed that they proceeded beyond Lorraine to America.

Thürnen

Heini Gisin, 53 years of age.
Verena Weibel, his wife, 45 years.
Their children:

1. Heinrich, bapt............................Jan.   7, 1731
2. Hans Jacob, bapt.........................Jan. 19, 1734

His liabilities surpassed his assets by 180 pounds.

Hans Jacob Märcklin, 56 years of age.
Anna Hofmann, his wife, 39 years.
Their children:

1. Anna, bapt...............................Dec. 25, 1717
2. Catharina, bapt.........................Sept. 21, 1720
3. Fridric(h), bapt........................Aug.   1, 1723
4. Anna Maria, bapt........................Febr. 26, 1730

He realized by his 'Gant' 266 pounds and owed 230.

Hans Martin, 41 years of age.
Eva Schaub, 43 years.
Their children:

1. Elsbeth..................................16 years old
2. Barbara.................................13 years old
3. Johannes, bapt.........................Nov. 27, 1731

Owned nothing.

These last three families must have emigrated in spite of their poverty. They are found on the final list of the Obervogt where in the case of Hans Buser and Rudi Schaub it is expressly remarked that they were not going. The latter reapplied, however, in 1738.

AMT MUENCHENSTEIN

Benken

Christoffel Spar, Spahr, linen-weaver.
Anna Gass, his wife.
Their children: Niclaus, bapt. Apr. 27, 1727, and three daughters, baptized later. Had only a little over two pounds left. They started for America, but did not get farther than Zweibrücken in the Palatinate. The son entered French military service and was never heard of again (GAV 19, July 5, 1784). The daughters were married in the territory of Zweibrücken and in the Canton of Basel.

Pratteln

Hans Meyer, the herdsman.
Elsbeth Guldenmann, of Gelterkinden, his wife.
Their children:

   1. Elsbeth, bapt.............................Aug. 13, 1713
   2. Hans Fridrich, bapt........................Nov. 24, 1733
   3–5. Two more sons and one more daughter mentioned in the final
      report of the Obervogt, whose names and dates could not be
      ascertained. Some other children of theirs had died.

His assets were lb. 880.6.6, his liabilities 661.12.8. Though not recorded in MP, he left with permission, and his actual emigration to Carolina is not only confirmed by the entry: 'In Carolina' in connection with the baptism of his son in KB, but also by verbal report. Hans Spring, who had come over to engage emigrants for Carolina, told in Muttenz in 1740 that the former herdsman of Pratteln had become proprietor of 300 acres of land and owner of a handsome lot of cattle in Carolina and was his nearest neighbor (AA).

Rotes Haus
   N. N., brother of the 'Lehnsmann' of that place. Went with others to America in May, 1736 (AA, Report of Obervogt, Sept. 4, 1736).
   Margreth Vögtlin and *Margreth Brüderlin*, her daughter, of Muttenz, and *Jacob Frey* of Pratteln do not seem to have availed themselves of their permission, for their names are not on the final list of Münchenstein (RP 107,429). Moreover Margreth Brüderlin reapplied for emigration again in 1749 and was also wavering in her resolution then.

AMT WALDENBURG

Bennwil

Barbara Börlin, daughter of the former Meyer Wernet B. of Bennwil, married to Hans Joggi Buser there March 10, 1733.

She had left her husband on account of his inordinate luxuriousness which had been impairing her health and making life with him unbearable. Instead of supporting her action the Marriage Court had finally gone so far as to lock her up with him in a prison cell of the Spahlen Gate until she should change her mind and promise to live with him again. After having borne this extremity for a while she had given the promise, but she was no sooner released than she sought refuge with her friends in the country and finally made her escape from the canton apparently not without the aid of members of Durs Thommen's family.

She came to Pennsylvania in the same ship with the other emigrants of 1736 and, while the Marriage Court at home pronounced her divorce '*excapite malitiosae desertionis*,' she like several members of the Thommen family found her way to the celibate community of the Seventhday Baptists or Dunkards at Ephrata, with whom Gerster reports her in 1740. About six years later, however, she had left Ephrata and, as is attested by Conrad Weiser, was married again. She was not manumitted till April, 1749, in connection with the release of her paternal inheritance to her new husband Wernhard Stohler, an emigrant of 1738. This is not recorded in MP, but in RL of 1750.

Eva Gysin, Gisin, daughter of Ulin G. and Salome Börlin, cousin of Barbara Börlin above, bapt. Apr. 1, 1710.

She had tried to get permission in the prescribed way, but the Council had denied her petition because it reached them after they had decided not to grant any more. Ten days later she succeeded however in attaining her end by another way. She was granted manumission for her marriage with Hans Georg Gerster above, and this gave her liberty to follow him wherever she pleased, even to America. Her manumission, recorded in MP Apr. 14, was not free of charge, but it was left to the 'Dreyer Amt,' the financial department of the city, to provide her with a 'viaticum.' She had earned and saved 70 pounds by then.

1737

Considerable time before the beginning of the year some eighteen subjects from Biel-Benken, Arisdorf and other places had come to Basel and expressed their desire to go to Carolina, but the Mayor had denied them the Chancery order to their Obervögte, and the Council had upheld his action (RP 108, Oct. 20, 1736). Still earlier the Council had learned of some 'plotting' at the house of the 'Lehnsmann,' fief holder or sub-tenant Lienert Heyer on the Rütihard, and ordered the Obervogt to look into the matter. The result of his investigation, embodied in his report of Sept. 4, 1736 (AA), was in substance as follows:

Lienert Heyer's brother and Antoni Rieger of Benken and Jacob Küntzlin, a carpenter, and Hans Kapp, a wagon-maker, of Münchenstein had discussed emigration to Pennsylvania. They had been actuated to do so partly by the letter of *Gondy*[1] in praise

---

[1] This letter of Antony Gondy was printed for the first time in the *American Historical Review* (1916), Vol. XXII, pp. 115–117, among the *Documents in Swiss Archives relating to Emigration to American Colonies in the Eighteenth Century*, contributed by A. B. Faust.

of Carolina, written in Charleston, S. C., in 1733, but only lately come into their possession through a man of Grenzach across the Rhine, and partly by their own unfavorable circumstances. The carpenter and the wagon-maker had complained of the growing competition in their trades and all of them had arrived at the conviction that their heavy debts and the 5 percent interest they had to pay in consequence of the mandate (see Introduction) combined with the tithes of grain and wine made it impossible for them to sustain themselves here any longer.

While Jacob Küntzlin and Hans Kapp gave up the thought of emigration for the present and did not go till three years later, Lienert Heyer and Antoni Rieger actively pushed their preparations and succeeded in obtaining the consent of the government. They claimed to have friends in the vicinity of Mannheim in the Palatinate and, if they did not find their fortunes there, they would seek it in another country. The following table of their families and their property is based on FAF and supplemented from AA and KB.

Benken

FAF Saturday, May 11, 1737. From
Rudolf Lützler, of Benken, (60 years of age),
Lienert Heyer, his son-in-law from there, (41 years of age), and
Clara Lützler, his wife, (32 years of age), who also intend to go to the Palatinate,
    Pro manumissione at lb. 10.......................... 30.—
    Tax on lb. 1200 worth of Rudolf Lützler's property at
    10 percent....................................120.—
    Tax on lb. 200 worth of Lienert Heyer's property at 10
    percent.................................... 20.—   170.—

Children of Lienert and Clara:
    1. Anna Barbara, bapt......................Febr. 22, 1724
    2. Elisabeth, bapt.........................June   17, 1725
    3. Leonhard, bapt.........................Dec.   25, 1727
    4. Hans Rudolf, bapt......................May   29, 1729
    5. Hans Ulrich, bapt......................July   29, 1731
    6. Clara.................................2½ years old
Ibidem. From

Anthoni Rieger, [KB Anthone Rüeger], of Benken, (47 years of age),
Barbara Würtzin, (from Wittinsburg), his wife, (also aged 47), and
Elsbeth Scholerin, (from Zunzgen), her mother, (72 years of age),
    who intend to go to the Palatinate,
    Pro manumissione at lb. 10.........................30.—
    Tax on lb. 500 worth of property drawn away at 10
    percent.....................................50.—   80.—

Children of Anthoni Rieger by Juditha Schaub, his first wife:
    1. Anthoni, shoemaker, bapt....................July   8, 1713
    2. Burkhard, tailor, bapt.....................Sept. 19, 1717
    3. Barbara, bapt.............................Apr.   5, 1719

His children by his present wife:

    1. Maria.................................7 years old
    2. Hans Jacob, bapt.......................Apr. 22, 1734

Ibidem. From the deceased *Jacob Schaub's* (and Barbara Würtz's) children of Wittisberg,

    1. Jacob, shoemaker, bapt.....................Sept. 9, 1714
    2. Anna, bapt.............................Jan. 31, 1719
    3. Martin, bapt...........................July 27, 1721
    Tax on their lb. 130 worth of property at 10 percent...........13.—

Another daughter, by the name of Elsbeth, bapt. Dec. 20, 1716, did not emigrate, for according to KB of Rümlingen she came to Waldenburg in 1743 though her family in America longed very much for her.

The further experiences of the two families are known through a letter by Lienert Heyer written two years after his emigration and an entry in RP 129, Aug. 7, 1756.   Lienert Heyer lost his youngest child, Clara, by the smallpox in England and the next youngest, Hans Ulrich, in America, but had another son Antoni.   In 1739 he and Antoni Rieger were living at 'Dolben Hagen,' apparently meant for Tulpehocken, Pa.   In 1756 the Junt brothers attest his presence in Virginia and report his willingness to renounce his claims to an inheritance in favor of his son-in-law who stayed in Switzerland.   Besides it can hardly be amiss to recognize him in the Lieni who renders such generous assistance to Jacob Pfau, the writer of the unsigned letter of Sept. 17, 1750, printed by A. B. Faust, *Jahrbuch der Deutsch-Amer. Hist. Ges. von Illinois*, 1918 19. He took his fellow-villager with his family and his things all the way up from the coast to Frederikstown, Virginia.

Since Gerster speaks of the safe arrival of four families from Basel in Philadelphia this year, we have to look for two more and may find them in Martin Heggendorn or Heckendorn with his wife and children and Hans Itin and his wife.   To be sure they petitioned only for permission to go to the Palatinate, or to Lorraine or the Palatinate (RP 108, Apr. 6 and 13), but they may likewise have used this only for a pretext, because permission to go to America would hardly have been obtainable this year.   The entries in FAF are as follows:

Saturday, May 11, 1737. From *Hans Itin* of Arristorff and Elsbeth Weber, his wife, who also intend to move away,
    pro Manumissione at lb. 10..........................20.—
    Tax on lb. 150 worth of property..................15.— (35.—)

Saturday, May 25, 1737. From *Martin Heckendorn* and Ursula Jenni, his wife, of Langenbruck,
    for Manumission at lb. 10..........................20.—
    10 percent tax on lb. 900 withdrawn................90.— (110.—)

Their seven children in KB: Elsbeth, bapt. March 2, 1718; Magdalena, March 19, 1719; Anna, Nov. 3, 1720; Sara, Nov. 7, 1723; Ursul, Nov. 3, 1726; Maria, Nov. 11, 1732; Barbara, Jan. 9, 1735.

1738

This year the government opened the gates for emigration to America again.   It did not discourage applications from the start, but required especially full particulars regarding the economic circumstances and moral conduct of the applicants and finally acceded to a proposition of its Emigrant Commission according to which they were divided into two classes.   Those who were moderately well situated and might be expected to get along if they put forth their best efforts, or who were particularly useful to their communities, as, *e.g.*, the schoolmaster at Buus, were told to remain. Those who either were more or less of a charge, in a few cases also an annoyance to their communities, were allowed to go, though their pastors and their Obervögte were required to make the usual efforts to dissuade them.   In this case they were provided with printed copies of a letter by Mauritz Göttschi's widow, which painted the condition of emigrants, especially of those who had to serve for their passage, in Pennsylvania in the darkest colors.[1] The schedule of distribution is preserved in CAM and shows that no less than 690 copies were sent out, of which, *e.g.*, Farnsburg and Waldenburg received 250 and 150 with the order to pass on 222 and 120 to the pastors of their district while they could retain the remainder for their own efforts.   Some large parishes like Sissach and Bubendorf received 48 copies each, and our investigation below proves that not a few emigrants desisted from their undertaking. Those who decided to go after all were however released from all payments of fees, a consideration which heretofore and hereafter was shown only to individuals.

We begin with a reproduction of the list on which the applicants appear divided into the two classes and arrange it in our usual alphabetical order of Aemter and villages.   It is without date, but must have been attached to the report of the Commission of March 29 (AA).

[1] A reprint of this letter can be found in *The American Historical Review* (1916), Vol. XXII, pp. 123–125, among the "Documents in Swiss Archives relating to Emigration to American Colonies in the Eighteenth Century," contributed by A. B. Faust.

List of Emigrants of 1738

[Amt Farnsburg]

Oltingen:
 Johannes Gisin, the 'Bahnbruder'
 [member of the Bann] maneat.
Sissach:
 Jacob Hoffmann emigr.
 Jacob Kestenholtz emigr.
 Sebastian Oberer emig.
 Sebastian Schaub emigret cum
 patre, if he is willing to go.
 Martin Tschudin emig.
Tennikhen:
 Joggi Thommen emigr.
Tieffligen:
 Hans Schneider emig.
Wenssligen:
 Hans Buss, the schoolmaster
 maneat.
Wintersingen:
 Heini and Bascheltin emig., if
 they take mother along.
Zuntzgen:
 Jacob Becher emig.
 Hans Boni emigr.
 Jacob Bossart emig.
 Heinrich Buser emig.

[Amt Homburg]

Buckten:
 Rudi Schaub emigr.
 Martin Thommen mane
Leuffelfingen:
 Hans Buser, Ganis emigr.
 Wernhard Gröber ⎫
 and Hans Gröber ⎭ mane
 Theodor Vögtlein emigr.

[Amt Liestal]

Lausen:
 Adam Buser maneat
 Martin Schaffner maneat
 Jacob Wäibel manet

[Amt Münchenstein]

Brattelen:
 Hans Recher go

[Amt Waldenburg]

Arbotschweil:
 Heini Rudin emigr.

Joggi Rudi emigr.
Agnes Schäublein shall remain.
Benweil:
 Hans Reufflein mane.
 Christen Schäubli emig.
Bubendorf:
 Emanuel Bürgin shall remain
 Hans Bürgin, Hans'son emig.
 Hans Rudi Bürgin has had his
 'Gant' (sale) and 8 children.
 lb. 400 worth of property.
 Dubit. emig.
 Heini Bürgin, Tailor Heini emig.
 Hans Neffzger shall remain.
 Hans Spitthaler may go.
 Adam Stohler emigret.
 Heirech(!) Thommen, Hans Joggi's
 son emig.
 Joggi Thommen. Should the pas-
 tor ask the children by the first
 marriage [added: and their
 Vogt], whether they wish to go
 along, and, if they do not wish
 to go, their share of the in-
 heritance should be retained and
 delivered to the Vögte (guar-
 dians).
 Hans Conrad Weiss remains.
 Imber Wissmer shall remain.
Lampenberg:
 Heini Fluebaher emigr.
 Peter Hemmig emig.
 Johannes Krayer maneat.
 Hans Regennas emigr.
 Heini Thommen emigr.
 Heini Tschudin emigr.
Lupsingen:
 Hans Rudi manet
Ramlispurg:
 Hans Adam Schelcker emig.
 Geörg Stohler emig., dissuade
 children from going.
 Adam Weibel emig.
Regotschweil:
 Fridlin Negelin emigr.
Ziffen:
 Fritz Recher emigret.
 Hans Recher emigr.
 Durs Schäublein maneat

AMT FARNSBURG

Diepflingen

Hans Schneider, unmarried.
Hopes to have 100 pounds left.—Leads a quiet life free from vice.

Sissach

* *Jacob Hoffmann*, lace-maker.
Barbara Tschudi, his wife. Their children: Elisabeth, Jan. 10, 1731; Barbara
  Esther, Susanna, Jacob, Verena, between Sept. 1732 and Febr. 1738.—As
  another son, Sebastian, was added to these in 1743, bapt. Apr. 19 and
  deceased soon afterwards, the family can neither have emigrated this year nor
  in 1740.

Jacob Kestenholtz, lace-maker.
Anna Maria Blinz, his wife.
Their children:

1.	Barbara, bapt.............................	May	18, 1727
2.	Hans Jacob, bapt..........................	Oct.	10, 1728
3.	Hans Geörg, bapt..........................	June	23, 1733
4.	Sebastian, bapt............................	Febr.	14, 1736

Does not expect to have anything left and depends for his passage upon an
aunt without children and aid promised by fellow emigrants. One of the four
children may have died before emigration.

Sebastian Oberer, miller's helper or day-labourer.
Salome Suter from Tenniken, his wife.
Their children:

1.	Elisabeth, bapt............................	Sept.	28, 1732
2.	Sebastian, bapt............................	Aug.	28, 1734

Expects to have 100 pounds left and does not feel quite sure as to whether his
father-in-law, Heini Suter of Tenniken, will contribute toward his expenses or
not. Since RP does not record that he asked for a 'Gant,' it is doubtful whether
he actually emigrated.

* *Sebastian Schaub*, lace-maker, Hans Heinrich Schaub, his father, a widower.
Elsbeth Tschudin, his wife. Their children: Elisabeth, bapt. Jan. 5, 1734, Hans
  Heinrich, Oct. 23, 1735. The birth of another daughter Anna, bapt. May
  7, 1739, proves that they did not go.

Martin Tschudi, lace-maker.
Rosina Schaffner from Tenniken, his wife.
Their children:

1.	Barbara, bapt.............................	Oct.	26, 1732
2.	Anna, bapt.................................	March 18, 1736
3.	Elisabeth, bapt............................	Dec.	8, 1737

Expects to have about 100 pounds left.

Tenniken

Joggi Thommen, day-labourer.
Barbara Bossart, his wife.
Their children:

1.	Anna Maria, bapt..........................	July	5, 1735
2.	Child, perhaps baptized elsewhere.		

Hopes to have a small balance in his favour and expects a contribution from
his father-in-law besides. His pastor attests his attendance upon divine service

and Holy Communion and his and his wife's industriousness. According to
GAV 20, 14 and 161, they emigrated, but were never heard of again.

Wintersingen

Ursula Freyvogel, widow of Heini Itin.
Her two sons:

     1. Heini Itin, bapt........................Febr. 23, 1721
     2. Basche Itin, bapt.......................Aug. 6, 1724

     Expect a balance of about 300 pounds.

Their pastor intimates that the parish might do quite well without them.
They did not possess much property and their mother was a pretty restless
kind of a woman, who frequently molested her neighbors, went rarely to church
and did not bring up her boys in the fear of the Lord. The community would
not only be content, but would greatly rejoice, if she were permitted to go. This
testimonial accomplished its ends. The permission granted to the boys was
conditioned upon the going of the mother.

Zunzgen

Jacob Becher, KB Bächer, lace-maker.
Catharina Oberer, from Sissach, his wife.
Their children:

     1. Elisabeth, bapt...........................May 3, 1722
     2. Johannes, bapt...........................March 19, 1724
     3. Heinrich, bapt...........................Febr. 17, 1726
     4. Anna, bapt..............................May 15, 1729

     Claims to have no property whatever and depends upon aid promised by fellow-
emigrants. One of the four children may have stayed in the Canton or died
before emigration.

* Hans Boni, KB Bonni, day-labourer.
Salome Meyer, from Kilchberg, his wife. Their children: Anna Margreth, bapt.
     Aug. 12, 1731, Johannes, Nov. 1733, Jacob, Dec. 1735.
     As these were followed by Anna, bapt. Nov. 9, 1738, Matthis, bapt. March 5
1741, deceased in 1755, etc., this family did not leave the country.

Jacob Bossart.
     Since KB does not give less than three Jacob Bossarts, it is not possible to
determine the names of his wife and three children. Moreover, he probably did
not emigrate, because his name is not on the list of those who applied for a 'Gant.'

Heinrich Buser, lace-maker.
     Had a wife and three children whose names cannot be given because there
are several Heinrich Busers. He seems to have emigrated, because he is among
those who asked for a 'Gant.'

AMT HOMBURG

Buckten

* Rudi Schaub, weaver, herdsman.
Anna Buser, his wife. Their children: Anna Maria, bapt. Aug. 8, 1724, with
     the note: 'Went to Zegligen 1744'; Catharina, bapt. Apr. 1729; Hans Jacob,
     bapt. July 1732, with the note: 'Went to Augst 1755, now in Corsica 1758';
     Anna, bapt. Sept. 1734, with the note: 'adultera.'
     The notes show that Rudi Schaub emigrated this year as little as he had done
in 1736.

Läufelfingen

Hans Buser, called Canis Hans, day-labourer.
Anna Schaub, from Sissach, his wife.
Their children:

1. Barbel, bapt.............................June 24, 1727
2. Hans Uhle, bapt..........................Aug. 31, 1730
3. Jacob, bapt.............................May 24, 1733
4. Anna, bapt.............................July 25, 1734
   A fifth child which is attributed to him in AA is not recorded in KB
   of Läufelfingen.

Thinks he may pay his debts by hook and crook. His pastor speaks of him in the highest terms. He had always been obliging, pious, industrious, one of the 'Stillen im Lande,' so that he should have been glad to see him stay. As was noted above, he had wished to emigrate in 1736.

Theodorr Vöglin, day-labourer.
Anna Schneider, from Diepflingen, his wife.
Hans, their child, bapt. Jan. 1, 1738.

May have a balance of 70 pounds. His pastor states that he had conducted himself blamelessly so that he could recommend him quite well to all fellow-Christians.

AMT LIESTAL

Seltisberg

Rudi Spinler.
Elsbeth Hafelfinger, his wife. Their children: Hans Joggi, bapt. Dec. 1731; Sebastian, bapt. Aug. 1733; Barbara, bapt. Febr. 1737.

Owned nothing. He is not on the list of the Commission, nor in RP, but only in an application in AA. A note in KB which states that his oldest son died in 1788 makes his emigration doubtful.

AMT MUENCHENSTEIN

Pratteln

Hans Recher from Ziefen.
Anna Tschudi, from Muttenz, his wife.
Their children:

1. Johannes, bapt............................Dec. 10, 1726
2. Anna Margreth, bapt......................July 18, 1728
3. Hans Friedrich, bapt.....................Febr. 21, 1730
4. Niclaus, bapt............................May 25, 1731
5. Anna Helena, bapt........................Aug. 31, 1732
6. Anna Barbara, bapt.......................Jan. 5, 1734

His 'Gant' was granted him Apr. 9. His emigration is confirmed by the notes added to his children's dates in KB. Four times: 'In Virginia,' once 'Is with the others in Virginia' and once 'Has gone to the New-land.'

AMT WALDENBURG

Since the testimonials granted by the pastors of this Amt for the most part cover quite a number of emigrants, it seems advisable to preface them in substance and to refer to them by the letters A, B, C and a.

Testimonial A: The following three honest men have never been called to appear before an Hon. Bann or Sessio on account of gambling, excessive use of wine or other offensive conduct and have never indulged in idleness, but have been industrious in their trades and obliging and peaceable toward their neighbours so that no complaint has come before me.

Testimonial B: They have conducted themselves honestly and 'bürgerlich,' attended divine service properly, not given particular offence to anybody, been diligent and industrious in their trades and nevertheless been unable to get on. I cannot remember either that I have been obliged to call one or the other before an Hon. Bann or Sessio.

Testimonial C: After consulting with the fellow members of my Bann I have learned that they have conducted themselves respectably as it behooves obedient subjects and also made a hard struggle to sustain themselves by the work of their hands.

Testimonial a: Upon inquiry from the magistrates of the three communities Bennwyl, Höhlstein and Lampenberg I have learned that they have conducted themselves well and without giving cause for complaint, and led Christian, honest and industrious lives with which I agree as far as I know them.

Arboldswill

Heini Rudin.
Verena Oberer, his wife.
Their children:

1.	Magdalena, bapt.	March	22,	1716
2.	Verena, bapt.	June	2,	1720
3.	Johannes, bapt.			?
4.	Ursula, bapt.	Apr.	23,	1724
5.	Elisabeth, bapt.	Oct.	7,	1725
6.	Barbara, bapt.	Apr.	20,	1732
7.	Heinrich, bapt.	Apr.	3,	1735

Failed in business about ten years ago. All his property was sold and did not suffice to pay his debts. Testim. B.

Joggi Rudi, called Stöcklin Joggi, aged 36.
Anna Thommen, his wife.
Their children:

1.	Jacob, bapt.	Febr.	12,	1725
2.	Heini, bapt.	Aug.	16,	1733

Was in foreign service for a while and had to be taken to task by an Hon. Bann upon his return. The admonitions bore good fruit. Failed some years ago, but recuperated and bought some property again.

Bennwil

Christen Schäublin, lace-maker, 50 years of age.
Anna Hemmig, his present wife.
Their children:

1.	Maria, bapt.	Jan.	31,	1723
2.	Hans Jacob, bapt.	Febr.	13,	1724
3.	Johannes, bapt.	Oct.	6,	1726
4.	Anna Cathrina, bapt.	Dec.	14,	1727
5.	Anna, a daughter by his first marriage.			

According to KB certificates of baptism were issued to Johannes in 1752 and to Anna Cathrina in 1756, which makes the emigration of the family very doubtful. Testim. A.

Bubendorf

Hans Bürgin, son of Hans, potter.
Wife and children cannot be ascertained because there are several by that name.
Expected balance of 30 pounds.   Testim. A.

Hans Rudi Bürgin, lace-maker, aged 44.
Maria Bürgi, his wife.
Their children:

1. Johann Rudolf, bapt.	Jan.	14,	1720
2. Heini, bapt.	Nov.	11,	1721
·3. Chrischona, bapt.	Dec.	5,	1723
4. Emanuel, bapt.	Dec.	9,	1725
5. Maria, bapt.	Aug.	1,	1728
6. Johannes, bapt.	July	2,	1730
7. Jacob, bapt.	May	3,	1733
8. Adam, bapt.	Jan.	1,	1736

Assets 1400 pounds, liabilities 1000.   Testim. B.

Heini Bürgin, tailor Heini.
Barbara Rudi, from Ziefen, his wife.
Their children:

1. Johannes, bapt.	Sept.	9,	1734
2. Heinrich, bapt.	Aug.	12,	1736
3. Barbara, bapt.	March	16,	1738

Expected balance of 150 pounds.   Testim. A.

Hans Spitteler, aged 25.
Barbara Bürgin, his wife.

Barbara, their daughter, bapt. . . . . March 31, 1737

Possessed a little vineyard estimated at 26 pounds and another little piece of ground worth 36, while he owed 16.   Testim. B.

Adam Stohler, lace-maker, 44 years of age.
Maria Schweitzer, his wife, aged 45.
Their children:

1. Anna, bapt.	July	19,	1722
2. Hans Jacob, bapt.	June	7,	1727
3. Maria, bapt.	June	19,	1729
4. Adam, bapt.	Oct.	28,	1731

Total value of his property estimated at 125 pounds, liabilities 100.   Testim. B. Although his reference to a letter of Riggenbacher in praise of Carolina does not make it improbable that they went there first, they cannot have stayed there because Maria Schweitzer is reported to have died at Bethlehem, Pa., at the age of 82 after having been connected by a second marriage with Felix Hauser.   An illegitimate grand-daughter of hers was married to Johannes Springer in Philadelphia and had two little daughters living at the time of her death in April 1774 (GAV 19, June 25, 1781).

Matthias Stohler, brother of Adam, herdsman.
A son of his, probably either Matthias, bapt. June 22, 1721, or Heinrich, May 30, 1726, though the petition on behalf of his emigration makes the son who goes with him 13 or 14 years old.

Matthias Stohler is not on the list of the Commission, but among the emigrants who were granted a 'Gant.'

Owing to the long illness of his wife, who had died only a short while ago, he had consumed all he possessed and been compelled to sustain himself by tending flocks and herds, which repeatedly appears to have been the ultimate resort of paupers.

Heirech Thommen, Hans Joggi's son.
Maria Mohler, his wife.
    1. Heinrich, their son, bapt..................Jan.   20, 1737
    Balance of 150 pounds. Testim. A.

Joggi Thommen, tailor, 46 years of age.
Anna Dietrich, his present wife.
a. Children by his first marriage with Maria Bürgi:
    1. Anna, bapt....................Oct.   30, 1718
    2. Hans Jacob, bapt....................Nov. 24, 1726
b. Children by his present marriage:
    1. Hans, bapt....................July   13, 1731
    2. Heinrich, bapt....................Dec. 27, 1733
c. Children of Anna Dietrich by her first marriage with Jacob Weber of Oberdorf,
    whose dates cannot be given owing to the loss of KB:
    1. Anna Weber. 2. Barbara Weber. 3. Hans Jacob Weber.
    Property estimated at 549 pounds, liabilities 330. Testim. B.

Lampenberg

Heini Fluebacher, Hemmenheini's son, day-labourer, aged 36.
Magdalena Walliser, his wife.
    Heini, their son, bapt. .... March 17, 1737.
    KB of Lampenberg and Binningen show that he had at least six more children,
Martin and Hans Jacob at Lampenberg in 1738 and 1741 and Anna Barbara
and three others at Binningen where he was herdsman in the employ of the castle.
Testim. a.

Peter Hemmig, lace-maker, some forty years of age.
Barbara Frey, his wife.
Their children:
    1. Barbara, bapt....................Aug.   6, 1724
    2. Hans Jacob, bapt....................Sept. 28, 1727
    3. Magdalena, bapt....................Oct.   3, 1734
    4. Peter, bapt....................Nov. 25, 1736
    Total value of property estimated at 340 pounds, liabilities 150. Testim. a.

Johannes Regenass, son of Johannes, lace-maker, aged 34.
Margreth Spilhofer, from Eptingen, his wife.
Their children:
    1. Hans, bapt....................Oct. 22, 1727
    2. Maria, bapt....................Aug. 20, 1730
    3. Elsbeth, bapt....................Febr. 27, 1735
    4. Salome, bapt....................Dec.   9, 1736
    5. Hans Jacob, bapt....................March 2, 1738
    Possessed nothing but a lace-loom on which he owed, including interest, more
than it was worth. Testim. a.

Heini Thommen, lace-maker, aged 37½.
Verena Rudi, his wife, and four children.
    Postponed their emigration till 1749.

Heinrich Tschudin, 37 years of age.
Barbara Jost, his wife, aged 38.
Their seven children: Heinrich, Johannes, Barbara, etc., baptized between Apr.
    1717 and Apr. 1737.
    They emigrated neither this year nor in 1740 when their village tried in vain
to get rid of them. They preferred begging at home and in Basel to working in
America.

Ramlinsburg

Hans Adam Schelcker, KB Schälcker, aged 51, whose wife is called Magdalena
Häner in AA, while the mother of his children is Magdalena Thommen, lit.
Thommännin, in KB.

Their children:

  1. Hans Jacob, bapt............................   ?
  2. Hans Adam, bapt...........................Oct.   28, 1727
  3. Johannes, bapt.............................Oct.   3, 1734

Property estimated at 245 pounds, liabilities 175.

Görg Stohler, day-labourer, 50 years of age.
Anna Rudi, his wife.
Their children:

 * 1. Johannes, bapt.............................Oct.   28, 1714
   2. Wernhard, bapt............................Dec.   29, 1715
 * 3. Heini, bapt...............................May   11, 1717
   4. Görg, bapt................................   ?

Owed as much as he possessed.   Wernhard and perhaps also Görg emigrated
with him, while not only Johannes, who assumed his reponsibilities, but also Heini
stayed.   Both are among those who offered to go security for Wernhard when he
returned from Pennsylvania in 1749 to collect the paternal inheritance of his
wife Barbara Börlin.—His pastor claims to have dissuaded him from emigrating
a year ago.   Testim. B.

* *Adam Weibel*, 30 years of age.
Anna Gysin, his wife and two children.

Postponed their emigration till 1749.

Reigoldswil

Fridlin Nägelin, baker.
Elsbeth Tschudi, from Muttenz, his wife.
Their children:

  1. Elsbeth, bapt.............................Dec.   5, 1717
  2. Margreth, bapt............................   ?
  3. Gertrud, bapt.............................Feb.   24, 1722
  4. Salome, born.............................March 16, 1724
  5. Johannes, born...........................Sept.   18, 1725
  6. Hans Rudolf, born........................Sept.   22, 1728
  7. Barbara, and with her Salome, Johannes and
        Hans Rudolf, bapt.......................May   3, 1732
  8. Samuel, bapt.............................June   26, 1735

Fridlin Nägelin, who, as the many entries and documents in RP
and KA show, so largely occupied the attention of the Council and
the Church, had quite a tragic fate.   First he grew utterly poor by
mishaps and ill management.   Then he became a fervent pietist
and thereby enlisted the interest of the pietistic circles in the city
of Basel, but brought new trouble upon his head at home.   He
might perhaps have been pardoned for holding other heterodox
views, but it was not to be condoned that he refused to bear arms
and take the oath of allegiance, and banishment was the inevitable
consequence.   It was only after ten years that he made his sub-

mission and was formally received into the Reformed Church again, on which occasion four of his children were baptized together. He was given a chance to make a new start at home, but the worst was still to come two years later in 1734.

His eldest son, a boy of nineteen, had been seized with the rage of the youth of his village for gambling and carousing and not being able to get the money he wanted at home he tried to find it in other ways. Seduced by a young companion who was ahead of him on the road of evil, he finally committed together with him a cold-blooded murder, all the circumstances of which up to their execution are related in minute detail in RP and a whole fascicle of original documents. The crime was ghastly and cruel the atonement. Their victims were a young married couple whose little boy they spared. First they tried to choke them to death. Then the woman's throat was cut and, when in spite of that she reappeared behind them, she was finished with an axe, as was her husband who was also giving signs of life again. In its turn Justice was not satisfied with taking their lives. After they had been subjected to torture to extort further confessions from them, they were sentenced first to receive eight strokes from below upward, then three heart-thrusts and if they were not yet dead, to be choked completely to death. After that their bodies were to be twined on wheels.

Four years later Fridlin Nägelin emigrated with his wife and remaining children when in addition to these experiences he was on the point of losing his homestead again. He could not be diverted from his purpose.

Ziefen

Fritz Recher, 30 years of age.
Anna Senn, his wife.
    1. Anna, 2. Esther, their children.
He expected a balance of 70 pounds. Testim. C.

Hans Recher, aged 38.
Kunigunda Liechtli, his wife.
Their children:

1. Maria, bapt.	Jan.	30, 1724
2. Durs, bapt.	Apr.	2, 1725
3. Anna, bapt.	June	15, 1727
4. Salome, bapt.	Jan.	9, 1729
5. Johannes, bapt.	Feb.	4, 1736

Failed about nine years ago and had not been getting on since. Supported himself by tending herds. Testim. C.

1739

The emigrants of this year whom we have been able to find left without permission.

Martin Schaffner, 'Bannbruder,' lace-maker, KB, cooper, aged 45.
Verena Tschudi, daughter of the 'Geschworener,' his wife.
Their children:

1. Barbara, bapt.............................Sept. 6, 1722
2. Margreth, bapt..........................July 28, 1726
3. Verena, bapt............................Aug. 15, 1728
4. Anna, bapt..............................Febr. 8, 1733

Hans Jacob Madöri, smith.
Esther Rudi, from Waldenburg, his wife.
Their children:

1. Hans Jacob, bapt........................Jan. 17, 1734
2. Sebastian, bapt.........................Oct. 13, 1737

Martin Schaffner is among those who were refused permission to emigrate the preceding year though he had tried every possible means to obtain it. He and some others had gone so far as to send a special quite pathetic supplication to the Council in which emigration was called the only resort looming up amidst the dark clouds of their misery that might better their condition and save them from utter ruin, and in which they offered to pray incessantly for the welfare of Council and country and rejoice at all good news from home if their request were granted. As a result of the refusal he left this year to the damage of his creditors and those who had gone bail for him, which, as Adam Buser stated to the Schultheiss in 1749 (AA, Report of March 11), would not have happened if he had received permission in 1738. The report read in Council May 30, 1739, presumes that he and Hans Jacob Madöri had gone to Carolina while Adam Buser speaks of his having gone to Pennsylvania.

Hans Joggi Hersperger and Hans Heinrich and Heini Wagner of Läufelfingen, who also started for America, returned to their families from London, and Jacob Degen of Mönchenstein will be found among our emigrants of uncertain date.

1740

This year there was once more a considerable number of applicants and among them fewer poor and paupers than in 1738. They were examined by the deputies to the 'Landessachen" to whom henceforth all matters of emigration not directly concerning the factories were referred. The applicants complained of lack of sufficient work and a decrease of their property in spite of their utmost efforts. Times were rather hard and it was scarcely possible for them to find means to pay the 5 percent interest which they had to give to their 'honourable' creditors. Since ruin was staring them in the face, they wished to seek homes and sustenance in another part of the world while they still had some property left. Their families were of the same mind as they were. Remonstrances

and warnings on the part of the deputies were in vain, all the
more so because they talked disparagingly against Carolina, while
it was to Pennsylvania that at least the emigrants from Muttenz
were firmly resolved to go, so firmly that even the agent Hans
Spring, who was enlisting emigrants for Carolina, could not divert
them from their purpose. The Council therefore consented to the
emigration of all who had applied up to March 16. Those who had
less than 100 pounds were released from the payment of dues as
they had been in 1736, but the others did not obtain any material
reduction in the computation of their ten percent tax and had to
pay five pounds for the manumission of each of their children.

In the absence of entries in MP we turn to the lists of emigrants
of March 5 and 16, found in CAM, and give them in our usual
order of Aemter and villages. After that we first introduce those
listed in FAF who paid their manumission fees and ten percent tax
and see then which of the remaining emigrated and which stayed
at home.—Those who sailed for Philadelphia this time had a very
bad passage. According to Gerster nearly sixty people from the
Canton of Basel died, mostly of hunger. 'For they have had a
very rough voyage with storm so that they have lost their provisions
and cooking-kettles.'

List of March 5, 1740

N.B.: In this list and that of March
16, '& f.,' = & family, is substituted for
'with wife and children.'

[Amt] Varnspurg
Arristorf:
Johannes Christen & f.
Heini Jäger & f., also his son's wife
and their children.
Martin Keller & f.
Bus:
Geörg Schneider, unmar.
Diegten:
Mathis Mohler, unmar.
Ormalingen:
Anna Barbara Anisshäusslein, [un-
mar.].
Riggenbach:
Hans Jacob Handschin & f.,
[also] his daughter's husband
Hans an der Eck and his
children.

[Amt] Liechstahl
Frenkendorf:
Heinrich Giger, unmar.
Fühlistorf:
Hans Fluebacher.

Gibenach:
Jacob Bitterlin & f.

[Amt] Mönchenstein
Mönchenstein:
Jacob Küentzlin & f.
Muttentz:
Heinrich Brodbeckh & f.
Jacob Brucker, unmar.
Hans Brüderlin with his sisters
and child, also Barbel Mössmer.
Heinrich Heu(!) & f.
Claus Meyer, unmar.
Hans Meyer & f.
Jacob Pfau, with wife, married
and unmarried children.
Bernhard Ramstein & f.
Jacob Ramstein & f.
Claus Seiler & f. and maid-servant.
Hans Seiler.
Hans Bernhard Seiler.
Claus Spänhauer & f.
Elsbeth Spittlerin, Jacob Spän-
hauer's widow, with children.

[Amt] Waldenburg
Bretzweil:
Durs Tschopp & f.

List of March 16, 1740

[Amt] Varnspurg
Augst:
Jacob Schmidhauser & f.
Diegten:
Martin Hefelfinger & f.
Rüneberg:
Martin Wagner & f. and
Heini Wagner, his brother.
Zeglingen:
Heinrich Riggenbacher & f.

[Amt] Homburg
Mettenberg:
Hans Jacob Buser & f.

[Amt] Liechstahl
Fühlistorf:
Hans(!) Häner & f.

Selbensperg:
Friderich Salathe & f.

[Amt] Mönchenstein
Mönchenstein:
Johannes Kapp, the waggon-
maker, & f.
Muttentz:
Hans Seiler, unmar.
Brattelen:
Hans Frey, the mason, & f.

[Amt] Waldenburg
Oberdorf:
Hans Krattiger & f.

I. Emigrants recorded in FAF

N.B.: What is put in parentheses and what follows after the financial statements is taken from other sources.

AMT FARNSBURG

Arisdorf

From *Hans Christen* of Arristorff, (33 years of age).
Ten percent tax on lb. 2870 worth of property.........287.—
Pro manumissione for himself and his wife............ 20.—
Ditto for their child.............................. 5.—   312.—

Elsbeth Giegelmann, his wife, 35 years of age.
Elsbeth, their child, bapt. July 27, 1732.
In Oct. 1748 he was at Lebanon, Pa., and signed a letter by Durs Thommen as
a witness. In 1763, or 1764 he visited his old home (AA).
From *Heini Jäger* of Arristorff, (60 years of age).
Ten percent tax on lb. 1470 worth of property.........147.—
Pro manumissione for himself and his wife............ 20.—
Ditto for their child.............................. 5.—

Furthermore pro manumissione for his son and his son's
wife... 20.—
Ditto for their 2 children........................ 10.—   202.—

Maria Heinimann, Heini Jäger's wife, 40 years of age.
Their children:
     1. Anna, bapt............................Nov.   9, 1721
     2. Heinrich, bapt.........................July   6, 1715
Ursel Würtz, Heinrich's wife, 24 years old.
Heinrich's and Ursel's children:
     1. Johannes, bapt........................May   14, 1737
     2. Heini, bapt...........................Oct. 20, 1739
From *Martin Keller* of Arristorff, (bapt. July 11, 1706).
Ten percent tax on lb. 2750 worth of property.........275.—
Pro manumissione for him and his wife.............. 20.—
Ditto for their 3 children........................ 15.—   310.—

Elisabeth Häring, his wife, bapt. Nov. 6, 1707.
Their children:

    1. Hans Jacob, bapt.............................March 7, 1729
    2. Elsbeth, bapt..............................July 27, 1732
    3. Martin, bapt..............................March 3, 1737

Dieglen

From *Martin Häfelfinger* of Dieckten, [called Wissen Martin, aged 41].
    Ten percent tax on lb. 1100 worth of property.........110.—
    Pro manumissione for him and his wife.............. 20.—
    Ditto for their 5 children.......................... 25.—   155.—

Anna Maria Gysin, his wife, 40 years of age.
Their children:

    1. Elsbeth, bapt...............................Oct.   14, 1725
    2. Verena, bapt...............................July   3, 1729
    3. Anna, bapt.................................July   29, 1731
    4. Martin, bapt...............................Nov.   22, 1733
    5. Johannes, bapt.............................Dec.   8, 1737
  Lost his wife on the voyage.
From *Mattis Mohler* of Dieckten, (aged 31).
    Ten percent tax on lb. 1035 worth of property.........103.10
    Pro manum. for him alone, being unmarried.......... 10.—   113.10

    Died on the voyage bequeathing if not all, at least a good deal of his money to fellow-emigrants. In 1749 his relatives at home 'sold' this inheritance to Jacob Joner (Gerster's letter of 1740 and CAM Apr. 23, 1749). Gerster says: 'Mathiss Mohler died on the sea. Wissen-Marti has inherited 12 doubloons of him and Juss Jocki as much and still others [have inherited as much].'

Rickenbach

From *Hans Joggi Handschi* of Riggenbach, late 'Lettensenn,' [47 years of age].
    Ten percent tax on lb. 170 worth of property...........17.—
    Pro manumissione for him and his wife................20.—
    Ditto for his daughter's husband and his daughter......20.—   57.—

Barbara Rickenbacher, his wife, 46 years of age.
Hans Andereck, their son in law.
Barbara Hantschi, their daughter.
Hans' and Barbara's children:

    1. Barbel Andereck.............................4 years old
    2. Hans Andereck..............................3 years old
Hans Joggi Hantschi's and Barbara Rickenbacher's other children:

    1. Anna Maria, bapt...........................Jan.   1, 1721
    2. Hans Ulrich, bapt..........................Aug.   9, 1722
    3. Anna, bapt.................................Febr. 24, 1726
    4. Elsbeth, bapt..............................May   30, 1728
    5. Hans Jacob............................... 10½ years old
    6. Ursula, bapt...............................March 19, 1730
    7. Heinrich, bapt............................. 4 years old
    8. Wernet, bapt.............................. 2 years old
    For the 10 children no manumission was charged. According to MP his daughter Barbara had been manumitted once before, Apr. 23, 1735, for her marriage with her present husband who was from Rumisberg, Canton of Bern.

Zeglingen

From *Heini Riggenbacher* of Zegligen, [44 years of age].
Ten percent tax on lb. 2420 worth of property.........242.—
Pro manumissione for him and his wife............... 20.—
Ditto for their 8 children a 5 lb...................... 40.— 302.—

Barbara Thommen, his wife, 39 years of age.
Their children:

1. Elsbeth, bapt................................July 30, 1724
2. Hans Adam, bapt..........................Nov. 18, 1726
3. Johannes, bapt.............................Oct. 24, 1728
4. Jacob, bapt................................June 25, 1730
5. Margreth, bapt............................March 18, 1732
6. Heinrich, bapt............................May 22, 1735
7. Barbara, bapt.............................Oct. 20, 1737
8. Anna, bapt................................Nov. 28, 1739

Lost his two youngest children on the voyage and his wife at Philadelphia and proceeded to Conestoga where he died before autumn 1748. His oldest daughter married Hans Kurtz and his two youngest children had Christen Gerber and Hans Gerber for guardians. His oldest son Hans Adam took a trip to Europe to collect an inheritance which his grandfather Adam Thommen, deceased in 1743, had left to him and his brothers and sisters. He arrived in March 1749, but did not get the money till he returned with the proper legal documents in 1750. Although he was a harmless, even timid young man, he was both times forced to leave the Canton after a very short stay and spent the intervening time in Holland and Germany.

AMT HOMBURG

Mettenberg

From *Jacob Buser* of the Metteberg, (lace-maker, aged 35).
Ten percent tax on lb. 130 worth of property...........13.—
Pro manumissione for him and his wife.................20.—
Ditto for their 3 children a 5 lb. ....15.— 48.—

Susanna Hefelfinger from Dieckten, his wife, aged 44.
Their children:

1. Anna, bapt................................May 9, 1728
2. Barbara, bapt.............................Febr. 25, 1731
3. Elsbeth, bapt.............................March 27, 1738

KB says with Anna and Barbara: 'Went to Carolina' and with Elsbeth: 'Went to Carolina with her parents who perished miserably on the sea.' Gerster tells their sad story more accurately. He died in England, Barbara and Elsbeth on the sea, and his wife a week after her arrival in Philadelphia. Anna had broken her left leg just below the hip in a gale and was getting restored at a physician's. Notice that the pastor uses Carolina for America.

AMT LIESTAL

Frenkendorf

From *Heini Giger* of Frenckendorff, (bapt. Jan. 24, 1719).
Ten percent tax on lb. 390 worth of property...........39.—
Pro manumissione for him alone, being unmarried.......10.— 49.—

Füllinsdorf

From *Hans Flubacher* of Filinstorff, (54 years of age).

Ten percent tax on lb. 340 worth of property...........34.—
Pro manumissione for him and his wife...............20.—
Ditto for their 3 children a 5 lb. ....20.—
Ten percent tax on the lb. 190 worth of property of his
son by his first marriage........................19.—
Pro manumissione for him, being unmarried...........10.—   103.—

Barbara Thommen, his wife, 44 years of age.
Their children:

    1. Hans Heinrich, bapt.......................March 26, 1730
    2. Anna, bapt...............................March 16, 1732
    3. Joseph, bapt.............................Dec.   19, 1734
    4. Elsbeth, bapt............................May   30, 1737
The son by his first marriage with Margreth Martin:
    Hans Jacob, bapt..........................Jan.   28, 1720

Gibenach

From *Jacob Bitterlin*, of Gibenacht, (38 years of age).

Ten percent tax on lb. 118 worth of property...........11.16
Pro manumissione for him and his wife...............20.—
Ditto for their 4 children...........................20.—   51.16

Anna Degen, his wife, 35 years of age.
Their children:

    1. Elsbeth, bapt. ?..........................   16 years old
    2. Anna, bapt. ?...:........................   14 years old
    3. Hans Jacob, bapt. ?.......................   5 years old
    4. Martin, bapt...............................June   7, 1739

AMT MUENCHENSTEIN

Münchenstein

From *Hans Kapp*, of Mönchenstein, (son of the Untervogt, wagon-maker, 37
years of age).

Ten percent tax on lb. 180 worth of property..........18.—
Pro manumissione for him and his wife...............20.—
Ditto for their 4 children a 5 lb.....................20.—   58.—

Judith Massmünster, his wife, 35 years of age.
Their children:

    1. Hans Jacob, bapt..........................Jan.   1, 1730
    2. Johannes, bapt...........................Febr. 20, 1735
    3. Leonhardt, bapt...........................Nov.   3, 1737
    4. Benedict, KB Benedichy, bapt...............March 1, 1739
In 1750 he was in Pennsylvania and sold an inheritance, which turned out to
be worth over 330 pounds, to Jacob Joner for 100 florins (RP 124, 271 and 281).
From *Jacob Küntzlin*, (KB Küntzli) of Mönchenstein, (carpenter), aged 48.

Ten percent tax on lb. 1600 worth of property.........160.—
Pro manumissione for him and his wife...............20.—
Ditto for their 2 children à 5 lb.....................10.—   190.—

Barbara Graf or Gräffin, his wife.
Their children:
    1. Hans Rudolf, bapt.........................Dec. 31, 1719
    2. Hans Jacob, bapt..........................Apr. 29, 1721

Muttenz

From *Jacob Brucker*, (Hans J.) of Muttentz, (orphan, bapt. Nov. 13, 1707).
    Ten percent tax on lb. 170 worth of property...........17.—
    Pro manumissione for him alone, unmarried............10.—   27.—

From *Heinrich Brodtbeck*, of Muttentz, (59 years of age).
    Ten percent tax on 1350 lb. worth of property.........135.—
    Pro manumissione for himself and his wife............20.—
    Ten percent tax(!) for their 5 children à 5 lb...........25.— 180.—

Elsbeth Spenhauer, his wife, 59 years of age.
Their children:
    1. Heinrich, bapt.............................Nov. 27, 1718
    2. Niclaus, bapt.............................Nov. 26, 1720
    3. Elsbeth, bapt.............................Nov. 15, 1723
    4. Barbel, bapt.............................Nov. 30, 1726
    5. Wernhard, bapt...........................Apr.   6, 1730
From *Hans Maria*, and *Catharina*, the *Brüderlein*, [Brüderlin] of Muttentz.
    Ten percent tax on lb. 560 worth of their property......56.—
    Pro manumissione for those three....................30.—
    Ditto for Catharina's(!) child.......................5.— 91.—

    Anna Maria Brüderlin, bapt.....................June 19, 1701
    Catharina Brüderlin, bapt......................Sept. 4, 1703
    Johannes Brüderlin, bapt.......................Febr. 28, 1706
    Ursula, according to KB, illegitimate daughter of
    Maria Brüderlin and Heinrich Heyd, bapt.......Jan. 2, 1735
From *Hans Meyer*, son of the "Geschworener" of Muttentz, (45 years of age)
    Ten percent tax on lb. 1910 worth of property.........191.—
    Pro manumissione for him and his wife..............20.—
    Ditto for their 2 children à 5 lb....................10.— 221.—

Dorothea Dägen, his wife.
Their children:
    1. Dorothea, bapt............. ....Apr. 13, 1721
    2. Jacob, bapt...............................Oct. 18, 1723
His 'Vogt' asserted that he emigrated because he felt vexed at having been proclaimed a 'prodigus.' According to a report of the Obervogt of March 14, 1749, he died on the voyage. His daughter Dorothea married Moritz Millhausen or Morris Millhouse of Lancaster Co., Pa. She and her brother availed themselves of Jacob Joner's services to collect the inheritance which their grandmother Ursula Meyer had left them. His first attempt to get it failed, but when he returned from America with a letter of attorney endorsed by William Peters, tabellion public of Philadelphia, he obtained it, though only after many tribulations and temporary imprisonment.
From *Hans Jacob Pfau*, the shoemaker of Muttentz, (aged 54).
    Ten percent tax on lb. 540 of his property............54.—
    Pro manumissione for himself and his wife............20.—
    Ditto for their 4 children à 5 lb....................20.— 94.—

Catharina Spenhauer, his wife.
Their children:

1. Johannes, bapt.............................Dec. 20, 1716
2. Joseph, bapt..............................Febr. 20, 1720
3. Catharina, bapt...........................May   2, 1723
4. Ursula, bapt..............................Apr. 8, 1725

He had to leave his two married children and a corresponding part of his property at home. He was living and doing well in America in 1748.
From *Jacob Ramstein*, of Muttentz, (45 years of age).

Ten percent tax on lb. 610 worth of property..........61.—
Pro manumissione for him and his wife................20.—
Ditto for their 8 children a 5 lb......................40.— 121.—

Barbara Welterlin, Wällterlin and -li, his wife, 45 years of age.
Their children:

1. Anna, bapt...............................Dec. 1, 1720
2. Jacob, bapt..............................Apr. 12, 1723
3. Elsbeth, bapt............................July 20, 1725
4. Heinrich, bapt...........................Aug. 3, 1728
5. Barbara, bapt............................Apr. 23, 1730
6. Maria, bapt..............................Dec. 14, 1732
7. Johannes, bapt...........................July 31, 1735
8. Ursula, bapt.............................Sept. 28, 1738

From *Claus Seyler* of Muttentz, (65 years of age).

Ten percent tax on lb. 2360 worth of property.........236.—
Pro manumissione for him and his wife.............. 20.—
Ditto for their 2 children......................... 10.— 266.—

Anna Uerbin, his wife, 50 years of age.

1. Niclaus, bapt...........................Febr. 7, 1717
2. Anna, bapt..............................Jan. 17, 1731

From the deceased *Wernet Spehauer's* (correctly *Spenhauer's*) widow (Elsbeth Spitteler) of Muttentz.

Ten percent tax on lb. 1000 worth of property.........100.—
Pro manumissione............................... 10.—
Ditto for the 4 children.......................... 20.— 130.—

Her children:

1. Heinrich, bapt...........................Aug. 2, 1716
2. Wernet, bapt............................July 16, 1719
3. Anna, bapt..............................Dec. 29, 1720
4. Barbara, bapt...........................Jan. 3, 1723

Heinrich also signed the letter by Durs Thommen of Oct. 27, 1748, mentioned above with Hans Christen. Soon afterwards he sailed for Europe to collect the inheritance which his grandfather had left to his mother. March 1, 1749, the Council consented (CAM), but two weeks later he and Jacob Joner were ordered to leave the Canton within 48 hours. They went to Bern to get Wernhard Stoler's (see 1738) papers legalized by the British Ambassador, were accused by the government of Bern of soliciting emigrants and stayed for a while at Muttenz and Pratteln without

permission, for which these two villages and their officials had
to suffer.

AMT WALDENBURG

Oberdorf

From *Hans Krattiger*, (son of Hans deceased), of Oberdorff, (aged 40).
    Ten percent tax on lb. 130 worth of property...........13.—
    Pro manumissione for him alone, no manumission being
        charged for his family...........................10.—   23.—

Barbel Sigrist, his wife, 39 years of age.
Their children whose ages cannot be verified:
    1. Barbel..8 years old
    2. Heinrich......................................5 years old
    3. Hans Ulrich...................................2 years old
He seems to be the carpenter of Oberdorf whose death is reported by Gerster
and whose wife and three children were in Philadelphia in a rather wretched
condition.

II. *Emigrants*

AMT FARNSBURG

Augst

* *Jacob Schmidhauser*, shoemaker, aged 54.
Margreth Gysin, his wife.
Their children: Verena, Hans Martin, Hans Heinrich, Salome, Anna Cathrina,
    Ester, bapt. between 1722 and 1737.
Gave up emigrating and died at Augst May 17, 1761.

Buus

Hans Geörg Schneider, orphan, bapt. Apr. 24, 1712.
    Has no property.
Verena Häfelfinger from Diegten, his wife, whom he must have married shortly
    before starting, because he is recorded as unmarried in a report read Apr. 20
    (RP 112). GAV 15, Oct. 30, 1747, and Jan. 26, 1750, their emigration is
    confirmed by relatives who have not heard from them.

Ormalingen

Anna Barbara Anisshäusslein, 25 years of age.
    Has no property. Her parents and brother and sister are in America. She
must therefore be identical with Barbara Anisshäusslein, daughter of Ester
Breiting, emigrant of 1736 above, and have postponed her emigration until the
present time.

Rünenberg

Heini Wagner, Jacob's son, dumb, unmarried, bapt. Dec. 6, 1711.
    Has no property.
Martin Wagner, his brother.
Maria Grieder, his wife.
Their children:
    1. Hans Jacob, bapt.........................June   1, 1732
    2. Maria, bapt..............................June   9, 1736
    Their emigration is not only attested by KB, which however erroneously
adds 'To the New-land' also to the name of Anna, bapt. Febr. 9, 1738, and

deceased Nov. 2, 1739, but also by Gerster who relates their sad fate: 'The dumb man of Rineburg has safely arrived. A Swiss woman of the Canton of Bern has received him. One child, the little boy, is still living and with him, the other child with its father and mother, his brother and brother's wife, have died on the sea.'

AMT LIESTAL

Füllinsdorf

* *Niclaus Häner* with his family.
   Postponed his emigration till the next year.

Seltisberg

* *Fridlin Salathe*, the tailor, aged 46, and his wife.
   Could probably not go on account of his debts. His failure the next year, by which his creditors lost 345 pounds, brought him a sentence of forced labour on a road.
   He emigrated secretly in 1751.

AMT MUENCHENSTEIN

Muttens

* *Heinrich Heyd* with wife and child. 'Heu' in the list is an error.
   Desisted from emigrating voluntarily (AA Report of March 17).
Barbara or Margreth Mössmer, cousin of the Brüderlin, may have accompanied them.
Claus Meyer, orphan. No indication what he did.
* *Jacob Pfau*, the young and his sister *Margreth*, children of the emigrating shoemaker, were ordered to stay, because Sara Heyd, the wife of the former, and * Bernhard Ramstein, the husband of the latter, changed their minds and refused to go, and the government objected to the separation of married people.
* *Hans Seiler*, unmarried, appears to be identical with the emigrant of that name in 1749. His financial status, which left him a balance of lb. 340, 19, would have enrolled him among the paying emigrants of FAF if he had left at the present time.
* *Hans Bennhard Seiler* desisted from emigrating (AA Report of March 17).
Claus Spänhauer, moler, 59 years of age.
Ursula Schwartz, his wife, aged 55.
Their children:
   1. Jacob, bapt.................................Jan.   17, 1723
   2. Mattheus, bapt...........................June   23, 1726
   His balance of only lb. 56.7.8 exempted him from the payment of dues.
Verena Tschudi, servant of Claus Seilers, may have accompanied the family.

Pratteln

Hans Frey, mason, 53 years of age.
Verena Brogli, his wife, 49 years of age.
Their children:
   1. Anna, bapt.................................Aug.   13, 1715
   2. Fridrich, bapt...........................Apr.   14, 1722
   3. Johannes, bapt...........................Febr.   20, 1725
   Their emigration is proved by the note: 'In Virginia' which in KB is added to the name of Johannes.

AMT WALDENBURG

Bretzwil

Durs Tschopp, Durs'son, 40 years of age.
Ursula Schäfer, Jacob's daughter, from Seltisberg, his wife.
Their children:

1. Barbara.................................... 14 years old
2. Anna, bapt...............................June 16, 1726
3. Salome, bapt............................July 20, 1727
4. Hans Jacob, bapt........................June   8, 1732
5. Durs, bapt..............................Apr. 17, 1734
6. Johannes, bapt..........................June 24, 1736
7. Samuel, bapt............................Nov. 15, 1739

His assets of lb. 1218.5.— were nearly balanced by his liabilities of 1217.11.6.
Nevertheless he could not be diverted from his purpose (AA Report of the Obervogt of Apr. 23) and must have found somehow the means of reaching the sea.

III. *Emigrants without Permission*

AMT FARNSBURG

Diegten

Jacob N. N., called *Juss Joggi*, with wife and children.

Gerster, from whose letter of 1740 we take this emigrant, is well
acquainted with him, but apparently never heard his family name
because he declares in his letter of 1737, where he wishes to address
him, that he does not know it.   Juss Joggi lost his youngest child
on the voyage, stopped at Gerster's at Germantown and then
moved on.

Diegten (?)

Martin N. N., the smith's son.

Mentioned by Gerster in his letter of 1740.   Had to serve for
his freight (passage-money) in Germantown, Pa.

———

Two others intended to emigrate, but failed to do so.   Matthis
Sigrist, an apprentice who was ill treated by his master's wife, did
not get beyond the vicinity of Basel because his master had sent
word to the shipmen not to take him aboard.   Rudolf Gättelin
returned only after an absence of some months.

1741

MP, where the entries are resumed this year, records only three
families.   We reproduce the entries and add the names and dates
of the children.

AMT LIESTAL
Füllinsdorf

Häner, Claus, of Fülistorff, [shoemaker, aged 35], was manumitted with his wife and six children, with whom he has a mind to go to Pennsylvania, and it was resolved that he should be released from the payment of the ten percent tax and from the payment of the manumission dues for his children, but pay the latter for himself and his wife. June 21, 1741.

```
Pays:  Pro manumissione.........................20.—
       Letters...................................  3.—      23.—
```

Elsbeth Roppel, his wife, aged 36.
Their children:

```
    1. Niclaus, bapt.............................June    16, 1726
    2. Johannes, bapt...........................Nov.     6, 1729
    3. Margreth, bapt...........................Sept.   23, 1731
    4. Elsbeth, bapt............................Sept.   15, 1733
    5. Joseph, bapt.............................Apr.    21, 1737
    6. Verena, bapt.............................Apr.    30, 1740
```
Had intended to emigrate the preceding year.

AMT MUENCHENSTEIN
Benken

Lützler, Lienert, of Benckhen, who has a mind to go to Pennsylvania with his two children, was released from bondage with these two children, the latter gratis, he however on payment of the manumission and ten percent tax dues. June 10, 1741. . . . [Reported that he has a balance of lb. 292.10. June 28].

```
Pays:  Pro manumissione.........................10.—
       Ten percent tax...........................29.5
       Letter....................................  1.10    40.15
```

The Land Commission had been opposed to his emigration 'because, as was well known, the journey was very unsafe and in America the war between Spain and England was waged very fiercely' (RP 113, June 10, 1741).
His children:

```
    1. Anna Elisabeth, bapt.....................Apr.    14, 1729
    2. Clara, bapt..............................Sept.   24, 1730
```

Bottmingen

Jundt, Jacob, of Bottmingen, who has a mind to go to Pennsylvania, was manumitted with
Elisabeth Märckhlin, his wife, and five young children on payment of the ten percent tax and manumission dues for himself and his wife. . . . (Reported that he has a balance of lb. 986.—). May 20, 1741.

```
Pays:  Pro manumissione.........................20.—
       Ten percent tax...........................98.12
       Letters...................................  3.—   121.12
```

Their children:

```
    1. Hans Jacob, bapt.........................Aug.    14, 1729
    2. Elisabeth, bapt..........................Febr.   11, 1731
    3. Hans Heinrich, bapt......................July    12, 1733
    4. Anna Maria, bapt.........................Febr.   27, 1736
    5. Matthias, bapt...........................Febr.    7, 1740
```

Jacob Seyler, emigrant of 1749, found them in poor circumstances in the vicinity of Philadelphia. They had no land of their own, had to buy their bread at the baker's and were daily taking milk to the market.

1742–1748

While the principal year of emigration from Zürich, which led to the preparation of the lists published in Volume I of this Series, fell in this period, there was no emigration of any consequence from Basel to the Colonies during this time. We know of one certain and a few possible cases which will be found below among the emigrants of uncertain date, and it is not probable that any considerable number of others will yet be discovered.

The news that nearly sixty of those who had started from Basel for Pennsylvania in 1740 had perished on the voyage or immediately afterward must have had a depressing effect which may have been intensified by the ghastly account of another voyage on which the survivors were said to have cooked and eaten the dead bodies of their starved comrades, printed in the 'Verbesserter und Neuer Vollkommener Staats-Calender, Genannt der Hinckende Bott' for 1743. To these were added the dangers of the war, which was raging not only on land, but also on the seas, and which was perhaps better known in Basel than in Zürich. Finally in 1748, when peace was restored, some families, numbering a hundred persons, allowed themselves to be lured to Surinam [1] by an agent who had come with a recommendation by the city of Amsterdam and had been endorsed by the government, instead of waiting for a chance to go to the American Colonies.

1749

Several circumstances conspired to make this year the principal year of emigration from Basel to the Colonies. Hard times and frequent and ill-arranged Fronungen, statute-labors, caused the poor people, who form the great majority of the emigrants of the year, to think that they could nowhere be worse off than at home, and at the same time the presence of three former countrymen from Pennsylvania who were followed by a fourth, Jacob Joner, Heinrich Spenhauer, Werner Stohler and Hans Adam Riggenbacher, brought the alluring prospects of the New-land palpably before their eyes. A report of the Obervogt of Farnsburg, dated March 14, describes the evil effects of the Fronungen (compulsory service) and the manner in which the emigration movement spread.

The poor people were chased about the country and nevertheless,

[1] In Dutch Guiana, South America.

10

owing to their living mostly far away from the place of the Fronung, did not get much work done.   But on the other hand they neglected thereby their work at home and were necessarily ruined on account of poor sustenance and the high price of the bread which they borrowed of the millers [because they could not pay for it].   In addition these poor day-laborers suffered from the fact that on account of the many Fronungen the peasants reduced as much as possible the number of their teams and were no longer willing to plough their poor land except at a higher price.

Regarding the emigration he says that those who desired leave to go were sitting continuously together and talking of the happy state they had in view.   This was causing a regular mania among the people, so that all sorts of persons reported for emigration, even young lace-maker boys and girls.   He then asks whether it might not be well to send the seducers and the worst of the emigrants as quickly as possible out of the country before still more confusion should arise.

The government adopted at once the first point of this suggestion and notified Joner and Spenhauer that they must leave within 48 hours and ordered the arrest with consequent expulsion of Stohler. A week later, March 22, it was resolved that all who had applied up to that time, numbering 382 with their families, should be permitted to go 'in order that they might see how foolishly they had acted' (CAM).   They should however not only forfeit their land-right and not set foot again upon the soil of the Canton under heavy penalties, but also leave eventual inheritances of theirs to the discretion of the government, and get out of the country as soon as they had settled their affairs.   The children were released from the payment of manumission, but, with a few exceptions, both manumission and emigration tax were exacted even of those who had less than 100 pounds.   Only those who had nothing but the household goods which they wished to take along went free.

When on March 29 the granting of further permissions was stopped, there were in Amt Münchenstein alone still twenty who wished to apply (RP 122, 196), and of course there were others in other districts who had failed to make up their minds in time. Some of these went without permission in the general turmoil, but it is not possible to ascertain all their names.   Probably they were less numerous than such as had received permission and stand recorded as emigrants in MP, but lost courage or found it impossible to go.   Those who left, departed about May 8, and went down the Rhine in four ships accompanied by Jacob Joner, whom one of them afterward accused of having taken undue advantage of them, a charge which we have not been able to verify. On the sea voyage they went in two ships, and in Joner's there died 5 adults and 16 children of the 'sea sickness.' In Pennsylvania they went to join their countrymen with whom they were acquainted as far as they had not first to work out their 'freight' (passage-money).

I. *Emigrants recorded in MP*

N.B.: MP furnishes the names of the single emigrants and of the heads of the families with the number of men, women and children of whom each party consisted (*e.g.*, 1.1.3 = one man, one woman, 3 children, —.1.— = one woman), and the dues which they paid. Everything else has been added from other sources.

The pastor of Sissach, to whose parish also Böckten, Itingen and Zunzgen belong, says in all his notes in KB that his emigrants went to Carolina instead of saying that they went to America.

Amt Farnsburg

Augst

Melchior Reinger, day-labourer, bapt. July 3, 1701.   1.1.—.
Released from payment of dues.
Verena Lüdin, his third wife.
No children.   Honest and industrious.

Boeckten

Marti Gass, carpenter.   1.1.5.
Released from payment of dues.
Anna Häring from Arisdorf, his wife.
Their children:
1. Anna, bapt., ... Oct.   19, 1738
2. Martin, bapt. . . . . June   5, 1740
3. Johannes, bapt. . . . . Sept.   9, 1742
4. Hans Jacob, bapt. . . . . Febr.   28, 1748
Heinrich, the fifth child, bapt. July 1747, died March 8, 1749, before the departure of the others.
KB confirms their actual emigration by the entry: 'Goes to Carol. with wife and children A. 1749 in May.' He is one of the two men, to whose testimonial the pastor of Sissach, who never makes an individual statement about the character of an emigrant, attached the note to the Landvogt, cited at the close of our Introduction. He was never heard of again (GAV, 20, 427).
Marti Gass, carpenter.   1.—.—.
Manumission . . . . 10.—
Probably identical with the preceding.

Buus

Sebastian Hassler, day-labourer.   1.1.1.
Released from payment of dues.   [Owned 100 pounds in cash.]
Barbara Degen from Muttenz, his wife.
1. Child of 12 weeks, not recorded in KB

Had received a dowry of only 100 pounds and not learned any trade.   Had given no cause for complaint.

Margret [Schaub] and
Catharina Schaub, her sister.   —.2.—.

Pays(!): Manumission............................20.—
    Ten percent tax...........................26.3   46.3

Catharina had lately been tried in Basel for several petty thefts and had been banished from the city and ordered to appear before the Bann of her parish.   She emigrated because she was afraid nobody would hire her as a servant on account of the 'misfortune' she had had.

Diepflingen

Martin Schneider.   1.1.4.

Ten percent tax(!)................................20.—
Manumission(!) 24.6.6   44.6.6

Eva Lüdin from Ramlinsburg, his wife.
Their children:
    1. Anna, bapt................................July   20, 1738
    2. Martin, bapt..............................Apr.   3, 1742
    3. Daniel, bapt..............................Febr.   7, 1745
    4. Johannes, bapt...........................June   4, 1747

Eptingen

* *Mathis Ritter*, carpenter.   1.—.4.   N.B.: MP omits the wives of all emigrants from Eptingen owing to a misunderstanding of the pastor's certificate.
    Released from payment of dues.
Verena Schäublin, his wife.
Their children: Hans Jacob, Barbara, Matthias, Martin, bapt. between July 1741 and Febr. 1747.—The birth of Verena in 1757, bapt. Apr. 19, proves that they did not emigrate.

Hans Jacob Schaffner, tailor, bapt. Jan. 26, 1721.   1.—.1.
    Released from payment of dues.
Anna Maria Newiker, his wife, bapt. Oct. 15, 1724.
    1. Anna, their child, bapt.....................March 19, 1747
    In RP Nov. 2, 1768, his emigration to Pennsylvania is confirmed.

* *Hans Jacob Schwander.*   1.—.7.
    Released from payment of dues.
    Anna Schäublin, his wife.
Their children: Anna, Barbara, Hans Jacob, Catharina, Matthis, Johannes, bapt. between Oct. 1729 and March 1748.—The birth of Jacob in 1752, bapt. July 2, shows that they did not go to America in 1749.

* *Hans Suter.*   1.—.3.
    Released from payment of dues.
Barbara Hug, his wife.
Their children: Hans Jacob, Anna Maria, Daniel, bapt. between Oct. 1744 and Febr. 1749.—The births of several other children: Hans Heinrich, bapt. Aug. 29, 1751, Elisabeth, June 3, 1753, Barbara, Oct. 10, 1756, prove that they stayed.

* *Adam Thommen*, herdsman, 57 years of age.   1.—.3.
    Released from payment of dues.
Margreth Suter, his wife.

Their children: Adam, Hans Jacob, Elsbeth, Barbara, bapt. between Nov. 1734 and Nov. 1746. KB tells that Adam Thommen did not die in Pennsylvania or Carolina, but at Eptingen: 'Adam Thommen, Gass Adam, the herdsman, who, while with the herd which he tended, was struck with paralysis . . . died the following day, Nov. 7 [1751]. His wife gave birth to a posthumous daughter Margreth, bapt. June 25, 1752.

Owing to their great poverty these emigrants from Eptingen had received 35 pounds from the village treasury as a contribution toward their travelling expenses. When the government heard of this in the following year, the Geschworene were reprimanded and those who had consented to the grant were ordered to refund the money to the treasury (RP 123, 186).

Gelterkinden

Anna Erni, Fridlin's daughter, lace-maker, bapt. Apr. 24, 1729. —.1.—.
  Released from payment of dues.
Fridli Erni, brother of Anna, lace-maker, bapt. July 24, 1727. 1.—.—.
  Released from payment of dues.
Anna Freyvogel, Johannes' daughter, lace-maker, bapt. Oct. 8, 1724. —.1.—.
  Released from payment of dues.
Basche Hirbin, KB U(e)rbi, Baschi's son, lace-maker, bapt. Dec. 18, 1731.
  1.—.—.
  Released from payment of dues.
Heini Gerster, Maritz' son. 1.—.—.
  Manumission.................................10.—.—
  Ten percent tax................................29. 8.10   39.8.10

Joggi Rohrer, father and son by the same name. 1.—.1.
  Ten percent tax(!)...10.—
  His failure some time ago had involved his son. Perhaps the latter did not emigrate till the next year.
Barbara Schaub, Hans Heinrich's daughter. —.1.—.
  Ten percent tax(!) ....10.—
Jacob Würtz, widower. 1.1.2(!).
  Pays: Manumission................................10.—
      Ten percent tax............................44.18   54.18

His children by Elsbeth Senn, deceased:
  1. Barbara, bapt.............................Febr.   3, 1732
  2. Son..   14 years old

The pastor of Gelterkinden attests that no complaint had been made about the conduct of any of these emigrants.

Hemmiken

* *Hans Jacob Alespach*, correctly *Alispach*. 1.1.2.
  Released from payment of dues.
Maria Schneider from Reigoldswil, his wife.
Their children: Barbara and Anna, bapt. Aug. 1747 and Febr. 1749.—The births
    of Maria, bapt. Dec. 20, 1750, and of Hans Jacob and Elisabeth in 1752 and
    1754 prove that they did not leave.
* *Martin Alispach*, unmarried. 1.—.—.
  Released from payment of dues.
  Was later on married to Elsbeth Fiechter, by whom he had several children,
1.,Martin, Jan. 4, 1757, etc.

Hans Joggi Beyer, correctly Hans *Geörg* Peyer or Beyer, unmarried.   1.—.—.
    Released from payment of dues.
    Pastor knows of nothing unfavourable to him.

Itingen

Hans Madöri, mason.   1.1.5.
    Released from payment of dues.
Anna Sigrist, his wife.
Their children:

    1. Hans Jacob, bapt.........................June   2, 1737
    2. Johannes, bapt............................Nov.   8, 1739
    3. Anna, bapt...............................Aug.   12, 1742
    4. Barbara, bapt............................Jan.   31, 1745
    5. Heinrich, bapt...........................March   3, 1748
    KB: 'Goes with wife and children to Carol. in May 1749.'

Maisprach

Jacob Blauck, carpenter.   1.1.—.
    Released from payment of dues.
Anna Margreth Gysin, his wife.
    Has two married daughters who desire to remain in the country. Is a good
industrious workman.

Bernhard Bowald, turner, 39 years of age.   1.1.7.
    Released from payment of dues.
Anna Speiser from Wintersingen, his wife.
Their children:

    1. Margreth, bapt...........................May   17, 1733
    2. Anna Maria, bapt.........................Dec.   11, 1735
    3. Barbara, bapt............................June   8, 1738
    4. Ursula, bapt.............................Oct.   9, 1740
    5. Hans Görg, bapt..........................June   16, 1743
    6. Friedrich, bapt..........................Oct.   3, 1745
    7. Rudolf, bapt.............................Oct.   6, 1748
    Is a good workman.

Jacob Bowald, weaver and herdsman.   1.1.3.
    Released from payment of dues.
Elsbeth Gruber, his wife.
Their children:

    1. Anna Maria, bapt.........................June   9, 1737
    2. Hans Heinrich, bapt......................Nov.   8, 1739
    3. Jacob, bapt..............................Nov.   24, 1743
    Pastor has not heard of anything unfavourable to him.

Hans Jacob Graff, Isac's son, linen-weaver, aged 45.   1.1.4.
    Manumission.....................................20.—
    Ten percent tax [on lb. 921.2] 92.2   112.2

Ursula Völmin from Ormalingen, his wife.
Their children:

    1. Hans Jacob, bapt.........................June   12, 1729
    2. Johannes, bapt...........................July   15, 1731
    3. Ursula, bapt.............................June   30, 1737
    4. Barbara, bapt............................Oct.   2, 1740
    Has endeavoured to lead a good Christian life.

Hans Komler, KB Kummler, 40 years of age. I.I.3.
    Released from payment of dues.
Anna Maria Grieder, his wife.
Their children:
    1. Johannes, bapt............................Apr.   26, 1739
    2. Hans Jacob, bapt..........................July   1, 1742
    3. Anna, bapt...............................Jan.   10, 1745

* *Hans Jacob Meyer*, swine-herd, 60 years of age. I.I.3.
    Released from payment of dues.
Margreth Rudi, his wife.
Their children: Salome, Hans Jacob, Martin, Fridli, bapt. 1721–1734. According
to a note on one of the Farnsburg lists he desired to remain in the country

Ormalingen

Hans Jacob Salin, correctly *Sälin*. I.I.2.
    Manumission.....................................20.—.—
    Ten percent tax.................................II. 6.10   31.6.10

Barbara Buss, his wife.
Their children:
    1. Hans Jacob, bapt.........................June   30, 1743
    2. Sebastian, bapt..........................May   31, 1746
Has led a Christian life.

Fridlin Schaub, mason. I.I.3.
    Released from payment of dues.
Catharina Buser, his wife.
Their children:
    1. Fridrich, bapt...........................Dec.   9, 1731
    2. Hans Jacob, bapt.........................Jan.   31, 1734
    3. Verena, bapt............................Febr.   19, 1736
    4. Sebastian, bapt.........................Febr.   8, 1739
One of these four children may have remained in the country or have died
before emigration.—Has led a good Christian life.

Rothenfluh

Jacob Hassler, cooper, about 30 years of age. I.I.3.
    Released from payment of dues.
Maria Märcklin, his wife, about the same age.
Their children:
    1. Child.................................... 4 years old
    2. Johannes, bapt..........................Dec.   13, 1746
    3. Eva, bapt...............................Nov.   17, 1748
Honest and industrious.

Hans Joggi Märcklin, 47 years of age. I.I.4.
    Released from payment of dues.
Elisabeth Hefelfinger, his wife, aged 46.
Their children:
    1. Hans Jacob, bapt.........................Oct.   3, 1728
    2. Hans Georg, bapt.........................Jan.   28, 1731
    3. Magdalena, bapt.........................Oct.   9, 1740
    4. Ursula, bapt............................July   21, 1744
Did not live up to the reputation of honesty which he enjoyed with his pastor,
but made use of the money of his wards (Vogtgelder) in his financial straits.

Was sent to the Schellenwerk (penitentiary), yet at the entreaties of his wife and children released after four days, 'because they wanted to go to Pennsylvania soon' (RP Apr. 19 and 23, 1749).

Mathis Spittheler from Bennwil, aged 61.   1.1.10.

Manumission	.20.—	
Ten percent tax	.39.—	59.—

Anna Raufft from Rothenfluh, his wife, aged 49.
Their children:

1. Hans Jacob, bapt.	July	14, 1720
2. Barbara, bapt.	March	22, 1722
3. Martin, bapt.	March	14, 1724
4. Anna, bapt.	March	10, 1726
5. Matthis, bapt.	Aug.	7, 1729
6. Elsbeth, bapt.	Aug.	26, 1731
7. Hans, bapt.	July	25, 1734
8. Ursula, bapt.	May	27, 1738
9. Verena, bapt.	Aug.	19, 1742
10. Jacob, bapt.	Febr.	2, 1749

Honest and industrious.

Rünenberg

Joggi Grieder, called Weaver Elsi's Joggi.   1.1.3.
     Released from payment of dues.
Barbara Grieder, Pfeiffer Hans Joggi's daguhter, called Pfeifferli, his wife.
Their children:

1. Johannes, bapt.	Jan.	16, 1746
2. Hans Joggi, bapt.	Sept.	2, 1747
3. Child probably baptized in Canton of Bern where he had lately stayed at his brother in law's.		

     KB: 'In Carolina' in connection with the dates of the children. Has led a quiet and honest life.—About 1754 his wife reported his death and that of the two older children (GAV 19, March 29, 1784).

Sissach

Joggi Gass, unmarried.   1.—.—.

Pays: Manumission	.10.—.—	
Ten percent tax	.21.12.10	31.12.10

Hans Georg Reinger.   1.1.2.

Manumission	.10.—	
Ten percent tax	.14.14	24.14.—

Anna Maria Dauber, his wife.
Their children:

1. Magdalena, bapt.	July	13, 1738
2. Hans Geörg, bapt.	Dec.	11, 1740

     KB: 'Goes with wife and children to Carolina in May 1749.'

Hans Ulrich Schaub.   1.1.2.
     Released from payment of dues.
Eva Horandt, his wife.
Their children:

1. Barbara, bapt.	Jan.	29, 1730
2. Child, bapt.	?	

* *Jacob Schweitzer.* 1.1.5.
> Released from payment of dues.

Elisabeth Senn, his wife.

Their children: Hans Jacob, Martin, Johannes, Elisabeth, Ambrosius, bapt.
> between Sept. 1740 and Apr. 1748.

> He decided to give up emigrating. The birth of another son in 1760 and the
deaths of Ambrosius in 1763 and Hans Jacob in 1804 show that his decision was
permanent.

Martin Tschudin, locksmith. 1.1.3.

> Manumission.................................20.—.—
> Ten percent tax................................19. 2. 4   39.2.4

Anna Schweitzer from Titterten, his wife.

Their children:

> 1. Jacob, bapt.............................Sept.   3, 1741
> 2. Anna, bapt.............................Dec. 11, 1742
> 3. Martin, bapt...........................Dec.   6, 1744

> KB: 'Goes to Carolina with wife and children 1749.'

* *Basche Zeller.* 1.1.3.
> Released from payment of dues.

Verena Schäublin, his wife.

Their children: Sebastian, Heinrich, Anna, bapt. between Febr. 1736 and Nov.
> 1743.

> A note on one of the Farnsburg lists says that he had not gone away. This is
confirmed by the death of his son Heinrich, bapt. Nov. 20, 1740, at Trani, Apulia
in 1771.

Tenniken

[*Hans Buser*], in whose place erroneously his 'Vogt' Hans Joggi Dalcher was
> entered in MP, unmarried. 1.—.—.

> Pays: Manumission...............................10.—
> Ten percent tax...........................87.4   97.4

> Hans or Johannes Buser died in Maryland early in the nineties, fifteen years
after he had been deserted by the woman whom he had married. His heirs in
the Canton of Basel sold what they inherited of him to Peter Ulrich, tradesman in
Philadelphia, for the sum of 286 Neuthaler and 12 Louisd'or (RP 167, 234 and 239,
June 4, 1794).

Wenslingen

Heini Schaffner. 1.1.1.
> Released from payment of dues.

Anna Wehrli from Rüttigen, Canton of Bern, his wife.

> 1. Jacob, their son, bapt........................Nov. 17, 1748

Wintersingen

Heini Bronner, KB Brunner, waggon-maker. 1.1.2.
> Released from payment of dues.

Barbara Möschinger, his wife.

Their children:

> 1. Anna, bapt..............................June 18, 1743
> 2. Fridrich, bapt...........................Aug. 30, 1744

Honest and industrious. Has long wished to go to Pennsylvania.

Zeglingen

Heinrich Sälin.   1.1.—.

    Ten percent tax(!) ....10.—.—

    Manumission(!) 10.18. 9   20.18.9

N. N. his wife.

Zunzgen

Verena Bossart.   —.1.—.

    Released from payment of dues.

Niclaus Madöri, mason, bapt. Febr. 2, 1721.   1.1.2.

    Released from payment of dues.

Elisabeth Trimmler from Brombach, his wife.

Their children:

    1. Simon, bapt.................................Aug.   2, 1744

    2. Anna Maria, bapt..........................Febr. 27, 1746

    3. Elisabeth, bapt...........................July   9, 1748

    KB: 'Goes with wife and children to Carol. in May 1749.'

AMT HOMBURG

Läufelfingen

Hans Grieber, correctly *Greber* or *Gröber.*   1.1.2.

    Pays: Ten percent tax [on lb. 2447.11]...............244.15

           Manumission dues......................... 20.—   264.15

Anna Wagner, his wife.

Their children:

    1. Johannes, bapt.............................Febr.   4, 1731

    2. Anna, bapt................................March 1, 1733

    Intended to emigrate with his aged father Wernet Greber (who then received an excellent testimonial from his pastor but died since) in 1738, but was refused permission. In America he lost his wife and married the widow of Joggi Grieder of Rünenberg above (GAV 19, 467, March 29, 1784).

AMT LIESTAL

Frenkendorf

Johannes Tschudin, Tschudi, Martin's son, cooper, bapt. Nov. 26, 1724.   1.1.—.

    Has paid for the letter [only].

Anna Maria Märcklin, daughter of Hans Joggi M. of Rothenfluh above, his wife, bapt. March 23, 1727.

    Was released from payment of dues because he claimed to have only 1 pound 19 sh. 2 d. left. Later on the papers of his father revealed however that he had been given 150 pounds before emigrating which enabled him to make such a start in Pennsylvania that he could undertake a business trip to Europe two years later. His wife died in 1749 or 1750.

Jacob Vogt, Hans' son, linen-weaver, bapt. Sept. 1, 1715.   1.1.1.

    Manumission.....................................20.—.—

    Ten percent tax [on lb. 76.8.4]................... 7.12.10   27.12.10

Anna Löliger, his wife.

    1. Johannes, their child, bapt..................Oct.   29, 1747

Lausen

Adam Buser, mason, 41 years of age. 1.1.2.

    Manumission.....................................20.—.—

    Ten percent tax [on lb. 310.6.—]..................31.—. 3   51.—.3

Barbara Bitterlin from Rünenberg, his wife.

Their children:

    1. Heinrich, bapt..............................March 18, 1732

    2. Anna Barbara, bapt........................Oct. 30, 1735

    Reminds the Schultheiss of Liestal that he and two others from Lausen had been refused permission to emigrate in 1738. See above Martin Schaffner 1739. Pastor attests that he has conducted himself all right.

Liestal

Adam Heinrich, Heinrich's son, linen-weaver, bapt. March 13, 1714. 1.1.2.

    Pays for: Manumission........................ 20.—.—

    Ten percent tax [on lb. 1028.12.6].......102.17. 3   122.17.3

Salome Gysi, his wife.

Their children:

    1. Hans Heinrich, bapt........................March 19, 1747

    2. Elisabeth, bapt.............................Aug. 27, 1748

    Pastor regards him as a drunkard.—According to GAV 16, Aug. 27, 1759, his wife was at that time in Pennsylvania and had inherited lb. 352.4.6 which her relatives wanted, giving security for them.

* *Johannes Hoch*, Samuel's son, saddler, bapt. March 26, 1713. 1.1.5.

    [Dues] unpaid.

Anna Maria Pfaff, Pantaleon's daughter, his wife.

Their children: Samuel, Hans Jacob, Adelheit, Johannes, Anna Maria, bapt.

    between Sept. 1738 and Nov. 1744.

    A report from Liestal dated May 2, 1749, announced his intention to remain in the country. Samuel died at Liestal in Febr. 1824.

AMT MUENCHENSTEIN

Benken

* *Johannes Muspach*, tailor, 36½ years old. 1.1.6.

    Permitted to leave gratis.

Elisabeth Weibel, his wife.

Their children: Hans Georg, Hans Ulrich, Elisabeth, Johannes, Anna Barbara,

    Fridrich, the last five bapt. between 1739 and 1747.

    A note on a Münchenstein list says that he had not gone away, and KB shows that he died at Benken. His son Hans Ulrich, however, settled in New Jersey, as we shall see, with the emigrants of uncertain date.

Jacob Pfau, saddler, 26 years of age. 1.1.4.

    Permitted to leave gratis.

Catharina Dyssly, Disslin, his wife, of the same age.

Their children:

    1. Elisabeth, bapt.............................March 15, 1744

    2. Anna Catharina, bapt.......................Dec. 26, 1745

    3. Abraham, bapt.............................May 14, 1747

    4. Magdalena, bapt...........................Dec. 1, 1748

This young saddler was so long delayed on his journey, first in England and afterward in 'Mehrenland,' (Maryland?), that he did not reach Frederickstown, Va., where he located, till next spring.   In England both Abraham and little Magdalena took the smallpox, and Magdalena died with them and was buried on 'Bartlome,' *i.e.*, Aug. 24, just before sailing.   In America his friends helped him to pay his 'freight' and Lieni, evidently his fellow villager Lienert Heyer, emigrant of 1737, employed a team of 4 horses for several weeks to bring his family and his things up to Frederickstown.   There he found plenty of work and meat, butter, cheese and good white bread every day, and after half a year he wrote that happy unsigned letter of Sept. 17, 1750, printed by A. B. Faust in '*Jahrbuch der Deutsch-Amer. Hist. Ges. von Illinois*, 1918–19, pp. 20–23 (No. 9). He thanks God day and night for having led him out of the 'school of the Cross' into the good land and wishes that all his friends might be with him.   If his dear old father were with him, he should suffer no care nor hunger nor want, he must not do any work and should have a horse of his own if he wanted one.

Later on he lost his wife and in 1756, or before, he was married to Madle Junt, emigrant of 1752, a fellow villager of his and well to do.

Philipp Schmid, mason, bapt. Jan. 22, 1713.   1.1.3.
   Pays: Ten percent tax [on lb. 43.10.8]. 4.7
      Manumission. . . . . .20.—   24.7

Maria Brun, Braun, from Zofingen, his wife, some 30 years old. Their children:
   1. Hans Jacob, bapt. . . . . .May   29, 1740
   2. Johannes, bapt. . . . . .June   3, 1742
   3. Ursula, bapt. . . . . .June   6, 1745
   Honest and industrious people.
Heinrich Spar, 52 years of age.   1.1.1.
   Permitted to leave gratis.
Anna Maria Kapp, his wife, 42 years of age.
      Anna Maria, their daughter, bapt. . . . . .Oct.   20, 1748
   Honest and industrious people.

Binningen

Stopfel Seiler, baker, 43 years of age.   1.1.6.
   Ten percent tax [on lb. 241.18]. 21.10
      Manumission. . . . . .20.—   41.10

Barbara Schultheiss from Riehen, his wife, 38 years of age.
Their children:
   1. Matthias, bapt. . . . . .Nov.   12, 1730
   2. Barbara, bapt. . . . . .June   21, 1733
   3. Hans Jacob, bapt. . . . . .June   12, 1735
   4. Anna Maria, bapt. . . . . .Oct.   27, 1737
   5. Margreth, bapt. . . . . .March 5, 1740
   6. Emanuel, bapt. . . . . .Oct.   28, 1742
   Remained at first in the vicinity of Philadelphia.

Hans Jacob Stehlin, Stölin, tailor, aged 47. 1.1.1.
    Permitted to leave gratis.
Elisabeth Pfaff from Liestal, his wife, aged 42.
    1. Johannes, their son, bapt.....................July   16, 1747

Bottmingen

Jacob Seyler, Hans Jacob, tailor, 51 years of age. 1.1.5.
    Ten percent tax [on lb. 214.14.7]...................21. 9. 6
    Manumission....................................20.—.—   41.9.6

Chrischona Brodbeck, his wife, 42 years of age.
Their children:
    1. Elsbeth, bapt...............................Nov.   19, 1730
    2. Anna Maria, bapt..........................Nov.   23, 1732
    3. Hans Jacob, bapt...........................June   2, 1737
    4. Johannes, bapt............................June   12, 1740
    5. Barbara, bapt..............................Sept.   22, 1743
    Is an honest citizen.—There is an interesting letter of his, printed by A. B. Faust in *The American Hist. Rev.*, XXII, pp. 119–121, in which he gives expression to the sense of relief he feels in Pennsylvania: 'No ground-rent, no tithes; everybody may do with his property as he pleases; neither statute-labour nor guard-duty; great liberty compared to the 'servitude of Egypt' in the Canton of Basel. He has bought 80 acres for 100 Basel pounds 20 'Stunden,' leagues, from Philadelphia.

Hans Ulrich Spar, 40 years of age. 1.1.9.
    Manumission dues.............................20.—.—
    Ten percent tax [on lb. 659.15].................65.19. 6 85.19.6

Margreth Seyler, his wife, aged 40.
Their children:
    1. Anna Barbara, bapt.......................Oct.   24, 1734
    2. Hans Ulrich, bapt.........................May   19, 1737
    3. Hans Jacob, bapt..........................Nov.   2, 1738
    4. Theodor, bapt.............................Jan.   10, 1740
    5. Matthias, bapt............................May   30, 1741
    6. Johannes, bapt............................July   22, 1742
    7. Wlatere(!), Walter(?), bapt..................July   26, 1744
    8. Anna Maria, bapt.........................Nov.   7, 1745
    9. Hans Heinrich, bapt.......................July   2, 1747
    Honest citizen.—Hans Heinrich died in Holland and Anna Maria in Philadelphia. Their father bought a farm 20 'Stunden' from Philadelphia.

Münchenstein

Lieni Busser, usually *Buser*, unmarried, 28 years of age. 1.—.—.
    Pays: Ten percent tax [on lb. 35.16.2]............. 3.11. 6
    Manumission............................10.—.— 13.11.6

Leaves because he has always had a great desire to travel and hopes to make his fortune in Pennsylvania.

Muttenz

Adam Brodbeck, Hans Jacob's son, weaver, aged 28. 1.1.2.
    Permitted to leave gratis.
Elisabeth Zehnder, Zehender, his wife, aged 29.
Their children:
    1. Anna, bapt. ....Nov.   10, 1743
    2. Anna Maria, bapt.........................June   18, 1748

Adam Brodbeck. 1.—.—.
    Manumission..10.—
    Ten percent tax [on lb. 324.—]......................32. 8   42.8

Leaves because he cannot stand life with his 'Xantippe.'
Claus Brodbek, brother of Adam just preceding. 1.1.—.
Permitted to leave gratis.
Magdalena Gysin, his wife.
Depends entirely upon his brother.
Hans Rudi Brodbek, carpenter, 30 years of age. 1.1.1.
    Manumission...................................20.—.—
    Ten percent tax [on lb. 249.11.7]..................24.19. 4 44.19.4

Margreth Boni from Frenkendorf, his wife, aged 22.
    1. Hans Rudolf, their son, bapt.................Apr. 25, 1745
Decided to stay and then left after all. Son must have died before 1794 when
Peter Ulrich of Philadelphia collected an inheritance for a daughter Margreth
born in America and married to Ludwig Müller in Pennsylvania (RP 167, 230
and 259).
Heinrich Brodbeck, Hans Heinrich, aged 31. 1.1.3.
    Manumission..20.—
    Ten percent tax [on lb. 676.8].......................67.13 87.13

Eva Hoffmann, his wife, aged 31.
Their children:
    1. Johannes, bapt.............................Aug. 22, 1741
    2. Anna Helena, bapt.........................Febr. 9, 1744
    3. Elisabeth, bapt............................June 18, 1747
Frid Bruker, usually *Brucker*, aged 60. 1.1.—.
    Ten percent tax [on lb. 492.4.2]....................49. 4. 6
    Manumission....................................20.—.— 69.4.6

Elisabeth Tschudin, his wife.
Had to leave half of his property for his son who remained.
Margret Brüderli, usually *Brüderlin*, daughter of Hans B. and Margret Vögtlin,
    unmarried, bapt. Jan. 10, 1697. —.1.—.
Permitted to leave gratis.
Did not avail herself of her permission to emigrate in 1736 and was wavering
again this time as to whether she should go or not.
Leonhard Heid, usually *Heyd*, waggon-maker, bapt. June 21, 1722. 1.1.—.
Permitted to leave gratis.
Elsbeth Weibel, Weiblin, his wife, daughter of Johan W. and Anna Maria Brod-
    beck, present wife of Stephan Wyrrslin, bapt. Aug. 29, 1728.
    Note on Münchenstein list: 'Has run off,' *i.e.*, he left without paying the
Chancery dues for the letter.
Hans Jacob Lüdin, day-labourer, bapt. May 29, 1712. 1.1.—.
    Ten percent tax [on lb. 254.—.10].....................25. 8
    Manumission..20.— 45.8

Ursula Pfirter, his wife, bapt. Apr. 24, 1712.
Hans Mössmer, Theodor's son, aged 34. 1.1.4.
    Ten percent tax [on lb. 259.6.6].......................25.19
    Manumission..20.— 45.19

Barbara Uerbin, his wife, aged 31.

Their children:
1. Theodor, bapt..............................Febr.   8, 1739
2. Maria, bapt...............................March 21, 1741
3. Johannes, bapt............................June 16, 1743
4. Barbara, bapt.............................March 5, 1747

Hans Mössmer, mason, 43 years of age.   1.1.1.
Permitted to leave gratis.
Chrischona Suter, his wife, aged 47.
1. Daughter...................................20 years old
The latter is urging her parents to emigrate.

Jacob Mössmer, Hans Jacob, Frid's son, aged 42. 1.1.2.
Permitted to leave gratis.
Catharina Spenhauer, his wife, aged 43.
Their children:
1. Margreth, bapt...........................Nov. 25, 1736
2. Hans Jacob, bapt..........................Apr. 16, 1741

Bernhard Ramstein, bapt. Oct. 25, 1707. 1.1.2.
Permitted to leave gratis.
Margreth Pfau, his wife, bapt. March 6, 1712.
Their children:
1. Margaretha, bapt.........................Febr. 10, 1739
2. Anna, bapt...............................March 10, 1748
See his refusal to go 1740. This time the success of his father in law in Pennsylvania made him desirous to follow him.

Hans Seiler, Heinrich's son, unmarried, bapt. Febr. 8, 1718. 1.—.—.
Ten percent tax [on lb. 292.—].....................29.4
Manumission......................................10.—   39.4

Appears to be identical with Hans Seiler who intended to emigrate in 1740.
Has always been honest in his dealings.
Martin Seiler, day-labourer, aged 37. 1.1.—
Manumission.....................................20.—.—
Ten percent tax [on lb. 112.11.4]...................11. 5. 4   31.5.4

Elisabeth Heyd, his wife, aged 31.
Stephan Spünhauer, day-labourer, bapt. Jan. 25, 1728. 1.1.1.
Permitted to leave gratis.
Ursula Brodbeck, his wife, aged 24.
1. Fridrich, their son, bapt......................May 19, 1748
Ursel Spänhauer, sister of Stephan, unmarried, bapt. July 12, 1723. —.1.—.
Manumission.....................................10.—.—
Ten percent tax [on lb. 157.15.6]..................15.15. 6   25.15.6

Jacob Tschudin, unmarried, bapt. Dec. 25, 1725(?). 1.—.—.
Ten percent tax [on lb. 46.2].......................... 4.12
Manumission.....................................10.—   14.12.—

His emigration considered hazardous on account of his frail constitution. A Jacob Tschudi who emigrated this year reported however Sept. 2, 1750, that he found work in Pennsylvania.
Jacob Tschudin. 1.—.—.
Permitted to leave gratis.
Apparently identical with the preceding. Neither the testimonials of the pastor nor the special lists of Münchenstein show two men by that name.

Johannes Tschudin, joiner. 1.1.1.
    Permitted to leave gratis.
Verena Mangold, his wife.
    1. Johannes, their son, bapt.....................March 19, 1748
Stepfan Wyrrslin's children. —.—.6.
    Ten percent tax [on lb. 397.17.10]........................39.15.—
Children of his wife by her first husband Joh. Weibel and one by him:
    1. Barbara Weibel, bapt.......................Jan.   23, 1731
    2. Anna Maria Weibel, bapt...................June 14, 1733
    3. Arbogast Weibel, bapt......................May 22, 1736
    4. Catharina Weibel, bapt....................Oct. 18, 1739
    5. Anna Weibel, bapt.........................Apr. 25, 1741
    6. Ursula Wyrrslin, bapt.....................Dec.   6, 1744
Hieron. d'Annone, the pastor of Muttenz, in his Diary, Vol. III, makes the following statement about the emigrants above and a few others, some of whom are not on any list: "May 8, [1749] many people from the Canton of Basel, among them also 66 persons from Muttenz, with whom I have had much to talk and to do, left by water [*i.e.*, on the Rhine] for the New-land. The government disliked to see it, and remonstrances have not been lacking, but because most of them were needy and 'übel gesittete' people, it was the easier to get over their loss."

March 28 he had said of Hans Rudi Brodbeck, Jacob Lüdin and Stefan Spänhauer that they had a good name, and Febr. 25 he had attested that Heinrich Brodbeck, Hans Mössmer, Theodor's son, Jacob Mössmer, Bernhard Ramstein and Stefan Würsslin were not compelled to emigrate on account of any ill conduct.

Pratteln

Niclaus Dill, correctly *Till*, linen-weaver, aged 26. 1.1.—.
    Manumission..20.—.—
    Ten percent tax [on lb. 154.4.6]..................15. 8. 6 35.8.6

Esther Schwillion, KB Chevillon, his wife, bapt. Dec. 20, 1722.
Hans Jacob Honecker, carpenter, 32 years of age. 1.1.1.
    Permitted to leave gratis.
Anna Bleyler from Zollikon, Canton of Zürich, his wife, aged 24.
    1. Hans Jacob, their son, bapt.................Apr. 14, 1748
    Have led a Christian life and not given cause for complaint.
Johannes Meyer, day-labourer, aged 27. 1.1.—.
    Ten percent tax [on lb. 490.6.10].......................49.1
    Manumission.......................................20.— 69.1

Elisabeth Schwillion, KB Chevillon, sister of Esther above, his wife, bapt. Aug. 14, 1718.
* *Hans Jacob Nebiger*, shoemaker, 43 years old. 1.1.—.
    Permitted to leave gratis.
Barbara Giger from Füllinsdorf, his wife, aged 41.
    Gave up emigrating. In the following year Jacob Joner claimed the credit for it (AA).

Amt Riehen

Hans Schuldheis, bapt. July 15, 1703. 1.1.2.
    Pays: Ten percent tax [on lb. 383.15].............33. 9. 4
    Manumission dues...........................20.—.— 53.9.4

Eva Soldner, his wife, bapt. Dec. 8, 1705.

Their sons:

1. Hans Georg, born or bapt.................Dec. 3, 1730
2. Hans, born or bapt........................Febr. 20, 1735

Parents quiet, industrious, without having given cause for complaint. Sons have the reputation of being pretty bad boys.

AMT WALDENBURG

Arboldswil

Hans Stohler, for a while school teacher. 1.1.—.

Ten percent tax [on lb. 79.—.8].........................7.18
[Manumission not charged.]

Ursula Thommen, his wife.

Has always conducted himself well.

Durs Thommen, Christen's son. 1.1.2.

Manumission.....................................20.—.—
Ten percent tax [on lb. 572.19]....................57. 5. 6   77.5.6

Elsbeth Rudin, KB Rayfftlin, his wife.
Their children:

1. Hans Jacob, bapt...........................Febr. 19, 1736
2. Anna, bapt................................Dec. 10, 1737

Has always endeavoured not to give cause for complaint.

Bennwil

Joggi Schwab, tinner. 1.1.2.

Manumission.................................. 20.—.—
Ten percent tax [on lb. 1553.15.4]................155. 7. 6   175.7.6

Maria Schwab, his wife.
Their children:

1. Margaretha, bapt..........................Sept. 28, 1738
2. Anna Maria, bapt.........................Jan.   10, 1745

Is entitled to good testimonials from the entire community.

Heini Vogt, day-labourer. 1.1.4.

Manumission.................................20.—.—
Ten percent tax [on lb. 198.18.4]..................19.17. 6   39.17.6

Barbara Roth, his wife.
Their children:

1. Heinrich, bapt............................March 21, 1728
2. Johannes, bapt...........................Jan. 22, 1730
3. Martin, bapt.............................Febr. 26, 1736
4. Barbara, bapt............................Jan. 15, 1741

Bubendorf

Joggi Weissner, [usually *Wissner*], Heini's son. 1.1.—.

for Manumission.....................................211.—
[Apparently released from payment of tax.]

Barbara Schaub, his wife.

Jacob Wissmer [Weissner], the young. 1.—.—.(!).

Dues not paid, [*i.e.*, gratis]. Has only 30 pounds.

Anna Buser, his wife.

1. Anna, their child, bapt.....................Apr. 30, 1748

Always industrious.

Höllstein

Hans Joggi Gisin, [Uhli's son], lace-maker. 1.1.2.
　　Manumission...20.—.—
　　Ten percent tax [on lb. 660.15.4]..................66. 1. 6   86.1.6

Barbara Rayfftlin, Raufftlin, his wife.
His children by Margreth Spiser, his first wife:
　　1. Anna, bapt................................Jan.　27, 1737
　　2. Barbara, bapt.............................Jan.　7, 1738
　　Has led a quiet, honest, God-fearing life.
* *Heini Merian*, teamster. 1.1.3.
　　Dues not paid [*i.e.*, gratis].
Barbara Würtz, his wife.
Their children: Anna, Heinrich, Eusebius, bapt. between March 1742 and Nov.
　　1747.—The birth of Friderich, bapt. Sept. 6, 1750, shows that they did not
　　emigrate.
Joggi Thommen, son of Fridlin, deceased. 1.1.4.
　　Manumission...20.—.—
　　Ten percent tax [on lb. 584.4.10]..................58. 8. 6   78.8.6

Barbara Handschin, his wife.
Their children:
　　1. Elsbeth, bapt.............................Oct.　15, 1724
　　2. Anna, bapt...............................Febr.　19, 1726
　　3. Magdalena, bapt..........................Jan.　16, 1729
　　4. Barbara, bapt............................Jan.　29, 1735
　　Has not given cause for complaint.

Lampenberg

Elsbet Christen, orphan, cousin of Heini below. —.1.—.
　　Dues not paid [*i.e.*, gratis].
　　Has not given cause for complaint.
Heini Christen, Heini's son, bapt. March 10, 1719. 1.1.5.
　　Manum. [incl. his mother's below]..................30.—
　　Ten percent tax [on lb. 1227.12.2]..................122.16   152.16

Maria Fluebacher, his wife.
Their children who according to another source were four:
　　1. Heinrich, bapt...........................Nov.　14, 1734
　　2. Anna, bapt..............................Apr.　7, 1737
　　3. Jacob, bapt.............................June　25, 1741
　　4. Son.................................... 3 years old
　　Has not given cause for complaint.
Hans Fluebacher. 1.1.6.
　　Dues not paid, [*i.e.*, gratis].
Margreth Häfelfinger, his wife.
Their children:
　　1. Elsbeth, bapt...........................Jan.　12, 1738
　　2. Johannes, bapt..........................Apr.　19, 1739
　　* 3. Heinrich, bapt..........................Jan.　8, 1741
　　4. Barbara, bapt...........................Febr.　17, 1743
　　5. Fridrich, bapt..........................Aug.　24, 1745
　　6. Stepdaughter from Hölstein, apparently Ursula
　　　　Gysin, bapt.............................Nov.　26, 1730
　　Heinrich died Apr. 17 before emigrating.
　　Has not given cause for complaint.

Madle Haussman, widow of Adam Thommen of Hölstein. —.1.6.
    Ten percent tax [on lb. 215.18.2]............................25.3.6
    [Manumission not charged.]
Her children:
    1. Adam Thommen, bapt......................Jan.   15, 1736
    2. Anna Thommen, bapt......................March 30, 1738
    3. Magdalena Thommen, bapt..................Jan.   14, 1741
    4. Martin Thommen, bapt.....................July   7, 1743
    5. Heinrich Thommen, bapt...................July   4, 1745
    6. Barbara Thommen, bapt....................Nov.   12, 1747
    Has not given cause for complaint.
Heini Thommen. 1.1.6.
    Manumission [half].......................................10.—
    Ten percent tax [on lb. 144.8.6].........................14. 8 24.8

Verena Rudin from Ziefen, his wife.
Their children:
    1. Barbara, bapt...............................Nov.   25, 1725
    2. Hans, bapt.................................Oct.   19, 1727
    3. Adam, bapt................................Jan.   18, 1729
    4. Verena, bapt...............................March 30, 1732
    5. Elsbeth, bapt..............................Oct.   11, 1739
    6. Heinrich, bapt.............................Jan.   5, 1744
    Has not given cause for complaint.
Anna Tschudi, mother of Heini Christen above, 64 years old. —.1.—.
    Dues not paid. [N.B. Manum. paid by son above.]

Lauwil

* *Hans Joggi Frey.* 1.1.3.
    Dues not paid, [*i.e.*, gratis].
Elsbeth Rudin, his wife.
Their children: Elsbeth, bapt. June 1746, and two others. The birth of Urs,
    bapt. Dec. 7, 1749, proves that they did not emigrate this year.

Liedertswil

Hans Degen, son of Heini, deceased, aged 32. 1.1.2.
    Manumission...20.—
    Ten percent tax [on lb. 641.12.8]......................64.3   84.3

Elsbeth Krattiger, his wife, about the same age.
Their children:
    1. Elsbeth, bapt..............................Dec.   18, 1746
    2. Catharina, bapt...........................March 17, 1748
    Have led a quiet honourable life and attended church assiduously.

Lupsingen

Hans Tschudi, son of Joggi, deceased. 1.—.—.(!). N.B.: MP has confounded
    Hans Tschudi with Hans Joggi Tschudin.
    Dues not paid, [*i.e.*, gratis].
Barbara Weyssner, Wissmer, his wife.
Their children:
    1. Maria, bapt...............................Jan.   16, 1746
    2. Jacob, bapt...............................March 20, 1748
    Bannbruder attests, that he had been honest and obliging toward everybody.
Had 67 pounds left which he used to dress himself and his family for the journey.
Jacob, which MP puts before Hans, may refer to his father.

Hans Joggi Tschudin, unmarried. 1.—.2.(!).
    Manumission...10.—
    Ten percent tax [on lb. 455.—].......................45.10 55.10

According to Bannbruder, honest and obliging toward everybody.

Niederdorf

Hans Rudolf Jund, usually *Junt*, stepson of the following, some 20 years old.
    Dues not paid, [*i.e.*, gratis].
    Observes the outward forms of religion.   God only knows his heart.
Hans Rudi Negelin, miller's helper. 1.1.1.
    Manumission.......................................20.—.—
    Ten percent tax [on lb. 261.10].....................25. 3. 6 45.3.6

Esther Thommen, his wife.
    Husband and true disciple of Jesus.   Wife eager for salvation.   Desirable
that these people, whose number is unfortunately so small, might stay.
Hans Weber. 1.1.9.
    Dues not paid, [not even the Chancery dues].
Barbara Schweitzer, his wife.
Their children:
        1–3. Names not ascertainable because KB does not begin till 1736.
        4. Madlen, bapt...............................Febr. 3, 1737
        5. Daniel, bapt...............................Dec.   16, 1738
        6. Anna, bapt.................................Aug.   21, 1740
        7. Hans Jacob, bapt...........................Jan.   28, 1742
        8. Hieronymus, bapt...........................Febr. 7, 1745
        9. Heinrich, bapt.............................Jan.   22, 1747
Has tried to sustain himself honestly.

Oberdorf

Hans Spitteler, saddler. 1.1.1.
    Manumission......................................20.—
    Ten percent tax [on lb. 635.—.6]...................63.10 83.10

Catharina Rinderknecht, his wife.
        1. Their child................................15 months old

Ramlinsburg

Anna Buser. —.1.3.
    Dues not paid, [*i.e.*, gratis].
        1–3. Three grown-up children whose names cannot be given because
            there are several Anna Buser in KB.
    Husband went into military service 8 years ago.
Martin Grimm. 1.1.2.
    Manumission......................................20.—.—
    Ten percent tax [on lb. 411.5.2]...................41. 2. 6 61.2.6

Elsbeth Weybel, his wife.
Their children:
        1. Hans Jacob, bapt...........................July   28, 1737
        2. Child, bapt................................   ?
    Has not given cause for complaint.
Joggi Grüenblat. 1.1.—.   N.B.: Children are omitted because Obervogt did
    not know their number.
    Dues not paid.
Barbara Lüdin, his wife.

Their children:
1. Catharina, bapt............................Sept. 25, 1729
2. Barbara, bapt..............................Apr. 12, 1733
3. Anna, bapt................................Dec. 4, 1735

Left before the time. His son Hans Jacob declared himself willing to pay his debts.

Anna Lüdin, lately married to Daniel, son of Heini below. —.1.—.
Manumission.....................................10.—.—
Ten percent tax [on lb. 397.17]...................39.15. 6   49.15.6

Heini Lüdin, son of Daniel, deceased. 1.1.3.
Manumission..20.—
Ten percent tax [on lb. 1076.13]..................107.13   127.13

Margreth Bidert from Bärenwil, his wife.
Their children:
1. Anna, bapt................................March 18, 1725
2. Daniel, bapt..............................Oct. 3, 1728
3. Johan Jacob, bapt.........................Jan. 15, 1730

Children can all work well. No cause for complaint.

Hans Schaub. 1.—.—.
Dues not paid.
Everybody speaks well of him.

Hans Stohler. 1.1.1.
Manumission......................................20.—
Ten percent tax [on lb. 699.1.10]..................69.18   89.18

Elsbeth Schwab, his wife.
1. Adam, their son, bapt.....................Jan. 1, 1740

Has not given cause for complaint.

Adam Weibel. 1.1.—. N.B.: Children omitted because Obervogt had not reported their number.
Dues not paid, [not even those for the Chancery].

Anna Gysin, his wife.
Their children:
1. Hans Joggi, bapt..........................Febr. 3, 1731
2. Chrischona, bapt..........................May 29, 1733
3. Anna, bapt...............................July 31, 1738
4. Johannes, bapt...........................June 2, 1742
5. Friedrich, bapt..........................March 19, 1747

Had obtained permission to emigrate in 1738 and not availed himself of it. No complaint about him.

Waldenburg

Muss Brodbeck, son of Andres. 1.1.3.
Dues not paid, [i.e., gratis].

Eva Weiss, his wife.
1–3. Children. Names not ascertainable because of loss of KB.

No complaint. Has lived quietly and attended church and the Lord's Supper pretty faithfully.

Baltz Strohman, Strauman, shoemaker, aged 26. 1.1.—.
Pays: Manumission dues...........................20.—
Ten percent tax [on lb. 263.4.10].................26.6   46.6

Verena Schwab, his wife, of the same age.
Has lived an honest Christian life and assiduously attended church and the Lord's Supper.

Johannes Strohman, mason, 1.1.7.
    Dues not paid, not even the 3 pounds for the Chancery.
Anna Jenni, his wife.
        1–7. Children of 18, 16, 11, 9, 7, 4 and ¼ years. Names not ascer-
            tainable.
    His wife a drunkard of the worst kind. Swallowed five quarts of wine on the
third day after childbirth, also suspected of other sins. Bad effects upon her
husband and children.

Ziefen

Hans Hemmig. 1.1.4.
        Pays for: Manumission dues........................ 20.—
                Ten percent tax [on lb. 2074.11.5]...........207.9   227.9

Eva Senn, his wife.
Their children:
        1. Elisabeth, bapt.............................June   23, 1737
        2. Johannes, bapt.............................Nov.   5, 1742
        3. Anna, bapt.................................Sept. 26, 1745
        4. Eva, bapt..................................Dec.   31, 1747
    Has led a quiet, honest, God-fearing life. Wishes to escape from various
circumstances that are annoying to him.
Martin Tschopp, son of Heini, deceased. 1.1.6.
        Manumission.................................. 20.—.—
        Ten percent tax [on lb. 1329.17.4]...............132.19. 6   152.19.6

Anna Tschopp, his wife.
Their children:
        1. Anna, bapt.................................Apr.   3, 1738
        2. Eva, bapt..................................Febr. 28, 1740
        3. Barbara, bapt..............................May   14, 1742
        4. Verena, bapt...............................Febr. 23, 1744
        5. Heinrich, bapt.............................Dec.   11, 1746
        6. Martin, bapt...............................March 10, 1748
    Both pastor and Geschworener attest that he has not been quarrelsome, but
peaceable in his intercourse with everybody.

II. *Emigrants not recorded in MP*

AMT FARNSBURG

Rothenfluh

Hans Walliser.
His wife and daughter whom we have not found in KB.
    According to report of Obervogt, read in Council May 14, 1749 (RP 122, 261),
they joined other emigrants without permission.

AMT LIESTAL

Seltisberg

Fridolin Salathe, son of Hans S. and Ursula Schäfer, bapt. Apr. 14, 1726.
Hans Jacob, his brother, bapt. Jan. 15, 1719.
    Their secret emigration, which undoubtedly took place in the year 1749,
came up in connection with their father's death in February 11 and May 2,
1750 (RP 123, 163 and 278 sq.). Their brother-in-law, Jeremias Vogt of Lauwil,

who was married to their sister Anna, asserted that they had emigrated after March 22, 1749, and without permission and hence had forfeited their claims to their paternal inheritance, while their 'Vogt' objected that they might have gone before that date. The report of the Waisenamt, adopted by the Council May 2, settled the matter as follows: In view of the wanton manner in which these two sons have forsaken their parents and of the necessity of maintaining their mother, the sons Jacob and Fridolin Salathe, who have gone to Pennsylvania, are excluded from the inheritance of their father, and the property [worth 1250 pounds] is turned over to Jeremias Vogt, Lauwil, on payment of the debts (lb. 988.7.4) on it and the promise to sustain his mother-in-law while she is living in good and evil days.

According to GAV 15, Apr. 27, 1750, the mother had received a letter from Philadelphia that one of her two sons had died in the meantime.

Amt Muenchenstein

Benken

Antoni Löw

His name is on the last list of emigrants from Amt Münchenstein among those who were too poor to pay the Chancery dues. We can therefore not tell whether he emigrated alone or with his family.

Muttens

Stephan Würsslin, cooper, 28 years of age.
Anna Maria Brodbeck, his wife, aged 42.

Although MP states only the emigration of Stephan Würsslin's children, five of whom were stepchildren, there can be no doubt that he and his wife emigrated with them. His name occurs on two of the special lists of Münchenstein, on that of the manumissions with the note 'gratis' and on that of the Chancery dues with the usual 3 pounds paid by a married couple.

Amt Waldenburg

Waldenburg

Catharina Brodbeck, sister of Muss, recorded above.

Her emigration is proved by RL 1753: 'And then from Muss and Catharina Brodbeck of Waldenburg who went to the Newly-found-land 3 years ago and inherited from their mother . . ., wife of the wheelwright Andres Brodbeck, lb. 66.18.4.

Per tax at 10 pro cento . . . . .6.14'

Daniel Schäublin.

His secret emigration and that of the following two men is announced in a report of the Obervogt, read in Council May 14, 1749 (RP 122, 261), in which it is presumed that they went to Pennsylvania. His own emigration is confirmed by RL 1753: 'First from Daniel Schäublin of Waldenburg who went to the Newly-found-land 3 years ago and at present inherited 50 pounds from his grandfather.

Per tax at 5 pro cento . . . . .5.—'

Jacob Schäublin, smith.
Jacob Tschopp, saddler.

Also these two emigrated secretly according to the same report of May 14. The latter left wife and children behind while the two Schäublins took them along. Their names can however not be given.

A number of others who probably emigrated this year will be found below among the emigrants of uncertain date.

1750

Though almost all the emigrants of this year left without being manumitted, MP contains a nearly full list of them. We reproduce it in our usual alphabetical arrangement with the omission of Martin Imhoff and Frid and Michel Schor, who had received permission, and of Hans Jacob Schweitzer, who did not emigrate.

Emigrants

May 9th, 1750 (Amt Farnsburg)
Gelterkinden:
  Heini Würtz, the glazier.
Zuntzgen:
  Hans Wagner: wife and child [1]
  [no place stated, but Gelterkinden].
  Hans Handtschin.
  Jacob Rohrer with wife and child.
  Shall 'Herr Landvogt' collect the dues and send them to the Chancery.

  May 16th (Amt Liestal)
Selbensperg:
  Hans Spinler with wife and child.

  May 13th (Amt Waldenburg)
Bubendorf:
  Fridli Miesch with wife and child.
Höllstein:
  Hans and Joggi Schäublin with wife and child.
Liedertschweil:
  Son and daughter of Heini Degen, deceased.

Ramlispurg:
  Hans Lüdin with wife and child.
  Shall 'Herr Landvogt' collect the dues and send them here.

  May 13th, 1750 (Amt Liestal)
Lausen:
  Sirach Tschudin with wife and child.
  Shall 'Herr Schuldheiss' collect the dues and send them here.

  May 20th, 1750 (Amt Waldenburg)
Höllstein:
  Hans Geörg Foltz, the smith.
Liederschweil:
  Heini Degen's widow.

  May 27th (Amt Waldenburg)
  Hans Tschopp, Höllsteiner's son.
  Shall 'Herr Landvogt' collect and pay all dues.

I. *Emigrants with Permission*

AMT FARNSBURG

Wintersingen

May 13, 1750

Martin im Hoff, [Jmhoff,[2] Martin's son] of Wintersingen receives permission to emigrate.
  Shall pay: Ten percent tax on lb. 1600 . . . . 160.—
       Manumission, he, wife, 2 children . . . . 40.—
       4 Letters at 18b [= Batzen] . . . . 6.—   206.—

Ursula Jtin, his wife.

---

[1] In the German, "Weib und Kind" may mean "wife and child" or "wife and children." Sometimes the one, sometimes the other is meant in this and the following documents, but the number is generally not given. "Child" as used here should therefore be understood to mean one or more children.

[2] I and J frequently appear as interchangeable in the old manuscripts. Jmhoff = Imhoff.

Their children:

1. Barbara, bapt.................................July 8, 1742
2. Martin, bapt.................................Febr. 9, 1744

The Council had decided that the children and one half of the property must remain in the country, but as the children insisted on going with their parents, this decision was reversed a week later (RP 123, 283 and 294).

AMT MUENCHENSTEIN

Muttenz

Frid Schor, Fridlin, 44 years of age.
Margreth Schneider, daughter of Jacob Schn. and Anna Pfau, his wife, bapt. Oct. 3, 1708.
Their children:

1. Fridrich, bapt.............................Oct. 23, 1731
2. Heinrich, bapt.............................Febr. 13, 1735
3. Johannes, bapt.............................May 24, 1739
4. Margreth, bapt.............................Oct. 21, 1742

Michel Schor, 42 years of age.
Anna Maria Schwartz, his wife, of the same age.
Their children:

1. Ursula, bapt..............................Dec. 13, 1738
2. Hans Jacob, bapt..........................Aug. 14, 1740
3. Anna Maria, bapt..........................Apr. 14, 1743

Both families had intended to emigrate in 1749 and received permission to do so. Their permission was renewed this year May 16 (RP), but there is no record of their making a payment of dues. Their pastor d'Annone is not sorry to see them go.

There is a letter by Frid Schor to his brother-in-law in which he announces the death of his wife and an infant of theirs, born a week after their arrival at Cowes, England. Their trip from Basel to Philadelphia had taken almost half a year, 25 weeks: 3 down the Rhine, 2 waiting for a ship in Holland, 1 across to Cowes, 4 waiting for another ship there and 15 more to Philadelphia. The infant had died when they were 3 weeks out, the mother followed after 7 more weeks, an often repeated tragedy of those early Colonial days.

II. *Emigrants without Permission*

AMT FARNSBURG

Gelterkinden

Hans Handschi, unmarried, bapt. July 27, 1732.
Note in KB: 'Went to Pennsylvania in 1750.'
Jacob Rohrer, lace-maker, presumably son of Jacob Rohrer and Anna Guldenmann, bapt. Oct. 24, 1723, and identical with Jacob Rohrer who is recorded among the emigrants of the preceding year in MP.
RP 123, 289, his destination is not mentioned, but the context and the fact that he was a stepbrother of Hans Handschi just above make it almost certain that he also went to Pennsylvania.
Heini Würz, the glazier.
Heini Müri of Wintersingen, who in pursuit of his debtor Vögtlin came across him in Rheinweiler, attested that he had said that he wanted to go to the New-land and that his wife had not been willing to come along. Had 400 pounds with him (GAV 15, Dec. 28, 1750). RP 124, 31, states that he went to Pennsylvania. Left wife and 5 children, among them one that was blind (RP 124, 290).

Ormalingen

Moritz Weber, Jacob's son, former miller.
Elsbeth Anisshäusslin, his wife.
Their children:

    1. Maria, bapt..............................Dec.   5, 1742
    2. Barbara, bapt............................March 28, 1745
    3. Maritz, bapt.............................Oct. 15, 1747

Barbara and Maritz are found in KB of Rümlingen, a parish in which he was 'Lehenmüller.'

He did not intend to emigrate without permission, but his petition, which was referred to the XIII, was either not acted upon or denied (RP 123, May 30). A few months later he took the matter into his own hands, sold his property to Daniel Meyer, the 'Blumenwirt,' landlord of the Flower in Basel, who afterwards claimed to have bought his 'debts,' and emigrated 'secretly' (RP 124, Nov. 25, 1750). Reports and hearings in the case extended for over a year till January 1752 and, if Daniel Meyer's statements could be believed, there was never less secrecy about a departure from Basel than about that of Moritz Weber. Daniel Meyer, who had been in America himself, gave himself the appearance of complete innocence though one may believe to see almost the twinkle in his eye as he makes his statements (AA, Report read in Council, Jan. 8, 1752): He did not know that the subjects needed permission to emigrate and he had not done anything to help Moritz Weber to get away. (N.B.: An order of May 9, RP 123, 289, forbade the shipmen to embark any one without due certificate.) Moritz Weber had spent a week at his inn and had moved about freely during that time. He had had his things carried openly to the landing place two hours before the ship started and had then followed himself. At all events the two men were well matched and played a successful game on the government. Moritz Weber's wife and children are only mentioned in his petition, but, as it is not stated that he left them behind, it may be supposed that he took them with him.

Hans Wagner.   *Zunzgen*
Catharina Buser, his wife.
Their children:

    1. Hans Jacob, bapt.........................Jan.   4, 1740
    2. Anna Maria, bapt........................Dec.   8, 1743
    3. Sebastian, bapt.........................Jan. 21, 1748
    4. Barbara, bapt...........................March 29, 1750

A report from Farnsburg, read May 9, said that he had left the country with his family and about 1500 pounds in cash and another report, read May 13, added that he had skipped the country by night. Seventeen years later this matter came up in Council again in connection with an inheritance of 2300 pounds which was claimed by the children. By that time their 'Vögte' had forgotten, or pretended to have forgotten, that they had left without permission. The parents had died on the voyage (RP 141, Jan. 23, 1768).

Amt Liestal

Sirach Tschudi, weaver.   *Lausen*
Barbara Madöri, his wife.

    1. Martin, their child, bapt...................Nov. 24, 1748

Matthis Vögtlin and his wife.

Two reports from Liestal, both read May 13, 1750 (RP 123, 290), announced that these two parties had betaken themselves out of the country, the latter on account of debts which he foresaw he could not pay. Both had gone to Kaiser-Augst, and Matthis Vögtlin had been seen there with Jacob Joner of Pennsylvania. It may therefore be assumed that they wanted to go to America with him.

Seltisberg

Hans Spinler, son of Heinrich, deceased.
His wife and children. RP 123, 299, does not say where he went.
As much indebted as his dilapidated house was worth.

AMT MUENCHENSTEIN

Münchenstein

* *Hans Ledermann* from Niederbipp, Canton of Bern, for 15 years tenant on an estate of Prof. Dr. Frey on Bruckfeld.
Had first been married to Anna Nebicker of Häfelfingen, and his oldest daughter Anna, bapt. March 13, 1735, was staying there at the house of her childless uncle and aunt Bürgi. When he wanted to go with his second wife and all his children to America, the Council decided that he might go where he pleased, but that he must leave his daughter Anna, who preferred to remain at her uncle's, in the country (RP 123, 310). Under the circumstances he gave up emigrating for the present, for KB reports the death of his second wife in February 1752 and his marriage to a third.

AMT WALDENBURG

Bubendorf

Fridlin Miesch.
Elisabeth Rudin, his wife.
Their children:
1. Johannes, bapt........................Sept.   4, 1729
2. Child, bapt..................   ....   ?
According to a report from Waldenburg, read in Council May 13 (RP 123, 291), he had skipped the country and started for the Newly-found-land. The Obervogt succeeded in recovering the government dues from the property which he had left behind. RL 1751: 'From F.. M.. at B.. who with his wife and 2 children has gone into the Newly-found-land and taken 592 pounds in money with him.
Tax at 10 pro cento.................................59.4
Manumission for 4 persons.........................40.—' 99.4

Höllstein

Hans Georg Foltz, smith.
Went to the Newly-found-land and left his wife and six children behind (RP 123, 303). One of his sons emigrated to America in 1771.
Hans Schäublin. Family not recorded in KB.
Joggi Schäublin, Hans Joggi, brother of Hans.
Anna Tschudi, his wife.
Their children:
1. Anna, bapt...............................Jan.   21, 1744
2. Catharina, bapt..........................Oct.   9, 1746
Both brothers skipped the country and started for the Newly-found-land (RP 123, 290 sq.).

Liedertswil

Son and *daughter* of *Heini Degen*, deceased, whose Christian names and dates cannot be given owing to the loss of KB.   Perhaps they were brother and sister of Hans Degen who emigrated the preceding year.   They were reported to have betaken themselves to Kaiser-Augst, where Jacob Joner stayed, on the way to the Newly-found-land (RP 123, 290).

Heini Degen's widow, their mother, followed them according to the report read May 20 (RP 123, 303).   The Obervogt collected the dues of all three.   RL 1751: 'From the widow, son and daughter of Heini Degen . . ., who have gone to the Newly-found-land and taken lb. 1207.10.10 in money with them. Tax at 10 pro cento. 120.15
Manumission for 3 persons. . . . . 30.—' 150.15

Ramlinsburg

Hans Lüdin, son of Daniel, deceased.
Magdalena Haussman, his wife.
Their children:

1. Johannes, bapt.	Sept.	8,	1737
2. Barbara, bapt.	Nov.	15,	1739
3. Anna, bapt.	Apr.	30,	1741

Has skipped the country and gone to the Newly-found-land (l.c. 291).

Hans Tschopp, Höllsteiner's son.
Left wife and children behind.   Destination not known (l.c. 310).

1751

Also most of the emigrants of this year left secretly and the few who went with permission were persons whom the government had a desire to retain.   Several of the secret emigrants belonged to the family of Johannes Tschudi of Frenkendorf, emigrant of 1749 and back on a business trip, whom both the governments of Basel and of Bern made vain efforts to arrest.   His personal description, which we owe to this circumstance, is as follows: 'Johannes Tschudi is a cooper by trade, 25 years old, has a broad, ruddy, well formed face and blonde (literally yellow) curly hair, is six feet tall and broad-set, wears a brown redingote and a doublet of blue cloth with like blue buttons, long blue city trousers, white stockings and city shoes, sports a couteau and a long stick.'

I. *Emigrants with Permission*

Sissach (Amt Farnsburg)

Barbara Senn, manumitted for her marriage with Hans Georg Lübert from 'Franckhenland,' Febr. 10, 1742.
Had no property at that time.
In 1748 she was staying in Basel where her husband was in service and her conduct from that time on leaves the impression that she was not only restless, but also not quite right in her mind.   She disobeyed regulations and, though told that she would be put in the 'Schellenwerk' (penitentiary), if she returned to the

city, came back twice and made herself obnoxious again. The result was two terms in the 'Schellenwerk,' imprisonment in the 'Waisenhaus' and, after she had once made her escape from there, the threat that an iron ball would be attached to her feet if she tried to run away again, finally deportation to Pennsylvania with her own consent. To make sure that she did not come back after all, it was resolved that she should not receive the main part of her money until she was in Holland aboard ship for America.

Frenkendorf (Amt Liestal)

Jacob Schaub, son of the schoolmaster Jacob Sch. and Anna Margreth Meyer, bapt. May 8, 1729. MP: 'Jacob Schaub, who has gone to Carolina(!)

Pays: Manumission.................................10.—
　　　Ten percent tax on 350 pounds.................35.— 45.—'

Ursula Till, daughter of Muss Till, who had left the country for destination unknown, his bride, bapt. Febr. 23, 1726. Her manumission was granted, but is not recorded in MP. She died in America in 1758, leaving a daughter Anna Margreth, born about 1755, whose attempts to obtain the inheritances which came to her in future years were in vain owing to the prepossession of the authorities against her father.

Jacob Schaub had the misfortune of losing his mother when he was scarcely eighteen, and coming by her death into possession of money which he did not know how to keep. Proclaimed a 'prodigus' and thereby deprived of the free use of it, he first enlisted and deserted a couple of times and then decided to emigrate to Pennsylvania, for which purpose the government allowed him to take with him 350 out of the 800 pounds which he had left, with the understanding that he was to receive the remainder on presentation of testimonials of good behavior.

Whether he was ashamed to ask for such papers in America or whether it was thought preposterous that he should do so, he made three applications without them, one for the 450 through Jacob Joner, one for the 2500, which he could claim after his father's death, through another agent and one himself in person. The government on the other hand had the paternalism, not to say pretention, to feel called upon to superintend his financial affairs even after he had managed to sustain himself and a family for fifteen years and more in America, and demanded a certificate of his financial status by the British government in addition to the testimonials. Not tolerated in the Canton and yet unwilling to return to America empty handed, he succumbed to the temptations which his wandering life in taverns brought with it and finally had to go back to America after all to procure those papers, and get them endorsed by the British ambassador at Bern before he received what was left of his 2500 pounds. He had no longer the moral energy to go back with this money to America at once, and the end was that he became penniless, was denied by the government a refuge which he hoped to find at his old home place Frenkendorf, was put on the pillory, led across the frontier and threatened with a flogging if he dared to return. A year later nothing was known of him at Basel any more, and it is uncertain whether he died of privations or disease or put a voluntary end to his life as he had threatened to do when he was denied the refuge at Frenkendorf (RP 141–144 in many places between Nov. 1768 and June 8, 1771, and Nord Amerika B 1, Sept. 11, 1772).

AMT RIEHEN

N. N. Trechslin, Christian name not mentioned in RP because he seems to have been well known to the Council.

He applied for permission to emigrate to Pennsylvania because, as he said, he was looked upon as infamous on account of his having been put to the rack. The Council did not only grant his request, but voted him 20 pounds as a contribution toward his travelling expenses, quite an unusual proceeding with a body which otherwise was so careful to avoid precedents. Unfortunately his antecedents cannot be given. His manumission is not recorded in MP.

II. *Emigrants without Permission*

AMT FARNSBURG

Augst

Johannes Strub.

He was engaged to be married to Elsbeth Tschudi below and received from her father a dowry of 116 pounds. Their marriage took place on the journey (Report by Schultheiss Hebdenstreit of Apr. 10, 1767).

Tenniken

Maria Magdalena Schafner, daughter of the Geschworener Hans Jacob Sch. and Anna Maria Häfelfinger, bapt. Apr. 17, 1729.

The story of her engagement to Johannes Tschudi of Frenkendorf, which took place at first sight, is told in the supplication which 'Ratsredner' Burckhard drew up on behalf of the latter (AA) and which was read in Council July 5, 1767. Their marriage occurred at Rotterdam, probably simultaneously with that of his sister and the young Strub above. In 1767 they had four children. In 1793 and 1795 she had not been heard from for so long that her relatives tried to get her pronounced legally dead in order to obtain the 1373 pounds which had been bequeathed to her in the meantime.

AMT LIESTAL

Frenkendorf

Fridlin Lander, KB Landerer, son of Hans L. and Anna Martin.

A report from Liestal, read in Council Apr. 17, 1751, announced that he had betaken himself out of the country and left scarcely enough to pay his debts, but. does not mention his destination. Only in GAV 20, 540, Febr. 22, 1796, it is said that he went to America.

Elsbeth Tschudi, daughter of Martin Tsch. and sister of Johannes above, bapt. July 10, 1729.

Weinbert Tschudi, their brother, bapt. Apr. 22, 1731.

Lorenz(?) Tschudi, son of the day-labourer Hans Tschudi and, if Lorenz is his correct name, bapt. Sept. 1, 1720.

The emigration of these three Tschudis was announced in a report from Liestal, read in Council June 12, 1751. Weinbert had received from his father 116 pounds before starting. Elsbeth died immediately upon her arrival in Pennsylvania (AA, Report of Apr. 10, 1767, cited above).

Gibenach

Johannes Ochsenmann.

He is one of nine applicants who were refused permission May 1, 1751 (RP 124, 251). A letter by the government to the Schultheiss, dated June 9 (CAM), shows that he did not acquiesce in this decision and skipped the country. The manumission dues (RP government dues), which had been collected from the property which he had left behind, were returned to his wife. No record of this in MP.

Seltisberg

Fridlin Salathe, the tailor, aged 57.

Verena von Arx, his wife, aged 43.

He now realized his desire to emigrate which he could not carry out in 1740. According to the report, read May 29, he had presumably betaken himself to Pennsylvania and left no property except an old bedstead and a trough.

AMT MUENCHENSTEIN

Benken

Heinrich Stöhlin.

A report, read in Council June 12 (RP 124, 300), announced that he had gone to Pennsylvania with the money he had realized from his 'Gant' and had left only a house worth 250 pounds. His wife received permission to sell the house and was not held responsible for the manumission dues and the ten percent tax which he had failed to pay.

AMT WALDENBURG

Bubendorf

Conrad Weiss, Hans Conrad.

Margreth Suter, his wife.

    1. Niclaus, their son, bapt. ....March 5, 1737

In view of the rare occurrence of the name Weiss in that period in KB, he must be identical with the emigrant Hans Conrad Weiss who was refused permission to go in 1738. It was supposed that he emigrated at the present time because he had bought the new property, which he had acquired after the sale of the old, at too high a price. The Obervogt succeeded in collecting the emigration dues. RL 1752: 'Item from Conrad Weiss of Bubendorf, who has gone there (*i.e.*, to the Newly-found-land), on account of

    Ten percent tax and manumission dues................lb. 119.17.2'

RP 124, 226, speaks of his wife and son, other places speak of his children probably erroneously.

Fridlin Rudin, exceptionally Ruodi, rope-maker.

Elisabeth Schäublin, his wife.

Their children:

1. Martin, bapt.................................Dec.   25, 1739
2. Catharina, bapt........................Febr.   2, 1744
3. Hieronymus, bapt........................Jan.   21, 1748
4. Friderich, bapt...........................July   6, 1749

A report, read in Council May 29 (RP 124, 281), announced that he had betaken himself out of the country the preceding week leaving only a pasture and some household goods. The Obervogt collected however the following dues. RL 1752: 'Item from Fridlin Rudin of that place [i.e., Bubendorf], who likewise left:

Ten percent tax on 750 pounds.....................75.—
Manumission for 6 persons........................60.—'   135.—

There is no direct evidence that he went to America, but there can be no doubt about it in view of the context.

1752

The emigrants of 1752, who can be given here, went likewise without permission and therefore are recorded in MP only in after years in connection with applications for release of their property.

Benken (Amt Münchenstein)

Adam Junt, KB Hans Adam, bapt. Dec. 4, 1729.

Matthias Junt, his brother.

Elisabeth Junt, their sister.

Madle Junt, KB Anna Magdalena, their other sister, bapt. Sept. 18, 1735, married in 1756 or before to Jacob Pfau of Benken, emigrant of 1749, who had lost his wife.

These four young people, repeatedly referred to as the 'Junt children,' left secretly in 1752 (RP 125, 285, July 12).[1] Four years later Adam and Matthias came back on a visit from Virginia and asked for their own and their sisters' manumission and release of the remainder of their property (RP 129, July 21, 1756). The Council resolved to grant their petition, but instructed the Obervogt to censure them for having left secretly and to watch out that they did not induce others to emigrate. The entry in MP reads as follows: 'Adam, Matthias, Elisabeth and Madle Junt of Bencken, lawfully begotten children of Hans Junt and Anna Flubacher . . ., who have gone to Virginia, have been released from serfdom July 21, 1756. The Landvogt on Mönchenstein has been ordered to levy the ten percent tax on their property and to carry it to account.

Pay: Pro manumissione............................40.—
Letters.. 6.—'   46.—

The tax in their case was very considerable, in fact the largest we have found before 1794. It amounted to lb. 1053.11 in addition to lb. 405.— accounted for in 1753, making a total of lb. 1458.15 on lb. 14,585.17.8 worth of property (RP 129, 286).

[1] Mat. Junt wrote an apologetic letter home to the Landvogt in behalf of the secret emigrants. See *American Historical Review*, op. cit., Vol. XXII, p. 121.

Bottmingen (Münchenstein)

Fridlin Seyler, KB Friederich, son of Theodor, deceased.
Anna Catharina Spaar, Sparr, his wife.
Their children:

1. Matthies, bapt................................Dec.   16, 1738
2. Hans Ulrich, bapt...........................July   7, 1743
3. Hans Jacob, bapt............................Apr.   17, 1746

Several entries in RP (125, 271, 299 and 342) show that the Council occupied itself repeatedly with his clandestine and fraudulent emigration. Nevertheless his three sons obtained in 1770 (RP 143, 80) the release of their property and their manumission. The entry in MP is as follows: 'Matthias, Ulrich and Hans Jacob Seyler, legitimate sons of Fridlin Sailer and Catharina Sparr of Botmingen, who have settled in Pennsylvania, have been manumitted together with their still living mother, who is also staying with them, by Our Gracious Lords March 28, 1770. Their property consisted of 572 pounds on which 'Herr Landvogt' on Münchenstein has collected the ten percent tax.

Pay: Manumission.................................40.—
      Letters....................................... 6.—' 46.—

At that time the sons were all married and located in Carlisle, Pa., the one being a tinner, the other a locksmith and the third a saddler. Their step-brother Leonhard Löw, whom we meet in 1763, seems to have emigrated with them in 1752 and gone back to live in the Canton of Basel once more until 1763.

1753

Bretzwil (Waldenburg)

Wernet Rieder, son of the smith, deceased.
According to a report from Waldenburg dated May 9, 1753 (AA), he went abroad with 200 pounds in money leaving behind wife and child who went to America in 1767. His married life had only lasted a few months as his wedding followed the baptism of the child. It took place four weeks later.

1754–1766

During this entire period we know only of a few emigrants. They are discussed among the emigrants of uncertain date with the exception of Johannes Leonhard Löw of whom there is a contemporary record in MP.

Holee (Amt Münchenstein)

'*Leonhard Löw*, (KB Johannes Leonhard), bapt. May 10, 1733, from the Holee, lawfully begotten son of Emanuel Löw . . . and Catharina Sparr (KB Anna Catharina), who intends to go to the American West Indies, has been released from serfdom March 30, Anno 1763 with
Anna Barbara Junt, his wife, and three children:

1. Elisabeth, [KB Anna Elisabeth], bapt..........Dec.   19, 1756
2. Anna Margreth, bapt........................Apr.   3, 1760
3. Anna Maria Löw, bapt.......................Dec.   13, 1761

Pays: Pro manumissione.......................... 20.—
      3 Letters.................................... 4.10
      Ten percent tax............................104.10' 189.—

His father, of whom his pastor says in KB that he was a fine man, died ten days after his birth. His mother married Fridlin Seyler, emigrant of 1752, and seems to have taken him along to America without being able to prevail on him to stay there. About the time of his second emigration he was talking however so much about America in his community that the Landvogt urged the Council to grant his request because he feared that his further presence might do more harm than good (AA, Letter of March 29, 1763).

1767

Apart from two families, whom we mention though their destination is uncertain, this year furnishes once more several parties of emigrants, amounting to thirty and some persons who went certainly to the Colonies. About half of these belonged again to the family of Johannes Tschudy of Frenkendorf, emigrant of 1749, reappearing in 1751 and now back again to collect inheritances for himself and his wife and on some other business. Although he was arrested and after an examination by the VII ordered to leave the Canton, he accomplished his ends through the intercession of the British ambassador in Bern, which is preserved in the original in AA. Also his old mother and his brother and sisters and their families finally obtained permission to emigrate, though with the stipulation of permanent exile. His cousin Niclaus and the other emigrants left without permission.

I. *Emigrants recorded in MP*

AMT LIESTAL

Füllinsdorf

'*Jacob Roppel* of Fühlinstorf,
Margreth Tschudy, [sister of Johannes], his wife, bapt. July 16, 1741, and his two
    children:
    1. Margreth, bapt........................   ?
    2. Jacob Roppel, (KB Hans Jacob), bapt.........Nov. 25, 1765
    who have gone to Pennsylvania, have been manumitted June 10, 1767.
    Possessed lb. 678.19 worth of property.
    Pays: For manumission...........................20.—
       Ten percent tax...........................67.16
       Letters.............................. 3.—' 93.16

Frenkendorf

'*Johannes Tschudy*, the carpenter of Frenkendorf, legitimate son of Johannes
    Tsch. . . . and Elisabeth Müller, bapt. Oct. 24, 1730, who is going to Pennsylvania, has been manumitted by Our Gracious Lords July 25, 1767.
    Possessed lb. 317.1.8 worth of property.
    Pays: For manumission...........................10.—
       Ten percent tax...........................31.4
       Letter................................ 1.10' 42.14

It is surprising that no charge was made for his wife nor for the wife of Martin Tschudy below.

Anna Tschudy, sister of Johannes, the emigrant of 1749.
Their children:

1. Johannes, bapt..............................Sept. 13, 1759
2. Elisabeth, bapt............................Oct. 11, 1761
3. Verena, bapt...............................Dec. 1, 1765

'*Martin Tschudy*, the cooper, legitimate son of Martin Tschudy of Frenckendorf and Elisabeth Tschudy, (brother of Johannes, the emigrant of 1749), bapt. July 31, 1735, who is going to Pennsylvania, has been manumitted by Our Gracious Lords July 25, 1767. Possessed lb. 252.8.10 worth of property.

Pays: For manumission............................10.—
      Ten percent tax.............................25.4
      Letter....................................... 1.10'   36.14

Anna Boni, his wife.
Their children:

1. Martin, bapt.............................Nov. 7, 1757
2. Johannes, bapt...........................March 4, 1759
3. Elisabeth, bapt..........................May 23, 1762
4. Anna, bapt...............................July 22, 1764

'*Elsbeth Tschudy*, Martin Tschudy's widow, legitimate daughter of Imbert Tschudy and Anna Reinger of Frenckendorf, aged 72, who has gone to Pennsylvania, has been manumitted by Our Gracious Lords July 25, 1767. Possessed lb. 520.7 worth of property.

Pays: For manumission............................10.—
      Ten percent tax.............................52.—
      Letter....................................... 1.10'   63.10

She had a great desire to see her grandchildren, children of her son Johannes, four in number, in Pennsylvania.

II. *Emigrants without Permission*

AMT FARNSBURG

Augst

Hans Regenass is mentioned RP 140, Sept. 16, among people who had left the country secretly, but there is only a possibility that he went to America. His wife was Elsbeth Hassler and three of the five children, whom he is supposed to have, are Anna Maria Ester, Salome and Johannes, bapt. 1758, 1760 and 1763.

Sissach

Niclaus Tschudi, illegitimate son of father of the same name and cousin of Johannes, the emigrant of 1749.

The examinations held with Niclaus Löliger and Jacob Würtz (AA), read in Council May 27 and June 10, reveal his ardent enthusiasm regarding the Newly-found-land and his efforts to persuade others to avail themselves of the great chance to make their fortunes. By night to his room-mate and by day to his companion on the road he talked America. He claimed that he himself, being well-read, had been promised by his cousin a place as a teacher, another, who was young and handsome, might make a good marriage. Perhaps some thirty would be coming along. Yet when his employer transmitted to him an order to appear at the Chancery, he ventured neither to go there nor to return to the factory, took a short leave of his father and crossed the boundary to be ready to join his cousin when he started back (RP 140, June 3, 1767).

AMT WALDENBURG

Arboldswil

Hans Rudi, called Trayer or Dräher Hans, is mentioned RP 140, 280 and 329, as a secret emigrant without indication of his destination. The names of his wife and four children cannot be given because his name is of too frequent occurrence.

Bretzwil

Johannes Häner, son of the joiner and later on schoolmaster Hans Häner and Elsbeth Plattner, also a joiner, bapt. Nov. 7, 1728.
Magdalena Gaissbuhler from Niederwil, Canton of Bern, his wife.
Their children:

1. Elsbeth, bapt.	March	5,	1752
2. Johannes, bapt.	May	6,	1753
3. Maria, bapt.	June	22,	1755
4. Magdalena, bapt.	Sept.	9,	1756
5. Hans Heinrich, bapt.	Jan.	7,	1759
6. Emanuel, bapt.	Oct.	4,	1761

His secret emigration is reported RP 140, 241, and that of his wife and children, whose number differs in the various reports, ibid., 280. Two letters relate their experiences in America. In the first, dated Aug. 23, 1769, printed by A. B. Faust, *Jahrb. d. D. Am. Ges. v. Ills.*, op. cit., No. 12, he tells that he was living at the house of Jacob Schaffner of Lausen (see Emigr. of uncertain date below) at Lebanon. His son Johannes was in service at Boston, his daughters in Philadelphia. He praised the new freedom he was enjoying. No restriction in the choice of a trade, no tithes, plenty of work, plenty to eat, not a day of 'Fronen' or guard duty yet. In a second letter, printed ibid., No. 13, he was thinking of moving farther West and showing a vivid conception of the immense possibilities of the country. In a Postscript he tells his friends with good-natured irony to while away the time in the guard-house with his letter and smoke a good pipe of tobacco with it.
Margreth Pfeiffer, divorced wife of Wernet Rieder, emigrant of 1753.
Hans Jacob Rieder, her son, bapt. Jan. 1, 1753.
July 11, 1767 (RP 140, 280), it is announced that she had betaken herself with her son to Neudorf in order to go to America. Their emigration is confirmed by an entry in GAV 21, Nov. 26, 1798, saying that her son had been absent about 40 (in reality 31) years.

Bubendorf

Martin Stohler.
RP 140, 277, July 11, 1767, he is reported to have left the country. Though it is not directly stated that he went to America, it is implied by the context.

Ziefen

Hans Tschopp, son of Hans.
Magdalena Stohler, his wife.
Their children:

1. Johannes, bapt.	July	12,	1761
2. Felix, bapt.	Dec.	4,	1763
3. Magdalena, bapt.	June	30,	1765

RP 140, 277, contains likewise the statement that he had found means to leave the country secretly with his wife and three children under age and that it was presumed that he had betaken himself to Johannes Tschudi, the emigrant of 1749. Fridlin Stohler, his father-in-law, had declared himself willing to meet his obligations.

1768

While other visitors from America used to come mainly on business purposes, and generally to collect inheritances for themselves or others and left their wives at home, there arrived in September, 1767, two men, father and son, with their wives, and asked to be received as subjects again. They were the son and grandson of Durs Thommen, the most prominent emigrant of 1736, Martin and Johannes, and had left the Canton, the former as a young man and the latter as a young child. They stayed all winter without coming to a decision on the purchase of some property and thereby increased the suspicion of the officials that they were not in earnest about their intentions. However this may be, when toward the close of April they were summoned to Basel to appear before the Land Commission, which had been authorized to keep them in Basel if they saw fit to do so, they preferred to disappear from the Canton again. Although often people from the neighboring villages had come to inquire of them about their relatives in America and according to a statement by Heinrich Strohman many in Ziefen should have liked to go if they could have disposed of their property, only three families and a bride who had been contemplating emigration anyway were so much influenced by them that they left the country.

I. *Emigrants recorded in MP*

Ziefen (Amt Waldenburg)

'*Michel Vogt*, [smith], and

Ursula Stohlerin, his wife, of Zyfen, who intend to go to Pennsylvania, have been manumitted by Our Gracious Lords July 9, 1768. Possessed 1038 pounds worth of property after deduction of 100 'Neuethaler' which were retained for their little four years old daughter and turned over to be administered by a 'Vogt.'

Pay for: Manumission.......................... 20.—
       Ten percent tax....................... 103.16
       2 Letters............................. 3.—' 126.16

   1. Catharina, their daughter, bapt..............Aug. 19, 1764

Michel Vogt had had a mind to emigrate in 1764, when his cousin Hans Christen of Arisdorf, emigrant of 1740, was back on a visit and had often regretted that he did not go then. Now, in 1767 and 1768, his desire had been revived by the good news he had received through the two Thommens concerning his relatives Durs and Michel Thommen of Arboldswil, the former an emigrant of 1749 (AA, Report of Apr. 6, 1768). He insisted however that the Thommens should not be blamed for it alone. He had also talked with a man from the Canton of Zürich (probably Joh. Hegetschwiler who had been in Basel in 1766). He can hardly have been long, if ever, in Pennsylvania, for Johannes Ernst says in a letter dated from South Carolina Oct. 12, 1773, printed by A. B. Faust, *The Amer. Hist. Rev.*, Vol. XXII, 122 sq., that his 'comrade' Michel Vogt had not made good his promise to pay for his passage and he had become a poor man. Two black Moors that he had bought had died. Also a letter by Jacob Balmer, dated Charleston, Aug. 6, 1788, speaks of him as being in Carolina, but by that time he had seven children and was evidently doing better (AA).

> '*Maria Tschopp*, lawful daughter of Hans Jacob Tschopp and Maria Schäublin of Zyfen, who has become engaged to be married to Johannes Ernst of Ihringen . . . Baaden Durlach, [the writer of the letter cited above] has been manumitted by Our Gracious Lords May 14, 1768. Has not yet any property of her own.
> Pays: Manum. lb. 10.—, Letter 1.10.'

This entry in MP does not record her as an emigrant for America, but we know from her husband's letter above that she followed him to Carolina to find an early grave, Sept. 29, 1769, and left him a son five months and a half old. Johannes Ernst had been helper in the smithy of Michel Vogt. He married again in Carolina in May, 1771.

II. *Emigrants without Permission*

Ziefen

Johannes Buser, Heinrich's son, baker, 34 years old.
Chrischona Strauman, sister of Heinrich Strohman or Strauman below, bapt. June 24, 1736.
Their children:

1. Anna, bapt. . . . . Apr.   18, 1758
2. Elisabeth, bapt. . . . . Sept.   6, 1761
3. Johannes, bapt. . . . . Dec.   25, 1763
4. Heinrich, bapt. . . . . Dec.   22, 1765

When called to appear before the Land Commission, he forswore any intention to emigrate (AA, Memorial of the Commission read in Council Apr. 27, 1768), yet only a little over two weeks later he had betaken himself out of the country (RP, Report from Waldenburg read in Council May 14).
Heinrich Strohman, Strauman, son of Heinrich Str. and Anna Krattiger, brother of Chrischona above, butcher, bapt. Oct. 16, 1740.
Elsbeth Plattner, his wife.
Their children:

1. Anna, bapt. . . . . June   24, 1766
2. Elsbeth, bapt. . . . . Nov.   29, 1769

In contrast with Joh. Buser, Heinrich Strohman frankly admitted before the Land Commission that he would be glad to emigrate if

he could sell his half of his house. Not the Thommens, who had
tried to discourage him, but the letter from his sister Elisabeth,
which he had received a year ago in February 1767 had awakened
in him the desire to go. He then laid the letter, printed by A. B.
Faust, *The Amer. Hist. Rev.*, XXII, 121 sq., before them and pointed
out that people over there were doing well. Seeing, however,
what obstacles and annoyances were placed in the way of Michel
Vogt in connection with his regular application, he did not wait to
make one and left the country two weeks later. The report from
Waldenburg, read in Council May 11, 1768, which announced this,
presumed that he would join the Thommens at Neudorf.

1769-1770

No case of emigration to the Colonies has come to our notice.

1771-1772

The emigration of these two years suddenly equals that of the
year 1749 and was undoubtedly caused by hard times. Apart
from other records, this is proved by the report of the Land Commission, read in Council May 6, 1772, which says that most of the
emigrants of the preceding years were poor and had sought other
countries and better sustenance on account of the high prices and
unemployment (Theurung und verdienstlose Zeiten). Thanks to
God, times were changing again and it might be confidently hoped
that the desire to emigrate would gradually abate. Also two
letters by the pastor Frantz Dietrich of Benken, dated Oct. 30 and
Nov. 3, 1771, attest the distress which was reigning among the
poor at the time and deserve to be given here in substance for the
vivid picture they present in the minds of the emigrants and the
thoughts and sentiments of a minister whose warmest sympathy
was going out to them: The sight of these people, the great number
of their children and their purpose, which was entirely unexpected
to him, touched his innermost heart as they must touch every one
who had not banished all sympathy from his breast. He had
therefore considered it his heartfelt duty to present to them all
reasons to the contrary which his scanty reading and experience
afforded him. The people heard only the voice of their present
distress and this made them blind to the greater misery to which
they exposed themselves. The inmates of Bedlam could not take
worse madness into their heads than these people who were dreaming
only of abundance and plenty.

The paltry means which they took with them would not carry

them over 50 leagues and it did not occur to any one to think of how he was to sustain himself and his family during the remaining 1600 or 1800 leagues of the way. And when this was represented to them, the answer was immediately ready. Heaven would not forsake them. Here in their native land the arm of God was too short for them, but on foreign soil he was to do miracles for them. Here they were not willing to trust Providence, but elsewhere they would rely on Him. Thus they were trifling with God. Besides these deluded people did not even really know where they were going and imagined the British possessions in North America, which extend over more than 30,000 square leagues, only as a large village where they hoped to meet all their distant relatives, if they had any, in one spot waiting to receive them with open arms.

A great majority of the emigrants of these two years applied for manumission, for the number of those who can be shown to have left without, including those given below with the 'Emigrants of Uncertain Date,' is comparatively small. The main reasons for this were that the authorities placed no obstacle in the way of emigration this time and that they had issued a new mandate according to which only those who went without permission should in the future be deprived of the right of inheriting, an ordinance which was made for the express purpose to induce the subjects not to leave secretly. As in case of the former large emigrations, also in these two years a good many who in their distress had applied for permission did not go or soon returned, among them also a well-to-do head of a family with his children. Some of them made special applications for readmission and, with one exception, all were allowed to stay.

While there are no particularly unfavorable reports concerning the voyage of the emigrants of 1771, that of 1772 became the most disastrous on record. They were 20 weeks out on their way to Philadelphia and, though the statement of Hans Plattner of Reigoldswil below, that almost all Swiss died, should not be taken too literally, it was reported that out of the 49 (?) emigrants from Benken, whom their pastor had tried so pathetically to dissuade from going, only 4 had reached Philadelphia alive.

1771

I. *Emigrants recorded in MP*

Apart from the names of the heads of the emigrating parties, MP this time records the members of each party both in words and in figures, *e.g.*, A with his wife and three children, and besides, as in 1749, the figures 1.1.3. We do not repeat this duplication and give only the figures. With the unmarried persons usually 'unmarried' is added. Otherwise only the tax and manumission dues paid or the release from them are recorded, with the exception of the manumissions from Amt Münchenstein and two from Waldenburg which are entered more fully. All other items are taken by us from other sources.

AMT FARNSBURG

Augst

* *Heini Blanck.* 1.1.2.
  Has paid nothing.
Barbara Schaub, his wife.
Their children: Margreth, bapt. Sept. 1769, and Barbara Nov. 1770. To these was added Anna, bapt. Jan. 16, 1773, which proves that they did not emigrate in 1771 or 1772.

Buus

Fridlin Schneider, son of the old messenger Jacob. 1.1.5.
  Has paid nothing.
Anna Meyer, his wife.
Their children, according to the letter of the Obervogt of July 1771 (AA), four instead of five in number.

    1. Hans Jacob, bapt.........................Sept.   1, 1765
    2. Anna, bapt..............................Sept.   11, 1768
    3. Elisabeth, bapt.........................Jan.   4, 1770
    4. Ursula, bapt............................Sept.   1, 1771
  The birth of Ursula makes it probable that they did not go till 1772.

Gelterkinden

Heinrich Buser, about 30 years of age. 1.1.3.
  Pays: Manumission.............................20.—
        Ten percent tax.........................71.—   91.—

Ursula Erni, his first wife, deceased.
    1. Friedrich, their son, bapt...............June   18, 1765
Barbara Schwab, his present wife.
Their children:
    1. Barbara, bapt............................Dec.   13, 1767
    2. Anna, bapt..............................July   21, 1771

Itingen

Hans Jacob Madöri, unmarried, bapt. Oct. 4, 1750. 1.—.—.
  Pays for the letter only.
  KB: 'Emigrates in Sept. 1771.'

Kilchberg

Hans Jacob Meyer, tailor's son. 1.1.3.
  Has paid nothing.
Elsbeth Würtz from Wenslingen, his wife.

Their children:
1. Child N. N., bapt.......................   ?
2. Barbara, bapt..............................Apr. 17, 1768
3. Hans Jacob, bapt.........................Jan. 29, 1771

Nusshof

Jacob Fiechter. 1.1.3.
    The letter has been paid for the children.
Anna Hug, his wife.
Their children:
1. Maria, bapt................................Sept. 10, 1761
2. Heinrich, bapt............................Apr.   1, 1764
3. Sebastian, bapt..........................Nov.   2, 1766

Oltingen

Tobias Gass, lace-maker. 1.1.3.
    Pay for the letter.
Ursula Thommen, his wife.
Their children:
1. Tobias, bapt..............................Aug. 10, 1762
2. Christian, bapt...........................Nov. 20, 1763
3. Barbara, bapt............................Aug. 16, 1767
    Had been obliged to sell his house and land on account of debts.
Fridrich Gysin, unmarried, 40 years of age. 1.—.—.
    Pays: Manumission...............................10.—
          Ten percent tax...........................18.—   28.—

Ormalingen

Jacob Bossart, Hans Jacob Bossert, linen-weaver. 1.1.2.
    Pays: Manumission............................... 20.—
          Ten percent tax..........................111.— 131.—

Anna Höli, his wife.
Their children:
1. Elisabeth, bapt..........................Sept.   5, 1767
2. Maria, bapt...............................May   21, 1771
    In 1791 he was located in Strassburg Township in Pa. (RP 165, 24).
* *Johannes Gerster*, day-labourer. 1.1.2.
    Has paid nothing.
Anna Catharina Hanhardt, his wife.
Their children: Daughter of 3 years, bapt. before coming to Orm., and Johannes,
    bapt. May 29, 1770, deceased in 1844. For lack of money they did not get
    beyond Basel (AA, Oct. 18, 1771). Another child Maria was bapt. June 7,
    1772, and died in 1776.

Rickenbach

Johannes Handschin, called Just Hans, son of Tailor Heini, herdsman. 1.1.5.
    Has paid nothing.
Margreth Mundweiler, his wife.
Their children:
1. Anna, bapt...............................Aug. 27, 1752
2. Heinrich, bapt...........................Apr. 28, 1754
3. Johannes, bapt..........................March 14, 1756
4. Isac, bapt...............................Oct.   8, 1758
5. Hans Jacob, bapt........................Dec.   2, 1764
    The deaths of Heinrich and Johannes, recorded in 1807 and 1811, make it
doubtful whether those two went to America.

Hans Jacob Mangold, about 46 years of age.   1.1.4.
    Pays: Manumission................................ 20.—
        Ten percent tax............................137.—   157.—

Anna Erni, his wife.
Their children:
    1. Maria, bapt................................Nov. 21, 1756
    2. Friedrich, bapt...........................Dec.   9, 1759
    3. Anna, bapt...............................Jan. 24, 1762
    4. Salome, bapt.............................Apr. 24, 1763
Martin Schäublin.   1.1.4.
    Pays: Manumission................................20.—
        Ten percent tax.............................78.—   98.—

Barbara Handschin, his wife.
Their children:
    1. Barbara, bapt............................Apr. 14, 1748
    2. Johannes, bapt...........................June 21, 1750
    3. Anna, bapt...............................Oct.   6, 1754
    4. Anna Maria, bapt.........................Nov. 27, 1757
Maria Schneider, Fridlin Erni's widow and mother-in-law of Hans Jacob Mangold
    above, about 60 years of age.   —.1.—.
    Has paid nothing.

Rothenfluh

* *Hans Ulrich Erni*, tailor, lace-maker.   1.1.4.
    Has paid nothing.
Maria Erni, Fridlin's daughter from Gelterkinden, his wife, bapt. Oct. 18, 1733.
Their children: Maria, bapt. March 1761, Elisabeth, Fridrich, Johannes and
    Hans Jacob, between Dec. 1764 and Sept. 17, 1769.—Another child, Hans
    Ulrich, was born Dec. 8, 1772, and died in 1774.   Furthermore KB says of
    Johannes: 'Went in 1804 with wife and children to America' and of Maria:
    '*Obiit* March 26, 1818.'   Plenty of evidence that this family did not emigrate
    in 1771 or 1772.
Joggi Rooss, widower, about 40 years of age.   1.—.4.
    Has paid nothing.
His wife, Barbara Schaub, had died in June 1770.
Their children:
    1. Elsbeth, bapt............................Febr. 27, 1757
    2. Ursula, bapt.............................Jan. 14, 1759
    3. Anna, bapt..............................Jan. 13, 1761
    4. Martin, bapt.............................Nov. 23, 1766
    The whole community urged him to go because he was a burden to them on
account of his poverty, but as the Council had forbidden him to go begging for
his travelling money, it is difficult to see how he got it.   Ursula died in 1816 in
Basel.

Rünenberg

Heini Bitterlin, day-labourer.   1.1.3.
    Has paid nothing.
Margreth Bürgi, his wife.
Their children:
    1. Heini, bapt..............................Apr. 20, 1756
    2. Elisabeth, bapt..........................Sept. 30, 1760
    3. Anna Barbara, bapt......................Oct. 27, 1765

Hans Grieder, day-labourer.   1.1.2.
> Has paid nothing.

Barbara Sigrist from Oberdorf, his wife.

Their children:

1. Jacob, bapt.......................................Aug.	30, 1767
2. Hans Joggi, bapt.........................Jan.	7, 1770

Heini Grieder, son of Weaver Heini, bapt. March 6, 1746.   1.1.1.

> Pays: Manumission...20.—
>
> Ten percent tax.............................31.—   51.—

Catharina Senn, his wife, aged 30.

> Anna Barbara, their child, bapt..................Oct.   13, 1770

Martin Grieder, day-labourer.   1.1.2.

> Pays: Manumission.................................. 20.—
>
> Ten percent tax...............................101.—   121.—

Anna Gysin, his wife.

Their children:

1. Jacob, bapt.................................June   22, 1766
2. Maria, bapt..............................May   8, 1770

Hans Jacob Ifert.   1.1.3.

> Pays: Manumission.................................20.—
>
> Ten percent tax..............................23.—   43.—

Maria Schafner, his wife.

Their children:

1. Anna, bapt................................Dec.   8, 1761
2. Ursula, bapt...............................Oct.   16, 1764
3. Verena, bapt...............................Jan.   7, 1770

Hans Jacob Sacker, Spurius, unmarried, bapt. March 18, 1753.   Later declared legitimate.

> Pays: Manumission.............................. 10.—
>
> Ten percent tax.............................. 8.—   18.—

Was without aid and without parents.   Wished to seek home and fortune abroad.

Hans Joggi Sigrist, day-labourer.   1.1.2.

> Has paid nothing.

Madle Tschudi, his wife.

Their children:

1. Heini, bapt................................Sept.   1, 1754
2. Hans Jacob, bapt.........................Febr.   13, 1763

Heinrich Sigrist, about 40 years of age.   1.1.3.

> Has paid nothing.

Anna Vögelin from Tecknau, his wife.

Their children:

1. Catharina, bapt............................Jan.   12, 1758
2. Heini, bapt...............................Febr.   15, 1761
3. Johannes, bapt............................March   6, 1768

Anna Tschudy, Jacob Sigrist's widow, and mother of Heinrich Sigrist, aged 60.   —.1.—.

> Pays: Manumission..................................10.—
>
> Ten percent tax.............................33.—   43.—

Sissach

Martin Hug, Niclaus' son, unmarried, bapt. May 27, 1753. 1.—.—.
    Pays: Manumission . . . . .10.—
    Ten percent tax . . . . .44.— 54.—

Jacob Schaub, mason, 1.1.3.
    Has paid nothing.
Salome Buser from Diegten, his wife.
Their children:

    1. Johannes, bapt. . . . . .Sept.   1, 1765
    2. Friderich, bapt. . . . . .Jan.   18, 1767
    3. Maria Salome, bapt. . . . . .Jan.   1, 1769

Jacob Schweitzer, alone. 1.—.—.
    Pays: Manumission . . . . .10.—
    Ten percent tax . . . . .12.— 22.—

According to one statement his youngest son Rudolf, about 10 years of age, emigrated with him and only his wife and the others remained at home.

Niclaus Schweitzer, Jacob's son, unmarried, bapt. May 2, 1751. 1.—.—.
    Has paid nothing.

Jacob Tschudy, son of Johannes below, bapt. March 12, 1747.
    Has paid nothing.
Margreth Völmi, his wife.

Johannes Tschudy, lace-maker. 1.1.7.
    Has paid nothing.
Maria Lang from Wintersingen, his wife.
Their children:

    1. Anna, bapt. . . . . .March 12, 1747
    2. Matthias, bapt. . . . . .May 25, 1749
    3. Anna Maria, bapt. . . . . .Aug. 24, 1751
    4. Child born away from Sissach . . . .   ?
    5. Elisabeth, bapt. . . . . .Jan. 13, 1760
    6. Verena, bapt. . . . . .July 18, 1762
    7. Margreth, bapt. . . . . .Jan. 12, 1766

Matthias may have come back from America or not have emigrated because his death is recorded in 1833.

Johannes Tschudy had emigrated once before in July, 1753, to Saxony and Prussia. The circumstances show the displeasure and suspicion with which the authorities viewed emigrants after the great exodus of 1749, particularly if they were lace-makers. When it became apparent that he wanted to go, he was arrested pending the decision of the Council. It was resolved that he must take all his five children with him, one of whom, Johannes, was only 4 months old and died at Berlin, for the entry of the note on his death with the first Johannes, who was baptized in 1746 and must have died before the birth of the second Johannes, is manifestly an error. Furthermore he and his family were forbidden to come back on pain of the 'Schellenwerk' and finally he must leave his lace-looms in the country. Though he possessed only 100 pounds worth of property, he had to pay 25.— and 4.10 Chancery dues for his release. Future developments show that he managed to come back after all.

AMT HOMBURG

Buckten

Hans Schmassmann, Hans Joggi's son, called Baderhans, ribbon-weaver. 1.1.3.
>Pays: Manumission....................................20.—
>Ten percent tax.............................. 9.—   29.—

Letter for two persons only.
Verena Müller, Hans' daughter, his wife, bapt. Oct. 13, 1737.
Their children:

>1. Hans Jacob, bapt.........................March 31, 1763
>2. Johannes, bapt............................Dec.   15, 1765
>3. Anna Maria, bapt..........................Nov. 15, 1767

Not long before his emigration his barn had been blown down by a gale and he had been granted 40 pounds by the government and 30 by the Deputaten (see Introduction) to rebuild it. These grants were withdrawn because he had not begun to rebuild it, and he could only keep the 30 which he had been allowed to collect himself.

Rümlingen

Martin Ifert, Yffert, Martin's son. 1.1.1.
>Pays: Manumission....................................20.—
>Ten percent tax.............................24.—   44.—

Maria Schafner from Wintersingen, his first wife, deceased.
>1. Matthias, their son, bapt. Jan. 29, 1764. Note 'in America '
Anna Furler, his present wife.

Thürnen

Hans Märklin, silk-reeller and day-labourer, bapt. March 2, 1732. 1.1.7.
>Pays: Manumission....................................20.—
>Ten percent tax.............................28.—   48.—

Barbara Tschopp from Bretzwil, his wife.

Their children:

>1. Anna, bapt...............................Jan.   6, 1756
>2. Hans Jacob, bapt.........................Jan.   8, 1758
>3. Heinrich, bapt...........................Apr.   8, 1762
>4. Anna Margreth, bapt......................Jan.   8, 1764
>5. Barbara, bapt............................Nov.   3, 1765
>6. Ester, bapt..............................Dec.   20, 1767
>7. Johannes, bapt...........................Oct.   10, 1769

Johannes with the note: 'Emigrates in September 1771'—Hans Märklin had a very hard time to sustain his large family. He was induced to emigrate by news of the success of a relative who had been as poor as he, but had paid for his freight in a few years and possessed now property sufficient for his sustenance in Pa.

Hans Jacob Mohler, lace-maker. 1.1.2.
    Pays nothing.
Elisabeth Gissler from Sissach, his wife.
Their children:
    1. Elisabeth, bapt...........................March 31, 1763
    2. Jacob, bapt..............................Oct.   30, 1764
Was urged to emigrate by his wife.

Amt Liestal

Seltisberg

Sebastian Spinnler, day-labourer. 1.1.4.
    No statement concerning payment of any dues. Has neither house nor land.
Barbara Hürst from Lupsingen, his wife.
Their children:
    1. Hans Jacob, bapt........................Febr.   4, 1759
    2. Anna Maria, bapt........................March 13, 1763
    3. Elsabeth, bapt. ....March 23, 1766
    4. Anna Barbara, bapt......................July   27, 1769
Desired to emigrate because nobody employed him since he stole a goat.

Amt Muenchenstein

Bottmingen

'*Heinrich Fiechter*, lawful son of Heinr. Fiechter and Elisabeth Gürtler of Bot-
    mingen, bapt. Hans Heinrich Oct. 24, 1745, who intends to go to Pennsyl-
    vania, has been manumitted by Our Gracious Lords May 1, 1771. Had lb.
    265.1.8 worth of property.
    Pays: Manumission................................10.—
           Ten percent tax.............................26.10
           Letter..................................... 1.10' 38.—

'*Leonhard Junt* of Botmingen with
Anna Glaser, his wife, and
    1. Leonhard, his son, bapt.....................Jan.   24, 1757
have received the permission to emigrate and manumission, May 1, 1771.
Have lb. 1423.— worth of property.
    Pay: Manumission............................. 20.—
          Ten percent tax...........................142.—
          3 Letters................................ 4.10' 166.10

'*Hans Jacob Rieger* and
Margreth Bay, his wife, of Botmingen,
    who intend to go to Pennsylvania with their children,
    1. Hans Rudolf, bapt.........................March 2, 1766
    2. Anna Barbara, bapt.......................Aug.   9, 1767
    3. Hans Jacob, bapt.........................Apr.   23, 1769
    4. Fridrich, bapt............................Sept. 23, 1770
have been manumitted by Our Gracious Lords (   ). Had lb. 491.—
worth of property.
    Pay: Manumission ,,............................20.—
          Ten percent tax........................ ,,,,..49.—
          6 Letters................................. 9.—' 78.—

Münchenstein

* [Anna] *Elisabeth Huggel*, lawful daughter of Heinrich Huggel and Magdalena,
Nebel . . . bapt. Aug. 21, 1725, has received manumission for emigration
May 1, 1771.   Had lb. 140.— worth of property.
    Pays: Manumission. . . . . .10.—
        Ten percent tax. . . . . .14.—' 24.—

She is put by mistake among the emigrants to America, for she made her
application from Holland (GAV 17, Apr. 30, 1771) and was received in the Home
for Old Women in Amsterdam about 1781 (GAV 20, Sept. 25, 1786).

AMT WALDENBURG

Bretzwil

Hans Häner, (first joiner, then schoolmaster), 74 years old, with Fridrich Häner,
his son, bapt. Dec. 9, 1736.   1.1.— instead of 1.—.1.
Have paid nothing.
Fridrich Häner was divorced on account of adultery and had only lately been
released from the 'Schellenwerk.'
Jacob Schneider, called 'im Winkel,' day-labourer, 50 years of age.   1.1.1.
    Pays: Manumission. . . . . 20.—
        Ten percent tax. . . . . .184.— 204.—

Anna Häner, daughter of Hans Häner above, his wife, bapt. Aug. 17, 1738.
    1. Barbara, their daughter, bapt. . . . . .June   4, 1769
Hans Häner and the other members of his family were induced to emigrate
by the letter of his son Johannes, secret emigrant of 1767, dated Lebanon, Pa.,
Aug. 23, 1769 (AA, printed by A. B. Faust, *Jahrb. d. D.-Am. Hist. Ges. v. Ill.*,
1918-19, No. 12).

Bubendorf

Heinrich Böhrlin, usually Börlin, Joggi's son, lace-maker, 40 years of age.   1.1.5.
    Pays: Manumission. . . . . .20.—
        Ten percent tax. . . . . .14.— 34.—

Barbara Bürgin, his wife, 38 years of age.
    1. Anna, bapt. . . . . .Febr.   3, 1754
    2. Barbara, bapt. . . . . .Apr.   3, 1760
    3. Elisabeth, bapt. . . . . .Febr. 21, 1762
    4. Heinrich, bapt. . . . . .June 24, 1764
    5. Maria, bapt. . . . . .July 10, 1770
Joggi Frey, day-labourer, 50 years of age.   1.1.—.
    Pays: Manumission. . . . . .20.—
        Ten percent tax. . . . . .60.— 80.—

Elsbeth Hägler, his wife, aged 30.
Heinrich Meyer, the older one, butcher, aged 48.   1.1.1.
    Pays: Manumission. . . . . .20.—
        Ten percent tax. . . . . .21.— 41.—

Anna Thommen, his wife, 50 years of age.
    1. Barbara, their daughter, bapt. . . . . .Jan.   9, 1752

Husband and wife died in March, 1796, in the neighborhood of Harrisburg, Pa., within an interval of only 2½ hours and were buried in the same grave. They left a handsome estate estimated at 600–700 pounds, probably Pennsylvania currency, which was administrated by their son-in-law and their grandson Nefzer. The heirs, presumably those two, had torn up their will (AA, Letter by Heinrich Buser, copy by Sebastian Sallade, dated Philadelphia, March 4, 1797).

Martin Thommen, day-labourer, 24 years of age. 1.1.—.
 Pays: Manumission.................................20.—
 Ten percent tax.............................71.— 91.—

Anna Nefzer, his wife, daughter of Jacob N. and Barbara Börlin of Bubendorf, bapt. Apr. 23, 1752.

Höllstein

' *Fridlin Foltz* . . ., lawful son of Hans Georg Foltz, and Verena Baderin, bapt. Jan. 13, 1750, May 22, 1771.

 Had lb. 170.7 worth of property.
 Pays: Manumission.................................10.—
 Ten percent tax.............................17.—' 27.—

 His father was one of the secret emigrants of 1750 above.
Anna Gysin, unmarried, bapt. Apr. 21, 1748. —.1.—.
 Pays: Manumission.................................10.— 10.—

 Had a great longing for Pennsylvania.
Martin Suter, teamster, bapt. May 16, 1734. 1.1.3.
 Pays: Manumission.................................20.—
 Ten percent tax.............................24.— 44.—

Elsbeth Bossart, his wife.
Their children:
  1. Martin, bapt...............................Apr. 15, 1764
  2. Elsbeth, bapt..............................May 7, 1766
  3. Verena, bapt...............................Jan. 19, 1768

Lampenberg

' *Jacob (Fluebacher)*, bapt. Aug. 17, 1755,
Anna (Fluebacher), bapt. Apr. 2, 1741, and
Magdalena Fluebacher, bapt. Sept. 9, 1753, lawful children of Heinrich Fl. . . and Ursula Buess . . ., have received manumission for emigration May 29, 1771. Jacob Fluebacher, 16 years old, takes one half of his property: lb. 124.15, his sisters have lb. 209.—.
 Pay: Manumission.................................30.—
 Ten percent tax.............................32.—' 62.—

Magdalena died soon in America. Jacob and Anna lived at Lancaster, Pa., whence they applied for an inheritance through Niclaus Kohl in 1789 (GAV 20, Aug. 31, 1789).

Oberdorf

Jacob Saner, Hans Jacob, day-labourer, aged 35.   1.1.2.
 Has paid nothing.
Maria Waldner, his wife, aged 36.
    1. Daughter.....................................6 years old
    2. Daughter.....................................4 years old
* *Durs Thommen*, KB marriage register Ursus, aged 29.   1.1.1.
 Has paid nothing.
Verena Seyler from Langenbruck, his wife, bapt. July 19, 1750.
    Their ship met with an accident ten leagues below Basel, which frightened the
wife so much that they returned (AA, Report of July 7, 1771).   The next year
they left secretly.

Titterten

Johannes Schweitzer, 29 years of age.   1.1.—.
 Has paid nothing.
N. N., his wife.
    Lately released from the 'Schellenwerk.'   Scum of dissolute and bold fellows.

Ziefen

Heinrich Buser, Heinrich's son.   1.1.3.
 Has paid nothing.
Verena Waldner, his wife.
Their children:
    1. Heinrich, bapt............................Dec.   30, 1759
    2. Johannes, bapt...........................Oct.   18, 1761
    3. Hans Jacob, bapt.........................Oct.   20, 1765
Anna Gysin, unmarried, bapt. Apr. 21, 1748.   —.1.—.
    Pays: Manumission..................................10.—   10.
                                               _____
Hans Joggi Schäublin, 31 years of age.   1.1.1.
    Pays: Manumission..................................20.—
                Ten percent tax............................12.—   32.—
                                               _____
Anna Maria Graber, his wife.
    1. Hans Jacob, their son, bapt.................Aug.   18, 1765
    Had been sent to the 'Schellenwerk' on account of several thefts.
Sebastian *Strohmann*, correct name is *Eusebius* Strauman or Strohman, bapt.
        Pentecost 1743.
    Has paid nothing.
Barbara Gysi, his wife, aged 28.
    1. Heinrich, their son, bapt...................Sept.   6, 1770
    Eusebius is a brother of Heinrich and Chrischona, emigrants of 1768.

II. *Emigrants without Permission*

AMT WALDENBURG

Langenbruck-Oberdorf

Johannes Müller, joiner of Langenbruck, former 'Hintersäss,' tenant or sub-
        tenant at Oberdorf.
Barbara Saner, his wife.
Their children:
    1. Esther, bapt. March 16, 1760, at Langenbruck.
    2 and 3. Probably baptized at Oberdorf where KB is missing.

According to report from Waldenburg, dated June 24, 1771, he left secretly with his wife and three children, presumably in order to go with other emigrants to Pennsylvania. This assumption was correct, for two years later he made an attempt to collect an inheritance through an agent from Lancaster, Pa. (RP 146, May 15, 1773).

Ziefen

Sebastian Schurch, son of Heinrich Sch., the innkeeper, bapt. Apr. 7, 1737.
Barbara Strauman, daughter of Heinrich Strohman or Strauman and Anna
    Krattiger, sister of Chrischona and Heinrich, emigrants of 1768, and Eusebius
    above, bapt. June 26, 1730.
Their children:

    1. Hans Jacob, bapt..........................Jan. 11, 1757
    2. Heinrich, bapt...........................May 21, 1758

There is some confusion in the records regarding the name of his wife which is sometimes given as Strauman and sometimes as Krattiger. *E.g.*, her marriage, which took place at Frenkendorf, where at that time young couples from all over the Canton were betaking themselves to get married, is recorded in KB of Frenkendorf with the name Strauman July 19, 1756, and in KB of Bubendorf, which includes Ziefen, with the name Krattiger and the inaccurate date of July 13, 1756. After the baptism of the first child the name Strauman prevails also in KB of Bubendorf.—Sebastian Schürch must probably be recognized in Ba—yan Shork—one or two letters between a and y are blurred or crossed out—in Jacob Balmer's letter of Aug. 6, 1788. He received all the merchandise which his brother Heinrich and Heinrich Tschudy brought with them in 1772.

1772

I. *Emigrants recorded in MP*

MP records the names of the heads of the emigrating parties followed by the number of the members of which each party consists in figures, the first denoting men, the second women and the third children. A few times also the father's name is added and usually 'unmarried' in case of the single persons. Besides, the tax and manumission dues paid, or the release from their payment, are recorded as in 1771. The amount of the property on which the tax was levied and all other items have been taken from other sources.

AMT FARNSBURG

Diegten

Hans Jacob Hägler, (of Mittel-Diegten). 1.1.—.
    Pays: Manumission.............................20.—
         Ten percent tax (on lb. 257.—)..............25.— 45.—

Anna Buser, his wife.
Martin Häuser, (Hüser). 1.1.3.
    Pays: Manumission.............................20.—
         Ten percent tax (on lb. 105.—)..............10.— 30.—

Barbara Häfelfinger, his wife.

Their children:
1. Hans Jacob, bapt...........................Aug.   4, 1767
2. Johannes, bapt............................Jan.   8, 1769
3. Anna Barbara, bapt.......................March 3, 1771

Hans Jacob Mohler, (son of Märtel, deceased). 1.1.5.
Has paid nothing because he has only lb. 15.1, which his creditors have left him.
Barbara Oberer from Sissach, deceased, his first wife.
Their children:
1. Verena, bapt..............................Sept. 9, 1756
2. Anna, bapt...............................Nov. 26, 1758
3. Esther, bapt.............................June 12, 1768
Verena Schäublin, not Gysin, his present wife to whom he was only married Jan. 22, 1771.
Children by the first marriage of this present wife with Hans Jacob Oberer of Tenniken:
1. Hans Jacob, KB Jacob, bapt.................March 4, 1753
2. Martin Oberer, bapt.......................   ?
In GAV 21, Aug. 1, 1803, it is asserted that the ship on which Verena Schäublin made her voyage was lost. It is more probable that she was one of the many who died aboard.

Jacob Mohler, Martin's son, KB Märtel's. 1.1.6.
Has paid nothing, having no property.
Elisabeth Mundweiler, his wife, from Tenniken.
Their children:
1. Hans Jacob, bapt.........................Apr. 16, 1758
2. Maria, bapt..............................Aug. 10, 1760
3. Martin, bapt............................Dec. 12, 1762
4. Anna, bapt..............................Aug. 11, 1765
5. Elisabeth, bapt.........................Dec. 18, 1768
6. Jacob, bapt.............................March 29, 1772

Martin Mohler, son of Märtel Marti, deceased. 1.1.2.
Has paid nothing, possessing only 37 pounds by the favour of the 'Deputaten Amt' which has released him from the payment of this sum.
Elsbeth Sigrist, Sigerist, his wife.
Their children:
1. Anna, bapt..............................Aug. 30, 1761
2. Anna Maria, bapt........................Nov.   5, 1769

Itingen

Heinrich Grimm, Christen's son, bapt. Jan. 22, 1736.
Pays: Manumission.................................20.—
Ten percent tax (on lb. 518.—)................51.— 71.—

Barbara Mohler from Ziefen, his wife.
Barbara, their daughter, bapt.................March 4, 1764
A note added to the baptismal date says: 'Emigrates to America in April 1772.'

Nusshof

Heinrich Imhof. 1.1.1.
Has paid nothing, possessing nothing.
Elisabeth Hägler, daughter of Hans Jacob Hägler above, his wife.
Hans, their son.....................................3 years old

Oltingen

Daniel Blatner, (Blattner, Platner). 1.1.3.
    Pays: Manumission................................20.—
    Ten percent tax (on lb. 220.—)................22.—   42.—

Veronica Thommen Froneck, his wife.
Their children:
    1. Anna, bapt...............................Febr. 17, 1765
    2. Johannes, bapt..........................May   4, 1766
    3. Barbara, bapt. ....Apr.   1, 1770

Ormalingen

Martin Riggenbacher, Martin's son, unmarried, bapt. Apr. 10, 1753. 1.—.—.
    Pays: Manumission................................10.—
    Ten percent tax [on lb. 800]....................80.—   90.—

His pastor says of him, March 18: 'Martin R., . . ., who desires to emigrate
and seems to have taken it into his head that he will find more comfortable days
in America than here, cannot be dissuaded from emigrating and has no other
reason than that he has been told that it was quite a good country. He wished
therefore to see whether it was true and, if he did not find it so, come back. His
father did not wish to hinder him.'—He was allowed to take one fourth of his
property with him and later on he first sent and then called for the rest. His
success induced Häring, the wealthy Untervogt of Arisdorf, who had married his
stepmother, to follow him with his whole family in 1794.
Josef Keller, son of Hans K. and Anna Gass, bapt. May 20, 1736. 1.1.4.
    Pays: Manumission................................20.—
    Ten percent tax (on lb. 244.—)................24.—   44.—

Margreth Hassler from Ormalingen, his first wife, died in childbirth.
Her children:
    1. Barbara, bapt............................Aug. 25, 1763
    2. Heinrich, bapt...........................Apr.   5, 1767
Margreth Suter, Anna Greth, his present wife.
Her children:
    1. Johannes, bapt..........................June   2, 1769
    2. Hans Jacob, bapt........................Nov. 10, 1771
    Josef K. had been denounced as a prodigal by his pastor some years ago.

Sissach

Bernhard Hersperger. 1.1.6.
    Pays: Manumission................................ 20.—
    Ten percent tax (on lb. 2024.—)..............202.—   222.—

Elisabeth Nebiger, his wife.
Their children:
    1. Heinrich, bapt.............................   ?
    2. Barbara, bapt............................Apr.   8, 1762
    3. Dorothea, bapt..........................July   3, 1763
    4. Elisabeth, bapt..........................June 23, 1766
    5. Maria, bapt.............................Dec.   6, 1767
    6. Eva, bapt...............................Jan. 22, 1771

Heinrich Hug, Niclaus' son, bapt. March 29, 1750. I.—.—.
    Pays: Manumission................................. 10.—
        Ten percent tax [on lb. 1100.—]...............110.— 120.—

Married his fellow emigrant Magdalena Frey, not recorded in AA nor MP, of Titterten upon arrival in Pennsylvania Oct. 18, 1772 (RP 146, 165). In 1786 both were living and obtained through Niclaus Kohl of Lancaster, Pa., the release of some property and of an inheritance (RP 159, 101).

Martin Schäublin. 1.1.3.
    Pays: Manumission.................................20.—
        Ten percent tax [on lb. 352.—].................35.— 55.—

Susanna Vogt, his wife.
Their children:
    1. Hans Jacob, bapt.........................Nov. 23, 1755
    2. Martin, bapt.............................May 20, 1759
    3. Elisabeth, bapt.........................Sept. 25, 1763

Hans Jacob Senn, former 'Kilchmeyer.' 1.1.2.
    Pays: Manumission................................ 20.—
        Ten percent tax [on lb. 1945.—]...............194.— 214.—

Barbara Seiler from Langenbruck, his wife.
Their children:
    1. Heinrich, bapt...........................July 8, 1766
    2. Johannes, bapt..........................Sept. 10, 1769
    The latter with the note: 'Emigrates in April 1772' in KB.

Sebastian Würtz, baker and day-labourer. 1.1.5.
    Pays: Manumission.................................20.—
        Ten percent tax [on lb. 184.—].................15.— 35.—

Anna Maria Haas, his wife.
Their children:
    1. Hans Jacob, bapt.........................June 10, 1755
    2. Barbara, bapt...........................Sept. 3, 1758
    3. Niclaus, bapt...........................Febr. 10, 1761
    4. Catharina, bapt.........................July 31, 1763
    5. Sebastian, bapt.........................May 6, 1770
    In KB the last with the note: 'Emigrates in April 1772.'

Tenniken

Martin Handschin. 1.1.1.
    Pays: Manumission.................................20.—
        Ten percent tax [on lb. 187.—].................18.— 38.—

Verena Dürrenberger, his wife.
    1. Heinrich, their son, 13 years old.

Wintersingen

* *Fridlin Imhof.* 1.—.3.
    Pays: Manumission................................ 10.—
        Ten percent tax [on lb. 2758.—]...............275.— 285.—

His children: Johannes, Hans Jacob, Elisabeth.
    Changed his mind and was readmitted as a subject May 23, 1772 (RP 145). Two months later his dues had not yet been refunded to him.

AMT HOMBURG

Buckten

Hans Jacob Buser, carpenter. 1.1.3.
    Pays: Manumission.................................20.—
        Ten percent tax [on lb. 234.—].................23.—   43.—

Barbara Grieder, his wife.
Their children:
    1. Elisabeth, bapt............................Febr. 25, 1759
    2. Eva, bapt................................Jan.   11, 1761
    3. Hans Jacob, bapt.........................July   1, 1766
Complained of the high price of victuals.

Häfelfingen

[*Hans*] *Jacob Pfeiffer*, lace-maker. 1.1.4.
    Pays: Manumission.................................20.—
        Ten percent tax [on lb. 177.—].................15.—   35.—

Anna Margreth Schafner from Anwil, his third wife.
Their children:
    1. Anna, bapt..............................Aug. 23, 1763
    2. Catharina, bapt.........................June 11, 1765
    3. Matthias, bapt..........................Dec. 14, 1766
    4. Salome, bapt............................May   24, 1768
Was induced to emigrate by a letter which he received a year ago from a younger brother who emigrated to South Carolina in 1737 and acquired considerable property by marrying the daughter of his employer. Five married children and one unmarried daughter of 22 remain in the Canton. In 1789 he was in Mecklenburg Co., N. C., and renounced his claim to the 200 pounds which he had inherited from his children Agnes and Jacob in favor of his other children.

Läufelfingen

Johannes Strub, small grocer. 1.1.1.
    Pays: Manumission.................................20.—
        Ten percent tax [on lb. 115.—].................11.—   31.—

Anna Catharina Minier, KB Munier, his wife.
    1. Hans Jacob, their child, bapt...............Nov.   3, 1771
Was induced to emigrate by a letter from a cousin of his wife in Maryland received some weeks ago in which the latter offered his assistance to relatives who felt like undertaking the journey. In 1806 a letter from Mecklenburg Co. [N. C.?] announced his death (GAV 21, 376).

AMT LIESTAL

Frenkendorf

Jacob Schaub, shoemaker. 1.1.4.
    Pays: Manumission.................................20.—
        Ten percent tax [on lb. 244.—].................24.—   44.—

Margreth Rudin, his wife.

Their children:

1. Anna, bapt.................................July   21, 1765
2. Margreth, bapt............................Oct.   4, 1767
3. Elisabeth, bapt...........................Jan.   30, 1770
4. Johannes, bapt............................May   5, 1771

In 1787 there arrived a certificate of the death of Margreth Rudi and five children of hers (GAV 20, Apr. 30, 1787).

Maria Vogt, Anna Maria, unmarried, '*arbeitselig*,' toilsome.   I.—.—.

Has paid neither manum. nor tax, possessing only 36 pounds.   A brother of hers in America, perhaps Jacob Vogt, emigrant of 1749, a man of means without children, had asked her several times to come over.

Füllinsdorf

Anna Maria Giger. —.I.I.

Pays: Manumission................................10.—
Ten percent tax [on lb. 94.—]................ 9.— [19.—]'

'These 19 pounds have been returned to the Gigerin by command of My Gracious Superiors and are therefore not carried to account.'

Hans Jacob Giger, her son, illegitimate, bapt......Jan. 22, 1765

Martin Roppel, bapt. May 26, 1737. I.I.2.

Pays: Manumission................................20.—
Ten percent tax [on lb. 376.—]..............37.—   57.—

Barbara Schäublin or Schaub from Wittinsburg, his wife, bapt. May 7, 1741. Their children:

1. Johannes, bapt............................July   22, 1764
2. Elsbeth, bapt.............................Sept.   11, 1768

In 1804 they sent a letter of attorney from South Carolina which however was not regarded as valid in Basel (GAV 22, May 4, 1813).

Lausen

Benedict Balmer. I.I.2.

Pays: Manumission................................20.—
Ten percent tax [on lb. 233.—]..............23.—   43.—

Barbara Wagner, his wife. Their children:

1. Barbara, bapt............................Jan.   8, 1769
2. Hans Jacob, bapt.........................Nov.   13, 1770

According to the letter of his brother Hans (?) Jacob Balmer below he seems to have been in New York in 1788.

* *Hans Balmer*, called Boppenhans, linen-weaver. I.I.3.

Paid for the letter only, having only 42 pounds in his possession.

Elsbeth Grieder, his third wife. His children: Johannes, bapt. Dec. 1768, deceased in 1850, Samuel, bapt. July 1771, and a daughter, 11 years old. His wife got ill on the journey and died on way back. Lausen declined unanimously to receive him again, and he was banished from the country (RP 14.5 May 9).

Hans Jacob Balmer, brother of Benedict above. I.I.I.

Pays: Manumission................................20.—
Ten percent tax [on lb. 382.—]..............35.—   55.—

Verena Hofer, his wife.

1. Barbara, their child.

Wrote a letter from Charleston, S. C., dated Aug. 6, 1788, in which he reported himself, a son and a daughter in good health so that his wife seems to have died (AA).

Hans Jacob Schweitzer, about 36 years of age.   1.1.—.
 Has paid neither manum. nor tax, possessing only lb. 21.9.2.
Barbara Hottinger, his wife.
 He was born illegitimate and a wretched cripple besides. His village would feel relieved if he left.

Peter Schweitzer, unmarried, bapt. Feb. 4, 1748.   1.—.—.
 Has paid neither manum. nor tax, possessing nothing.
 He said he desired only a passport, but sailed for America and died on that disastrous voyage (Letter by Jacob Balmer above of Aug. 6, 1788).

* *Fridrich Tschudy.*   1.1.—.
 Has paid neither manum. nor tax, his creditors losing with him.
Engela Rudin, his wife.
 Returned to Lausen after a few months and was allowed to stay there again (RP 145, Sept. 16, 1772).

Hans and *Martin* Tschudy, unmarried.   2.—.—.
 Pay: Manumission................................20.—   20.—

Released from payment of tax, possessing only lb. 54.11 each. If Hans is identical with John Shutte in Jacob Balmer's letter cited above, he died in Philadelphia, probably soon after the voyage.

Hans Jacob Tschudy, cooper.   1.1.5.
 Pays: Manumission................................20.—
       Ten percent tax [on lb. 272.—]..................27.—   47.—

Barbara Balmer, his wife.
Their children:
  1. Hans Jacob, bapt.............................June   3, 1759
  2. Elisabeth, bapt.............................Oct.   5, 1760
  3. Johannes, bapt.............................July   17, 1763
  4. Heinrich, bapt.............................Oct.   12, 1766
  5. Barbara, bapt.............................Sept.   6, 1770
Heinrich Tschudy.   1.—.—.
 Pays: Manumission................................10.—
       Ten percent tax [on lb. 200.—].................20.—   30.—

His wife with her child was not willing to accompany him, but did not object to his going. He died soon after his arrival in Philadelphia (Letter by Jacob Balmer cited above and GAV 23, Dec. 6, 1814). According to the latter source he died in the hospital.

Liestal

Wilhelm Pfaff, miller's helper.   1.1.4.
 Has paid neither manum. nor tax, possessing nothing.
Anna Strohman, not Krattiger, his wife.
Their children:
  1. Ursula, bapt...............................Dec.   4, 1760
  2. Margreth, bapt...........................June   4, 1765
  3. Anna, bapt.................................Oct.   6, 1768
  4. Elisabeth, bapt...........................Dec.   2, 1770
 The parish registers show with reference to the names of Strohman and Krattiger in this case the same confusion above with Sebastian Schürch of Ziefen,

emigrant of 1771. Only this time Anna Strohman, probably a sister of Barbara and bapt. March 9, 1732, is called Krattiger on the marriage register of Frenkendorf and Strohman, or Strohman with Krattiger marked out, in Liestal.

Wilhelm Zeller, son of Hans Jacob Z. and Elisabeth Baumgartner, cooper, bapt. May 26, 1740. I.I.I.

> Pays: Manumission.................................20.—
>   Tax at five per 100 [on lb. 136.—].............. 6.10   26.10

Dorothe Strub, his wife.

>   1. Johann Jacob, their son, bapt................March 4, 1770

A letter of his which he wrote on his voyage from London was the last that was heard of him (GAV 22, Apr. 13, 1813).

AMT MUENCHENSTEIN

Benken

Burkart Hayer, correctly here and below *Heyer*, weaver.   I.I.2.

> Manumission...20.—
> Ten percent tax [on lb. 330]........................30.—   50.—

Elsbeth Schwab from Bennwil, his wife.
Their children:

>   1. Anna Maria, bapt..........................Oct.   26, 1749
>   2. Hans Jacob, bapt..........................Jan.   10, 1764

Hans Ulrich Hayer, lace-maker.   I.I.5.

> Pays: Manumission.................................20.—
>   Ten percent tax [on lb. 760.—]................70.—   90.—

Anna Dietrich, his wife.
Their children:

>   1. Hans Ulrich, bapt........................Aug.   30, 1750
>   2. Hans Lucas, bapt.........................Aug.   20, 1754
>   3. Anna Maria, bapt.........................Jan.   14, 1759
>   4. Johann Friederich, bapt...................March 27, 1763
>   5. Anna Barbara, bapt........................June   9, 1771

Hans Plattner, one of the emigrants from Reigoldswil below, reports the death of this whole family, evidently on the voyage (AA, joint letter of 1774). In agreement with this it is said in RP, Febr. 23, 1828, that they had never been heard from.

Ulrich Hayer, tailor, Hans Ulrich, 48 years.   I.I.2.

> Pays: Manumission.................................20.—
>   Ten percent tax [on lb. 175.—].................15.—   35.—

Verena Wiedmer from Seen, Canton of Zürich, his wife.
Their children:

>   1. Hans Caspar, bapt........................Dec.   9, 1755
>   2. Maria Elisabeth, bapt....................Oct.   16, 1757

Some of his relatives in America in good circumstances.

Hans Ulrich Leu, Löw, weaver.   I.I.6.
Pays only for the letter. Has 40 pounds worth of property.
Chrischona Heyer, his wife.

Their children:
1. Elisabeth, bapt.........................Febr.   9, 1755
2. Chrischona, bapt.......................June   8, 1756
3. Anna Margreth, bapt....................Nov. 20, 1757
4. Maria Magdalena, bapt..................July   8, 1760
5. Catharina, bapt........................Apr. 27, 1762
6. Ursula, bapt...........................May 22, 1763

Heinrich Schäublin, carpenter, 46 years.   1.1.7.
Has not paid.   Has nothing.
Anna Barbara Deck, his wife.
Their children:
1. Hans Heinrich, bapt....................March 25, 1755
2. Ursula, bapt...........................Febr.   2, 1758
3. Anna Barbara, bapt.....................Nov. 17, 1761
4. Anna Margreth, bapt....................Jan. 22, 1764
5. Anna Maria, bapt.......................June 30, 1766
6. Johannes, bapt.........................May 12, 1768
7. Jacob, bapt............................Febr. 11, 1770

Small earnings in summer, none in winter.
Jacob Sparr, Hans Jacob, Spahr, day-labourer, 43 years old.   1.1.5.
Pays: Manumission..................................20.—
Ten percent tax [on lb. 190.—].................15.—   35.—

Elsbeth Tschudy, his wife.
Their children:
1. Hans Jacob, bapt.........................   ?
2. Elisabeth, bapt.........................March 23, 1756
3. Catharina, bapt........................Nov.   5, 1758
4. Anna Barbara, bapt.....................Dec. 14, 1760
5. Johannes, bapt.........................Dec. 29, 1765

Said he had two brothers and a sister in America, probably Heinrich, emigrant
of 1749, Anna Cathrina of 1752 and ?
Jacob Stöcklin, Hans Jacob, unmarried, bapt. March 25, 1753.   1.—.—.
Pays:..10.—
Ten percent tax [on lb. 170.—]......................15.—   25.—

Had been put for half a year in the 'Zuchthaus,' house of correction, for thefts
and had lately committed a new theft there.
Jacob Weisskopf, Hans Jacob, linen-weaver, aged 41.   1.1.4.
Pays: Manumission..................................20.—
Ten percent tax [on lb. 110.—].................10.—   30.—

Ursula Deck, his wife.
Their children:
1. Magdalena, bapt........................Aug. 22, 1756
2. Anna Margreth, bapt....................Oct. 23, 1757
3. Hans Jacob, bapt.......................Jan.   1, 1764
4. Johannes, bapt.........................June   9, 1765

Bottmingen

Jacob Dietrich, formerly coachman, aged 57.   1.—.1.
Pays: Manumission ,,....................................10.—
Ten percent tax [on lb. 516 of his own property and
on that of his son]........................60.—   70.—

1. Hans Heinrich, his son, bapt.................June 24, 1753

His dull-witted wife was wavering as to whether she should go or not and finally stayed.

Hans Ulrich Schaub, tailor, bapt. June 3, 1725.   I.I.—.

Pays: Manumission...................................20.—

Ten percent tax [on lb. 447.—]................44.—   64.—

Muttenz

Heinrich Berger, weaver. I.I.3.

Pays toward manumission...............................16,13.4,

being released from the payment of lb. 17.16.8 of his dues.

Anna Margreth Jausslin, his wife.

Their children:

1. Hans Heinrich, bapt........................Sept.   5, 1756
2. Sabina, bapt...............................Apr.   22, 1759
3. Anna Margreth, bapt.......................June   21, 1767

Both husband and wife were guilty of having sold yarn which had been entrusted to them.   May 25, 1771, it was announced that they had fled, but in June the wife was sentenced to the Schellenwerk until she would be pardoned and in July the husband received a year in the hardest class of the Schellenwerk (RP July 13, 1771).   Wanted to emigrate because nobody would give him any work after his release.

AMT RIEHEN

Jacob Felgenhauer, son of Hans F. and Maria Peter, unmarried, bapt. Nov. 5, 1752. I.—.—.

Has nothing.

AMT WALDENBURG

Lampenberg

Adam Fluebacher, Heinrich's son, unmarried.   I.—.2 instead of I.—.—, because the recorder mistook his parents for his children and put them down as emigrants.

Pays: Manumission................................10.—

Ten percent tax [on lb. 273.—]................27.—   37.—

Spoke of having an uncle and a brother and two sisters in America, but, as indicated under 1771 above, one of the sisters had died, and he himself died on the voyage.   The captain found in his chest money amounting to £ 140.14 Pennsylvania currency, which was a great deal more than he had declared in Basel (RP 145, Apr. 15, 1772, and Nord-Amerika B1).

Lauwil

* *Hans Joggi Dürrenberger*, mason. I.I.I.

Has paid nothing.   Has less than nothing.   Prefers begging to working.

Elsbeth Müller, his wife.

Hans Heinrich, their son, bapt......................Jan. 1769.

Was unable to start for lack of means and readmitted Sept. 16, 1772.

Hans Jacob, another son of theirs, is recorded Febr. 7, 1774.

Hans Frey. I.I.2.

Has paid nothing.   Has nothing.

Salome Schweitzer, his wife.

Their children:

1. Hans Jacob, bapt..........................March 29, 1767
2. Elsbeth, bapt.............................May   14, 1769

Heini Schweitzer, the younger one.
    Has paid nothing. Has less than nothing. Prefers begging to working.
Eva Nägelin from Reigoldswil, his wife.
       1. Heinrich, their són, bapt..................Sept. 29, 1771
Heini Wytstich, Weitstich, son Heinrich W. and Maria Dürrenberger, bapt.
    March 5, 1738. I.I.4.
    Has paid nothing. Has nothing.
Magdalena Schweitzer, his wife.
Their children:
       1. Maria, bapt...............................Febr. 21, 1762
       2. Magdalena, bapt..........................Oct. 30, 1763
       3. Elsbeth, bapt............................Nov. 2, 1766
       4. Heinrich, bapt...........................Dec. 31, 1769

Lupsingen

Emanuel Ammann, Fridlin's son, bapt. Nov. 10, 1742. I.I.2.
    Has paid nothing. [Had only 11 pounds.]
Catharina Häring, his wife.
Their children:
       1. Fridrich, bapt...........................May 4, 1766
       2. Anna, bapt. ?........................... 2 years old
Jacob Dürrenberger. I.I.4.
    Has paid nothing. [Has nothing.]
Verena Bürgin, his wife.
Their children:
       1. Verena, bapt............................Febr. 12, 1758
       2. Jacob, bapt.............................Nov. 30, 1760
       3. Barbara, bapt...........................March 20, 1763
       4. Maria, bapt.............................Jan. 31, 1768

Niederdorf

Hans Thommen, the young, called 'Wydenhans.' I. I. 2.
    Pays: Manumission...................................20.—
    Ten percent tax [on lb. 132.—]................10.— 30.—

Elsbeth Heckendorn, Heggendorn, his wife.
Their children:
       1. Johannes, bapt..........................Nov. 29, 1761
       2. Fridrich, bapt..........................Jan. 1, 1764
Josef Tschudy. I.I.2.
    Has paid nothing. [Has nothing.]
Catharina Bürgi, his wife.
Their children:
       1. Fridrich, bapt..........................June 21, 1761
       2. Jacob, bapt.............................March 24, 1765

Oberdorf

Wernhard Meyer, lace-maker. I.I.5.
    Pays: Manumission...................................20.—
    Ten percent tax [on lb. 131.—]................10.— 30.—

Anna Buser, his wife, married to him Jan. 6, 1756.
Their children:
       1. Jacob. 2. Wernhard. 3. Maria. 4. Anna. 5. Elsbeth.

Jacob Roht, lace-maker.   1.1.5.
    Pays: Manumission.................................20.—   20.—

    Released from other payments because he had only lb. 65.17.
Barbara Grimm, his wife.
Their children:
        1. Barbara.   2. Maria.   3. Elsbeth.   4. Jacob.   5. Ursula.
Heinrich Spyser, Speiser, lace-maker.   1.1.2.
    Pays: Manumission.................................20.—
          Ten percent tax [on lb. 325.—]..................30.—   50.—

Catharina Suter, his wife.
Their children: 1. Hans.   2. Martin.

Reigoldswil

Hans Baltasar Bürgi, orphan, unmarried.   1.—.—.
    Pays: Manumission.................................10.—
          Ten percent tax [on lb. 90.—]..................9.—   19.—

Hans Frey, son of the 'Meyer' Jacob F., lace-maker, bapt. Dec. 6, 1739.   1.1.3.
    Has paid nothing.   Has no property.
Anna Catharina Dettweiler, KB Anna Catharina, his wife, bapt. Sept. 1738.
Their children:
        1. Hans Jacob, bapt...........................Febr. 10, 1765
        2. Urs, KB Durs, bapt.........................Nov.   6, 1768
        3. Niclaus, bapt..............................Febr.   3, 1771
    Parents and children died on the voyage (AA, Hans Plattner in joint letter,
A. B. Faust, *Jahrb. etc.*, 1918–19, No. 13).
Romay Frey, lace-maker, bapt. Jan. 27, 1737.   1.1.3.
    Has paid nothing.   Has nothing.
Verena Nägelin, his wife, bapt. Sept. 1742.
Their children:
        1. Verena, bapt...............................March 4, 1764
        2. Romay, bapt...............................Jan.   26, 1766
        3. Hans Georg or Jacob, bapt.................Sept. 24, 1769
    The parents and the youngest son died on the voyage.   The other two children
reached Philadelphia (AA, Hans Plattner in letter just cited).
Hans Plattner, here spelt Blatner, Daniel's son.   1.1.4.
    Pays: Manumission.................................20.—
          Ten percent tax [on lb. 696.—]..................69.—   89.—

Barbara Frey, his wife.
Their children:
        1. Romay, bapt...............................July   18, 1756
        2. Daniel, bapt..............................Apr.   29, 1759
        3. Barbara, bapt.............................May   2, 1762
        4. Hans, bapt................................Febr.   9, 1772
    In the letter repeatedly cited Hans Plattner writes: 'We have had a hard
voyage.   The Swiss have almost all died on the sea.   For 20 weeks the ship was
our dwelling-house.   On the 15th day of August 1772 my wife Bara(!) Frey has
died and our little child two weeks before.'   July 13, 1773, he married Anna Liesa
Eschbach, a good housekeeper, with 600 Basel pounds worth of property, while he
had only one Louis d'or left.   At the time when he was writing, in 1774, he had
already a daughter by her and had moved 100 miles farther West.

Anna Roht, Jacob Bürgi's widow, 65 years of age. —.1.—.
    Pays: Manumission..................................10.—
        Ten percent tax [on lb. 75.—].................. 5.— [15.—]

Titterten

Ulrich Frey, lace-maker. 1.1.4.
    Pays: Manumission..................................20.—
        Ten percent tax [on lb. 93.—].................. 5.— 25.—

Elisabeth Tschopp, his wife.
Their children:
    1. Martin. 2. Ludwig. 3. Elisabeth. 4. Catharina.
Heinrich Schweitzer, shoemaker. 1.1.5.
    Pays: Manumission..................................20.—
        Ten percent tax [on lb. 31.—].................. 3.— 23.—

For letter nothing. Dues reduced because there would have been only 45 pounds left to him.
Anna Baumann, his wife.
Their children:
    1. Esther. 2. Anna. 3. Maria. 4. Catharina. 5. Heinrich.

Ziefen

Joggi Rudy, single. 1.—.—.
    Pays: Manumission..................................10.—
        Ten percent tax [on lb. 300.—].................30.— 40.—

Heinrich Schürch, son of the innkeeper Heinrich Sch. and brother of Sebastian, emigrant of 1771, lace-maker, bapt. Oct. 19, 1732. 1.1.2.
    Pays: Manumission..................................20.—
        Ten percent tax [on lb. 598.—].................59.— 79.—

Elisabeth Rudy, his wife, married to him Dec. 4, 1752.
Their children:
    1. Elisabeth, bapt............................Nov. 18, 1753
    2. Heinrich, bapt............................ ?
Heinrich Schürch must be identical with Heinri Schurk in Jacob Balmer's letter of 1788 cited above, who had invested in merchandise together with Heinrich Tschudy, but died on the voyage or immediately afterward. Since the goods went to his brother it is not probable that his wife and children had survived.

II. *Emigrants not recorded in MP*

Sissach (Amt Farnsburg)

Anna Würtz from Rümlingen, stepdaughter of Bernhard Hersperger above
    Had permission and paid for the letter through her stepfather (AA, 'Ausfertigung der Frenlassungen'), but was not recorded in MP. In 1784 (GAV 19, 452) Martin Riggenbacher collected lb. 646.10 for her.

Oberdorf (Amt Waldenburg)

Durs Thommen (see above, 1771).
    Report from Waldenburg, dated Apr. 25, 1772, announced that he had left the country by night with wife and child presumably in order to start on the journey with other emigrants anew.

Titterten

Magdalena Frey.
Married her fellow emigrant Heinrich Hug upon arrival in Philadelphia.

1773

After the disastrous voyage of the emigrants of 1772 there seem to have been made only four applications this year, two of which were granted and two refused. Those granted are recorded in MP.

Lausen (Amt Liestal)

'*Eva Buess*, widow of Heinrich Schaub of Lausen with two children:

    1. Anna [Schaub], bapt.........................Apr.   30, 1752
    2. Johannes [Schaub], bapt.....................March 7, 1756
the Schaubs, who emigrate to Pennsylvania, has been released Apr. 29, 1779. Possess together 632 pounds worth of property.
Pays: Manumission...............................20.—
     Ten percent tax.............................63.—
     Letters.................................. 4.10' 87.10

Ziefen (Amt Waldenburg)

'*Christen Müller*, the smith, [wheelwright], of Zyfen, has been manumitted and exiled by Our Gracious Lords May 15, 1773. Has 100 pounds worth of property on which according to their decision the dues have been paid by his wife and children(!).
Pays: Manumission...............................10.—
     Ten percent tax.............................10.—
     Letter.................................. 1.10' 21.10

He was induced to emigrate by the good reports from his brother Martin, who, as he said, had emigrated five years ago and was back on a clandestine visit to the Canton at that time (see Emigrants of Uncertain Date). Since his wife and only son were not willing to accompany him, he was entitled to take only one third of his property, *i.e.*, 150 pounds, with him, but, when the Council reduced this sum to 100, he flew into such a rage that his village became afraid of him and he was transported to the prison in Basel. Here he gave such confused answers that the Council found it advisable to have his state of mind examined by a minister and the city physician who found that he was all right and had simply been drunk. Because he had been in such a rage, he was however escorted to the frontier by two 'Hartschierer,' policemen, and told that he would be put in the 'Schellenwerk' if he dared to come back (AA, Report of Oct. 31, 1772; RP 146, 144, 150, 154 and 157).

1774–1783

During this period which largely coincides with the Revolutionary War and the beginning of which may also still have stood under the influence of the disastrous voyage of 1772, we know only of one emigrant who settled in New Jersey about 1779 and who will be found among those of uncertain date.

1784

Three parties, two of which are recorded in MP, from *Ormalingen* (Amt Farnsburg). The baptismal dates are supplied from KB.

'1784, Apr. 1.

Heinrich [*Buess*, KB Hans Heinrich], bapt. Apr. 12, 1761, and

Hans Jakob(!) *Buess*, [KB Joh. Jacob], bapt. Dec. 22, 1765, of Ormelingen, sons of Heinrich Buess and Elisabeth Handschin of that place. Their father is still living; their mother has died. Their property consists of 390 pounds. They want to go to America.

Ten percent tax....................................39.—
Manumission.....................................20.—
2 Letters.. 3.— 62.—'

They had an uncle in America who had made some money (RP 157, 137).
'1784, May 5.

Hans Jakob(!) *Schaub*, 'Hartschierer,' policeman, of Ormelingen, and
Anna Maria Zeller, his wife, and 3 sons:

    1. Hans Jakob, bapt. ....July 19, 1772
    2. Fridrich, bapt.............................June 16, 1778
    3. Johannes, bapt...........................Febr. 6, 1780
the oldest of whom is 12, the youngest 4 years old, are going to West India. Their property consists of lb. 223.2.10.

Manumission....................................20.—
Ten percent tax.................................20.—
2 Letters.. 3.— 43.—'

West India includes the U. S. KB adds 'in America' to the date of each of the three boys. These and the following people had desired to emigrate 12 years ago, and the women were as anxious or still more anxious to go than the men (RP 157, 182).

Heinrich Freyburger.
Susanna Wälchli from Brittnau, Canton of Bern.
Their children:

    1. Johannes, bapt............................Jan. 20, 1765
    2. Margretha, bapt..........................Aug. 6, 1769
    3. Hans Heinrich, bapt......................May 31, 1772
    4. Hans Jacob, bapt.........................Apr. 23, 1775
    5. Jacob, bapt..............................Apr. 16, 1778
    6. Anna Barbara, bapt.......................March 12, 1780

KB adds 'in America' to the dates of Hans Heinrich, Hans Jacob and Jacob.
Induced to emigrate by his poverty and a description of America in the calendar of 1782 and an American newspaper, which Martin Riggenbacher had left behind as waste paper. Pastor states that there is a larger and larger increase of poor people in the parish and that they might do very well without this family and some others (AA, Report of May 2, 1784).

1785–1787

Only one family in 1786 recorded in MP.

Rothenfluh

'1786, February 25.
Christen Bertschin and
Anna Maria, née Baumann, [Buman from the Canton of Bern], with 2 little sons:
    1. Christian, 11 years old, bapt. June 30, 1775, and
    2. Johannes, 8 years old, bapt. March 1, 1778, of Rotenfluh.
  Their property amounted to lb. 346.18.3. By decision of the Council the
ten percent tax and manumission dues were presented to their daughter Ursula
who remains in the country.
    Manumission.............................20.—.—
    Ten percent tax..........................34.13. 9
    Letters................................. 3.—.—   Pays 57.13.9'

KB adds 'in America' to the dates of both of the children.

1788

Five families, all recorded in MP, the first four together under
the title: 'Emigrants to America in consequence of decision of
March 8, 1788.'

Böckten (Amt Farnsburg)

Jacob Weibel, son of Martin, deceased, of Böckten, with
[Ursula Würtz from Gelterkinden] his wife and five children:
    1. [Hans] Jacob, bapt........................Febr. 13, 1774
    2. Martin, bapt.............................Apr.   4, 1776
    3. Catharina, bapt..........................Nov.   1, 1778
    4. Barbara, bapt............................Jan. 28, 1781
    5. Fried, bapt............................... ?
  Has lb. 1317.8 worth of property.
    Manumission............................ 20.—
    Ten percent tax..........................129.14
    Letters................................. 3.—   Pays: 152.14'

'*Johannes Weibel*, [butcher's son], of Böggten, with
[Ursula Freyburger from Ormalingen] his wife, and three children:
    1. Hans Jacob, bapt.........................Dec. 17, 1780
    2. Johannes, bapt...........................Dec. 22, 1782
    3. Heinrich, bapt........................... ?
  According to certificate from the 'Landschreiberey' he has lb. 135.19.2 worth
of property.
    Manumission............................20.—
    Ten percent tax..........................11.10
    Letters................................. 3.—   Pays: 34.10'

Itingen

'*Elssbeth Gunzenhauser* of Itingen, unmarried, has lb. 338.13.11 worth of property.
    Manumission............................10.—
    Ten percent tax..........................32.16.8
    Letter................................. 1.10   Pays: 44.6.8'

Sissach

'*Jacob Senn* of Sissach with
[Elisabeth Frey, his] wife, and three children:

    1. Anna Maria, bapt.............................Sept. 6, 1778
    2. Jacob, bapt.................................Sept. 21, 1779
    3. Heinrich, bapt.............................   ?
Has lb. 74.4.9 worth of property.
Manumission..................................20.—
Ten percent tax................................ 7.8
Letters....................................... 3.—   Pays 30.8'

Lausen (Amt Liestal)

'1788, June 4.
* *Martin Buser* of Lausen and
Anna Keller, his wife, and Sara, their child, who wish to betake themselves to
    America, were manumitted and released from payment of manumission dues.
    Have no property whatever.'
Spent about 5 years in America 20 years ago and had a desire to emigrate again.
Parish glad to get rid of these people and to give them some travelling money
(RP 161, 171).
    Back after 10 weeks. Got only as far as Holland. Allowed to stay again on
good behaviour (RP 161, 246).

1789–1791

While we know of no emigrants in 1789 or 1791, there are quite
a number in 1790. They are all recorded in MP with the heading:
'Emigrants to America, April 13, 1790.' Only one, who did not
emigrate, follows in June by himself. All but one came from
Amt Farnsburg.

1790

Maisprach

'*Johannes Gruber*, the locksmith of Maysprach.
    Has lb. 105.10 worth of property. Released from payment of manumission,
tax and letter dues.'
'*Johannes Gruber*, son of the preceding, the turner, . . . with Anna Keller, his
    wife, and five children:
    1. Johannes, bapt.............................Jan.   1, 1781
    2. Anna, bapt................................Nov.   3, 1783
    3. Anna Maria, bapt..........................Febr. 6, 1785
    4. Hanns Georg, bapt.........................Febr. 20, 1787
    5. Ursula, bapt..............................Jan. 17, 1790
Has lb. 545.1.1 worth of property.
Manumission..................................20.—
Letters....................................... 3.—
Ten percent tax...............................52.4   75.4'

Ormalingen

'*Hanns Handschin* of Ormelingen, unmarried, bapt. Dec. 3, 1765.
    Has 58 pounds worth of property. Released from payment of manumission
and tax.'

Rothenfluh

'*Gedeon Gass*, [called Höfer Gedi], former sergeant, of Rothenflue, with Anna Maria Frach, his wife, and four children:

    1. Barbara, bapt..............................June 14, 1775
    2. Martin, bapt..............................Dec. 14, 1776
    3. Anna Maria, bapt.........................Jan. 16, 1780
    4. Friedrich, bapt...........................March 4(?) 1784

[KB with each child: 'To America.']
Has lb. 1688.3.4 worth of property.

    Manumission............................... 20.—
    Letters...................................   3.—
    Ten percent tax...........................166.10   Pays 189.10'

'*Heini Gass* of Rothen Flue, Martin's son, unmarried.
    Has lb. 158.7.8 worth of property
    Manumission...............................10.—
    Letter.................................... 1.10
    Ten percent tax...........................14.12   Pays 26.2'

'*Hanns Carle*, [Johannes Karly], weaver, of Rothenflue, with [Catharina] Elisabeth Bussinger, [of Ormalingen], his wife, and five children:

    1. Anna Barbara, bapt........................Aug. 17, 1780
    2. Verena, bapt.............................Nov. 24, 1781
    3. Johannes, bapt...........................March 30, 1785
    4. Hanns Jacob, bapt........................July 21, 1787
    5. Anna Catharina, bapt.....................Febr. 20, 1790

Has no property. Released from payment of manumission, tax and letter dues.'

Notes in KB with the date of Hans Jacob: 'To America,' with that of Anna Catharina: 'Have gone to America.'

Had misappropriated state yarn and is willing to replace it with the money which he has left from the sale of his house, but is condemned to wear the 'Lasterstecken' for 4 weeks and appear with it in the church (RP 163, 78, March 10, 1790).

'*Hans Jacob Keller*, of Rothenflue, and
Barbara Schmassmann, [from Buckten], his wife, bapt. Nov. 16, 1727.
    Has 1275 pounds worth of property.
    Manumission............................... 20.—
    Letters...................................   3.—
    Ten percent tax...........................125.4   Pays: 148.4'

'*Hans Jacob Keller*, son of the preceding, bapt. July 29, 1759, and
Verena Freyburger of Ormalingen, his wife, with two children:
    1. Johannes, bapt...........................Febr. 10, 1785
    2. Barbara, bapt............................May   9, 1789

Has no property. Released from payment of manumission and letter dues.'

KB: 'To America' with both children and 'Emigrated' added to the record of the marriage of the parents.

'*Johannes Keller*, brother of the last named, bapt. Jan. 10, 1762, and
Ursula Rudi, daughter of Heinrich R. and Verena Kommler, from Oltingen, his wife, bapt. Febr. 3, 1765.

Has also no property. Released from payment of manumission and letter dues.'

KB: 'Emigrated' with the record of their marriage, May 12, 1789.

Wintersingen

Elisabeth Imhoof of Wintersingen, [herdswoman at Maisprach], 40 years of age.
and

      1. Matthis, her illegitimate boy, bapt............July   23, 1775
Has no property whatever. Released from payment of all dues.' The father
of the boy was from the Canton of Bern and had run off.
' *Fridlin Müri* of Wintersingen and
Anna Graf, his wife, bapt. Dec. 16, 1747, and three children:

      1. Heinrich, bapt.............................Dec.   22, 1771
      2. Maria, bapt................................June   5, 1774
      3. Hanns Jacob, bapt.........................Oct.   19, 1783
Has lb. 476.17.2 worth of property.
Manumission.......................................20.—
Letters.. 3.—
Ten percent tax....................................45.6   68.6'

Entries in KB report the deaths of Hans Jacob and the mother. Hans Jacob:
'Died in Nov. 1790 in America.' Anna Graf: 'Died in America of dropsy in
March 1791.' Her husband Fridli Müri wrote it. He had to serve his master in
Maryland near Baltimore 3 years in serfdom.

Lausen (Amt Liestal)

'*Hans Jacob Schweitzer* of Lausen and
Barbara Tschopp, his wife, with three children:

      1. Judith, bapt................................Oct.   22, 1775
      2. Hanns Jacob, bapt.........................Oct.   3, 1779
      3. Hanns Heinrich, bapt.....................March 3, 1789
Has lb. 103.11.8 worth of property. Released from payment of manumission
and tax.'
The first two children are by his first wife, Margreth Gass, deceased Aug. 11,
1783. Another daughter, Margreth, bapt. Nov. 20, 1768, did not emigrate.

Sissach (Amt Farnsburg)

'1790, June 11, the manumission letter was granted to
* *Jacob Mangold* of Sissach, who wishes to go to America with Anna Ehrsam of
    Rümlingen, his wife, and his two children Ester and Hanns Jacob. . . .
    Has . . . not the least property.—Released from payment of man. and
    clerical dues.'
He begged travelling money, got the first time as far as Konstanz and the
second as far as Ulm. Was exiled and not received again (RP 163, 221 and 164,
170 sq.).

1792–1794

There are again some emigrants in 1792 and 1794.

1792

Although serfdom and payment of manumission had been
abolished in December 1790, most emigrants of this year are still
found in MP because the ten percent tax was recorded there for a
while longer. They are all from Amt Farnsburg.

I. *Emigrants recorded in MP*
Ormalingen

'1792, Apr. 17.

Johannes Buser of Ormelingen, who with the consent of the government is going
to America, paid the ten percent tax on the property he withdraws, lb.
961.19.8 . . . [with several deductions].

Ten percent tax...81.4

On the same day the above paid the tax on the property of his stepson
Hanns Jacob Völlmi of Ormelingen, bapt. Sept. 25, 1774, which amounted to
lb. 79.4.6.

Ten percent tax...7.18'

KB has the note 'in America' both with the date of this stepson and that of
his brother of the same name who was baptized Febr. 23, 1772, and buried less
than three months afterward.

Joh. Buser claimed to have a son and a daughter in America in good circumstances (RP 165, March 14). If they bear his name and are from Ormalingen,
they emigrated secretly.

Rothenfluh

'1792, Apr. 24. By the emigrant
Fried Bütscher, [usually Bitscher, tailor], of Rothenflue, the tax on lb. 403.—.10
was paid.

[Ten percent tax]..40.6'

Barbara Buser from Diepflingen, his wife.

Their children:

    1. Friedrich, bapt............................Dec.   5, 1773
    2. Barbara, bapt............................Jan.   28, 1777
    3. Abraham, bapt............................Aug. 15, 1780

KB: 'To America' with the date of Friedrich.

He is allowed to take 60 pounds to his mother who according to his statement
emigrated in 1759 (CAM, 1792, March 7, and GAV 18, July 31, 1775).

'1792, Apr. 26. By
Martin Gass, [tailor], bapt. July 16, 1767, the tax on lb. 143.13.8 [was paid].

[Ten percent tax]..14.6'

'1792, Apr. 21. The emigrant
Hans Gerster of Rothenflue, [unmarried], paid the tax on lb. 842.2.8.

Ten percent tax...84.4'

'On the same day also
Hans Jacob Gerster of Rothenflue, [brother of the preceding, unmarried], bapt.
May 22, 1768, paid the tax on lb. 523.19.

Ten percent tax...52.8'

'1792, Apr. 26. By [*Barbara Würtz*], widow of
Hans Jacob Keller, the joiner, of Rothenfluh, the tax on lb. 834.5.8 was paid.

[Ten percent tax]..83.8'

'Ditto. By
Elisabeth Keller, [daughter of the preceding], bapt. Dec. 6, 1767, on lb. 340.17.18.

[Ten percent tax]..34.0'

The last two are mother and sister of Johannes Keller who emigrated to
America in or after 1771. His visit home was the principal cause of their emigration. See also 'Emigrants of Uncertain Date' below.

II. *Emigrants not recorded in MP*
Buus

Hans Jacob Kaufmann, son of sergeant Jacob K. . . and Ursula Bürgin, unmarried, bapt. Jan. 2, 1770.

Ten percent tax on 175 pounds..............................17.10

He left without permission.   His father, who was summoned to Basel, said that the Landvogt and pastor had told his son that he must ask for permission, but that the other emigrants of Rothenfluh had told him that he had not to pay anything.   The father had not only to pay the tax on the money which the young man had received from his brother, his grandfather and himself, but was also fined 10 pounds for the benefit of the 'Armenseckel,' poor relief, of his village (RP June 2, 1792).

Ormalingen

Jacob Bussinger, lace-maker.
Anna Meyer, his wife.
    1. Mathias, their son, bapt....................March 14, 1790

Rothenfluh

Johann Rudolf Bitscher, son of Fried above, bapt. June 28, 1767.
    Released from payment of tax (RP 165, March 14).
Anna Maria Roth from Basel, his wife.   KB adds to their marriage date June 3,
    1788: 'Emigrated' and to his baptismal date: 'To America.'
    1. Daughter, 1½ years old, not recorded in KB.

Wenslingen

Hans Jacob Börlin, tailor (RP 165, Febr. 22).
Elisabeth Gysin, his wife.
    1. Hans Jacob, bapt..........................March 31, 1782
    2. Eva, bapt....,.........................May   17, 1783
    3. Elisabeth, bapt...........................March 5, 1786
Another tailor by the same name was married to Barbara Buser and had a son Heinrich in 1796.   A third Hans Jacob Börlin, whose profession is not stated, was married to Salome Pegetz and had a son Hans Jacob in 1796.   It seems therefore that it must have been the first who emigrated.   One of his children probably died before emigration.

1794

The emigrants of this year are not found in MP.   They came again all from Amt Farnsburg.

Arisdorf

Heinrich Häring, rarely Heering, former Untervogt.
Barbara Weber, from Ormalingen, his present wife.
His children by Margreth Thommen from Wenslingen, his first wife, deceased:
    1. Hans Jacob, bapt..........................Oct.   23, 1763
        Barbara Rickenbacher, daughter of Barbara Weber above, his wife, to
          whom he was married on the same day, June 16, 1789, when his
        father married her mother.
        Their children:
          1. Elisabetha, bapt...................Jan.   17, 1790
          2. Margaretha, bapt...................Sept.   4, 1791
    2. Heinrich, other son of the Untervogt, bapt. July 20, 1766, unmarried.
    Ten percent tax on lb. 34,814.—..............3481.8 (RP 167, 108).
Since it was discovered that the old Häring had failed to declare lb. 5162.11.10 worth of his property and his explanations and those of his elder son were considered unsatisfactory, he was fined 50 pounds and had to pay 100 Neuthaler for the benefit of the 'Armenseckel' of his parish (RP 167, 114, March 15).   The

total of his tax, exclusive of fines, nearly reached the total of taxes and manumission dues paid by all emigrants together in the principal year of emigration
1749 and surpassed it after the deductions made for Chancery dues.

In spite of their wealth the Härings were induced to emigrate by the good news
which their son Heinrich had brought home from a three years' trip on which he
had also visited his new stepbrother Martin Riggenbacher, stepson of Barbara
Weber, emigrant of 1772. Since he had found the latter in excellent condition,
they all hoped to live a happier and more enjoyable life with their friends and
acquaintances over there than in their own country (RP 167, 26).

Diegten

Sebastian Hägler, miller's helper, unmarried.
    Possessed only his savings of 50 florins (RP 167, March 22).

Gelterkinden

Johannes Fricker, son of the messenger, unmarried, 25 years old.
    Possessed 230 pounds. Could not sustain himself without touching his capital
(RP 167, March 8).

Rothenfluh

Friedrich Gass im Hof (RP 167, Jan. 8).
Anna Wirz, his wife.
Their children:

1. Fridrich, bapt.	Jan.	30,	1774
2. Anna, bapt.	Nov.	8,	1777
3. Martin, bapt.	June	3,	1783
4. Anna Maria, bapt.	Oct.	25,	1784

    KB: 'To America' with each of these children.
In spite of hard work his property had been decreasing for some years.

Tecknau

Hans Jacob Schäublin, the father (RP 167, March 8).
Hans Jacob Schäublin, the son.
Anna Gysin, his wife.
Their children:

1. Jacob, bapt.	Apr.	29,	1781
2. Johann Rudolf, bapt.	Oct.	2,	1785
3. Maria, bapt.	Sept.	10,	1789
4. Hans Jacob, bapt.	June	3,	1792
5 and 6.		?	

    The dates of the two other children with which they are credited in RP are
not found in KB.

Zeglingen

Hans Jacob Thommen, probably son of Hans Jacob Th. and Anna Riggenbacher,
    bapt. Jan. 7, 1772.
    While Heinrich Häring, the younger, above, may have taken his trip to America
at least partly with a view to settle there, Hans Jacob Thommen undertook it
for the outspoken purpose of seeing friends over there and then come back home
again. He therefore asked only for a passport and permission to take so much of
his 5000 pounds worth of property as he would need for his trip. Whereupon the
Council resolved to let him take 200–300 Neuthaler and to remember the ten
percent tax on the whole, *i.e.*, to collect it, in case he should not come back
(RP 167, March 12).

VIII

Emigrants of Uncertain Date

While the year of emigration of all who have been treated so far is established beyond doubt by the existence of contemporary records, the year of those given in this section is only known from later sources of varying definiteness and reliability. If, *e.g.*, it is said in RL 1752 that somebody emigrated two years ago, this may mean 1749 or 1750 according as the statement was penned in 1751 or between New Year and Oculi 1752, or if a statement is made so long a time after emigration as is often the case in GAV, the principal source of this section, the very length of the interval leaves often room for doubt and sometimes it can be proved that it is erroneous. The same uncertainty applies to some of the late notes in KB.

We have included in this section some emigrants of whom it can only be shown that they reached countries in the vicinity of the Colonies and a few with whom even this is uncertain.

BASEL

Christian Bürgi, son of Leonhard B. and Anna Catharina Faesch, born or bapt. March 31, 1735.

Emigrated in 1755 (GAV 21, 4) or 1756 (GAV 20, 74). After many adversities he settled at Missilimakinac, Canada, where he suffered many more adversities and died between Sept. 19, 1779, the date of his last letter, and 1781, when his death was learned by vice-sergeant Goetz. He seems to have died unmarried.

Hans Ulrich Faesch.

According to GAV 22, 176 (Dec. 1811), he sailed from Amsterdam to the West Indies in 1770. His last letter, dated May 5, 1774, said that he was intending to go to St. Domingue.

Hans Lux Falkeysen, son of Theodor F. and Catharina Burkhardt, born or bapt. Febr. 7, 1702(?).

He was a tradesman belonging to the weavers' guild and had married Margreth Iselin, sister of Dr. Joh. Rudolf Iselin, 'Praepositus Collegii Superioris,' by whom he had three daughters, Maria, Catharina and Margreth, between 1731 and 1734. He became a radical pietist, neglected his business and his wife (RP 107, Nov. 19, 1735, and Apr. 4, 1736) and rather left both than to take the oath of allegiance. Finally he went to Pennsylvania whence we hear twice of him through the Diary of Hieronymus d'Annone, with whom he had been on friendly terms in the past.

Apr. 26, 1746, d'Annone learned that during the presence of Count Zinzendorf in Pennsylvania (probably in 1742) he had once tried to force the count to discuss a package of pamphlets with him. The count had finally accepted the package and written on it: 'God does everything in proper time, but Mr. Falkeysen calls at an improper time' whereupon the latter had withdrawn with angry words and mien. May 1751 d'Annone heard from an American Frenkendorf man (*i.e.*, Johannes Tschudi) a great deal about the continuing 'Schwärmereien' of poor Falkeysen. See also: Paul Wernle, Der Schweizerische Protestantismus im 18. Jahrh. I, 331.

N. N. Heu (?).

First name not known, second doubtful.   He was together with Nicolaus Heu one of the three heirs of Peter Heu, who died on the coast of Madras in 1760, and supposed to be in America at the time (GAV 16, Nov. 24, 1760).

Hans Rudolf Huber, son of Dr. Joh. Werner H. and Marg. Beck, born or bapt. Feb. 25, 1731.

Left British military service near Halifax in 1754 (GAV 22, 104).

Rudolf Hug.

Barbara Nägelin, his wife, deceased(?).

Their children:

     1. Margreth, born or bapt.....................May   23, 1748

     2. Hieronymus, born or bapt...................Febr.   26, 1750

Sold his 'Gantrodel' to the detriment of his creditors and went secretly with his children to America in 1753 (GAV 18, Sept. 26, 1774).

Joh. Fridrich Schmid, born away from Basel at Speier, according to a book of his sister in 1725.   Went to America in 1777 (GAV 22, 128).

Samuel Schneider, son of Rudolf Sch. and Ursula Gysin, bapt. March 6, 1725.

GAV 16, Nov. 30, 1761, it is stated that he had then been absent for 18 years (*i.e.*, since 1743) and inherited 200 florins which were deposited for him with the tanners' guild.   In 1773 he was located in Frederick Co., Md., and sent Conrad Graf of Lancaster Co., Pa., to collect the money for him (GAV 18, 167).

AMT FARNSBURG

Buus

Hans Jacob Hassler, son of Fridlin H. and Elsbeth Hassler, bapt. Apr. 29, 1697.

GAV 15, Febr. 23, 1750, it says that he had been absent some 30 years and gone across the sea.   America is not mentioned.

Heinrich Schaub, son of Heini Sch., the cooper, and Ursula Wipff, bapt. Nov. 23, 1749.

According to GAV 22, June 5, 1810, he went to America in 1767.

Diepflingen

Heinrich Würz, son of Heini W. and Elsbeth Heiniman, bapt. Febr. 19, 1747.

GAV 22, June 29, 1813, it is stated that he emigrated to America in 1771.

Eptingen

Hans Rudolf Schaffner, son of Martin Sch. and Anna Jenny, brother of Hans Jacob, emigrant of 1749 above, bapt. July 6, 1726.

Nov. 2, 1768, relatives of his applied for an inheritance which had come to him and his brother, alleging that both had gone to Pennsylvania 19 years ago without permission (which was only true of him), and had never been heard of (RP 141, 331).   A few years later, Jan. 29, 1772, he gave an unmistakable sign of life by claiming the inheritance himself through Christoph Lochner of Philadelphia and obtaining it (RP 145, 27).

Gelterkinden

Johannes Bossart, son of Hans Ulrich B. and Anna Maria Deck, bapt. May 29, 1731.

GAV 22, Febr. 6, 1810, it is said that he had gone to America over 50 years ago, *i.e.*, before 1760, with the consent of the government, but there is no record of it in MP.

Kilchberg

Anna Maria Heller, daughter of Urs Heller from the Canton of Bern and Anna Meyer of Kilchberg, bapt. Oct. 12, 1748. KB adds to this date: 'in Carolina.' Perhaps her parents emigrated also.

Oltingen

Jacob Rudin, son of Heini R. and Barbara Kommler and brother of Ursula, emigrant of 1790.

GAV 21, May 5, 1807, says that he left the Canton 14 years ago (*i.e.*, in 1793), leaving behind wife and children. A destination is not given. He may have followed his sister to America.

Ormalingen

N. N. Bossart, brother of Jacob, emigrant of 1771.

He died in Pennsylvania before 1792 (RP 165, March 31, 1792).

Niclaus Völmi, son of Johannes V. and Verena Buser, bapt. Jan. 31, 1730.

According to GAV 22, July 3, 1810, he went to America 40 years ago, which would be 1770, or more probably 1771 or 1772.

Hans Jacob Zeller, shoemaker.

Claimed property through the two Thommens 1767–68 in vain (RP 140, 414, and 141, 21) and through Martin Riggenbacher of Ormalingen successfully in 1783–84 (RP 156, 399, and GAV 19, 453), on which occasions it is stated that he emigrated in 1749 without permission. In 1783 he was located in Maryland.

Rothenfluh

Fridrich Bitscher's mother.

July 31, 1775 (GAV 18, 297), the son reported in connection with an inheritance which had come to her from her father in Baden that she had gone to Pennsylvania 16 years ago (*i.e.*, in 1759) without permission and would then be over 60 years old if she was living. In 1792, when he emigrated himself, he was authorized to take the 60 pounds in question to her (CAM 1792, March 7). Her maiden name is not mentioned.

Johannes Keller, son of the Geschworener Hans Jacob K. and Barbara Würtz, bapt. Aug. 8, 1751.

According to RP 165, Jan. 28, 1792, he left the Canton 21 years ago (*i.e.*, in 1771) as a joiner journeyman and went to America where he settled in Baltimore, Pa.(!), and married a native (American). On the occasion of his visit in 1792 he took his mother and sister together with property of his own and others back with him to America.

Martin Keller, brother of Johannes above, bapt. Dec. 6, 1767.

Was located as a turner in Baltimore in 1791 (RP 165, l.c.). Time of emigration not ascertainable.

Rünenberg

David Grieder, son of Basche G., the Geschworener's son, and Barbara Bürgi from Rothenfluh, bapt. March 23, 1749.

GAV 22, Apr. 13, 1813, it is asserted that he went to America 41 years ago (*i.e.*, in 1772), with permission, but he is not recorded in MP.

Tecknau

Heini Handschin.

Jan. 25, 1762 (GAV 16, 347), his brother Joggi produced a certificate of his death from Bethlehem 'not far from Pennsylvania in the West Indies'(!).

Wintersingen

Heini Rohrer, son of Hans R., the smith's son, and Barbara Lang, bapt. Dec. 10, 1719.

According to RP 122, Febr. 8, 1749, he emigrated in May 1740 and wrote to his 'Vogt' from Rotterdam and Philadelphia, but apparently not afterwards.

Jacob Speiser.

In 1794 he was located in Philadelphia and offered to present his brother Christen in Wintersingen with 34 pounds and his half of a vineyard worth 100 florins (GAV 20, Oct. 27, 1794). Had also said so during a recent visit. Particulars about him not ascertained because the name Speiser is common in his village.

Zeglingen

Jacob Grieder, son of Hans Joggi Grieder and Elsbeth Schaub, bapt. May 21, 1736.

In connection with his birth KB adds 'Gone to the New-land' by the side of his parents. This may however be an error.

Marti Raufft, son of Marti R. and Barbara Gisin, bapt. Nov. 20, 1719.

His identity is ascertained by the fact that KB also contains the birth dates of his brothers and sister who apply for his scanty property in his absence: Anna, Dec. 10, 1721, Hans Jacob, March 6, 1725, and Johannes, Aug. 22, 1728. There are two dates given for the time of his emigration, GAV 15, Apr. 26, 1751, the year 1741, and GAV 19, 449, the year 1749. The former date would seem to be more nearly correct.

Margreth Thommen, daughter of Heini Th. and Margreth Gysi, bapt. July 22, 1736.

In connection with her birth KB adds again: 'Gone to the New-land.' It is not impossible that this is an error and that Heini Th. was confounded with Jacob Th., the emigrant of 1736.

AMT HOMBURG

Bucklen

Hans Ulrich Müller, son of Hans M., called the Graw, and Barbara Buser, bapt. Apr. 15, 1736.

GAV May 8, 1806, says he emigrated 50 years ago, *i.e.*, in 1756. There is however no evidence that he went to America where his sister Verena went in 1771.

Anna Schaub, daughter of Sebastian Sch., the weaver, and Ursel Lieberknecht, bapt. Apr. 30, 1730.

Our knowledge of her emigration rests on the note in KB: 'came A. 1749 in Carolinam.'

Häfelfingen

Hans Jacob Pfeiffer's brother.

According to report from Homburg of March 5, 1772 (AA), Hans Jacob Pfeiffer claimed to have received a year ago a letter from a younger brother of his who had gone to Carolina in 1737 and had obtained possession of considerable property by his marriage to the daughter of his former employer.

Känerkinden

Elisabeth Buser, daughter of Heinrich B., lace-maker, and Verena Buser, bapt. Oct. 6, 1748.

GAV 22, March 5, 1811, puts her at Metteberg in the same Amt and says that she emigrated to America in 1771.

Hans Heinrich Buser, son of Wernhard B. and Anna Helena Anishäusslein, bapt. Oct. 16, 1729.

His emigration is claimed by the note: 'came in Carol.' in KB.

Läufelfingen

Heini Schneider, son of Martin Sch., the joiner, and Elsbeth Fiechter, bapt. May 7, 1730.

According to RP 137, 60 (1764), he had left the country in 1749, ostensibly as a joiner journeyman, though it had appeared suspicious at the time that he had taken a comparatively large sum of money, 300 pounds, with him without the knowledge of the Landvogt. His belated manumission, which took place in 1764 together with the release of some property, reads in MP as follows:

'Heini Schneider . . ., lawfully begotten son of Martin Sch. . . . and Elsbeth F. . . ., who has gone to Pennsylvania, has 299 pounds worth of property and has been released from serfdom March 10, 1764.

Pays pro Manumission . . . . .10.—
Tax on 299 pounds at 10 percent . . . . .29.18   39.18'

AMT KLEINHUENINGEN

Mattis Hofer, son of Johannes H. and Verena Gisel, born or bapt. Apr. 6, 1719.

Apr. 14, 1766 (GAV 17, 274), Joh. Hegetschwiler makes a vain attempt to recover 400 pounds for him. It is stated on that occasion that Mattis H. had already tried to obtain them 19 years ago (*i.e.*, in 1747). In 1765 he was living with his family in Pennsylvania.

AMT LIESTAL

Frenkendorf

Andreas Boni, probably son of Martin B. and Margaretha Müller and bapt. Nov. 11, 1708.

Our knowledge of his emigration rests upon a long extract from a letter of his made by the Chancery of Basel and preserved in the Generallandesarchiv at Karlsruhe, Akten Baden Generalia 9847. It is dated Oct. 16, 1736, and from Pennsylvania and directed to his cousin Martin, whose full name and address were not reproduced by the copyist and could therefore not be given with any degree of certainty. It shows an intimate familiarity with the journey down the Lower Rhine, names a person in Greufeldt, probably Crefeld, and another in Rotterdam who might be of assistance to emigrants, and, as it suggests the unusual alternative of making the journey on foot instead of by ship, it was probably written by a young man who tried it. Also the remarks about the facility with which young and industrious people could make their way in America, while it must be left to God how old people would get along, point to a young man and seem to exclude the possibility that the letter was written by the noted Andres Boni who was exiled on account of his religious views in 1706. This Andres Boni had lost a wife in the Palatinate before that time, was living in Friesland, far away from the Lower Rhine, in 1726, and must have been in 1736 over fifty years old.

The writer of the letter is also a truly religious man and begins and ends with an expression of trust in God and faith in his guidance. He has some acquaintance with the conditions and prospects of immigration both in New York and Pennsylvania and can therefore not have arrived in America any later than 1735 or early in 1736. We do not know whether cousin Martin found the means of joining him there.

Lausen

Jacob Schaffner, in some reports called Hans Jacob, son of Jacob Schaffner, 'Scheurenmeyer' at Basel.

According to a report by Schultheiss Hebdenstreit of Sept. 11, 1772 (Nord Amerika B1), he emigrated in 1754 without applying for manumission or paying the ten percent tax. He settled in Pennsylvania and kept a store at Lebanon where he was quite accommodating to countrymen who came that way. In 1769–70 he ventured to revisit his old home and even succeeded in collecting the inheritance for the Seyler boys who, as we have seen under 1752, had likewise emigrated without permission, 'because he made the impression of being an honest man.' Two years later, however, when he reappeared once more, he aroused suspicion and his clandestine emigration came up in Council. As a result he was told to apply for his manumission within two weeks or expect to be arrested (RP 145, Dec. 23, 1772). He evidently preferred to leave the country within the limit, for his manumission is not recorded till 15 years later when he desired the release of an inheritance of his own:

'1787, June 23, Jacob Schafner of Lausen, who went to America Anno 1754 . . . .

Manumission . . . . 10.—.—
Letter 1.10
Ten percent tax . . . . 98.—. 4' 109.10.4

Liestal

Daniel Hoch.

Is mentioned twice in GAV. 15, March 25, 1748, it is stated that he had been gone for 15 years (*i.e.*, since 1733), and 19, July 3, 1780, that he left as a butcher journeyman 47 years ago (*i.e.*, again in 1733) and thereupon went to Carolina whence he wrote to his relatives in 1734.

Adam Gysin, son of Peter G. and Elisabeth Habillon, bapt. Oct. 10, 1717.

According to GAV 21, Dec. 4, 1804, he had then been absent for about 60 years (*i.e.*, since the middle of the forties), and given the last sign of life 1749. It was rumored that he had been missing after an engagement in the war of the North American States, which, if true, could hardly refer to the Revolutionary War.

AMT MUENCHENSTEIN

Benken

Joh. Ulrich Muspach, son of Johannes, the tailor, and Elsbeth Weibel, bapt. Nov. 8, 1739.

While his father abstained from making use of his permission to go to America in 1749, he and his brother Johannes, bapt. Jan. 27, 1743, went into the wide world without being manumitted and perhaps at first without the intention to remain abroad. Johannes wandered all the way to the borders of Asia and established himself at Sarepta and Joh. Ulrich reached America and settled in New Jersey about 1779 (GAV 20, 205, and RP 162, 73). After their father's death, which occurred Dec. 16, 1787, both applied for their inheritance and manumission. That of Joh. Ulrich reads as follows: '1789 Apr. 18, Joh. Ulrich Muspach of Bencken, at present located in Sussex Co. in nova Caesarea, was manumitted. According to his 'Vogt's' account of Apr. 25 his property amounts to lb. 453.6.9. . . .

Manumission . . . . 10.—
Ten percent tax 44.6
Letter . . . . 1.10 55.16'

Hans Jacob Schmid, son of Hans Jacob Sch., carpenter, and Anna Barbara Deck, bapt. Jan. 1, 1727.

According to GAV 21, 382, June 3, 1806, he is said to have emigrated to America unmarried in 1749.

Münchenstein

Catharina Banga, daughter of the cooper Jacob B. and Cathrina Kapp (deceased Nov. 20, 1740), bapt. Oct. 26, 1717.

RP 124, March 6, 1751, it is stated that she emigrated to Pennsylvania in 1739 and had not given sign of life. Apr. 3, 1751, her four brothers and sisters, Barbara, Hans Jacob, Johannes and Anna Margreth, were allowed the 80 pounds which she had inherited from their grandfather Matthis Kapp, deceased, in 1743, on giving joint security (CAM). She must have been related to Hans Kapp, emigrant of 1740.

Hans Jacob Degen, son of the Geschworener Jacob D. and Catharina Seiler, bapt. Nov. 25, 1714.

The earliest official information concerning his emigration is found in RL 1750: 'From Daniel Degen as 'Vogt' of Jacob Degen, son of the Geschworener, who went to Pennsylvania 10 years ago

Ten percent tax on the inheritance from his mother deceased....50.—'

Also two statements in GAV point to 1739 as the time of his emigration. 16, Apr. 28, 1757, says that he went to the Newly-found-land 18 years ago, and 20, May 30, 1791, that he went there in 1739 with the consent of the government. We have however not found any contemporary record of it.

Anna Margreth Huggel, daughter of Heinrich H. and Magdalena Näbel, sister of Elisabeth, who is listed among the emigrants to America of 1771 by mistake, bapt. Febr. 6, 1724.

There are three references to her emigration in GAV: 19, Nov. 29, 1784, 20, Sept. 20, 1786, and 22, Sept. 3, 1811. In the second her sister Elisabeth speaks of her as having gone to America over 30 years ago (*i.e.*, before 1756).

Maria Massmünster.

GAV 19, July 5, 1779, it is stated that she had then been absent for about 40 years (*i.e.*, since 1739 or 1740), which would be the time when Judith Massmünster, the wife of Hans Kapp, went to America. Perhaps she accompanied her.

Muttenz

Hans Fridrich Lützler, son of 'Meister' Johannes L. and Catharina Lang from Kleinhüningen, bapt. June 24, 1714.

According to GAV 20, Dec. 26, 1791, he went about 48 years ago (*i.e.*, about 1743) unmarried to America. A Frenkendorf man, who was in this country about 20 years ago, apparently Jacob Schaub, told that he had died there single.

Jacob Mössmer.

Went to America in 1794 and died in Baltimore. Certificate of his death by Dr. Christian Becker p. t. preacher in Baltimore, July 25, 1810 (GAV 23, Jan. 2, 1817).

Pratteln

Niclaus Tschudy, son of Hans Jacob Tsch., the turner, and Maria Vögtlin, bapt. Sept. 11, 1712.

There is no contemporary reference to his emigration in RP, but he must be the 'boy' of Pratteln who is mentioned by Gerster in his letter of 1737 as one of his fellow emigrants of the preceding year. His case did not come up in Council till 1766 when he applied through Joh. Hegetschwiler for his paternal inheritance. It then was found that he had left 30 years ago (*i.e.*, in 1736), and had never been manumitted (RP 166, March 26). The entry in MP is in part as follows: 'Claus

Tschudy of Brattelen, who has gone to Pennsylvania . . . has been manumitted
Apr. 16, 1766. . . . Pays for manumission lb. 10.—, for the letter 1.10.' The
ten percent tax had been paid in the castle of Mönchenstein.

In accordance with the fact that his parents were pietists and that his mother
was considered one of the most uncompromising and at the same time most
harmless among them, because she did not try to convert anybody to her views,
a letter of his, dated Oct. 27, 1750, breathes a pronounced religious spirit. Fearing
that they will never see each other in the flesh again, he expresses the hope that
they will meet in eternity and asks them to pray for him as he is going to do for
them. At the time he was married and had two boys, but was apparently not in
very brilliant circumstances, because he begs his parents to repay his cousin Jacob
Joner for aid rendered him when nobody else would help him.

Amt Waldenburg
Arboldswil

Anna Rudin, daughter of Fritz R.

RL 1755: 'First from Anna Rudin of Arbotschweyl, who has gone to the
Newly-found-land and inherited from her father Fritz Rudin during his lifetime
and her mother deceased together lb. 667.10

   Tax at 10 pro cento made. . . . . .63.15'

Michel Thommen.

Mentioned by Michel Vogt, emigrant of 1768, as a cousin of his in America.
Since we have not found him in KB, he may be a son of Durs, emigrant of 1749,
and be born in America.

Bennwil

Basche Spittahler, Spitteler.
Anna Tschudin from Lausen, his wife.
Their children:

   1. Verena, bapt. . . . . .Dec.   9, 1725
   2. Anna, bapt. . . . . .March 21, 1728
   3. Johannes, bapt. . . . . .July   30, 1730
   4. Sebastian, bapt. . . . . .Oct.   25, 1733
   5. Friderich, bapt. . . . . .May   12, 1737
   6. Jacob, bapt. . . . . .May   25, 1738

Authority for his emigration is GAV 17, Nov. 24, 1766, where it is stated
that he and his brother Hans had gone with their wives and children to Pennsylvania thirty years ago. The year 1736 is in fact the time when his brother
left (see 1736 above), but he must have gone later because of the birth of his son
Jacob in 1738.

Bubendorf

Emanuel Bürgi, 34 years of age.
Anna Rudin, daughter of Fritz R.

   1. Emanuel, their son, bapt. . . . . .June   4, 1730

He is one of the applicants of 1738 who were refused permission, but it cannot
be said whether he emigrated then or later. GAV 15, Febr. 24, 1749, contains a
statement regarding the fate of this family which Wernhard Stohler, emigrant of
1738, located in Pennsylvania, made and signed on the occasion of his visit in 1749.
According to that Emanuel Bürgi, the father, had died on the voyage, the mother
had married again and the son had died in Pennsylvania in his seventeenth year.

Lampenberg

Hans Fluebacher, son of Stoffel Hans Fl. and Anna Fluebacher, bapt. June 27, 1717.
Elsbeth Mohler from Diegten, his wife, to whom he was married Apr. 28, 1749,
   just previous to the great emigration of that year.

This Hans Fluebacher, who should not be confounded with his namesake, listed among the emigrants of 1749 in MP, is referred to as an emigrant without permission in RL 1755: 'From Hans Fluebacher, son of Hans deceased, of Lampenberg, who without most gracious permission went with his wife to the Newly-found-land and inherited 357 pounds from his father and mother, deceased:

Tax at 10 pro cento makes........................35.14
For manumission for both........................20.—' 55.14

He seems to have died without wife and children, for in 1792 there arrived the report from America that he had died in Lancaster Co., Pa., and bequeathed his property to his brother Christoffel, bapt. Febr. 1, 1722, without knowing that he had died also. He is called there Johannes instead of Hans (RP 165, 73, and GAV 20, Apr. 30, 1792).

Langenbruck

Christen Gerber from Sumiswald, Canton of Bern.

It is perhaps possible that he is identical with one of the guardians of the two youngest children of Heini Riggenbacher of Zeglingen, emigrant of 1740. He was married and had a daughter Anna, bapt. March 12, 1730.

Lukas Jenni, son of Joh. J. and Elisabeth Tauber.

According to GAV 23, March 14, 1815, he was born in 1770. His last letter was dated May 1, 1791, Cape Français, St. Domingue.

Lauwil

Jonas Vogt.

1. Jonas, his son, said to have been born about 1740.

RP 166, March 27 and May 11, 1793, and GAV 20, Apr. 29, 1793, furnish the following information concerning him. After having left the Canton once before on account of debts, he is said to have emigrated secretly with his son Jonas in 1749. In America he had five more children: Barbara, Michel, Eva, Anna and Elisabeth, and died between 1790 and 1792. His son Jonas had died before. In 1793 Benjamin Herr of Northumberland Co., Pa., appeared with a power of attorney, dated Sunbury, July 4, 1791, and claimed an inheritance of lb. 352.17 for the five children. The release, however, was refused for three reasons. His name was not found in MP so that he 'seemed' to have emigrated without consent. His children had never been subjects of Basel. The applicants at home were needy.

Titterten

Esther Schweitzer, said to be baptized in 1750.

GAV 23, July 12, 1814, says that she went to America unmarried in 1772. In the absence of KB it cannot be ascertained whether she was a daughter of Heinrich Schweitzer, emigrant of 1772, by a first wife or not.

Hans Schweitzer's mother.

RL 1752 offers the following entry: 'And then from Hans Schweitzer and his brothers and sisters, who have inherited 745 pounds from their mother who has gone to the Newly-found-land:

Per tax at 10 percent.....................................74.10'

In the absence of KB it cannot be decided whether she had left her children in the Canton to follow a second husband to America or not, or whether she figures on one of our lists above or not.

Ziefen

Elisabeth Furler, daughter of Hans Jacob F. and Barbara Tschopp, bapt. March 7, 1751.

GAV 22, Apr. 13, 1813, it is stated that she emigrated to America in 1772. She is, however, not recorded in MP.

15

Martin Müller, brother of Christen, emigrant of 1773.
Ursula Schäublin, his wife.

     1. Heinrich, their son, bapt....................Sept.   9, 1753

According to a report from Waldenburg, dated Oct. 31, 1772 (AA), his brother said that he had emigrated five years ago (*i.e.*, in 1767) and was doing well. Though he had left without permission, he ventured to come back on a visit with Jacob Schaffner 1772–73 (joint letter, printed by A. B. Faust, *J. d. D.-Am. H. Ges. v. Ill.*, No. 13). His presence remained, however, not undiscovered and an order was sent to Liestal to arrest him (CAM, Apr. 17, 1773).

N. N. Rudin, son of Fritz, deceased.

RL 1752: 'First from Fritz Rudin's heirs of Zyfen on account of their brother, who went to the Newly-found-land 2 years ago, and the property which he inherited from his father deceased mentioned above consisting of lb. 163.7:

    Per tax at 10 pro cento..............................16.7
    Per manumission.....................................10.—' 26.7

Martin Schob, probably rather *Tschopp*, which is sometimes spelt Tschobb, then Schaub.

He is mentioned in the letter of Elisabeth Strohman below as having come with her to America and as a father of three girls and a boy and owner of a large farm within visiting distance from her place. E. Str.'s letter is found in AA and was printed by A. B. Faust, *The Am. Hist. Rev.*, XXII, 121 sq.

Elisabeth Strohman, daughter of Heinrich Str. and Anna Krattiger, sister of Chrischona and Heinrich, emigrant of 1768, and Barbara, Eusebius and perhaps also Anna, emigrants of 1771, all of whom seem to have been induced to come to America by her letter, bapt. July 7, 1728.

These data as well as the time of her emigration, of which there is no contemporary record, may be determined by a chain of circumstantial evidences. The first clue is furnished by the facts that Heinrich Strohman, emigrant of 1768, refers to her before the Land Commission as his sister and gives her age (AA). Then KB revealed the names of their parents and these led to the discovery of the record of her own birth in 1728. Furthermore her letter, mentioned above with Martin Schob, intimates that she left the country with many others, for she says that Martin Schob is the only one of those with whom she came to America of whom she knows. In particular she does not know anything about Johannes Degen, an emigrant of 1749. At the same time the year 1749 is the only year of a collective emigration which can come into consideration because she was too young to go in 1749 when she was only 12 years of age, and between 1749 and 1766 there had been only sporadic cases of emigration.

When she wrote her letter, probably in autumn 1766, because her family received it in February 1767, she was married, had three boys and one girl, helped her husband, whose name she fails to tell us, in his weaving and owned 35 acres of land. Every line breathes happiness and success.

With the following emigrants it is doubtful from what place in the Canton they came.

Friedrich Gass.

Hans Martin, emigrant of 1735, tells in his letter to the Candidate Ryhiner, dated Nov. 6, 1735, that he bought his farm upon the advice of Friedrich Gass without explaining who he is. He must therefore have been known to both of them and surely be from the Canton of Basel, perhaps from Pratteln. He may have arrived in Pennsylvania in 1734 or even earlier.

Jacob Müller,
Johannes Müller and
Margreth Müller, brothers and sister of Adam Müller.

According to GAV 18, March 29 and Apr. 30, Adam Müller, who in the first entry is assigned to Muttenz and in the second to Tenniken, claimed that Jacob and Margreth had left 47 years ago (*i.e.,* in 1715), and according to GAV 16, Aug. 30, 1762, he said they had been 48 years (*i.e.,* since 1714) in the New World. They had started therefore about 20 years before a real emigration from the Canton to America began, probably in common with Johannes, who had died before 1749 when the negotiations concerning the inheritance which he had bequeathed to his brother Adam, between the latter and Jacob Joner began. Christian Sinzenig, who is mentioned in that connection, was evidently the husband of Margreth. The time of her and her brother Jacob's death cannot be determined. Sinzenig lived in Pennsylvania.

Sebastian Salade, also Sallade.

He was established in Philadelphia. In a letter, dated Philadelphia, March 4, 1797, he transmitted the copies of two letters and some other information concerning the estate left by Heinrich Meyer, emigrant of 1771, with the declaration that he was too busy and too far away from Harrisburgh to occupy himself further with the matter. In GAV 23, Sept. 4, 1817, he is designated as merchant and tradesman in Philadelphia in connection with a letter of attorney which he had sent to his brother Martin Salade at Frenkendorf (Amt Liestal).

Johan Conrad Schweighauser.

He is mentioned in 1743 in a letter of Anna Thommen, emigrant of 1736, written in Ephrata, Aug. 12, the delivery of which she confided to him as a friend who was about to take a trip to Basel (Briefe an Hieron. d'Annone). Again John Conrad Schweighauser of Philadelphia, either he himself or a son of his by the same name, is found in the papers which deal with the delivery of the estate of Adam Fluebacher, emigrant of 1772, deceased on the voyage, to his mother at Lampenberg (Nord Amerika B1). He signs himself John C. Schweighauser on his bill of exchange and is called John Conrad in the endorsement of his account by the notary Peter Miller. The Schweighausers were a noted family in the City and Canton of Basel at the time.

INDEX *

The name of the father, usually, is followed by that of the mother, whose maiden name appears in parenthesis, and the children follow in alphabetical order. A strictly alphabetical individual arrangement has not been attempted, family units and a chronological arrangement are largely used. The entire paragraphs in the index should be read.—G. M. B.

* Prepared by Gaius Marcus Brumbaugh, Washington, D. C.

www.ingramcontent.com/pod-product-compliance
Lightning Source LLC
Chambersburg PA
CBHW031115020426
42333CB00012B/96